ng-book

The Complete Guide to Angular

Felipe Coury

Ari Lerner

Nate Murray

Carlos Taborda

Technical Editor:
Frode Fikke

FULLSTACK.*io*

ng-book

The Complete Guide to Angular

Written by Nate Murray, Felipe Coury, Ari Lerner, and Carlos Taborda

© 2018 Fullstack.io
ISBN-13: 978-1985170285

Questions? Email us at: us@fullstack.io
Sample code download available at: ng-book.com/code

Published in San Francisco, California by Fullstack.io.

We'd like to thank our contributors to this book including:

- *Frode Fikke for technical edits*
- *Nic Raboy, and Burke Holland for their contribution to the NativeScript chapter*
- *Travas Nolte for his work on many chapters*
- *Daniel Rauf for his edits on RxJS, Redux, and Routing*

Contents

Book Revision

Revision 68p for paper print - Covers up to Angular 6 (6.0.0, 2018-05-08)

Sample Code Download

This book comes with example code - see the next page for details on how to download it.

Bug Reports

If you'd like to report any bugs, typos, or suggestions just email us at: us@fullstack.io[1].

Chat With The Community!

We're experimenting with a community chat room for this book using Gitter. If you'd like to hang out with other people learning Angular 2, come join us on Gitter[2]!

Be notified of updates via Twitter

If you'd like to be notified of updates to the book on Twitter, follow @fullstackio[3]

We'd love to hear from you!

Did you like the book? Did you find it helpful? We'd love to add your face to our list of testimonials on the website! Email us at: us@fullstack.io[4].

---

[1] mailto:us@fullstack.io?Subject=ng-book%202%20feedback

[2] https://gitter.im/ng-book/ng-book

[3] https://twitter.com/fullstackio

[4] mailto:us@fullstack.io?Subject=ng-book%202%20testimonial

How to Read This Book

This book aims to be the single most useful resource on learning Angular. By the time you're done reading this book, you (and your team) will have everything you need to build reliable, powerful Angular apps.

Angular is a rich and feature-filled framework, but that also means it can be tricky to understand all of its parts. In this book, we'll walk through everything from installing the tools, writing components, using forms, routing between pages, and calling APIs.

But before we dig in, there are a few guidelines I want to give you **in order to get the most out of this book**. Briefly, I want to tell you:

- how to approach **the code examples** and
- **how to get help** if something goes wrong

Running Code Examples

This book comes with a library of runnable code examples. The code is available to download from the same place where you downloaded this book.

We use the program npm[5] to run **every example** in this book. This means you can type the following commands to run any example:

```
1  npm install
2  npm start
```

> If you're unfamiliar with npm, we cover how to get it installed in the Getting Started section in the first chapter.

After running npm start, you will see some output on your screen that will tell you what URL to open to view your app.

If you're ever unclear on how to run a particular sample app, check out the README.md in that project's directory. Every sample project contains a README.md that will give you the instructions you need to run each app.

---

[5] https://www.npmjs.com/

FULLSTACK

Download the Example Code

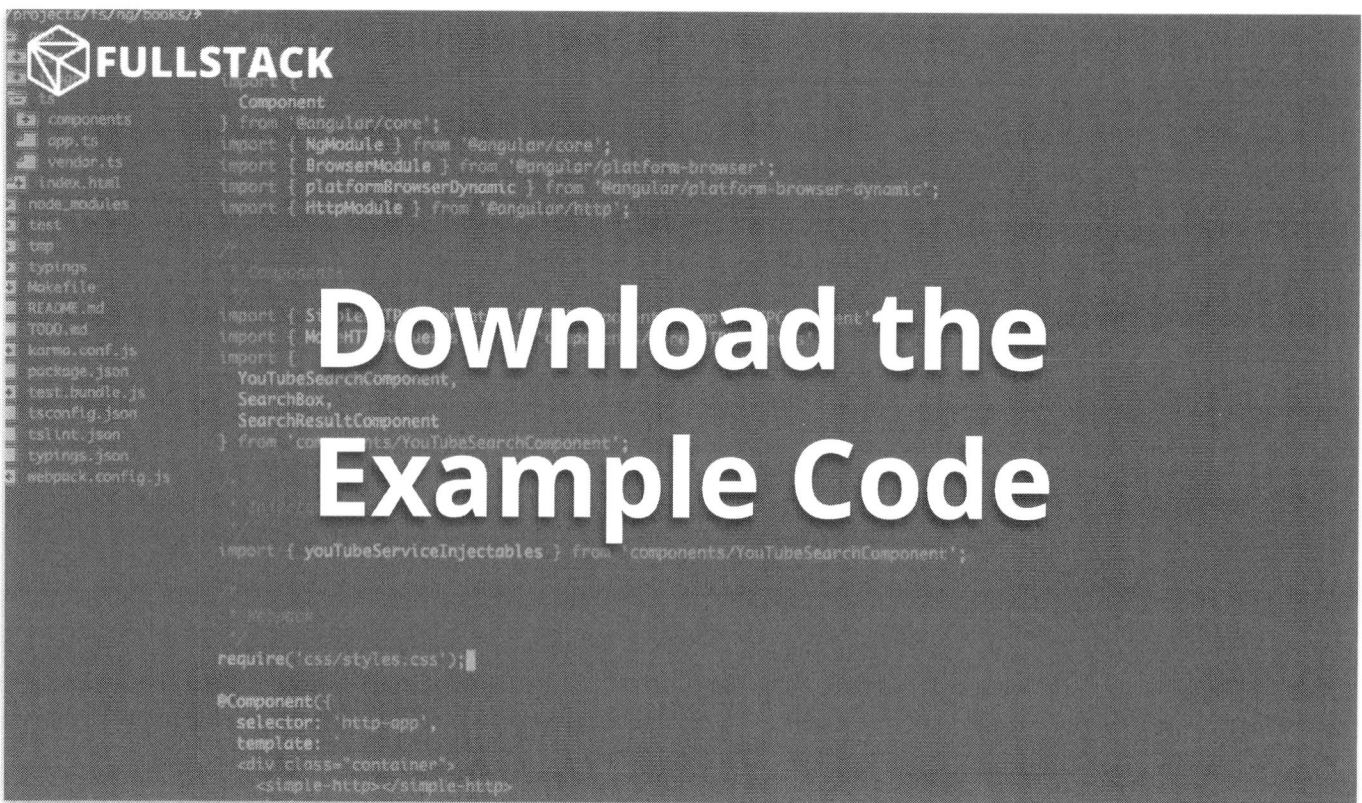

This book contains several example apps and code samples. Because you purchased the paperback version you can **download this code for free** at our website.

Note: because of page restrictions, the *Typescript* chapter has been removed and is **available as a free PDF** when you download the example code:

URL	https://ng-book.com/code/
BOOK SERIAL CODE	AMZ-82SA

To download the code, visit the URL above and enter your email and serial code and we'll email you the code download.

Learn more at: ng-book.com/code/

DOWNLOAD

For instance, in the Dependency Injection chapter you may see a code block with the filename: `price.service.1.ts`. When you see the `.N.ts` syntax that means we're building up to the ultimate file, which will **not** have a number. So, in this case, the final version would be: `price.service.ts`. We do it this way so that a) we can unit test the intermediate code and b) you can see the whole file in context at a particular stage.

A Word on Versioning

As you may know, the Angular covered in this book is a descendant of an earlier framework called "AngularJS". This can sometimes be confusing, particularly when reading supplementary blogs or documentation.

The official branding guidelines state that "*AngularJS*" is a term reserved for AngularJS 1.x, that is, the early versions of "Angular".

Because the new version of Angular used TypeScript (instead of JavaScript) as the primary language, the 'JS' was dropped, leaving us with just *Angular*. For a long time the only consistent way to distinguish the two was folks referred to the *new* Angular as *Angular 2*.

However, the Angular team in 2017 switched to *semantic versioning* with a new major-release upgrade slated for every 6 months. Instead of calling the next versions *Angular 4*, *Angular 5*, and so on, the number is also dropped and it's just *Angular*.

In this book, when we're referring to *Angular* we'll just say *Angular* or sometimes *Angular X*, just to avoid confusion. When we're talking about "the old-style JavaScript Angular" we'll use the term *AngularJS* or *AngularJS 1.x*.

Getting Help

While we've made every effort to be clear, precise, and accurate you may find that when you're writing your code you run into a problem.

Generally, there are three types of problems:

- A "bug" in the book (e.g. how we describe something is wrong)
- A "bug" in our code
- A "bug" in your code

If you find an inaccuracy in how we describe something, or you feel a concept isn't clear, email us! We want to make sure that the book is both accurate and clear.

Similarly, if you've found a bug in our *code* we definitely want to hear about it.

If you're having trouble getting your own app working (and it isn't *our* example code), this case is a bit harder for us to handle.

Your first line of defense, when getting help with your custom app, should be our unofficial community chat room[7]. We (the authors) are there from time-to-time, but there are hundreds of other readers there who may be able to help you faster than we can.

If you're still stuck, we'd still love to hear from you, and here are some tips for getting a clear, timely response.

Emailing Us

If you're emailing us asking for technical help, here's what we'd like to know:

- What revision of the book are you referring to?
- What operating system are you on? (e.g. Mac OS X 10.8, Windows 95)
- Which chapter and which example project are you on?
- What were you trying to accomplish?
- What have you tried[8] already?
- What output did you expect?
- What actually happened? (Including relevant log output.)

The **absolute best way to get technical support** is to send us a short, self-contained example of the problem. Our preferred way to receive this would be for you to send us a Plunkr link by using this URL[9].

That URL contains a runnable, boilerplate Angular app. If you can copy and paste your code into that project, reproduce your error, and send it to us **you'll greatly increase the likelihood of a prompt, helpful response**.

When you've written down these things, email us at us@fullstack.io[10]. We look forward to hearing from you.

Technical Support Response Time

We perform our free, technical support **once per week**.

If you need a faster response time, and help getting **any** of your team's questions answered, then you may consider our premium support option[11].

---

[7] https://gitter.im/ng-book/ng-book

[8] http://mattgemmell.com/what-have-you-tried/

[9] https://angular.io/resources/live-examples/quickstart/ts/eplnkr.html

[10] mailto:us@fullstack.io

[11] mailto:us@fullstack.io?Subject=Angular%20Premium%20Support&Body=Hello%21%20I%27m%20interested%20in%20premium%20Angular%20support%20for%20our%20team

Chapter Overview

Before we dive in, I want to give you a feel for the rest of the book and what you can expect inside.

The first few chapters provide the **foundation** you need to get up and running with Angular. You'll create your **first apps**, use **the built-in components**, and start **creating your components**.

Next we'll move into intermediate concepts such as using **forms**, using **APIs**, **routing** to different pages, and using *Dependency Injection* to organize our code.

After that, we'll move into more **advanced concepts**. We spend a good part of the book talking about *data architectures*. Managing state in client/server applications is hard and we dive deep into two popular approaches: using **RxJS Observables** and using **Redux**. In these chapters, we'll show how to build the same app, two different ways, so you can compare and contrast and evaluate what's best for you and your team.

After that, we'll discuss how to write complex, **advanced components** using Angular's most powerful features. Then we talk about how to write **tests** for our app and how we can **upgrade our Angular 1 apps** to Angular. Finally, we close with a chapter on writing **native mobile apps** with Angular using **NativeScript**.

By using this book, **you're going to learn how to build real Angular apps** faster than spending hours parsing out-dated blog posts.

So hold on tight - you're about to become an Angular expert, and have a lot of fun along the way. Let's dig in!

- Nate (@eigenjoy[12])

---

[12] https://twitter.com/eigenjoy

Writing Your First Angular Web Application

Simple Reddit Clone

In this chapter we're going to build an application that allows the user to **post an article** (with a title and a URL) and then **vote on the posts**.

You can think of this app as the beginnings of a site like Reddit[13] or Product Hunt[14].

In this simple app we're going to cover most of the essentials of Angular including:

- Building custom components
- Accepting user input from forms
- Rendering lists of objects into views
- Intercepting user clicks and acting on them
- Deploying our app to a server

By the time you're finished with this chapter you'll know how to take an empty folder, build a basic Angular application, and deploy it to production. After working through this chapter you'll have a good grasp on how Angular applications are built and a solid foundation to build your own Angular app.

Here's a screenshot of what our app will look like when it's done:

---

[13]http://reddit.com

[14]http://producthunt.com

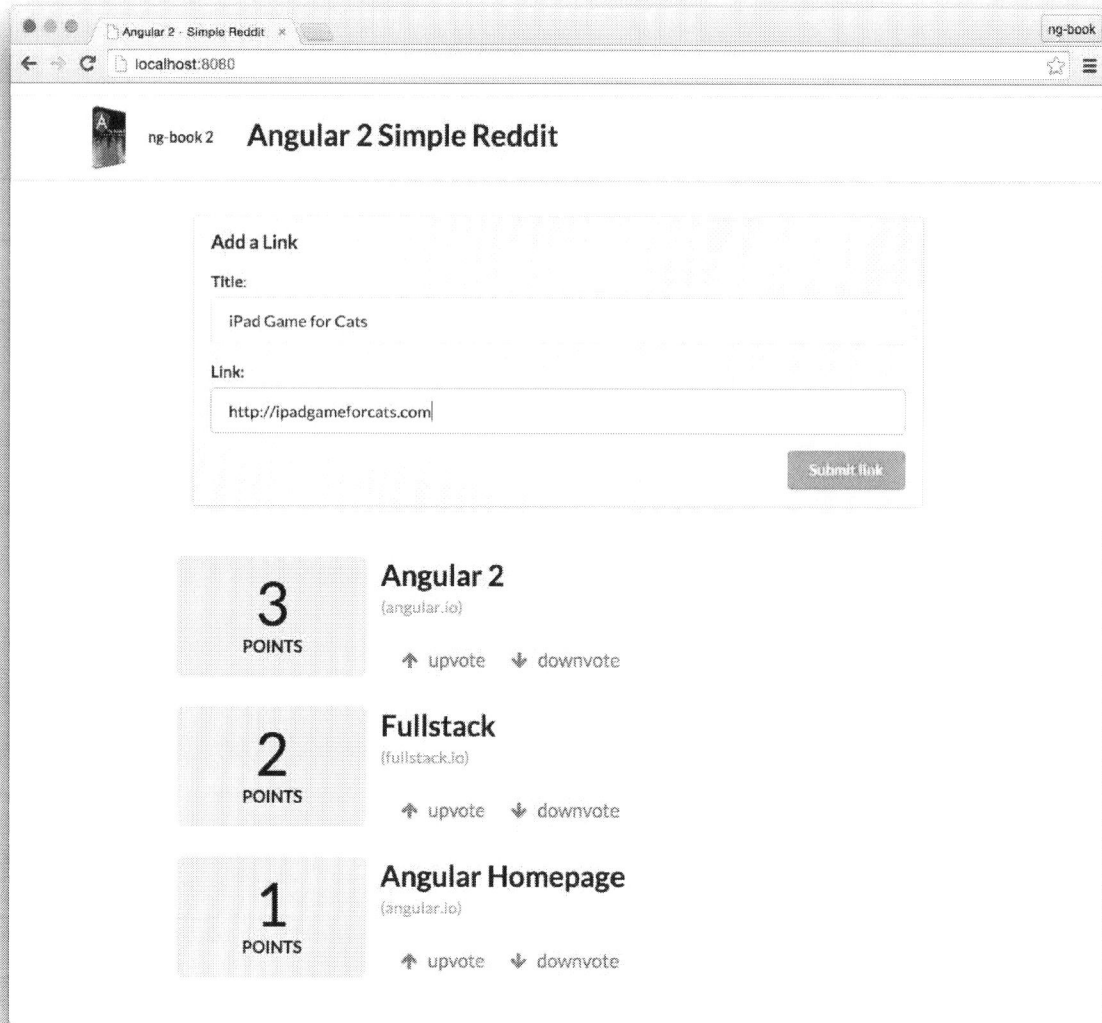

Completed application

First, a user will submit a new link and after submitting the users will be able to upvote or downvote each article. Each link will have a score and we can vote on which links we find useful.

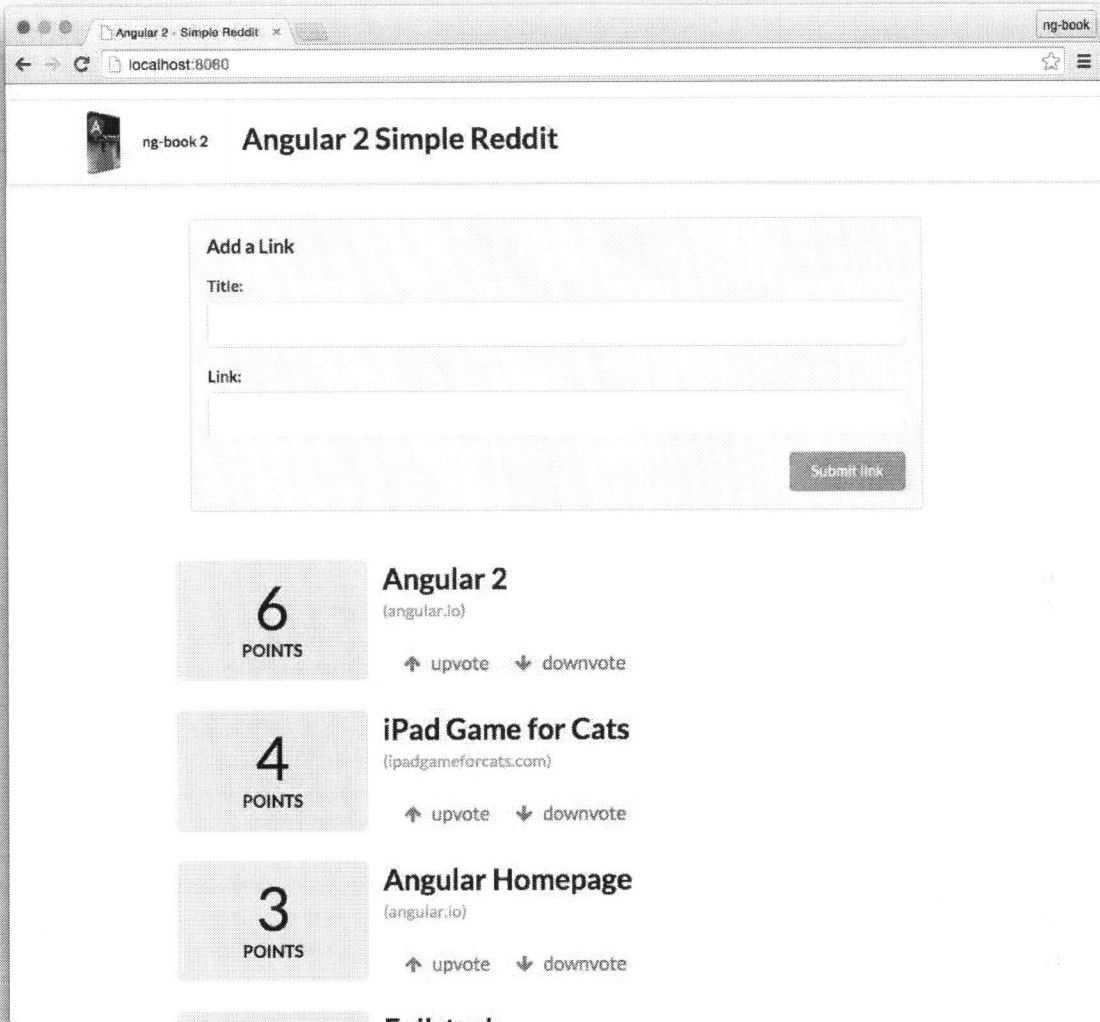

App with new article

In this project, and throughout the book, we're going to use TypeScript. TypeScript is a superset of JavaScript ES6 that adds types. We're not going to talk about TypeScript in depth in this chapter, but **we'll go over TypeScript more in depth in the next chapter.**

Don't worry if you're having trouble with some of the new syntax. If you're familiar with ES5 ("normal" JavaScript) / ES6 (ES2015) you should be able to follow along and we'll talk more about TypeScript in a bit.

Getting started

Node.js and npm

To get started with Angular, you'll need to have Node.js installed. There are a couple of different ways you can install Node.js, so please refer to the Node.js website[15] for detailed information.

Make sure you install Node 8.9.0 or higher.

> ⚠️ If you're on a Mac, your best bet is to install Node.js directly from the Node.js website instead of through another package manager (like Homebrew). Installing Node.js via Homebrew is known to cause some issues.

The Node Package Manager (npm for short) is installed as a part of Node.js. To check if npm is available as a part of our development environment, we can open a terminal window and type:

```
$ npm -v
```

If a version number is not printed out and you receive an error, make sure to download a Node.js installer that includes npm.

Your npm version should be 5.6.0 or higher.

TypeScript

Once you have Node.js setup, the next step is to install TypeScript. Make sure you install at least version 2.1 or greater. To install it, run the following npm command:

```
1   $ npm install -g typescript
```

> ℹ️ **Do I have to use TypeScript?** No, you don't *have* to use TypeScript to use Angular, but you probably should. Angular does have an ES5 API, but Angular is written in TypeScript and generally that's what everyone is using. We're going to use TypeScript in this book because it's great and it makes working with Angular easier. That said, it isn't strictly required.

---

[15]https://nodejs.org/download/

Browser

We highly recommend using the Google Chrome Web Browser[16] to develop Angular apps. We'll use the Chrome developer toolkit throughout this book. To follow along with our development and debugging we recommend downloading it now.

Special instruction for Windows users

Throughout this book, we will be using Unix/Mac commands in the terminal. Most of these commands, like ls and cd, are cross-platform. However, sometimes these commands are Unix/Mac-specific or contain Unix/Mac-specific flags (like ls -1p).

As a result, be alert that you may have to occasionally determine the equivalent of a Unix/Mac command for your shell. Fortunately, the amount of work we do in the terminal is minimal and you will not encounter this issue often.

Windows users should be aware that our terminal examples use Unix/Mac commands.

Angular CLI

Angular provides a utility to allow users to create and manage projects from the command line. It automates tasks like creating projects, adding new controllers, etc. It's generally a good idea to use Angular CLI as it will help create and maintain common patterns across our application.

To install Angular CLI, just run the following command:

```
1   $ npm install -g @angular/cli
```

Once it's installed you'll be able to run it from the command line using the ng command. When you do, you'll see a lot of output, but if you scroll back, you should be able to see the following:

```
1   $ ng --version
```

If everything installed correctly, you should see the current version output to your terminal. Congratulations!

---

[16]https://www.google.com/chrome/

If you're running OSX or Linux, you might receive this line in the output:

```
1   Could not start watchman; falling back to NodeWatcher for file system events.
```

This means that we don't have a tool called **watchman** installed. This tool helps Angular CLI when it needs to monitor files in your filesystem for changes. If you're running OSX, it's recommended to install it using Homebrew with the following command:

```
1   $ brew install watchman
```

If you're on OSX and got an error when running brew, it means that you probably don't have Homebrew installed. Please refer to the page http://brew.sh/ to learn how to install it and try again.

If you're on Linux, you may refer to the page https://ember-cli.com/user-guide/#watchman for more information about how to install watchman.

If you're on Windows instead, you don't need to install anything and Angular CLI will use the native Node.js watcher.

If you're curious about all of the things that Angular CLI can do, try out this command:

```
1   $ ng --help
```

Don't worry about understanding all of the options - we'll be covering the important ones in this chapter.

Now that we have Angular CLI and its dependencies installed, let's use this tool to create our first application.

Example Project

Open up the terminal and run the ng new command to create a new project from scratch:

```
1   $ ng new angular-hello-world
```

Once you run it, you'll see (roughly) following output:

```
 1   CREATE angular-hello-world/README.md (1034 bytes)
 2   CREATE angular-hello-world/angular.json (3504 bytes)
 3   CREATE angular-hello-world/package.json (1323 bytes)
 4   CREATE angular-hello-world/tsconfig.json (384 bytes)
 5   CREATE angular-hello-world/tslint.json (2805 bytes)
 6   CREATE angular-hello-world/.editorconfig (245 bytes)
 7   CREATE angular-hello-world/.gitignore (503 bytes)
 8   CREATE angular-hello-world/src/environments/environment.prod.ts (51 bytes)
 9   CREATE angular-hello-world/src/environments/environment.ts (631 bytes)
10   CREATE angular-hello-world/src/favicon.ico (5430 bytes)
11   CREATE angular-hello-world/src/index.html (304 bytes)
12   CREATE angular-hello-world/src/main.ts (370 bytes)
13   CREATE angular-hello-world/src/polyfills.ts (3194 bytes)
14   CREATE angular-hello-world/src/test.ts (642 bytes)
15   CREATE angular-hello-world/src/assets/.gitkeep (0 bytes)
16   CREATE angular-hello-world/src/styles.css (80 bytes)
17   CREATE angular-hello-world/src/browserslist (375 bytes)
18   CREATE angular-hello-world/src/karma.conf.js (964 bytes)
19   CREATE angular-hello-world/src/tsconfig.app.json (194 bytes)
20   CREATE angular-hello-world/src/tsconfig.spec.json (282 bytes)
21   CREATE angular-hello-world/src/tslint.json (314 bytes)
22   CREATE angular-hello-world/src/app/app.module.ts (314 bytes)
23   CREATE angular-hello-world/src/app/app.component.css (0 bytes)
24   CREATE angular-hello-world/src/app/app.component.html (1141 bytes)
25   CREATE angular-hello-world/src/app/app.component.spec.ts (986 bytes)
26   CREATE angular-hello-world/src/app/app.component.ts (207 bytes)
27   CREATE angular-hello-world/e2e/protractor.conf.js (752 bytes)
28   CREATE angular-hello-world/e2e/src/app.e2e-spec.ts (299 bytes)
29   CREATE angular-hello-world/e2e/src/app.po.ts (208 bytes)
30   CREATE angular-hello-world/e2e/tsconfig.e2e.json (213 bytes)
31   ...
32   added 1146 packages in 105.319s
33       Successfully initialized git.
```

> Note: the exact files that your project generates may vary slightly depending on the version of @angular/cli that was installed.

This will run for a while while it's installing npm dependencies. Once it finishes we'll see a success message.

There are a lot of files generated! Don't worry about understanding all of them yet. Throughout the book we'll walk through what each one means and what it's used for.

Let's go inside the `angular-hello-world` directory, which the `ng` command created for us and see what has been created:

```
1   $ cd angular-hello-world
2   $ tree -F -L 1
3   .
4   |-- README.md                // a useful README
5   |-- angular.json             // angular-cli configuration file
6   |-- e2e/                     // end-to-end tests
7   |-- node_modules/            // installed dependencies
8   |-- package-lock.json        // npm dependencies lockfile
9   |-- package.json             // npm configuration
10  |-- src/                     // our application's code
11  |-- tsconfig.json            // typescript config
12  `-- tslint.json              // linting config
13
14  3 directories, 6 files
```

The `tree` command is completely optional. But if you're on OSX it can be installed via `brew install tree`

For now, the folder we're interested in is `src`, where we'll put our custom application code. Let's take a look at what was created there:

```
1   $ cd src
2   $ tree -F
3   .
4   |-- app/
5   |   |-- app.component.css
6   |   |-- app.component.html
7   |   |-- app.component.spec.ts
8   |   |-- app.component.ts
9   |   `-- app.module.ts
10  |-- assets/
11  |-- browserslist
12  |-- environments/
13  |   |-- environment.prod.ts
14  |   `-- environment.ts
15  |-- favicon.ico
16  |-- index.html
17  |-- karma.conf.js
```

```
18  |-- main.ts
19  |-- polyfills.ts
20  |-- styles.css
21  |-- test.ts
22  |-- tsconfig.app.json
23  |-- tsconfig.spec.json
24  `-- tslint.json
25
26  3 directories, 18 files
```

Using your favorite text editor, let's open `index.html`. You should see this code:

code/first-app/angular-hello-world/src/index.html

```html
1   <!doctype html>
2   <html lang="en">
3   <head>
4     <meta charset="utf-8">
5     <title>AngularHelloWorld</title>
6     <base href="/">
7
8     <meta name="viewport" content="width=device-width, initial-scale=1">
9     <link rel="icon" type="image/x-icon" href="favicon.ico">
10  </head>
11  <body>
12    <app-root></app-root>
13  </body>
14  </html>
```

Let's break it down a bit:

code/first-app/angular-hello-world/src/index.html

```html
1   <!doctype html>
2   <html lang="en">
3   <head>
4     <meta charset="utf-8">
5     <title>AngularHelloWorld</title>
6     <base href="/">
7
8     <meta name="viewport" content="width=device-width, initial-scale=1">
9     <link rel="icon" type="image/x-icon" href="favicon.ico">
10  </head>
```

If you're familiar with writing HTML files, this first part is straightforward, we're declaring the core structure of the HTML document and a few bits of metadata such as page `charset`, `title` and base `href`.

If we continue to the template body, we see the following:

code/first-app/angular-hello-world/src/index.html

```
11  <body>
12    <app-root></app-root>
13  </body>
14  </html>
```

The `app-root` tag is **where our application will be rendered**.

But what *is* the `app-root` tag and where does it come from? `app-root` is a *component* that is defined by our Angular application. In Angular **we can define our own HTML tags** and give them custom functionality. The `app-root` tag will be the "entry point" for our application on the page.

Let's try running this app as-is and then we'll dig in to see how this component is defined.

Writing Application Code

Running the application

Before making any changes, let's load our app from the generated application into the browser. Angular CLI has a built in HTTP server that we can use to run our app.

To use it, head back to the terminal, and change directories into the root of our application.

```
1  $ cd angular-hello-world
2  $ ng serve
3  ** NG Live Development Server is running on http://localhost:4200. **
4  // ...
5  // a bunch of other messages
6  // ...
7  Compiled successfully.
```

Our application is now running on `localhost` port 4200. Let's open the browser and visit:

http://localhost:4200[17]

---

[17] http://localhost:4200

Note that if you get the message:

```
1    Port 4200 is already in use. Use '--port' to specify a different port
```

This means that you already have another service running on port 4200. If this is the case you can either 1. shut down the other service or 2. use the --port flag when running ng serve like this:

```
1    ng serve --port 9001
```

The above command would change the URL you open in your browser to something like: http://localhost:9001

Another thing to notice is that, on some machines, the domain localhost may not work. You may see a set of numbers such as 127.0.0.1. When you run ng serve it should show you what URL the server is running on, so be sure to read the messages on your machine to find your exact development URL.

Running application

Now that we have the application setup, and we know how to run it, it's time to start writing some code.

Making a Component

One of the big ideas behind Angular is the idea of *components*.

In our Angular apps, we write HTML markup that becomes our interactive application, but the browser only understands a limited set of markup tags; Built-ins like `<select>` or `<form>` or `<video>` all have functionality **defined by our browser creator**.

What if we want to **teach the browser new tags**? What if we wanted to have a `<weather>` tag that shows the weather? Or what if we want to create a `<login>` tag that shows a login panel?

This is the fundamental idea behind components: we will **teach the browser new tags** that have custom functionality attached to them.

> If you have a background in AngularJS 1.X, you can think of **components as the new version of directives**.

Let's create our very first component. When we have this component written, we will be able to use it in our HTML document using the `app-hello-world` tag:

```
1  <app-hello-world></app-hello-world>
```

To create a new component using Angular CLI, we'll use the **generate** command.

To generate the **hello-world** component, we need to run the following command:

```
1  $ ng generate component hello-world
2  CREATE src/app/hello-world/hello-world.component.css (0 bytes)
3  CREATE src/app/hello-world/hello-world.component.html (30 bytes)
4  CREATE src/app/hello-world/hello-world.component.spec.ts (657 bytes)
5  CREATE src/app/hello-world/hello-world.component.ts (288 bytes)
6  UPDATE src/app/app.module.ts (414 bytes)
```

So how do we actually define a new Component? A basic Component has two parts:

1. A Component decorator
2. A component definition class

Let's look at the component code and then take these one at a time. Open up our first TypeScript file: `src/app/hello-world/hello-world.component.ts`.

code/first-app/angular-hello-world/src/app/hello-world/hello-world.component.ts

```
1   import { Component, OnInit } from '@angular/core';
2
3   @Component({
4     selector: 'app-hello-world',
5     templateUrl: './hello-world.component.html',
6     styleUrls: ['./hello-world.component.css']
7   })
8   export class HelloWorldComponent implements OnInit {
9
10    constructor() { }
11
12    ngOnInit() {
13    }
14
15  }
```

This snippet may seem scary at first, but don't worry. We're going to walk through it step by step.

> ℹ️ Notice that we suffix our TypeScript file with `.ts` instead of `.js` The problem is our browser doesn't know how to interpret TypeScript files. To solve this gap, the `ng serve` command live-compiles our `.ts` to a `.js` file automatically.

Importing Dependencies

The `import` statement defines the modules we want to use to write our code. Here we're importing two things: `Component`, and `OnInit`.

We `import` `Component` from the module `"@angular/core"`. The `"@angular/core"` portion tells our program **where to find the dependencies** that we're looking for. In this case, we're telling the compiler that `"@angular/core"` defines and exports two JavaScript/TypeScript objects called `Component` and `OnInit`.

Similarly, we `import` `OnInit` from the same module. As we'll learn later, `OnInit` helps us to run code when we initialize the component. For now, don't worry about it.

Notice that the structure of this `import` is of the format `import { things } from wherever`. In the `{ things }` part what we are doing is called *destructuring*. Destructuring is a feature provided by ES6 and TypeScript. We will talk more about it in the next chapter.

The idea with `import` is a lot like `import` in Java or `require` in Ruby: we're **pulling in these dependencies from another module** and making these dependencies available for use in this file.

Component Decorators

After importing our dependencies, we are declaring the component:

code/first-app/angular-hello-world/src/app/hello-world/hello-world.component.ts

```
3  @Component({
4    selector: 'app-hello-world',
5    templateUrl: './hello-world.component.html',
6    styleUrls: ['./hello-world.component.css']
7  })
```

If you're new to TypeScript then the syntax of this next statement might seem a little foreign:

```
1  @Component({
2    // ...
3  })
```

What is going on here? These are called *decorators*.

We can think of decorators as **metadata added to our code**. When we use @Component on the HelloWorld class, we are "decorating" HelloWorld as a Component.

We want to be able to use this component in our markup by using a <app-hello-world> tag. To do that, we configure the @Component and specify the selector as app-hello-world.

```
1  @Component({
2    selector: 'app-hello-world'
3    // ... more here
4  })
```

The syntax of Angular's component selectors is similar to CSS selectors (though Angular components have some special syntax for selectors, which we'll cover later on). For now, know that with this selector we're **defining a new tag** that we can use in our markup.

The selector property here indicates *which DOM element* this component is going to use. In this case, any <app-hello-world></app-hello-world> tags that appear within a template will be compiled using the HelloWorldComponent class and get any attached functionality.

Adding a template with templateUrl

In our component we are specifying a templateUrl of ./hello-world.component.html. This means that we will load our template from the file hello-world.component.html in the same directory as our component. Let's take a look at that file:

code/first-app/angular-hello-world/src/app/hello-world/hello-world.component.html

```
1  <p>
2    hello-world works!
3  </p>
```

Here we're defining a p tag with some basic text in the middle. When Angular loads this component it will also read from this file and use it as the template for our component.

Adding a template

We can define templates two ways, either by using the template key in our @Component object or by specifying a templateUrl.

We could add a template to our @Component by passing the template option:

```
1  @Component({
2    selector: 'app-hello-world',
3    template: `
4      <p>
5        hello-world works inline!
6      </p>
7    `
8  })
```

Notice that we're defining our template string between backticks (` ... `). This is a new (and fantastic) feature of ES6 that allows us to do **multiline strings**. Using backticks for multiline strings makes it easy to put templates inside your code files.

> ℹ️ **Should you really be putting templates in your code files?** The answer is: it depends. For a long time the commonly held belief was that you should keep your code and templates separate. While this might be easier for some teams, for some projects it adds overhead because you have switch between a lot of files.
>
> Personally, if our templates are shorter than a page, we much prefer to have the templates alongside the code (that is, within the .ts file). When we see both the logic and the view together, it's easy to understand how they interact with one another.
>
> The biggest drawback to mixing views and our code is that many editors don't support syntax highlighting of the internal strings (yet). Hopefully, we'll see more editors supporting syntax highlighting HTML within template strings soon.

Adding CSS Styles with `styleUrls`

Notice the key `styleUrls`:

```
1    styleUrls: ['./hello-world.component.css']
```

This code says that we want to use the CSS in the file `hello-world.component.css` as the styles for this component. Angular uses a concept called "style-encapsulation" which means that styles specified for a particular component *only apply to that component*. We talk more about this in-depth later on in the book in the Styling section of Advanced Components.

For now, we're not going to use any component-local styles, so you can leave this as-is (or delete the key entirely).

> ℹ️ You may have noticed that this key is different from `template` in that it accepts *an array* as it's argument. This is because we can load multiple stylesheets for a single component.

Loading Our Component

Now that we have our first component code filled out, how do we load it in our page?

If we visit our application again in the browser, we'll see that nothing changed. That's because we only **created** the component, but we're not **using** it yet.

In order to change that, we need to add our component tag to a template that is already being rendered. Open up the file: `first_app/angular-hello-world/src/app/app.component.html`

Remember that because we configured our `HelloWorldComponent` with the selector `app-hello-world`, we can use the `<app-hello-world></app-hello-world>` in our template. Let's add the `<app-hello-world>` tag to `app.component.html`

Delete the content in `app.component.html` and replace it with:

code/first-app/angular-hello-world/src/app/app.component.html

```
1   <h1>
2     {{title}}
3
4     <app-hello-world></app-hello-world>
5   </h1>
```

Now refresh the page and take a look:

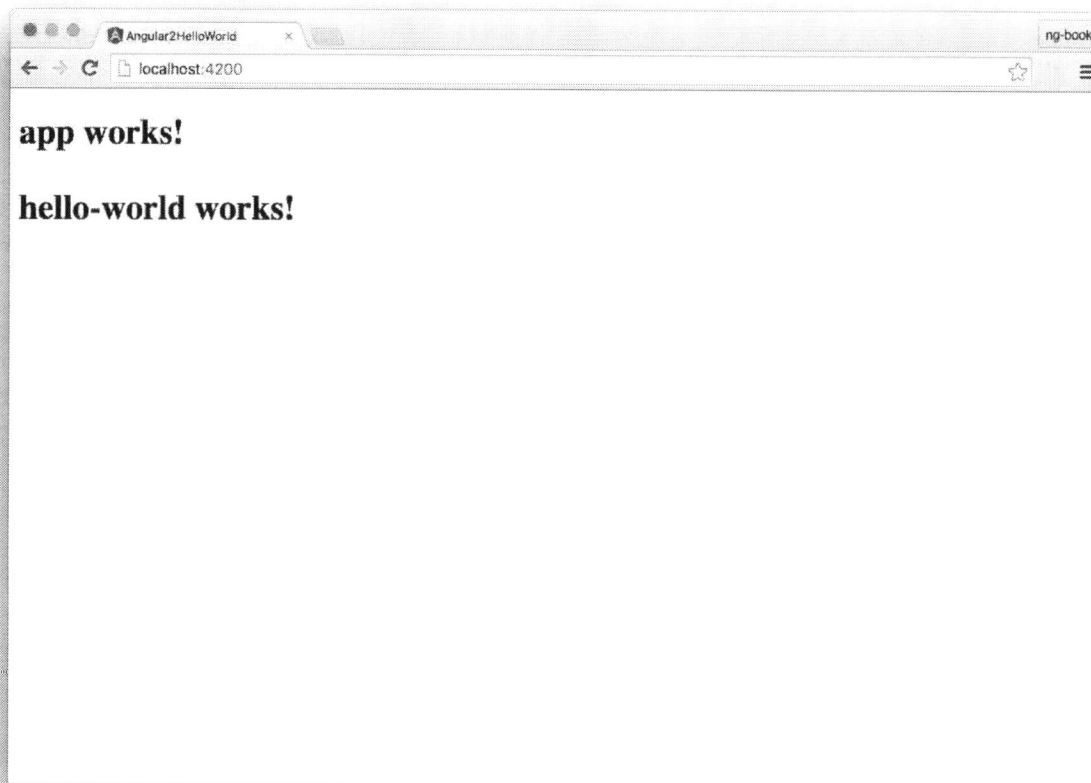

Hello world works

It works!

Adding Data to the Component

Right now our component renders a static template, which means our component isn't very interesting.

Let's imagine that we have an app which will show **a list of users** and we want to show their names. Before we render the whole list, we first need to render an individual user. So let's create a new component that will show a user's name.

To do this, we will use the `ng generate` command again:

```
1   ng generate component user-item
```

Remember that in order to see a component we've created, we need to add it to a template.

Let's add our `app-user-item` tag to `app.component.html` so that we can see our changes as we make them. Modify `app.component.html` to look like this:

code/first-app/angular-hello-world/src/app/app.component.html

```
1  <h1>
2    {{title}}
3
4    <app-hello-world></app-hello-world>
5
6    <app-user-item></app-user-item>
7  </h1>
```

Then refresh the page and confirm that you see the user-item works! text on the page.

We want our UserItemComponent to show the name of a particular user .

Let's introduce name as a new *property* of our component. By having a name property, we will be able to reuse this component for different users (but keep the same markup, logic, and styles).

In order to add a name, we'll introduce a property on the UserItemComponent class to declare it has a local variable named name.

code/first-app/angular-hello-world/src/app/user-item/user-item.component.ts

```
8  export class UserItemComponent implements OnInit {
9    name: string; // <-- added name property
10
11   constructor() {
12     this.name = 'Felipe'; // set the name
13   }
14
15   ngOnInit() {
16   }
17
18 }
```

Notice that we've changed two things :

1. name Property

On the UserItemComponent class we added a *property*. Notice that the syntax is new relative to ES5 JavaScript. When we write name: string; it means that we're declaring the name property to be of *type* string.

Being able to assign a type to a variable is what gives *TypeScript* it's name. By setting the type of this property to string, the compiler ensures that name variable is a string and it will throw an error if we try to assign, say, a number to this property.

This syntax is also the way TypeScript defines instance properties. By putting name: string in our code like this, we're giving every instance of UserItemComponent a property name.

2. A Constructor

On the `UserItemComponent` class we defined a *constructor*, i.e. a function that is called when we create new instances of this class.

In our constructor we can assign our `name` property by using `this.name`

When we write:

code/first-app/angular-hello-world/src/app/user-item/user-item.component.ts

```
11    constructor() {
12      this.name = 'Felipe'; // set the name
13    }
```

We're saying that whenever a new `UserItemComponent` is created, set the name to `'Felipe'`.

Rendering The Template

When we have a property on a component, we can show that value in our template by using two curly brackets `{{ }}` to display the value of the variable in our template. For instance:

code/first-app/angular-hello-world/src/app/user-item/user-item.component.html

```
1    <p>
2      Hello {{ name }}
3    </p>
```

On the `template` notice that we added a new syntax: `{{ name }}`. The brackets are called *template tags* (or sometimes *mustache tags*).

Whatever is between the template tags will be expanded as an *expression*. Here, because the `template` is *bound* to our Component, the `name` will expand to the value of `this.name` i.e. `'Felipe'`.

Try It Out

After making these changes reload the page and the page should display `Hello Felipe`

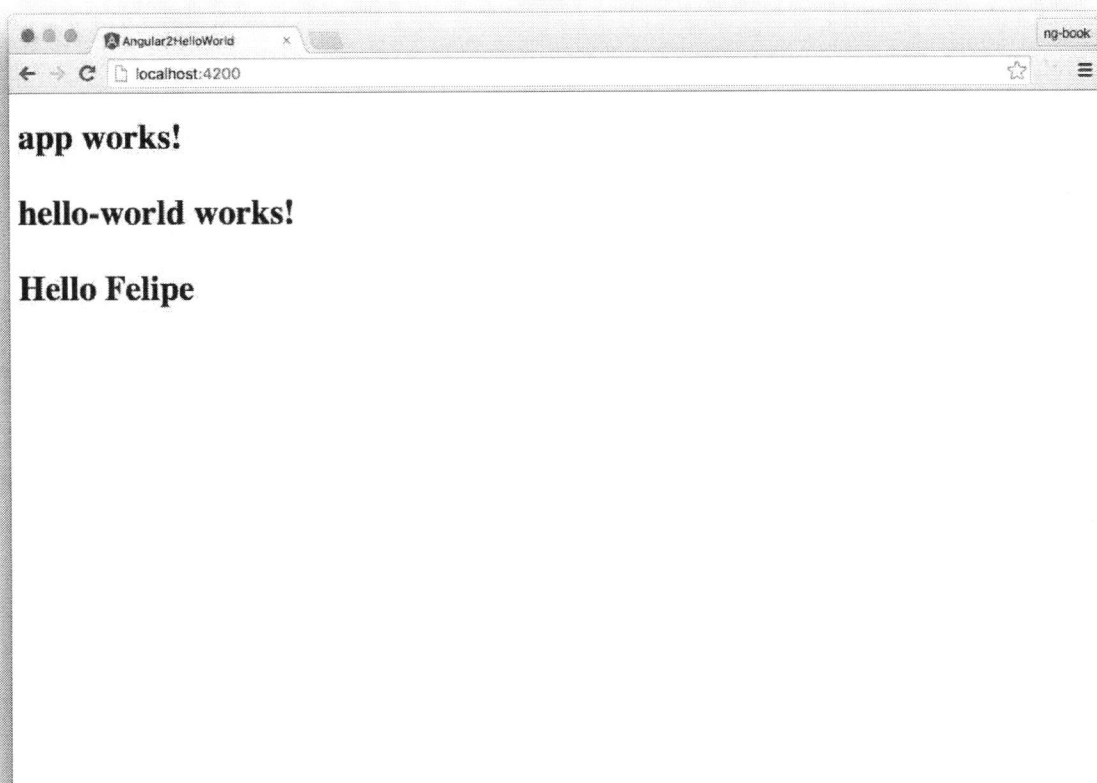

Application with Data

Working With Arrays

Now we are able to say "Hello" to a single name, but what if we want to say "Hello" to a collection of names?

In Angular we can iterate over a list of objects in our template using the syntax *ngFor. The idea is that we want to **repeat the same markup for a collection of objects**.

> If you've worked with AngularJS 1.X before, you've probably used the ng-repeat directive. NgFor works much the same way.

Let's create a new component that will render a *list* of users. We start by generating a new component:

```
1  ng generate component user-list
```

And let's replace our `<app-user-item>` tag with `<app-user-list>` in our `app.component.html` file:

code/first-app/angular-hello-world/src/app/app.component.html
```
1  <h1>
2    {{title}}
3
4    <app-hello-world></app-hello-world>
5
6    <app-user-list></app-user-list>
7  </h1>
```

In the same way we added a `name` property to our `UserItemComponent`, let's add a `names` property to this `UserListComponent`.

However, instead of storing only a single string, let's set the type of this property to *an array of strings*. An array is notated by the `[]` after the type, and the code looks like this:

code/first-app/angular-hello-world/src/app/user-list/user-list.component.ts
```
8   export class UserListComponent implements OnInit {
9     names: string[];
10
11    constructor() {
12      this.names = ['Ari', 'Carlos', 'Felipe', 'Nate'];
13    }
14
15    ngOnInit() {
16    }
17
18  }
```

The first change to point out is the new `string[]` property on our `UserListComponent` class. This syntax means that `names` is typed as an `Array` of `strings`. Another way to write this would be `Array<string>`.

We changed our constructor to set the value of `this.names` to `['Ari', 'Carlos', 'Felipe', 'Nate']`.

Now we can update our template to render this list of names. To do this, we will use `*ngFor`, which will

- iterate over a list of items and
- generate a new tag for each one.

Here's what our new template will look like:

code/first-app/angular-hello-world/src/app/user-list/user-list.component.html

```
1  <ul>
2    <li *ngFor="let name of names">Hello {{ name }}</li>
3  </ul>
```

We updated the template with one `ul` and one `li` with a new `*ngFor="let name of names"` attribute. The `*` character and `let` syntax can be a little overwhelming at first, so let's break it down:

The `*ngFor` syntax says we want to use the `NgFor` directive on this attribute. You can think of `NgFor` akin to a `for` loop; the idea is that we're creating a new DOM element for every item in a collection.

The value states: `"let name of names"`. `names` is our array of names as specified on the `UserList-Component` object. `let name` is called a *reference*. When we say `"let name of names"` we're saying loop over each element in `names` and assign each one to a *local* variable called `name`.

The `NgFor` directive will render one `li` tag for each entry found on the `names` array and declare a local variable `name` to hold the current item being iterated. This new variable will then be replaced inside the `Hello {{ name }}` snippet.

We didn't have to call the reference variable `name`. We could just as well have written:

```
1    <li *ngFor="let foobar of names">Hello {{ foobar }}</li>
```

But what about the reverse? Quiz question: what would have happened if we wrote:

```
1    <li *ngFor="let name of foobar">Hello {{ name }}</li>
```

Answer: We'd get an error because `foobar` isn't a property on the component.

NgFor repeats the element that the `ngFor` is called. That is, we put it on the `li` tag and **not** the `ul` tag because we want to repeat the list element (`li`) and not the list itself (`ul`).

Note that the capitalization here isn't a typo: `NgFor` is the capitalization of the *class* that implements the logic and `ngFor` is the "selector" for the attribute we want to use.

If you're feeling adventurous you can learn a lot about how the Angular core team writes Components by reading the source directly. For instance, you can find the source of the NgFor directive here[18].

---
[18]https://github.com/angular/angular/blob/master/packages/common/src/directives/ng_for_of.ts

When we reload the page now, we'll see that we now have one `li` for each string in the array:

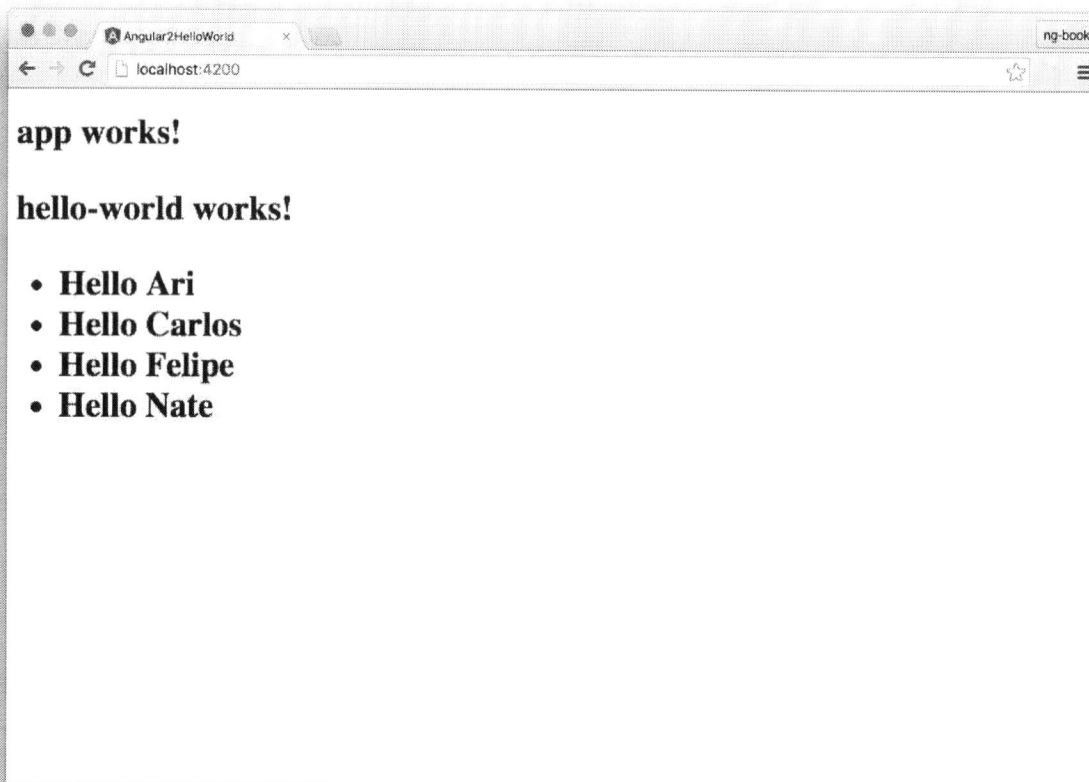

Application with Data

Using the User Item Component

Remember that earlier we created a `UserItemComponent`? Instead of rendering each name within the `UserListComponent`, we ought to use `UserItemComponent` as a *child component* - that is, instead of rendering the text `Hello` and the name directly, we should let our `UserItemComponent` specify the template (and functionality) of **each item in the list**.

To do this, we need to do three things:

1. Configure the `UserListComponent` to render to `UserItemComponent` (in the template)
2. Configure the `UserItemComponent` to accept the `name` variable as an *input* and
3. Configure the `UserListComponent` template to **pass the name** to the `UserItemComponent`.

Let's perform these steps one-by-one.

Rendering the UserItemComponent

Our UserItemComponent specifies the selector app-user-item - let's add that tag to our template:

code/first-app/angular-hello-world/src/app/user-list/user-list.component.html

```
1  <ul>
2    <li *ngFor="let name of names">
3      <app-user-item></app-user-item>
4    </li>
5  </ul>
```

Notice that we swapped out the text Hello and the name for the tag app-user-item.

If we reload our browser, this is what we will see:

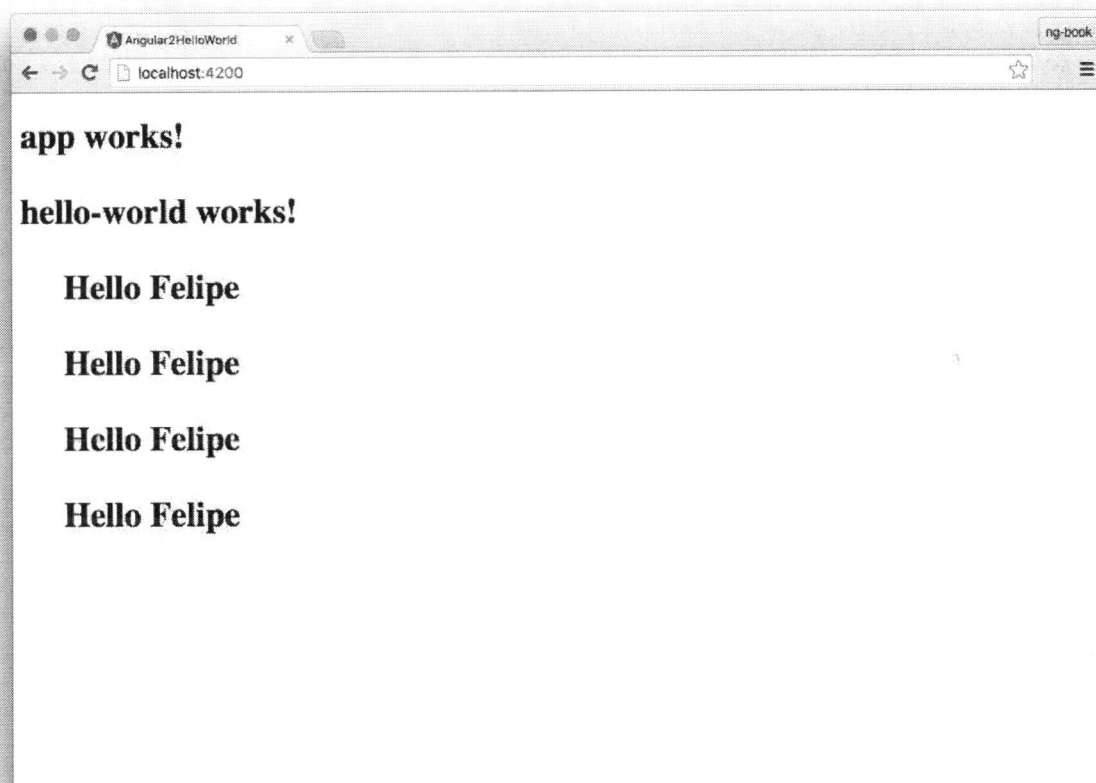

Application with Data

It repeats, but something is wrong here - every name says "Felipe"! We need a way to *pass data into the child component.*

Thankfully, Angular provides a way to do this: the @Input decorator.

Accepting Inputs

Remember that in our UserItemComponent we had set this.name = 'Felipe'; in the constructor of that component. Now we need to change this component to accept a value for this property.

Here's what we need to change on our UserItemComponent:

code/first-app/angular-hello-world/src/app/user-item/user-item.component.ts

```
 1  import {
 2    Component,
 3    OnInit,
 4    Input // <--- added this
 5  } from '@angular/core';
 6
 7  @Component({
 8    selector: 'app-user-item',
 9    templateUrl: './user-item.component.html',
10    styleUrls: ['./user-item.component.css']
11  })
12  export class UserItemComponent implements OnInit {
13    @Input() name: string; // <-- added Input annotation
14
15    constructor() {
16      // removed setting name
17    }
18
19    ngOnInit() {}
20  }
```

Notice that we changed the name property to have an *decorator* of @Input. We talk a lot more about Inputs (and Outputs) in the next chapter, but for now, know that this syntax allows us to pass in a value *from the parent template* .

In order to use Input we also had to add it to the list of constants in import.

Lastly, we don't want to set a default value for name so we remove that from the constructor.

So now that we have a name Input, how do we actually use it?

Passing an Input value

To pass values to a component we use the *bracket* [] syntax in our template - let's take a look at our updated template:

code/first-app/angular-hello-world/src/app/user-list/user-list.component.html

```
1  <ul>
2    <li *ngFor="let name of names">
3      <app-user-item [name]="name"></app-user-item>
4    </li>
5  </ul>
```

Notice that we've added a new attribute on our app-user-item tag: [name]="name" . In Angular when we add an attribute in brackets like [foo] we're saying we want to pass a value to the *input* named foo on that component.

In this case notice that the name on the right-hand side comes from the let name ... statement in ngFor. That is, consider if we had this instead:

```
1    <li *ngFor="let individualUserName of names">
2      <app-user-item [name]="individualUserName"></app-user-item>
3    </li>
```

The [name] part designates the Input on the UserItemComponent. Notice that we're *not* passing the literal string "individualUserName" instead we're passing the *value* of individualUserName, which is, on each pass, the value of an element of names.

We talk more about inputs and outputs in detail in the next chapter. For now, know that we're:

1. Iterating over names
2. Creating a new UserItemComponent for each element in names and
3. Passing the value of that name into the name Input property on the UserItemComponent

Now our list of names works!

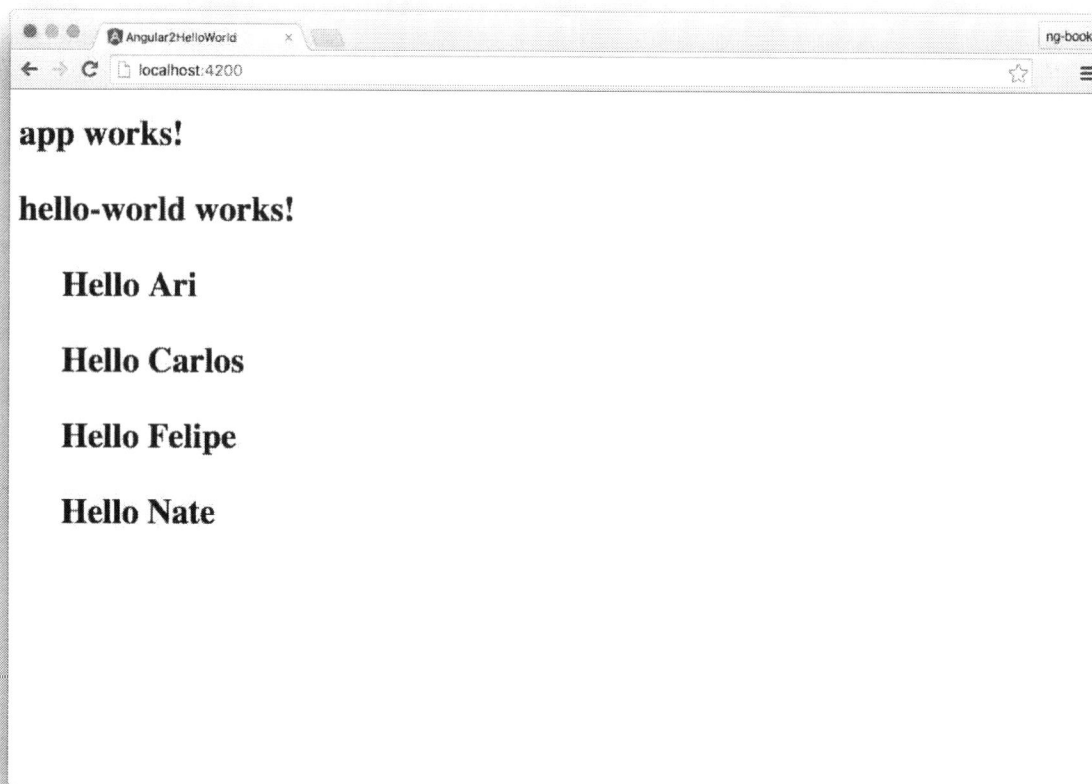

Application with Names Working

Congratulations! You've built your first Angular app with components!

Of course, this app is very simple and we'd like to build much more sophisticated applications. Don't worry, in this book we'll show you how to become an expert writing Angular apps. In fact, in this chapter we're going to build a voting-app (think Reddit or Product Hunt). This app will feature user interaction, and even more components!

But before we start building a new app, let's take a closer look at how Angular apps are bootstrapped.

Bootstrapping Crash Course

Every app has a main entry point. This application was built using Angular CLI (which is built on a tool called Webpack). We run this app by calling the command:

```
1   ng serve
```

ng will look at the file angular.json to find the entry point to our app. Let's trace how ng finds the components we just built.

At a high level, it looks like this:

- `angular.json` specifies a "main" file, which in this case is `main.ts`
- `main.ts` is the entry-point for our app and it *bootstraps* our application
- The bootstrap process boots **an Angular module** – we haven't talked about modules yet, but we will in a minute
- We use the `AppModule` to bootstrap the app. `AppModule` is specified in `src/app/app.module.ts`
- `AppModule` specifies which *component* to use as the top-level component. In this case it is `AppComponent`
- `AppComponent` has `<app-user-list>` tags in the template and this renders our list of users.

For now the thing we want to focus on is the Angular module system: `NgModule`.

Angular has a powerful concept of *modules*. When you boot an Angular app, you're not booting a component directly, but instead you create an `NgModule` which points to the component you want to load.

Take a look at this code:

code/first-app/angular-hello-world/src/app/app.module.ts

```
 9  @NgModule({
10    declarations: [
11      AppComponent,
12      HelloWorldComponent,
13      UserItemComponent,
14      UserListComponent
15    ],
16    imports: [
17      BrowserModule
18    ],
19    providers: [],
20    bootstrap: [AppComponent]
21  })
22  export class AppModule { }
```

The first thing we see is an `@NgModule` decorator. Like all decorators, this `@NgModule( ... )` code **adds metadata to the class immediately following** (in this case, `AppModule`).

Our `@NgModule` decorator has four keys: `declarations`, `imports`, `providers`, and `bootstrap`.

declarations

declarations specifies the components that are **defined in this module**. This is an important idea in Angular:

You have to declare components in a `NgModule` before you can use them in your templates.

You can think of an `NgModule` a bit like a "package" and `declarations` states **what components are "owned by" this module**.

You may have noticed that when we used `ng generate`, the tool automatically added our components to this `declarations` list! The idea is that when we generated a new component, the `ng` tool assumed we wanted it to belong to the current `NgModule`.

imports

`imports` describes which *dependencies* this module has. We're creating a browser app, so we want to import the `BrowserModule`.

If your module depends on other modules, you list them here.

> **`import` vs. `imports`?**
>
> You might be asking the question, "What's the difference between `import`ing a class at the top of the file and putting a module in `imports`?"
>
> The short answer is that you put something in your `NgModule`'s `imports` if you're going to be using it in your templates or with *dependency injection*. We haven't talked about *dependency injection*, but rest assured, we will.

providers

`providers` is used for dependency injection. So to make a service available to be injected throughout our application, we will add it here.

> Learn more about this in the section on `Dependency Injection`.

bootstrap

`bootstrap` tells Angular that when this module is used to bootstrap an app, we need to load the `AppComponent` component as the top-level component.

Expanding our Application

Now that we know how to create a basic application, let's build our Reddit clone. Before we start coding, it's a good idea to look over our app and break it down into its logical components.

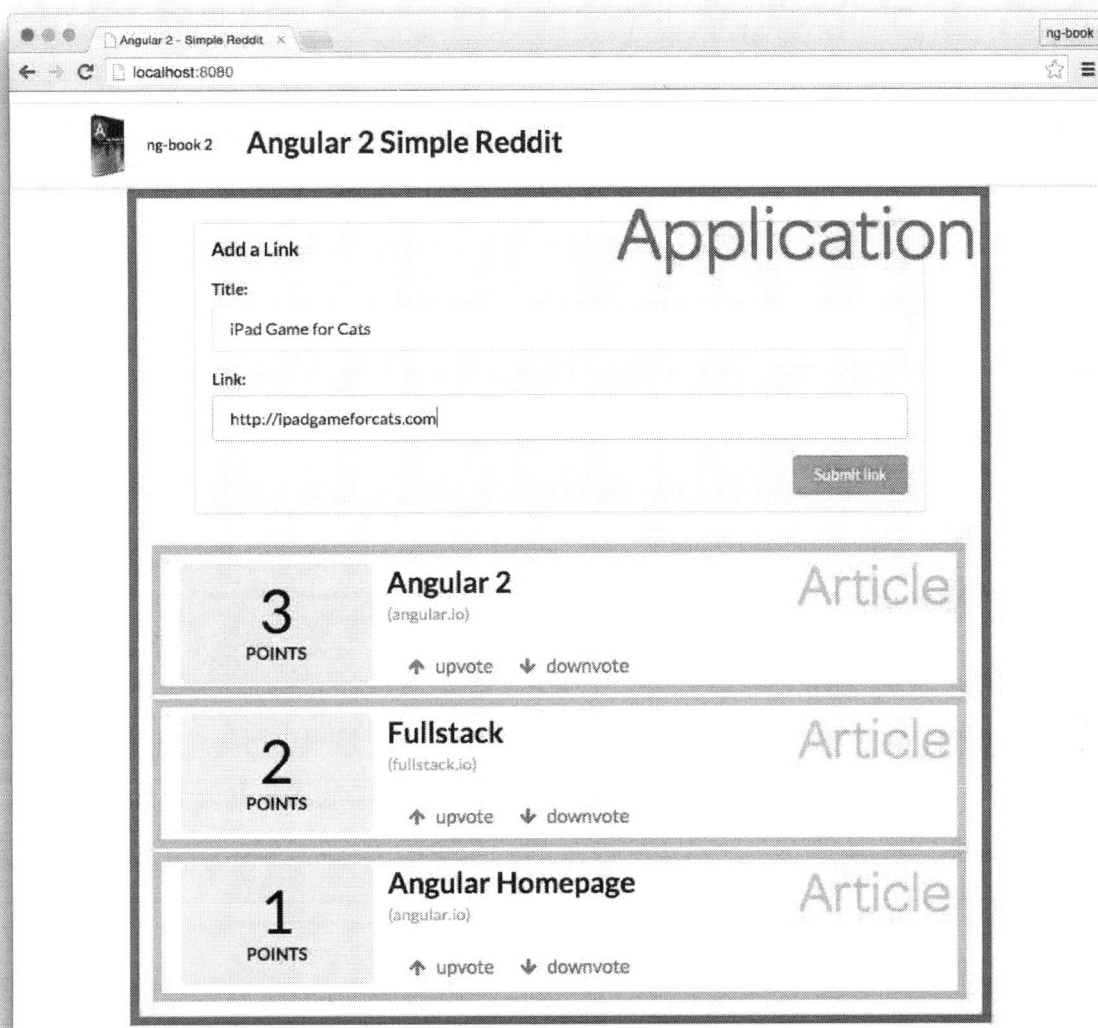

Application with Data

We're going to make two components in this app:

1. The overall application, which contains the form used to submit new articles (marked in magenta in the picture).
2. Each article (marked in mint green).

In a larger application, the **form** for submitting articles would probably become its own component. However, having the form be its own component makes the data passing more complex, so we're going to simplify in this chapter and have only two components.

For now two components will work fine, but we'll learn how to deal with more sophisticated data architectures in later chapters of this book.

But first thing's first, let's generate a new application by running the same **ng new** command we ran before to create a new application passing it the name of the app we want to create (here, we'll create an application called `angular-reddit`):

```
1   ng new angular-reddit
```

We've provided a completed version of our `angular-reddit` in the example code download. If you ever need more context, be sure to check it out to see how everything fits together.

Adding CSS

First thing we want to do is add some CSS styling so that our app isn't completely unstyled.

If you're building your app from scratch, you'll want to copy over a few files from our completed example in the `first_app/angular-reddit` folder.

Copy:

- `src/index.html`
- `src/styles.css`
- `src/app/vendor`
- `src/assets/images`

into your application's folder.

For this project we're going to be using Semantic-UI[19] to help with the styling. Semantic-UI is a CSS framework, similar to Zurb Foundation[20] or Twitter Bootstrap[21]. We've included it in the sample code download so all you need to do is copy over the files specified above.

---

[19] http://semantic-ui.com/

[20] http://foundation.zurb.com

[21] http://getbootstrap.com

The Application Component

Let's now build a new component which will:

1. store our current list of articles
2. contain the form for submitting new articles.

We can find the main application component on the `src/app/app.component.ts` file. Let's open this file. Again, we'll see the same initial contents we saw previously.

code/first-app/angular-reddit/src/app/app.component.ts

```
1   import { Component } from '@angular/core';
2
3   @Component({
4     selector: 'app-root',
5     templateUrl: './app.component.html',
6     styleUrls: ['./app.component.css']
7   })
8   export class AppComponent {
9     title = 'app works!';
10  }
```

Notice that the `title` property was automatically generated for us on the `AppComponent`. Remove that line, because we aren't using the component `title`.

Below we're going to be submitting new links that have a 'title', which could be confused with the `AppComponent` title that was auto-generated by Angular CLI. When we add a 'title' to the new links we submit below the form title is a separate form field.

Let's change the template a bit to include a form for adding links. We'll use a bit of styling from the `semantic-ui` package to make the form look a bit nicer:

code/first-app/angular-reddit/src/app/app.component.html

```
1    <form class="ui large form segment">
2      <h3 class="ui header">Add a Link</h3>
3
4      <div class="field">
5        <label for="title">Title:</label>
6        <input name="title">
7      </div>
8      <div class="field">
9        <label for="link">Link:</label>
10       <input name="link">
11     </div>
12   </form>
```

We're creating a `template` that defines two `input` tags: one for the `title` of the article and the other for the `link` URL.

When we load the browser you should see the rendered form:

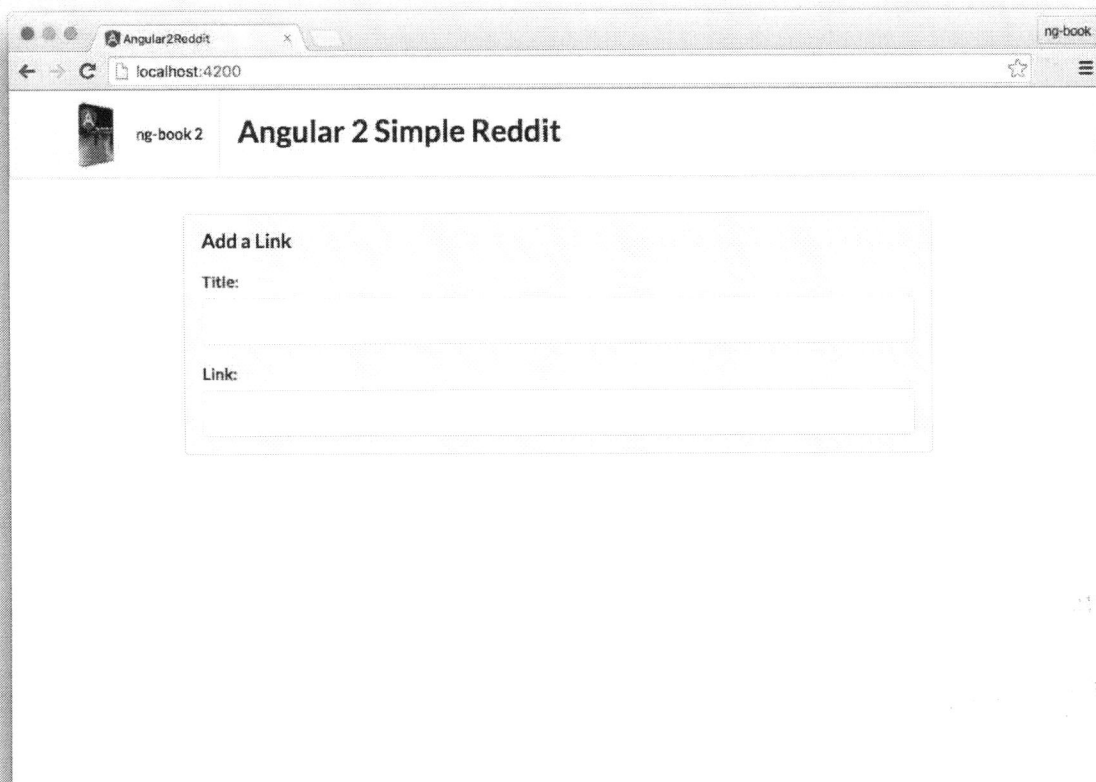

Form

Adding Interaction

Now we have the form with input tags but we don't have any way to submit the data. Let's add some interaction by adding a submit button to our form.

When the form is submitted, we'll want to call a function to create and add a link. We can do this by adding an interaction event on the ‹button /› element.

We tell Angular we want to respond to an event by surrounding the event name in parentheses (). For instance, to add a function call to the ‹button /› onClick event, we can pass it through like so:

```
1  <button (click)="addArticle()"
2        class="ui positive right floated button">
3    Submit link
4  </button>
```

Now, when the button is clicked, it will call a function called addArticle(), which we need to define on the AppComponent class. Let's do that now:

code/first-app/angular-reddit/src/app/app.component.ts

```
8   export class AppComponent {
9     addArticle(title: HTMLInputElement, link: HTMLInputElement): boolean {
10      console.log(`Adding article title: ${title.value} and link: ${link.value}`);
11      return false;
12    }
13  }
```

With the addArticle() function added to the AppComponent and the (click) event added to the <button /> element, this function will be called when the button is clicked. Notice that the addArticle() function can accept two arguments: the title and the link arguments. We need to change our template button to pass those into the call to the addArticle().

We do this by populating a *template variable* by adding a special syntax to the input elements on our form. Here's what our template will look like:

code/first-app/angular-reddit/src/app/app.component.html

```
1   <form class="ui large form segment">
2     <h3 class="ui header">Add a Link</h3>
3
4     <div class="field">
5       <label for="title">Title:</label>
6       <input name="title" #newtitle>  <!-- changed -->
7     </div>
8     <div class="field">
9       <label for="link">Link:</label>
10      <input name="link" #newlink> <!-- changed -->
11    </div>
12
13    <!-- added this button -->
14    <button (click)="addArticle(newtitle, newlink)"
15            class="ui positive right floated button">
16      Submit link
17    </button>
18
19  </form>
```

Notice that in the input tags we used the # (hash) to tell Angular to assign those tags to *a local variable*. By adding the #newtitle and #newlink to the appropriate <input /> elements, we can **pass them as variables** into the addArticle() function on the button!

To recap what we've done, we've made **four** changes:

1. Created a `button` tag in our markup that shows the user where to click
2. We created a function named `addArticle` that defines what we want to do when the button is clicked
3. We added a `(click)` attribute on the `button` that says "call the function `addArticle` when this button is pressed".
4. We added the attribute `#newtitle` and `#newlink` to the `<input>` tags

Let's cover each one of these steps in reverse order:

Binding `input`s to values

Notice in our first input tag we have the following:

```
1   <input name="title" #newtitle>
```

This markup tells Angular to *bind* this `<input>` to the variable `newtitle`. The `#newtitle` syntax is called a *resolve*. The effect is that this makes the variable `newtitle` available to the expressions within this view.

`newtitle` is now an **object** that represents this `input` DOM element (specifically, the type is `HTMLInputElement`). Because `newtitle` is an object, that means we get the value of the input tag using `newtitle.value`.

Similarly we add `#newlink` to the other `<input>` tag, so that we'll be able to extract the value from it as well.

Binding actions to events

On our `button` tag we add the attribute `(click)` to define what should happen when the button is clicked on. When the `(click)` event happens we call `addArticle` with two arguments: `newtitle` and `newlink`. Where did this function and two arguments come from?

1. `addArticle` is a function on our component definition class `AppComponent`
2. `newtitle` comes from the resolve (`#newtitle`) on our `<input>` tag named `title`
3. `newlink` comes from the resolve (`#newlink`) on our `<input>` tag named `link`

All together:

```
1   <button (click)="addArticle(newtitle, newlink)"
2           class="ui positive right floated button">
3     Submit link
4   </button>
```

> **ℹ** The markup `class="ui positive right floated button"` comes from Semantic UI and it gives the button the pleasant green color.

Defining the Action Logic

On our `class AppComponent` we define a new function called `addArticle`. It takes two arguments: `title` and `link`. Again, it's important to realize that `title` and `link` are both **objects** of type `HTMLInputElement` and *not the input values directly*. To get the value from the `input` we have to call `title.value`. For now, we're just going to `console.log` out those arguments.

code/first-app/angular-reddit/src/app/app.component.ts

```
9    addArticle(title: HTMLInputElement, link: HTMLInputElement): boolean {
10     console.log(`Adding article title: ${title.value} and link: ${link.value}`);
11     return false;
12   }
```

> **🔑** Notice that we're using backtick strings again. This is a really handy feature of ES6: backtick strings will expand template variables!
>
> Here we're putting `${title.value}` in the string and this will be replaced with the value of `title.value` in the string.

Try it out!

Now when you click the submit button, you can see that the message is printed on the console:

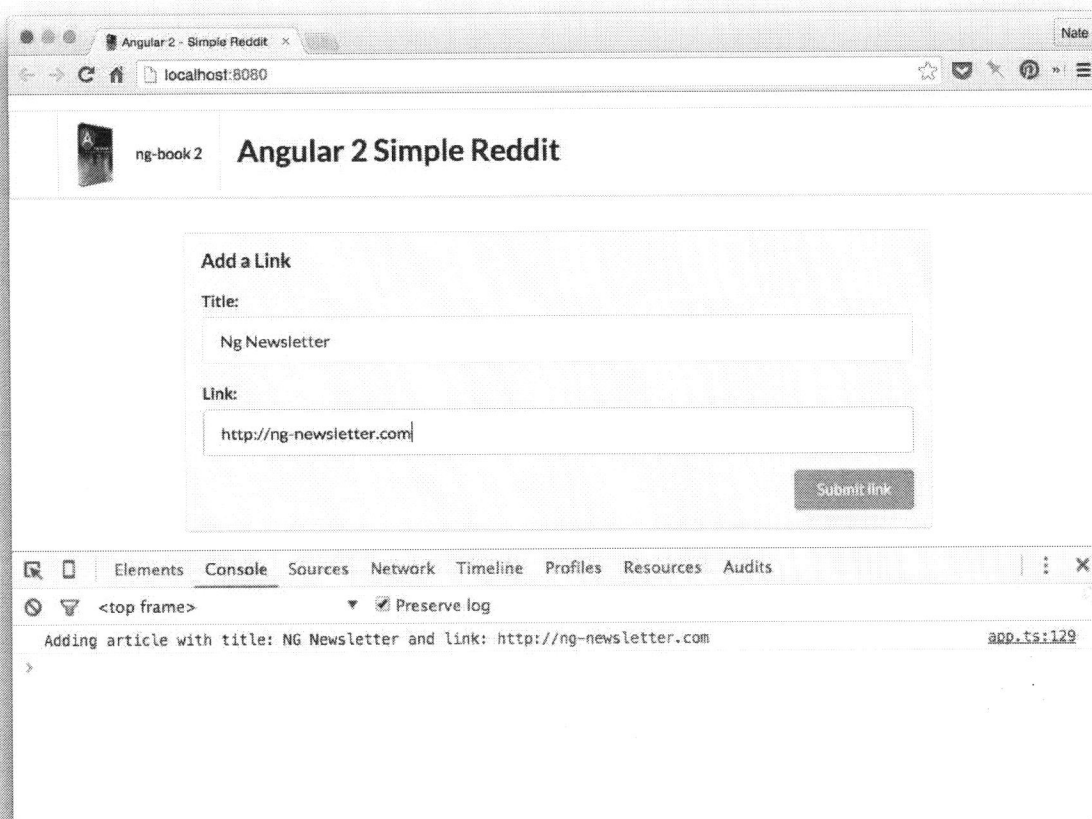

Clicking the Button

Adding the Article Component

Now we have a form to submit new articles, but we aren't showing the new articles anywhere. Because every article submitted is going to be displayed as a list on the page, this is the perfect candidate for a new component.

Let's create a new component to represent the individual submitted articles.

A reddit-article

For that, let's use the ng tool to generate a new component:

```
1   ng generate component article
```

We have three parts to defining this new component:

1. Define the `ArticleComponent` view in the template
2. Define the `ArticleComponent` properties by annotating the class with `@Component`
3. Define a component-definition class (`ArticleComponent`) which houses our component logic

Let's talk through each part in detail:

Creating the `ArticleComponent` template

We define the template using the file `article.component.html`:

code/first-app/angular-reddit/src/app/article/article.component.html

```
1   <div class="four wide column center aligned votes">
2     <div class="ui statistic">
3       <div class="value">
4         {{ votes }}
5       </div>
6       <div class="label">
7         Points
8       </div>
9     </div>
10  </div>
11  <div class="twelve wide column">
12    <a class="ui large header" href="{{ link }}">
13      {{ title }}
14    </a>
15    <ul class="ui big horizontal list voters">
16      <li class="item">
17        <a href (click)="voteUp()">
18          <i class="arrow up icon"></i>
19            upvote
20          </a>
21      </li>
22      <li class="item">
23        <a href (click)="voteDown()">
24          <i class="arrow down icon"></i>
25          downvote
26        </a>
```

```
27        </li>
28      </ul>
29    </div>
```

There's a lot of markup here, so let's break it down :

A Single reddit-article Row

We have two columns:

1. the number of votes on the left and
2. the article information on the right.

We specify these columns with the CSS classes `four wide column` and `twelve wide column` respectively (remember that these come from SemanticUI's CSS).

We're showing `votes` and the `title` with the template expansion strings `{{ votes }}` and `{{ title }}`. The values come from the value of `votes` and `title` property of the `ArticleComponent` class, which we'll define in a minute.

Notice that we can use template strings in **attribute values**, as in the `href` of the a tag: `href="{{ link }}"`. In this case, the value of the `href` will be dynamically populated with the value of `link` from the component class

On our upvote/downvote links we have an action. We use `(click)` to bind `voteUp()`/`voteDown()` to their respective buttons. When the upvote button is pressed, the `voteUp()` function will be called on the `ArticleComponent` class (similarly with downvote and `voteDown()`).

Creating the `ArticleComponent`

code/first-app/angular-reddit/src/app/article/article.component.ts

```
 7  @Component({
 8    selector: 'app-article',
 9    templateUrl: './article.component.html',
10    styleUrls: ['./article.component.css'],
11  })
```

First, we define a new Component with @Component. The selector says that this component is placed on the page by using the tag <app-article> (i.e. the selector is a tag name).

So the most essential way to use this component would be to place the following tag in our markup:

```
1  <app-article>
2  </app-article>
```

These tags will remain in our view when the page is rendered.

Creating the ArticleComponent Definition Class

Finally, we create the ArticleComponent definition class:

code/first-app/angular-reddit/src/app/article/article.component.ts

```
12  export class ArticleComponent implements OnInit {
13    @HostBinding('attr.class') cssClass = 'row';
14    votes: number;
15    title: string;
16    link: string;
17
18    constructor() {
19      this.title = 'Angular 2';
20      this.link = 'http://angular.io';
21      this.votes = 10;
22    }
23
24    voteUp() {
25      this.votes += 1;
26    }
27
28    voteDown() {
29      this.votes -= 1;
30    }
```

```
31
32    ngOnInit() {
33    }
34
35  }
```

Here we create four properties on `ArticleComponent`:

1. `cssClass` - the CSS `class` we want to apply to the "host" of this component
2. `votes` - a `number` representing the sum of all upvotes, minus the downvotes
3. `title` - a `string` holding the title of the article
4. `link` - a `string` holding the URL of the article

We want each `app-article` to be on its own row. We're using Semantic UI, and Semantic provides a CSS class for rows[22] called `row`.

In Angular, a component *host* is **the element this component is attached to**. We can set properties on the host element by using the `@HostBinding()` decorator. In this case, we're asking Angular to keep the value of the host elements class to be in sync with the property `cssClass`.

> We import `HostBinding` from the package `@angular/core`. For instance we can add `HostBinding` like this:

```
1  import { Component, HostBinding } from '@angular/core';
```

By using `@HostBinding()` the **host element** (the `app-article` tag) we want to set the `class` attribute to have "`row`".

> Using the `@HostBinding()` is nice because it means we can encapsulate the `app-article` markup *within* our component. That is, we don't have to both use an `app-article` tag **and** require a `class="row"` in the markup of the parent view. By using the `@HostBinding` decorator, we're able to configure our host element from *within* the component.

In the `constructor()` we set some default attributes:

---

[22] http://semantic-ui.com/collections/grid.html

code/first-app/angular-reddit/src/app/article/article.component.ts

```
18    constructor() {
19      this.title = 'Angular 2';
20      this.link = 'http://angular.io';
21      this.votes = 10;
22    }
```

And we define two functions for voting, one for voting up voteUp and one for voting down voteDown:

code/first-app/angular-reddit/src/app/article/article.component.ts

```
24    voteUp() {
25      this.votes += 1;
26    }
27
28    voteDown() {
29      this.votes -= 1;
30    }
```

In voteUp we increment this.votes by one. Similarly we decrement for voteDown.

Using the app-article Component

In order to use this component and make the data visible, we have to add a ‹app-article›‹/app-article› tag somewhere in our markup.

In this case, we want the AppComponent to render this new component, so let's update the code in that component. Add the ‹app-article› tag to the AppComponent's template right after the closing ‹/form› tag:

```
1    <button (click)="addArticle(newtitle, newlink)"
2            class="ui positive right floated button">
3      Submit link
4    </button>
5  </form>
6
7  <div class="ui grid posts">
8    <app-article>
9    </app-article>
10 </div>
```

If we generated the ArticleComponent using Angular CLI (via ng generate component), by default it should have "told" Angular about our app-article tag (more on that below). However, if we created this component "by hand" and we reload the browser now, we might see that the <app-article> tag wasn't compiled. Oh no!

Whenever hitting a problem like this, the first thing to do is open up your browser's developer console. If we inspect our markup (see screenshot below), we can see that the app-article tag is on our page, but it hasn't been compiled into markup. Why not?

Unexpanded tag when inspecting the DOM

This happens because the AppComponent component **doesn't know about the** ArticleComponent **component** yet.

> **Angular 1 Note**: If you've used Angular 1 it might be surprising that our app doesn't know about our new app-article component. This is because in Angular 1, directives match globally. However, in Angular you need to explicitly specify which components (and therefore, which selectors) you want to use.
>
> On the one hand, this requires a little more configuration. On the other hand, it's great for building scalable apps because it means we don't have to share our directive selectors in a global namespace.

In order to tell our AppComponent about our new ArticleComponent component, we need to **add the ArticleComponent to the list of declarations in this NgModule**.

> We add ArticleComponent to our declarations because ArticleComponent is part of this module (AppModule). However, if ArticleComponent were part of a *different* module, then we might import it with imports.
>
> We'll discuss more about NgModules later on, but for now, know that when you create a new component, you have to put in a declarations in NgModules.

code/first-app/angular-reddit/src/app/app.module.ts

```
 6  import { AppComponent } from './app.component';
 7  import { ArticleComponent } from './article/article.component';
 8
 9  @NgModule({
10    declarations: [
11      AppComponent,
12      ArticleComponent // <-- added this
13    ],
```

See here that we are:

1. importing ArticleComponent and then
2. Adding ArticleComponent to the list of declarations

After you've added ArticleComponent to declarations in the NgModule, if we reload the browser we should see the article properly rendered:

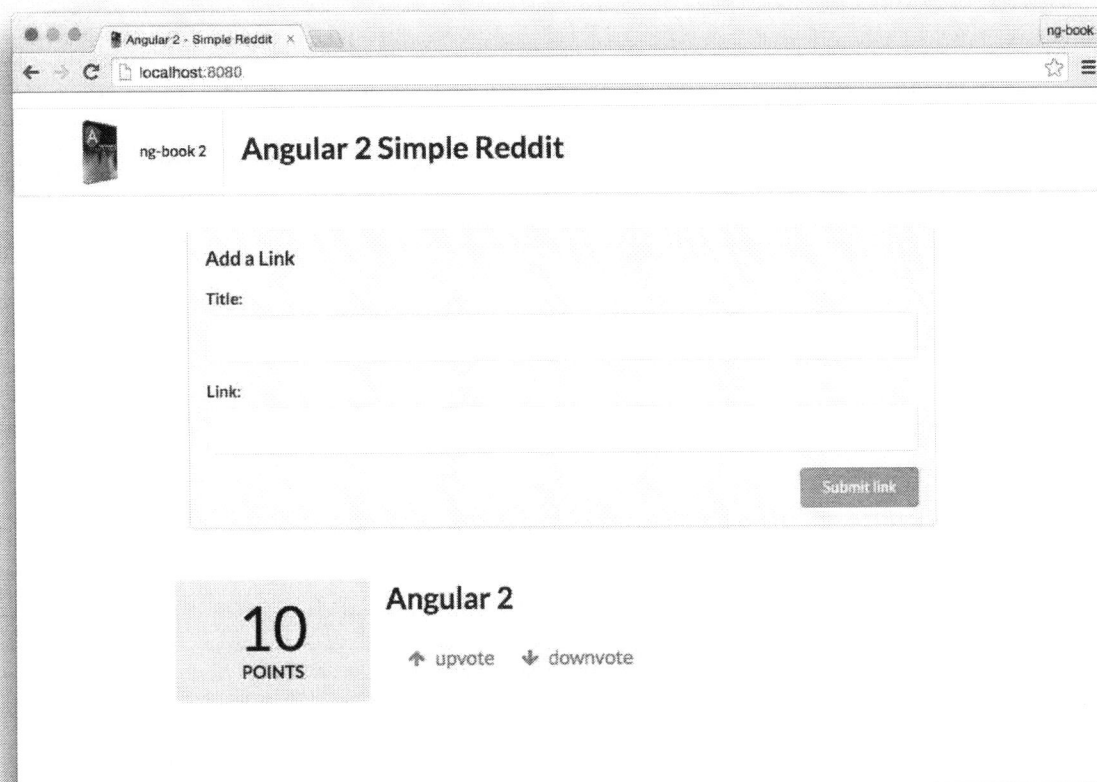

Rendered ArticleComponent component

However, clicking on the **vote up** or **vote down** links will **cause the page to reload** instead of updating the article list.

JavaScript, by default, **propagates the `click` event to all the parent components**. Because the `click` event is propagated to parents, our browser is trying to follow the empty link, which tells the browser to reload.

To fix that, we need to make the click event handler to return `false`. This will ensure the browser won't try to refresh the page. Let's update our code so that each of the functions `voteUp()` and `voteDown()` return a boolean value of `false` (tells the browser *not* to propagate the event upwards):

```
1  voteDown(): boolean {
2    this.votes -= 1;
3    return false;
4  }
5  // and similarly with `voteUp()`
```

Now when we click the links we'll see that the votes increase and decrease properly without a page refresh.

Rendering Multiple Rows

Right now we only have one article on the page and there's no way to render more, unless we paste another `<app-article>` tag. And even if we did that all the articles would have the same content, so it wouldn't be very interesting.

Creating an Article class

A good practice when writing Angular code is to try to isolate the data structures we are using from the component code. To do this, let's create a data structure that represents a single article. Let's add a new file `article.model.ts` to define an `Article` class that we can use.

code/first-app/angular-reddit/src/app/article/article.model.ts

```
1   export class Article {
2     title: string;
3     link: string;
4     votes: number;
5
6     constructor(title: string, link: string, votes?: number) {
7       this.title = title;
8       this.link = link;
9       this.votes = votes || 0;
10    }
11  }
```

Here we are creating a new class that represents an `Article`. Note that this is a **plain class and not an Angular component**. In the Model-View-Controller pattern this would be the **Model**.

Each article has a `title`, a `link`, and a total for the `votes`. When creating a new article we need the `title` and the `link`. The `votes` parameter is optional (denoted by the `?` at the end of the name) and defaults to zero.

Now let's update the `ArticleComponent` code to use our new `Article` class. Instead of storing the properties directly on the `ArticleComponent` component let's **store the properties on an instance of the** `Article` **class**.

First let's import the class:

code/first-app/angular-reddit/src/app/article/article.component.ts

```
6   import { Article } from './article.model';
```

Then let's use it:

code/first-app/angular-reddit/src/app/article/article.component.ts

```
13  export class ArticleComponent implements OnInit {
14    @HostBinding('attr.class') cssClass = 'row';
15    article: Article;
16
17    constructor() {
18      this.article = new Article(
19        'Angular 2',
20        'http://angular.io',
21        10);
22    }
23
24    voteUp(): boolean {
25      this.article.votes += 1;
26      return false;
27    }
28
29    voteDown(): boolean {
30      this.article.votes -= 1;
31      return false;
32    }
33
34    ngOnInit() {
35    }
36
37  }
```

Notice what we've changed: instead of storing the title, link, and votes properties directly on the component, we're storing a reference to an article. What's neat is that we've defined the type of article to be our new Article class.

When it comes to voteUp (and voteDown), we don't increment votes on the component, but rather, we need to increment the votes on the article.

However, this refactoring introduces another change: we need to update our view to get the template variables from the right location. To do that, we need to change our template tags to read from article. That is, where before we had {{ votes }}, we need to change it to {{ article.votes }}, and same with title and link:

code/first-app/angular-reddit/src/app/article/article.component.html

```
1  <div class="four wide column center aligned votes">
2    <div class="ui statistic">
3      <div class="value">
4        {{ article.votes }}
5      </div>
6      <div class="label">
7        Points
8      </div>
9    </div>
10 </div>
11 <div class="twelve wide column">
12   <a class="ui large header" href="{{ article.link }}">
13     {{ article.title }}
14   </a>
15   <ul class="ui big horizontal list voters">
16     <li class="item">
17       <a href (click)="voteUp()">
18         <i class="arrow up icon"></i>
19           upvote
20         </a>
21     </li>
22     <li class="item">
23       <a href (click)="voteDown()">
24         <i class="arrow down icon"></i>
25         downvote
26       </a>
27     </li>
28   </ul>
29 </div>
```

Reload the browser and everything still works.

This situation is better but something in our code is still off: our voteUp and voteDown methods break the encapsulation of the Article class by changing the article's internal properties directly.

> voteUp and voteDown currently break the Law of Demeter[23] which says that a given object should assume as little as possible about the structure or properties of other objects.

The problem is that our ArticleComponent component knows too much about the Article class

---

[23] http://en.wikipedia.org/wiki/Law_of_Demeter

internals. To fix that, let's add `voteUp` and `voteDown` methods on the `Article` class (we'll also add a `domain` function, which we'll talk about in a moment):

code/first-app/angular-reddit/src/app/article/article.model.ts

```
1  export class Article {
2    title: string;
3    link: string;
4    votes: number;
5
6    constructor(title: string, link: string, votes?: number) {
7      this.title = title;
8      this.link = link;
9      this.votes = votes || 0;
10   }
11
12   voteUp(): void {
13     this.votes += 1;
14   }
15
16   voteDown(): void {
17     this.votes -= 1;
18   }
19
20   // domain() is a utility function that extracts
21   // the domain from a URL, which we'll explain shortly
22   domain(): string {
23     try {
24       // e.g. http://foo.com/path/to/bar
25       const domainAndPath: string = this.link.split('//')[1];
26       // e.g. foo.com/path/to/bar
27       return domainAndPath.split('/')[0];
28     } catch (err) {
29       return null;
30     }
31   }
32 }
```

We can then change `ArticleComponent` to call these methods:

code/first-app/angular-reddit/src/app/article/article.component.ts

```
13  export class ArticleComponent implements OnInit {
14    @HostBinding('attr.class') cssClass = 'row';
15    article: Article;
16
17    constructor() {
18      this.article = new Article(
19        'Angular 2',
20        'http://angular.io',
21        10);
22    }
23
24    voteUp(): boolean {
25      this.article.voteUp();
26      return false;
27    }
28
29    voteDown(): boolean {
30      this.article.voteDown();
31      return false;
32    }
33
34    ngOnInit() {
35    }
36
37  }
```

? Why do we have a voteUp function in both the model and the component?

The reason we have a voteUp() and a voteDown() on both classes is because each function does a slightly different thing. The idea is that the voteUp() on the ArticleComponent relates to the **component view**, whereas the Article model voteUp() defines what *mutations* happen **in the model**.

That is, it allows the Article class to encapsulate what functionality should happen **to a model** when voting happens. In a "real" app, the internals of the Article model would probably be more complicated, e.g. make an API request to a webserver, and you wouldn't want to have that sort of model-specific code in your component controller.

Similarly, in the ArticleComponent we return false; as a way to say "don't propagate the event" - this is a view-specific piece of logic and we shouldn't allow the Article model's voteUp() function to have to knowledge about that sort of view-specific API. That is, the Article model should allow voting apart from the specific view.

After reloading our browser, we'll notice everything works the same way, but we now have clearer, simpler code.

> ℹ️ Checkout our `ArticleComponent` component definition now: it's so short! We've moved a lot of logic **out** of our component and into our models. The corresponding MVC guideline here might be Fat Models, Skinny Controllers[24]. The idea is that we want to move most of our logic to our models so that our components do the minimum work possible.

Storing Multiple `Articles`

Let's write the code that allows us to have a list of multiple `Articles`.

Let's start by changing `AppComponent` to have a collection of articles:

code/first-app/angular-reddit/src/app/app.component.ts

```
1   import { Component } from '@angular/core';
2   import { Article } from './article/article.model'; // <-- import this
3
4   @Component({
5     selector: 'app-root',
6     templateUrl: './app.component.html',
7     styleUrls: ['./app.component.css']
8   })
9   export class AppComponent {
10    articles: Article[]; // <-- component property
11
12    constructor() {
13      this.articles = [
14        new Article('Angular 2', 'http://angular.io', 3),
15        new Article('Fullstack', 'http://fullstack.io', 2),
16        new Article('Angular Homepage', 'http://angular.io', 1),
17      ];
18    }
```

Notice that our `AppComponent` has the line:

```
1     articles: Article[];
```

---

[24] http://weblog.jamisbuck.org/2006/10/18/skinny-controller-fat-model

The `Article[]` might look a little unfamiliar. We're saying here that `articles` is an `Array` of `Articles`. Another way this could be written is `Array<Article>`. The word for this pattern is *generics*. It's a concept seen in Java, C#, and other languages. The idea is that our collection (the `Array`) is typed. That is, the `Array` is a collection that will only hold objects of type `Article`.

In order to have access to the `Article` class, we first have to `import` it, as we do up top.

We populate this `Array` by setting `this.articles` in the constructor:

code/first-app/angular-reddit/src/app/app.component.ts

```
12    constructor() {
13      this.articles = [
14        new Article('Angular 2', 'http://angular.io', 3),
15        new Article('Fullstack', 'http://fullstack.io', 2),
16        new Article('Angular Homepage', 'http://angular.io', 1),
17      ];
18    }
```

Configuring the `ArticleComponent` with inputs

Now that we have a list of `Article` *models*, how can we pass them to our `ArticleComponent` *component*?

Here again we use `Inputs`. Previously we had our `ArticleComponent` class defined like this:

code/first-app/angular-reddit/src/app/article/article.component.ts

```
13    export class ArticleComponent implements OnInit {
14      @HostBinding('attr.class') cssClass = 'row';
15      article: Article;
16
17      constructor() {
18        this.article = new Article(
19          'Angular 2',
20          'http://angular.io',
21          10);
22      }
```

The problem here is that we've hard coded a particular `Article` in the constructor. The point of making components is not only encapsulation, but also reusability.

What we would really like to do is to configure the `Article` we want to display. If, for instance, we had two articles, `article1` and `article2`, we would like to be able to reuse the `app-article` component by passing an `Article` as a "parameter" to the component like this:

```
1  <app-article [article]="article1"></app-article>
2  <app-article [article]="article2"></app-article>
```

Angular allows us to do this by using the Input decorator on a property of a Component:

```
1  class ArticleComponent {
2    @Input() article: Article;
3    // ...
```

Now if we have an Article in a variable myArticle we could pass it to our ArticleComponent in our view. Remember, we can pass a variable in an element by surrounding it in square brackets [variableName], like so:

```
1  <app-article [article]="myArticle"></app-article>
```

Notice the syntax here: we put the name of the input in brackets as in: [article] and the value of the attribute is what we want to pass into that input.

Then, and this is important, the this.article on the ArticleComponent instance will be set to myArticle. We can think about the variable myArticle as being passed as a *parameter* (i.e. input) to our components.

Here's what our ArticleComponent component now looks like using @Input:

code/first-app/angular-reddit/src/app/article/article.component.ts

```
1  import {
2    Component,
3    OnInit,
4    Input,        // <-- added,
5    HostBinding
6  } from '@angular/core';
7  import { Article } from './article.model'; // <-- added
8
9  @Component({
10   selector: 'app-article',
11   templateUrl: './article.component.html',
12   styleUrls: ['./article.component.css']
13 })
14 export class ArticleComponent implements OnInit {
15   @HostBinding('attr.class') cssClass = 'row';
16   @Input() article: Article;
17
```

```
18    constructor() {
19      // article is populated by the Input now,
20      // so we don't need anything here
21    }
22
23    voteUp(): boolean {
24      this.article.voteUp();
25      return false;
26    }
27
28    voteDown(): boolean {
29      this.article.voteDown();
30      return false;
31    }
32
33    ngOnInit() {
34    }
35
36 }
```

Don't forget to `import`!

Notice that we `import` the `Input` class from `@angular/core`. We've also imported our `Article` model as we did with the `AppComponent` earlier.

Rendering a List of Articles

Earlier we configured our `AppComponent` to store an array of `articles`. Now let's configure `AppComponent` to *render* all the `articles`. To do so, instead of having the `<app-article>` tag alone, we are going to use the `NgFor` directive to iterate over the list of `articles` and render a `app-article` for each one:

Let's add this in the `template` of the `AppComponent` `@Component`, just below the closing `<form>` tag:

```
    Submit link
  </button>
</form>

<!-- start adding here -->
<div class="ui grid posts">
  <app-article
    *ngFor="let article of articles"
    [article]="article">
  </app-article>
</div>
<!-- end adding here -->
```

Remember when we rendered a list of names as a bullet list using the NgFor directive earlier in the chapter? This syntax also works for rendering multiple components.

The *ngFor="let article of articles" syntax will iterate through the list of articles and create the local variable article (for each item in the list).

To specify the article input on a component, we are using the [inputName]="inputValue" expression. In this case, we're saying that we want to set the article input to the value of the local variable article set by ngFor.

> We are using the variable article many times in that previous code snippet, it's (potentially) clearer if we rename the temporary variable created by NgFor to foobar:

```
1    <app-article
2      *ngFor="let foobar of articles"
3      [article]="foobar">
4    </app-article>
```

So here we have three variables:

1. articles which is an Array of Articles, defined on the AppComponent
2. foobar which is a single element of articles (an Article), defined by NgFor
3. article which is the name of the field defined on inputs of the ArticleComponent

Basically, NgFor generates a temporary variable foobar and then we're passing it in to app-article

Reloading our browser now, we will see all articles will be rendered:

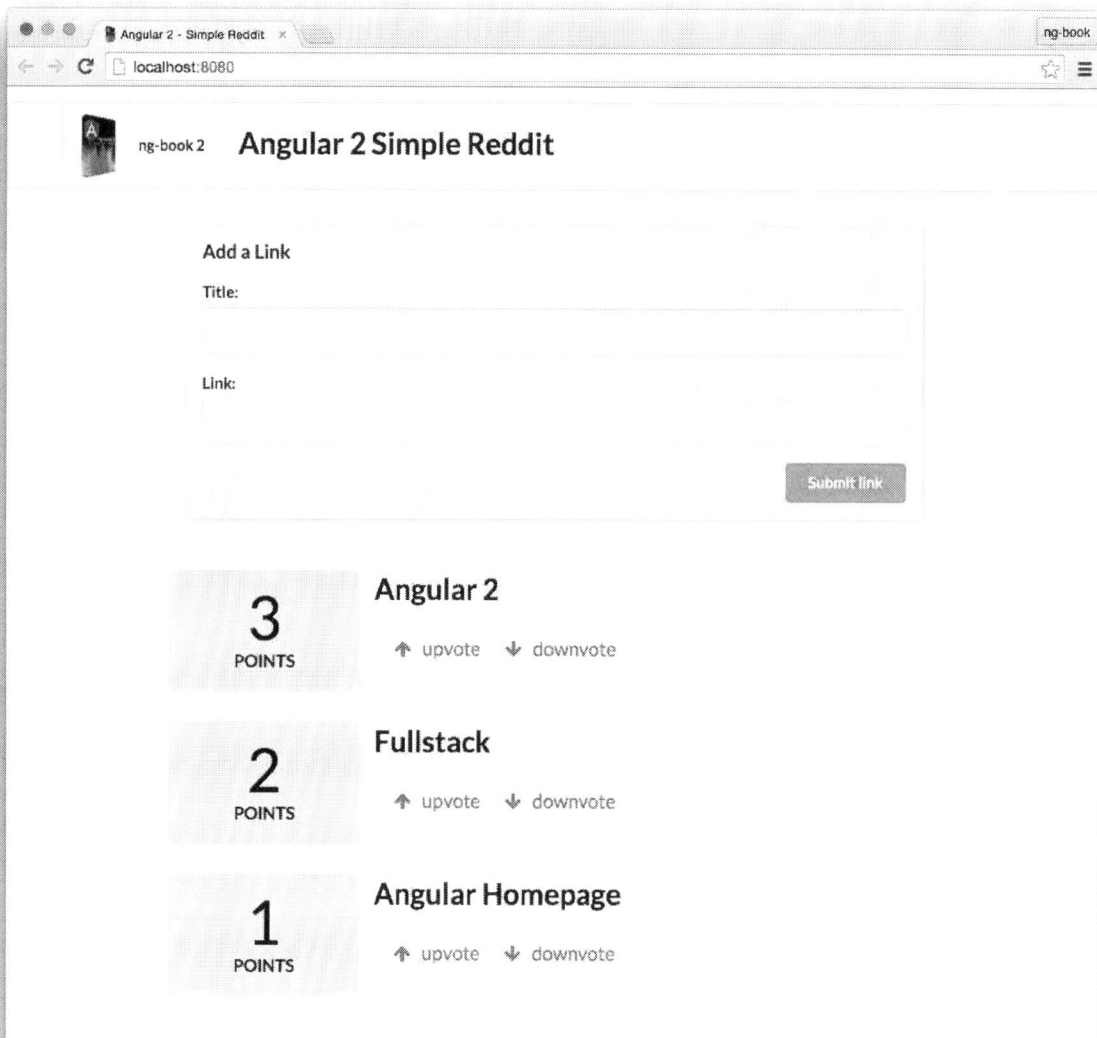

Multiple articles being rendered

Adding New Articles

Now we need to change addArticle to actually add new articles when the button is pressed. Change the addArticle method to match the following:

code/first-app/angular-reddit/src/app/app.component.ts

```
20    addArticle(title: HTMLInputElement, link: HTMLInputElement): boolean {
21      console.log(`Adding article title: ${title.value} and link: ${link.value}`);
22      this.articles.push(new Article(title.value, link.value, 0));
23      title.value = '';
24      link.value = '';
25      return false;
26    }
```

This will:

1. create a new `Article` instance with the submitted title and URL
2. add it to the array of `Articles` and
3. clear the `input` field values

> How are we clearing the `input` field values? Well, if you recall, `title` and `link` are `HTMLInputElement` *objects*. That means we can set their properties. When we change the `value` property, the `input` tag on our page changes.

After adding a new article in our input fields and clicking the **Submit Link** we will see the new article added!

Finishing Touches

Displaying the Article Domain

As a nice touch, let's add a hint next to the link that shows the domain where the user will be redirected to when the link is clicked.

Let's add a `domain` method to the `Article` class:

code/first-app/angular-reddit/src/app/article/article.model.ts

```
22    domain(): string {
23      try {
24        // e.g. http://foo.com/path/to/bar
25        const domainAndPath: string = this.link.split('//')[1];
26        // e.g. foo.com/path/to/bar
27        return domainAndPath.split('/')[0];
28      } catch (err) {
29        return null;
30      }
31    }
```

Let's add a call to this function on the ArticleComponent's template:

```
1  <div class="twelve wide column">
2    <a class="ui large header" href="{{ article.link }}">
3      {{ article.title }}
4    </a>
5    <!-- right here -->
6    <div class="meta">({{ article.domain() }})</div>
7    <ul class="ui big horizontal list voters">
8      <li class="item">
9        <a href (click)="voteUp()">
```

And now when we reload the browser, we will see the domain name of each URL (note: URL must include *http://*).

Re-sorting Based on Score

Clicking and voting on articles, we'll see that something doesn't feel quite right: our articles don't sort based on the score! We definitely want to see the highest-rated items on top and the lower ranking ones sink to the bottom.

We're storing the articles in an Array in our AppComponent class, but that Array is unsorted. An easy way to handle this is to create a new method sortedArticles on AppComponent:

code/first-app/angular-reddit/src/app/app.component.ts

```
28    sortedArticles(): Article[] {
29      return this.articles.sort((a: Article, b: Article) => b.votes - a.votes);
30    }
```

ES6 Arrow Function

The above code snippet uses "arrow" (=>) functions from ES6. You can read more about arrow functions here[25]

sort() We're also calling the sort() function, which is a built-in which you can read about here[26]

In our ngFor we can iterate over sortedArticles() (instead of articles directly):

```
1  <div class="ui grid posts">
2    <app-article
3      *ngFor="let article of sortedArticles()"
4      [article]="article">
5    </app-article>
6  </div>
```

Deployment

Now that we have an app that runs, let's get it live on the internet, so that we can share it with our friends!

Deployment and performance in production-ready apps is an intermediate topic that we'll cover in a future chapter. For now, we're going to gloss over the details and just show how easy a basic deployment can be.

Deploying our app is the act of pushing our code to a server, where it can be accessed by others.

Broadly speaking, the idea is that we're going to:

- *compile* all of our TypeScript code into JavaScript (which the browser can read)
- *bundle* all of our JavaScript code files into one or two files
- and then *upload* our JavaScript, HTML, CSS, and images to a server

Ultimately, this Angular app is an HTML file that *loads JavaScript code*. So we need to upload our code to a computer somewhere on the internet.

But first, let's **build** our Angular app.

---

[25] https://developer.mozilla.org/en-US/docs/Web/JavaScript/Reference/Functions/Arrow_functions
[26] https://developer.mozilla.org/en-US/docs/Web/JavaScript/Reference/Global_Objects/Array/sort

Building Our App for Production

The Angular CLI tool we used to generate this app can be used to build our app for production. In fact, we just type a single command.

In `first_app/angular-reddit`, type the following:

```
1   ng build --target=production --base-href /
```

This command tells the `ng` tool to **build** our application for a `production` environment. We also set the `--base-href` to a single slash `/`.

The base-href describes what the 'root' URL of our application will be. So, for instance, if you wanted to deploy your app to a subfolder on your server under `/ng-book-demo/`, you could base `--base-href` `/ng-book-demo/`

This command will run for a little while and when it finishes you should have a `dist` folder on your disk.

```
1   $ ls dist/
2   136B   assets/
3   5.3K   favicon.ico
4    27K   flags.9c74e172f87984c48ddf.png
5   306K   icons.2980083682e94d33a66e.svg
6   119K   icons.706450d7bba6374ca02f.ttf
7    55K   icons.97493d3f11c0a3bd5cbd.woff2
8    70K   icons.d9ee23d59d0e0e727b51.woff
9    59K   icons.f7c2b4b747b1a225eb8d.eot
10  1.1K   index.html
11  1.4K   inline.44deb5fed75ee6385e18.bundle.js
12   17K   main.c683e6eda100e8873d71.bundle.js
13   82K   polyfills.b81504c68200c7bfeb16.bundle.js
14  503K   styles.7f23e351d688b00e8a5b.bundle.css
15  440K   vendor.cc4297c08c0803bddc87.bundle.js
```

These files are the full compiled result of your app. Notice that there is a long string of characters in the middle of each file such as:

```
1   main.c683e6eda100e8873d71.bundle.js
```

Those characters are a hash of the content (and may not match on your computer). If you look at each file, you can see that we have some icons, the `index.html`, a `main.js`, a `polyfills.js`, a `vendor.js`, and some `styles.css`. Now all the need to do is upload these to our server.

Uploading to a Server

There are **lots** of ways to host your HTML and JavaScript. For this demo, we're going to use the easiest way possible: now[27].

> If you don't want to use now, you're free to use whatever method you want. For instance, you can host sites on Heroku, AWS S3, upload files to your own server via FTP, etc.
>
> The important thing is that the server exposes all of the files in our dist folder onto the internet.

Installing now

We can install now using npm:

```
1  npm install -g now
```

To deploy a site with now is very easy:

```
1  cd dist # change into the dist folder
2  now
```

The now command should ask you a couple of questions (such as your email address) and you'll need to check your email and click the link inside.

After you've confirmed your account (or if you had one already), now will **upload your code** and then **give you a URL** to view to see your application.

Visit that URL and view your app. If it works, try sending the URL to a friend!

Congratulations! You've built and deployed your first Angular app!

Full Code Listing

We've been exploring many small pieces of code for this chapter. You can find all of the files and the complete TypeScript code for our app in the example code download included with this book.

---

[27]https://zeit.co/now

Wrapping Up

We did it! We've created our first Angular App. That wasn't so bad, was it? There's lots more to learn: understanding data flow, making AJAX requests, built-in directives, routing, manipulating the DOM etc.

But for now, bask in our success! Much of writing Angular apps is just as we did above:

1. Split your app into components
2. Create the views
3. Define your models
4. Display your models
5. Add interaction

In the future chapters of this book we'll cover everything you need to write sophisticated apps with Angular.

Getting Help

Did you have any trouble with this chapter? Did you find a bug or have trouble getting the code running? We'd love to hear from you!

- Come join our community and chat with us on Gitter[28]
- Email us directly at us@fullstack.io[29]

Onward!

---

[28]https://gitter.im/ng-book/ng-book
[29]mailto:us@fullstack.io

How Angular Works

In this chapter, we're going to talk about the high-level concepts of Angular. We're going to take a step back so that we can see how all the pieces fit together.s

> If you've used AngularJS 1.x, you'll notice that Angular has a new mental-model for building applications. Don't panic! As AngularJS 1.x users ourselves we've found Angular to be both straightforward and familiar. A little later in this book we're going to talk specifically about how to convert your AngularJS 1.x apps to Angular.

In the chapters that follow, we won't be taking a deep dive into each concept, but instead we're going to give an overview and explain the foundational ideas.

The first big idea is that an Angular application is made up of *Components*. One way to think of Components is a way to teach the browser new tags. If you have an Angular 1 background, Components are analogous to *directives* in AngularJS 1.x (it turns out, Angular has directives too, but we'll talk more about this distinction later on).

However, Angular Components have some significant advantages over AngularJS 1.x directives and we'll talk about that below. First, let's start at the top: the Application.

Application

An Angular Application is nothing more than a tree of Components.

At the root of that tree, the top level Component is the application itself. And that's what the browser will render when "booting" (a.k.a *bootstrapping*) the app.

One of the great things about Components is that they're **composable**. This means that we can build up larger Components from smaller ones. The Application is simply a Component that renders other Components.

Because Components are structured in a parent/child tree, when each Component renders, it recursively renders its children Components.

For example, let's create a simple inventory management application that is represented by the following page mockup:

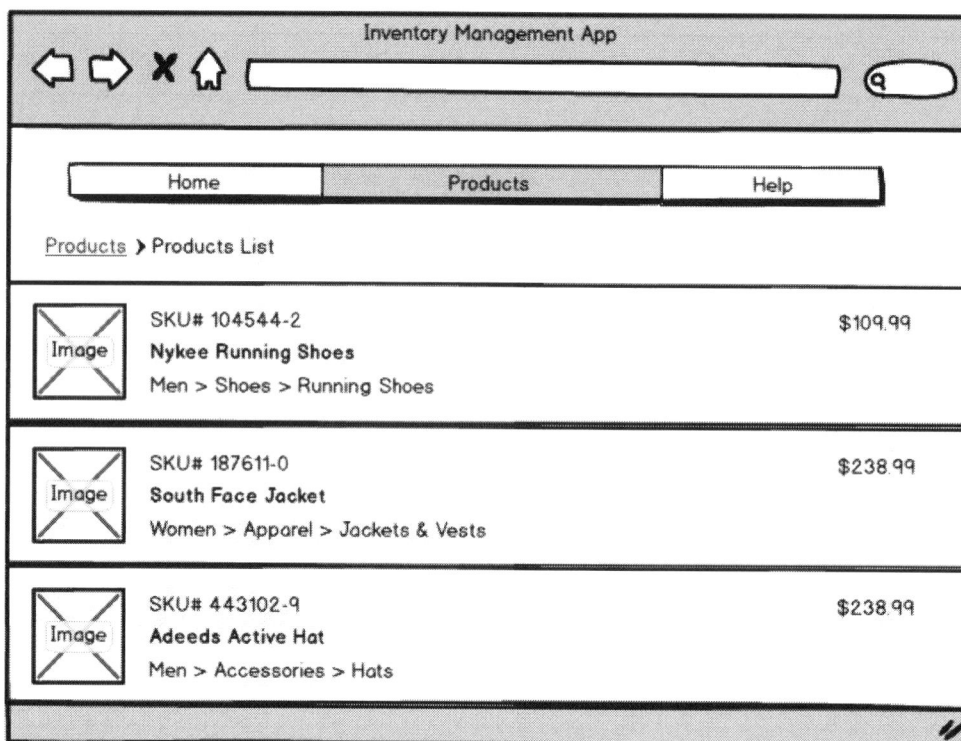

Inventory Management App

Given this mockup, to write this application the first thing we want to do is split it into components.

In this example, we could group the page into three high level components

1. The Navigation Component
2. The Breadcrumbs Component
3. The Product List Component

The Navigation Component

This component would render the navigation section. This would allow the user to visit other areas of the application.

Navigation Component

The Breadcrumbs Component

This would render a hierarchical representation of where in the application the user currently is.

The Product List Component

The Products List component would be a representation of a collection of products.

Product List Component

Breaking this component down into the next level of smaller components, we could say that the Product List is composed of multiple Product Rows.

Product Row Component

And of course, we could continue one step further, breaking each Product Row into smaller pieces:

- the **Product Image** component would be responsible for rendering a product image, given its image name
- the **Product Department** component would render the department tree, like *Men > Shoes > Running Shoes*
- the **Price Display** component would render the price. Imagine that our implementation customizes the pricing if the user is logged in to include system-wide tier discounts or include shipping for instance. We could implement all this behavior into this component.

Finally, putting it all together into a tree representation, we end up with the following diagram:

App Tree Diagram

At the top we see **Inventory Management App**: that's our application.

Under the application we have the Navigation, the Breadcrumb and the Products List components.

The Products List component has Product Rows, one for each product.

And the Product Row uses three components itself: one for the image, the department, and the price.

Let's work together to build this application.

You can find the full code listing for this chapter in the downloads under `how-angular-works/inventory-app`.

Here's a screenshot of what our app will look like when we're done:

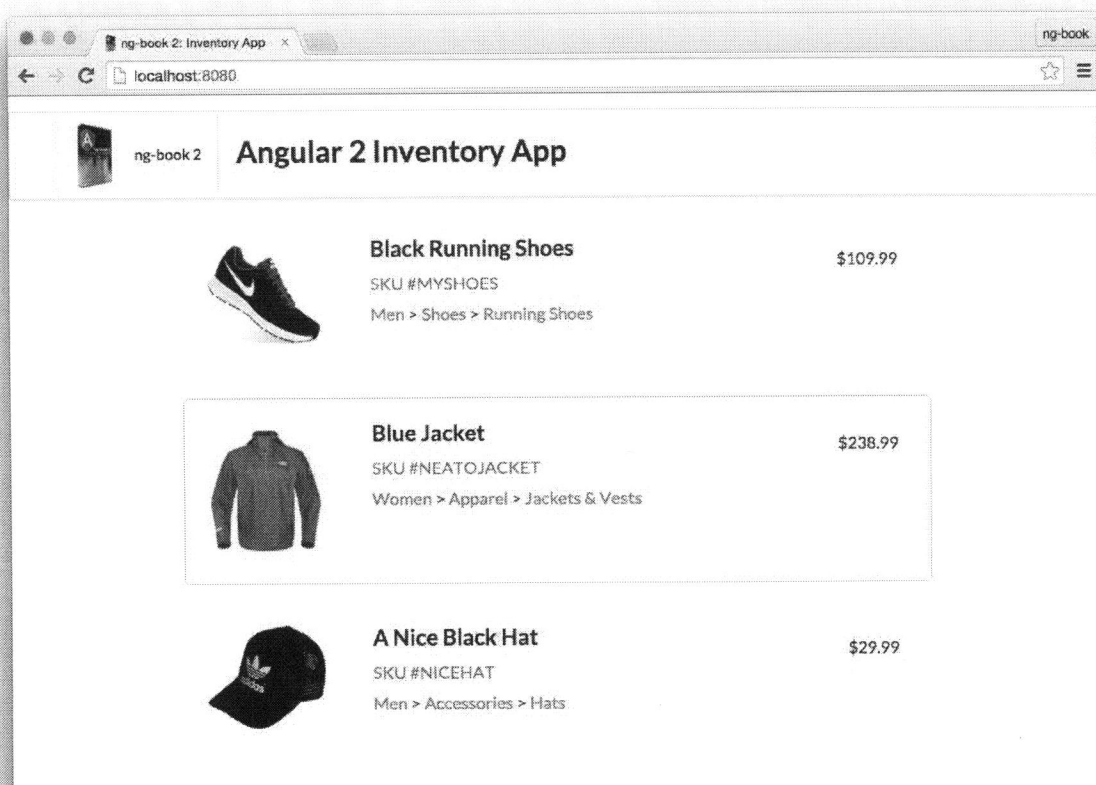

Completed Inventory App

How to Use This Chapter

In this chapter we're going to explain the fundamental concepts required when building Angular apps by walking through an app that we've built. We'll explain:

- How to break your app into components
- How to make reusable components using *inputs*
- How to handle user interactions, such as *clicking* on a component

In this chapter, we've used `angular-cli`, just as we did before. This means you can use all of the normal `ng` commands such as:

```
1  ng serve # runs the app
```

Also, in this chapter, we're not going to give step-by-step instructions on how to create each file in the app. If you'd like to follow along at home, when we introduce a new component you can run:

```
1  ng generate component NameOfNewComponentHere
```

This will generate the files you need, and you're free to type in your code there or copy and paste code from the book or from our example code.

We've provided the entire, completed application in the code download folder under how-angular-works/inventory-app. If you ever feel lost or need more context, take some time to look at the completed example code.

Let's get started building!

Product Model

One of the key things to realize about Angular is that it **doesn't prescribe a particular model library**.

Angular is flexible enough to support many different kinds of models (and data architectures). However, this means the choice is left to you as the user to determine how to implement these things.

We'll have **a lot** to say about data architectures in future chapters. For now, though, we're going to have our models be plain JavaScript objects.

code/how-angular-works/inventory-app/src/app/product.model.ts

```
1   /**
2    * Provides a `Product` object
3    */
4   export class Product {
5     constructor(
6       public sku: string,
7       public name: string,
8       public imageUrl: string,
9       public department: string[],
10      public price: number) {
11    }
12  }
```

If you're new to ES6/TypeScript this syntax might be a bit unfamiliar.

We're creating a new Product class and the constructor takes 5 arguments. When we write public sku: string, we're saying two things:

- there is a public variable on instances of this class called sku

- `sku` is of type `string`.

If you're already familiar with JavaScript, you can quickly catch up on some of the differences, including the `public constructor` shorthand, here at learnxinyminutes[30]

This `Product` class doesn't have any dependencies on Angular, it's just a model that we'll use in our app.

Components

As we mentioned before, Components are the fundamental building block of Angular applications. The "application" itself is just the top-level Component. Then we break our application into smaller child Components.

When building new Angular applications, we often follow this process: we mockup the design in wireframes (or on paper) and then we break down the parts into Components.

We'll be using Components a lot, so it's worth looking at them more closely.

Each component is composed of three parts:

- Component *Decorator*
- A View
- A Controller

To illustrate the key concepts we need to understand about components, we'll start with the top level Inventory App and then focus on the **Products List** and child components:

---

[30]https://learnxinyminutes.com/docs/typescript/

Products List Component

Here's what a basic, top-level `AppComponent` looks like:

```
1   @Component({
2     selector: 'inventory-app-root',
3     template: `
4     <div class="inventory-app">
5       (Products will go here soon)
6     </div>
7     `
8   })
9   export class AppComponent {
10    // Inventory logic here
11  }
```

If you've been using Angular 1 the syntax might look pretty foreign! But the ideas are pretty similar, so let's take them step by step.

The `@Component` is called a **decorator**. It adds metadata to the class that follows it (`AppComponent`). The `@Component` decorator specifies:

- a `selector`, which tells Angular what element to match
- a `template`, which defines the view

The Component **controller** is defined by a `class`, the `AppComponent` class, in this case.

Let's take a look into each part now in more detail.

Component Decorator

The `@Component` decorator is where you configure your component. One of the primary roles of the `@Component` decorator is to configure how the outside world will interact with your component.

> **ⓘ** There are lots of options available to configure a component (many of which we cover in the Advanced Components Chapter). In this chapter we're just going to touch on the basics.

Component `selector`

With the `selector` key, you indicate how your component will be recognized when used in a template. The idea is similar to CSS or XPath selectors. The `selector` is a way to define what elements in the HTML will match this component. In this case, by saying `selector: 'inventory-app-root'`, we're saying that in our HTML we want to match the `inventory-app-root` tag, that is, we're defining a new tag that has new functionality whenever we use it. E.g. when we put this in our HTML:

```
1   <inventory-app-root></inventory-app-root>
```

Angular will use the `AppComponent` component to implement the functionality.

Alternatively, with this selector, we can also use a regular `div` and specify the component as an attribute:

```
1   <div inventory-app-root></div>
```

Component `template`

The view is the visual part of the component. By using the `template` option on `@Component`, we declare the HTML template that the component will use:

```
1   @Component({
2     selector: 'inventory-app-root',
3     template: `
4     <div class="inventory-app">
5        (Products will go here soon)
6     </div>
7        `
8   })
```

For the `template` above, notice that we're using TypeScript's backtick multi-line string syntax. Our template so far is pretty sparse: just a `div` with some placeholder text.

We can also move our template out to a separate file and use `templateUrl` instead:

```
1   @Component({
2     selector: 'inventory-app-root',
3     templateUrl: './app.component.html'
4   })
5   export class AppComponent {
6     // Inventory logic here
7   }
```

Adding A Product

Our app isn't very interesting without `Products` to view. Let's add some now.

We can create a new `Product` like this:

```
1    // this is just an example of how to use Product,
2    // we'll do something similar in our Angular code in a moment
3
4    // first, we have to import `Product` so that we can use it
5    import { Product } from './product.model';
6
7    // now we can create a new `Product`
8    let newProduct = new Product(
9        'NICEHAT',                              // sku
10       'A Nice Black Hat',                     // name
11       '/assets/images/products/black-hat.jpg', // imageUrl
12       ['Men', 'Accessories', 'Hats'],         // department
13       29.99);                                 // price
```

Our constructor for `Product` takes 5 arguments. We can create a new `Product` by using the `new` keyword.

> Normally, I probably wouldn't pass more than a few arguments to a function. Another option here is to configure the `Product` class to take an Object in the constructor, then we wouldn't have to remember the order of the arguments. That is, `Product` could be changed to do something like this:

```
1    new Product({sku: "MYHAT", name: "A green hat"})
```

But for now, this 5 argument constructor is easy to use.

We want to be able to show this `Product` in the view. In order to make properties accessible to our template **we add them as instance variables to the Component.**

For example, if we want to access `newProduct` in our view we could write:

```
1  class AppComponent {
2    product: Product;
3
4    constructor() {
5      let newProduct = new Product(
6            'NICEHAT',
7            'A Nice Black Hat',
8            '/resources/images/products/black-hat.jpg',
9            ['Men', 'Accessories', 'Hats'],
10           29.99);
11
12     this.product = newProduct;
13   }
14 }
```

or more concisely:

```
1   class AppComponent {
2     product: Product;
3
4     constructor() {
5       this.product = new Product(
6             'NICEHAT',
7             'A Nice Black Hat',
8             '/resources/images/products/black-hat.jpg',
9             ['Men', 'Accessories', 'Hats'],
10            29.99);
11    }
12  }
```

Notice that we did three things here:

1. **We added a `constructor`** - When Angular creates a new instance of this Component, it calls the `constructor` function. This is where we can put setup for this Component.
2. **We described an instance variable** - On `AppComponent`, when we write: `product: Product`, we're specifying that the `AppComponent` instances have a property `product` which is a `Product` object.
3. **We assigned a `Product` to `product`** - In the `constructor` we create an instance of `Product` and assigned it to the instance variable

Viewing the `Product` with Template Binding

Now that we have `product` assigned to the `AppComponent` instance, we could use that variable in our view template:

```
1   <div class="inventory-app">
2       <h1>{{ product.name }}</h1>
3       <span>{{ product.sku }}</span>
4   </div>
```

Using the {{...}} syntax is called *template binding*. It tells the view we want to use the value of the expression inside the brackets at this location in our template.

So in this case, we have two bindings:

- {{ product.name }}
- {{ product.sku }}

The product variable comes from the instance variable product on our Component instance of AppComponent.

What's neat about template binding is that the code inside the brackets is *an expression*. That means you can do things like this:

- {{ count + 1 }}
- {{ myFunction(myArguments) }}

In the first case, we're using an operator to change the displayed value of count. In the second case, we're able to replace the tags with the value of the function myFunction(myArguments). Using template binding tags is the main way that you'll show data in your Angular applications.

Adding More Products

In the code above, we're only able to show a single product in our app, but we want to be able to show a list of products. Let's change our AppComponent to store an array of Products rather than a single Product:

```
1  class AppComponent {
2    products: Product[];
3
4    constructor() {
5      this.products = [];
6    }
7  }
```

Notice that we've renamed the variable product to products, and we've changed the type to Product[]. The [] characters at the end mean we want products to be an Array of Products. We also could have written this as: Array<Product>.

Now that our AppComponent holds an array of Products. Let's create some Products in the constructor:

code/how-angular-works/inventory-app/src/app/app.component.ts

```
15  export class AppComponent {
16    products: Product[];
17
18    constructor() {
19      this.products = [
20        new Product(
21          'MYSHOES',
22          'Black Running Shoes',
23          '/assets/images/products/black-shoes.jpg',
24          ['Men', 'Shoes', 'Running Shoes'],
25          109.99),
26        new Product(
27          'NEATOJACKET',
28          'Blue Jacket',
29          '/assets/images/products/blue-jacket.jpg',
30          ['Women', 'Apparel', 'Jackets & Vests'],
31          238.99),
32        new Product(
33          'NICEHAT',
34          'A Nice Black Hat',
35          '/assets/images/products/black-hat.jpg',
36          ['Men', 'Accessories', 'Hats'],
37          29.99)
38      ];
39    }
```

This code will give us some Products to work with in our app.

Selecting a Product

We (eventually) want to support user interaction in our app. For instance, the user might *select* a particular product to view more information about the product, add it to the cart, etc.

Let's add some functionality here in our AppComponent to handle what happens when a new Product is selected. To do that, let's define a new function, productWasSelected:

code/how-angular-works/inventory-app/src/app/app.component.ts

```
41    productWasSelected(product: Product): void {
42      console.log('Product clicked: ', product);
43    }
```

This function accepts a single argument product and then it will log out that the product was passed in. We'll use this function in a bit.

Listing products using `<products-list>`

Now that we have our top-level AppComponent component, we need to add a new component for rendering a list of products. In the next section we'll create the implementation of a ProductsList component that matches the selector products-list. Before we dive into the implementation details, here's how we will *use* this new component in our template:

code/how-angular-works/inventory-app/src/app/app.component.html

```
1  <div class="inventory-app">
2    <products-list
3      [productList]="products"
4      (onProductSelected)="productWasSelected($event)">
5    </products-list>
6  </div>
```

There is some new syntax here, so let's talk about each part:

Inputs and Outputs

When we use products-list we're using a key feature of Angular components: inputs and outputs:

```
1      <products-list
2        [productList]="products"                          <!-- input -->
3        (onProductSelected)="productWasSelected($event)"> <!-- output -->
4      </products-list>
```

The [squareBrackets] pass inputs and the (parentheses) handle outputs.

Data flows *in* to your component via *input bindings* and events flow *out* of your component through *output bindings*.

Think of the set of input + output bindings as defining the **public API** of your component.

[squareBrackets] **pass inputs**

In Angular, you pass data into child components via *inputs*.

In our code where we show:

```
1    <products-list
2      [productList]="products"
```

We're using an *input* of the `ProductList` component.

It can be tricky to understand where `products`/`productList` are coming from. There are two sides to this attribute:

- `[productList]` (the left-hand side) and
- `"products"` (the right-hand side)

The left-hand side `[productList]` says we want to use the `productList` *input* of the `products-list` component (we'll show how to define that in a moment).

The right-hand side `"products"` says that we want to send the *value of the expression* `products`. That is, the array `this.products` in the `AppComponent` class.

> ❓ You might ask, "how would I know that `productList` is a valid input to the `products-list` component? The answer is: you'd read the docs for that component. The `inputs` (and `outputs`) are part of the "public API" of a component.
>
> You'd know the inputs for a component that you're using in the same way that you'd know what the arguments are for a function that you're using.
>
> That said, we'll define the `products-list` component in a moment, and we'll see exactly how the `productList` input is defined.

(`parens`) handle outputs

In Angular, you send data out of components via *outputs*.

In our code where we show:

```
1    <products-list
2      ...
3      (onProductSelected)="productWasSelected($event)">
```

We're saying that we want to listen to the `onProductSelected` *output* from the `ProductsList` component.

That is:

- `(onProductSelected)`, the left-hand side is the name of the `output` we want to "listen" on

- "productWasSelected", the right-hand side is the **function we want to call** when something new is sent to this output
- $event is a *special variable* here that represents **the thing emitted on** (i.e. sent to) the output.

Now, we haven't talked about **how to define inputs or outputs** on our own components yet, but we will shortly when we define the ProductsList component. For now, know that we can pass data to child components through *inputs* (like "arguments" to a function) and we can receive data out of a child component through *outputs* (sort of like "return values" from a function).

Full AppComponent Listing

We broke the AppComponent up into several chunks above. So that we can see the whole thing together, here's the full code listing of our AppComponent:

code/how-angular-works/inventory-app/src/app/app.component.ts

```
1   import {
2     Component,
3     EventEmitter
4   } from '@angular/core';
5
6   import { Product } from './product.model';
7
8   /**
9    * @InventoryApp: the top-level component for our application
10   */
11  @Component({
12    selector: 'inventory-app-root',
13    templateUrl: './app.component.html'
14  })
15  export class AppComponent {
16    products: Product[];
17
18    constructor() {
19      this.products = [
20        new Product(
21          'MYSHOES',
22          'Black Running Shoes',
23          '/assets/images/products/black-shoes.jpg',
24          ['Men', 'Shoes', 'Running Shoes'],
25          109.99),
26        new Product(
27          'NEATOJACKET',
```

```
28            'Blue Jacket',
29            '/assets/images/products/blue-jacket.jpg',
30            ['Women', 'Apparel', 'Jackets & Vests'],
31            238.99),
32        new Product(
33            'NICEHAT',
34            'A Nice Black Hat',
35            '/assets/images/products/black-hat.jpg',
36            ['Men', 'Accessories', 'Hats'],
37            29.99)
38        ];
39    }
40
41    productWasSelected(product: Product): void {
42      console.log('Product clicked: ', product);
43    }
44 }
```

and the template:

code/how-angular-works/inventory-app/src/app/app.component.html

```
1 <div class="inventory-app">
2   <products-list
3     [productList]="products"
4     (onProductSelected)="productWasSelected($event)">
5   </products-list>
6 </div>
```

The ProductsListComponent

Now that we have our top-level application component, let's write the ProductsListComponent, which will render a list of product rows.

We want to allow the user to select **one** Product and we want to keep track of which Product is the currently selected one. The ProductsListComponent is a great place to do this because it "knows" all of the Products at the same time.

Let's write the ProductsListComponent in three steps:

- Configuring the ProductsListComponent @Component options
- Writing the ProductsListComponent controller class
- Writing the ProductsListComponent view template

Configuring the ProductsListComponent @Component Options

Let's take a look at the @Component configuration for ProductsListComponent:

code/how-angular-works/inventory-app/src/app/products-list/products-list.component.ts

```
1  import {
2    Component,
3    EventEmitter,
4    Input,
5    Output
6  } from '@angular/core';
7  import { Product } from '../product.model';
8
9  /**
10  * @ProductsList: A component for rendering all ProductRows and
11  * storing the currently selected Product
12  */
13 @Component({
14   selector: 'products-list',
15   templateUrl: './products-list.component.html'
16 })
17 export class ProductsListComponent {
18   /**
19    * @input productList - the Product[] passed to us
20    */
21   @Input() productList: Product[];
22
23   /**
24    * @output onProductSelected - outputs the current
25    *          Product whenever a new Product is selected
26    */
27   @Output() onProductSelected: EventEmitter<Product>;
```

We start our ProductsListComponent with a familiar option: selector. This selector means we can place our ProductsListComponent with the tag <products-list>. We've also defined two properties productList and onProductSelected. Notice that productList has a @Input() annotation, denoting that it is an *input* and onProductSelected has an @Output() annotation, denoting that it is an *output*.

Component inputs

Inputs **specify the parameters we expect our component to receive**. To designate an input, we use the @Input() decoration on a component class property.

When we specify that a Component takes an input, it is expected that the definition class **will have an instance variable** that will receive the value. For example, say we have the following code:

```
1    import { Component, Input } from '@angular/core';
2
3    @Component({
4      selector: 'my-component',
5    })
6    class MyComponent {
7      @Input() name: string;
8      @Input() age: number;
9    }
```

The name and age inputs map to the name and age properties on instances of the MyComponent class.

> If we need to use two different names for the attribute and the property, we could for example write @Input('firstname') name: String;. But the Angular Style Guide[31] suggests to avoid this.

If we want to use MyComponent from another template, we write something like: `<my-component [name]="myName" [age]="myAge"></my-component>`.

Notice that the attribute name matches the input name, which in turn matches the MyComponent property name. However, these don't always have to match.

For instance, say we wanted our attribute key and instance property to differ. That is, we want to use our component like this:

```
1    <my-component [shortName]="myName" [oldAge]="myAge"></my-component>
```

To do this, we would change the format of the string in the inputs option:

```
1    @Component({
2      selector: 'my-component'
3    })
4    class MyComponent {
5      @Input('shortName') name: string;
6      @Input('oldAge') age: number;
7    }
```

- The **property name** (name, age) represent how that incoming property will be **visible ("bound") in the controller.**
- The **@Input argument** (shortName, oldAge) configures how the property is **visible to the "outside world".**

---
[31] https://angular.io/docs/ts/latest/guide/style-guide.html

Passing products through via the inputs

If you recall, in our AppComponent, we passed products to our products-list via the [productList] input:

code/how-angular-works/inventory-app/src/app/app.component.html

```
1  <div class="inventory-app">
2    <products-list
3      [productList]="products"
4      (onProductSelected)="productWasSelected($event)">
5    </products-list>
6  </div>
```

Hopefully this syntax makes more sense now: we're passing the value of this.products (on the AppComponent) in via an input on ProductsListComponent.

Component outputs

When you want to send data from your component to the outside world, you use *output bindings*.

Let's say a component we're writing has a button and we need to do something when that button is clicked.

The way to do this is by binding the *click* output of the button to a method declared on our component's controller. You do that using the (output)="action" notation.

Here's an example where we keep a counter and increment (or decrement) based on which button is pressed:

```
1  @Component({
2    selector: 'counter',
3    template: `
4      {{ value }}
5      <button (click)="increase()">Increase</button>
6      <button (click)="decrease()">Decrease</button>
7    `
8  })
9  class Counter {
10   value: number;
11
12   constructor() {
13     this.value = 1;
14   }
```

```
15
16    increase() {
17      this.value = this.value + 1;
18      return false;
19    }
20
21    decrease() {
22      this.value = this.value - 1;
23      return false;
24    }
25  }
```

In this example we're saying that every time the first button is clicked, we want the `increase()` method on our controller to be invoked. And, similarly, when the second button is clicked, we want to call the `decrease()` method.

The parentheses attribute syntax looks like this: `(output)="action"`. In this case, the output we're listening for is the `click` event on this button. There are many other built-in events we can listen to such as: `mousedown`, `mousemove`, `dbl-click`, etc.

In this example, the event is *internal* to the component. That is, calling `increase()` increments `this.value`, but there's no effect that leaves this component. When creating our own components we can also expose "public events" (component `outputs`) that allow the component to talk to the outside world.

The key thing to understand here is that in a view, we can listen to an event by using the `(output)="action"` syntax.

Emitting Custom Events

Let's say we want to create a component that emits a custom event, like `click` or `mousedown` above. To create a custom output event we do three things:

1. Specify `outputs` in the `@Component` configuration
2. Attach an `EventEmitter` to the output property
3. Emit an event from the `EventEmitter`, at the right time

Perhaps `EventEmitter` is unfamiliar to you. Don't panic! It's not too hard.

An `EventEmitter` is an object that helps you implement the Observer Pattern[32]. That is, it's an object that will:

1. maintain a list of subscribers and
2. publish events to them.

That's it.

Here's a short and sweet example of how you can use `EventEmitter`

```
1  let ee = new EventEmitter();
2  ee.subscribe((name: string) => console.log(`Hello ${name}`));
3  ee.emit("Nate");
4
5  // -> "Hello Nate"
```

When we assign an `EventEmitter` to an output *Angular automatically subscribes* for us. You don't need to do the subscription yourself (though in a special situation you could add your own subscriptions, if you want to).

Here's an example of how we write a component that has outputs:

```
1  @Component({
2    selector: 'single-component',
3    template: `
4      <button (click)="liked()">Like it?</button>
5    `
6  })
7  class SingleComponent {
8    @Output() putRingOnIt: EventEmitter<string>;
9
10   constructor() {
11     this.putRingOnIt = new EventEmitter();
12   }
13
14   liked(): void {
15     this.putRingOnIt.emit("oh oh oh");
16   }
17 }
```

---

[32] https://en.wikipedia.org/wiki/Observer_pattern

Notice that we did all three steps: 1. specified outputs, 2. created an EventEmitter that we attached to the output property putRingOnIt and 3. Emitted an event when liked is called.

If we wanted to use this output in a parent component we could do something like this:

```
 1  @Component({
 2    selector: 'club',
 3    template: `
 4      <div>
 5        <single-component
 6          (putRingOnIt)="ringWasPlaced($event)"
 7          ></single-component>
 8      </div>
 9    `
10  })
11  class ClubComponent {
12    ringWasPlaced(message: string) {
13      console.log(`Put your hands up: ${message}`);
14    }
15  }
16
17  // logged -> "Put your hands up: oh oh oh"
```

Again, notice that:

- putRingOnIt comes from the outputs of SingleComponent
- ringWasPlaced is a function on the ClubComponent
- $event contains the thing that was emitted, in this case a string

Writing the ProductsListComponent Controller Class

Back to our store example, our ProductsListComponent controller class needs three instance variables:

- One to hold the list of Products (that come from the productList input)
- One to output events (that emit from the onProductSelected output)
- One to hold a reference to the currently selected product

Here's how we define those in code:

code/how-angular-works/inventory-app/src/app/products-list/products-list.component.ts

```
17  export class ProductsListComponent {
18    /**
19     * @input productList - the Product[] passed to us
20     */
21    @Input() productList: Product[];
22
23    /**
24     * @output onProductSelected - outputs the current
25     *          Product whenever a new Product is selected
26     */
27    @Output() onProductSelected: EventEmitter<Product>;
28
29    /**
30     * @property currentProduct - local state containing
31     *             the currently selected `Product`
32     */
33    private currentProduct: Product;
34
35    constructor() {
36      this.onProductSelected = new EventEmitter();
37    }
```

Notice that our productList is an Array of Products - this comes in from the inputs.

onProductSelected is our output.

currentProduct is a property internal to ProductsListComponent. You might also hear this being referred to as "local component state". It's only used here within the component.

Writing the ProductsListComponent View Template

Here's the template for our products-list component:

code/how-angular-works/inventory-app/src/app/products-list/products-list.component.html

```
1  <div class="ui items">
2    <product-row
3      *ngFor="let myProduct of productList"
4      [product]="myProduct"
5      (click)='clicked(myProduct)'
6      [class.selected]="isSelected(myProduct)">
7    </product-row>
8  </div>
```

Here we're using the `product-row` tag, which comes from the `ProductRow` component, which we'll define in a minute.

We're using `ngFor` to iterate over each `Product` in `productList`. We've talked about `ngFor` before in this book, but just as a reminder the `let thing of things` syntax says, "iterate over `things` and create a copy of this element for each item, and assign each item to the variable `thing`".

So in this case, we're iterating over the `Products` in `productList` and generating a local variable `myProduct` for each one.

> Style-wise, I probably wouldn't call this variable `myProduct` in a real app. Instead, I'd probably call it `product`, or even `p`. But here I want to be explicit about what we're passing, and `myProduct` is slightly clearer because it let's us distinguish the 'local template variable' from the input `product`.

The interesting thing to note about this `myProduct` variable is that we can now use it *even on the same tag*. As you can see, we do this on the following three lines.

The line that reads `[product]="myProduct"` says that we want to pass `myProduct` (the local variable) to the input `product` of the `product-row`. (We'll define this input when we define the `ProductRow` component below.)

The `(click)='clicked(myProduct)'` line describes what we want to do when this element is clicked. `click` is a built-in event that is triggered when the host element is clicked on. In this case, we want to call the component function `clicked` on `ProductsListComponent` whenever this element is clicked on.

The line `[class.selected]="isSelected(myProduct)"` is a fun one: Angular allows us to set classes conditionally on an element using this syntax. This syntax says "add the CSS class `selected` if `isSelected(myProduct)` returns `true`." This is a really handy way for us to mark the currently selected product.

You may have noticed that we didn't define `clicked` nor `isSelected` yet, so let's do that now (in `ProductsListComponent`):

clicked

code/how-angular-works/inventory-app/src/app/products-list/products-list.component.ts

```
39    clicked(product: Product): void {
40      this.currentProduct = product;
41      this.onProductSelected.emit(product);
42    }
```

This function does two things:

1. Set this.currentProduct to the Product that was passed in.
2. Emit the Product that was clicked on our output

isSelected

code/how-angular-works/inventory-app/src/app/products-list/products-list.component.ts

```
44    isSelected(product: Product): boolean {
45      if (!product || !this.currentProduct) {
46        return false;
47      }
48      return product.sku === this.currentProduct.sku;
49    }
```

This function accepts a Product and returns true if product's sku matches the currentProduct's sku. It returns false otherwise.

The Full ProductsListComponent Component

Here's the full code listing so we can see everything in context:

code/how-angular-works/inventory-app/src/app/products-list/products-list.component.ts

```
1    import {
2      Component,
3      EventEmitter,
4      Input,
5      Output
6    } from '@angular/core';
7    import { Product } from '../product.model';
8
9    /**
10     * @ProductsList: A component for rendering all ProductRows and
```

```
11   * storing the currently selected Product
12   */
13  @Component({
14    selector: 'products-list',
15    templateUrl: './products-list.component.html'
16  })
17  export class ProductsListComponent {
18    /**
19     * @input productList - the Product[] passed to us
20     */
21    @Input() productList: Product[];
22
23    /**
24     * @output onProductSelected - outputs the current
25     *          Product whenever a new Product is selected
26     */
27    @Output() onProductSelected: EventEmitter<Product>;
28
29    /**
30     * @property currentProduct - local state containing
31     *            the currently selected `Product`
32     */
33    private currentProduct: Product;
34
35    constructor() {
36      this.onProductSelected = new EventEmitter();
37    }
38
39    clicked(product: Product): void {
40      this.currentProduct = product;
41      this.onProductSelected.emit(product);
42    }
43
44    isSelected(product: Product): boolean {
45      if (!product || !this.currentProduct) {
46        return false;
47      }
48      return product.sku === this.currentProduct.sku;
49    }
50
51  }
```

and the template:

code/how-angular-works/inventory-app/src/app/products-list/products-list.component.html

```
1  <div class="ui items">
2    <product-row
3      *ngFor="let myProduct of productList"
4      [product]="myProduct"
5      (click)='clicked(myProduct)'
6      [class.selected]="isSelected(myProduct)">
7    </product-row>
8  </div>
```

The `ProductRowComponent` Component

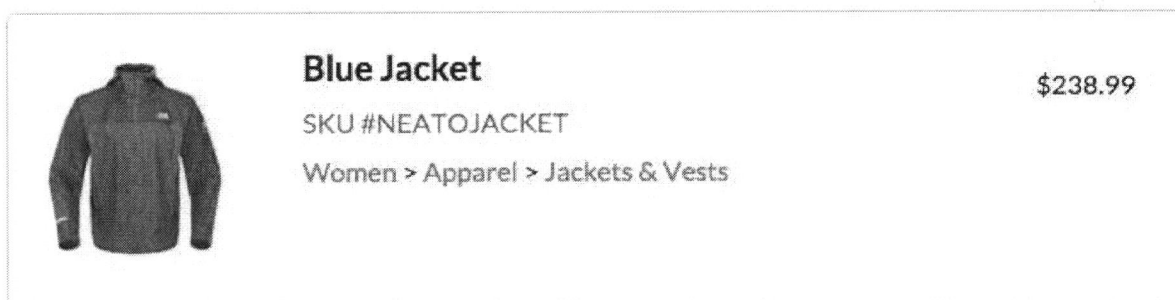

A Selected Product Row Component

Our `ProductRowComponent` displays our `Product`. `ProductRowComponent` will have its own template, but will also be split up into three smaller Components:

- `ProductImageComponent` - for the image
- `ProductDepartmentComponent` - for the department "breadcrumbs"
- `PriceDisplayComponent` - for showing the product's price

Here's a visual of the three Components that will be used within the `ProductRowComponent`:

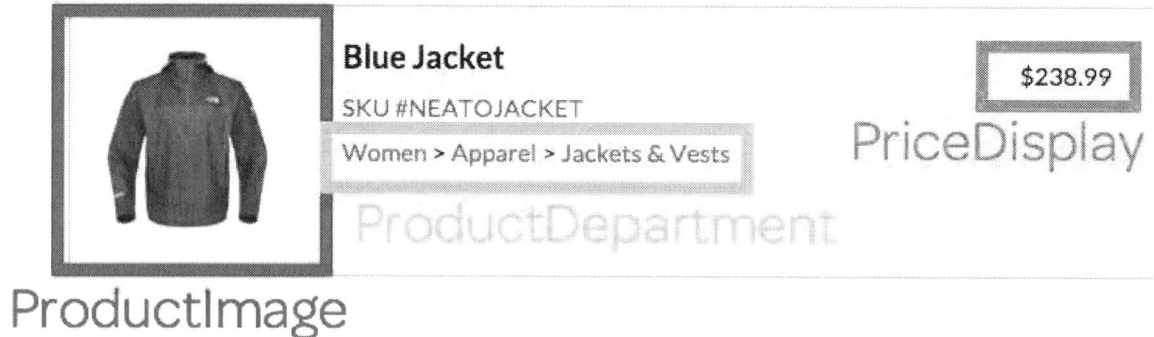

ProductRowComponent's Sub-components

Let's take a look at the ProductRowComponent's Component configuration, definition class, and template:

ProductRowComponent **Configuration**

The ProductRowComponent uses a lot of the ideas we've covered so far:

code/how-angular-works/inventory-app/src/app/product-row/product-row.component.ts

```
1   import {
2     Component,
3     Input,
4     HostBinding
5   } from '@angular/core';
6   import { Product } from '../product.model';
7
8   /**
9    * @ProductRow: A component for the view of single Product
10   */
11  @Component({
12    selector: 'product-row',
13    templateUrl: './product-row.component.html',
14  })
15  export class ProductRowComponent {
16    @Input() product: Product;
17    @HostBinding('attr.class') cssClass = 'item';
18  }
```

We start by defining the selector of product-row. We've seen this several times now - this defines that this component will match the tag product-row.

Next we define that this row takes an @Input of product. This instance variable will be set to the Product that was passed in from our parent Component.

The HostBinding decoration is new - it lets us **set attributes on the host element**. The *host* is the element this component is attached to.

In this case, we're using the Semantic UI item class[33]. Here when we say @HostBinding('attr.class') cssClass = 'item'; we're saying that we want to attach the CSS class item to the host element.

> Using host is nice because it means we can configure our host element from *within* the component. This is great because otherwise we'd require the host element to specify the CSS tag and that is bad because we would then make assigning a CSS class part of the requirement to using the Component.

Instead of putting a long template string in our TypeScript file, instead we're going to move the template to a separate HTML file and use a templateUrl to load it. We'll talk about the template in a minute.

ProductRowComponent template

Now let's take a look at the template:

code/how-angular-works/inventory-app/src/app/product-row/product-row.component.html

```
1   <product-image [product]="product"></product-image>
2   <div class="content">
3     <div class="header">{{ product.name }}</div>
4     <div class="meta">
5       <div class="product-sku">SKU #{{ product.sku }}</div>
6     </div>
7     <div class="description">
8       <product-department [product]="product"></product-department>
9     </div>
10  </div>
11  <price-display [price]="product.price"></price-display>
```

Our template doesn't have anything conceptually new.

In the first line we use our product-image directive and we pass our product to the product input of the ProductImageComponent. We use the product-department directive in the same way.

We use the price-display directive slightly differently in that we pass the product.price, instead of the product directly.

---

[33]http://semantic-ui.com/views/item.html

The rest of the template is standard HTML elements with custom CSS classes and some template bindings.

Now let's talk about the three components we used in this template. They're relatively short.

The `ProductImageComponent` Component

In the `ProductImageComponent` the template is only one line, so we can put it inline:

code/how-angular-works/inventory-app/src/app/product-image/product-image.component.ts

```
 8   /**
 9    * @ProductImage: A component to show a single Product's image
10    */
11   @Component({
12     selector: 'product-image',
13     template: `
14     <img class="product-image" [src]="product.imageUrl">
15     `
16   })
17   export class ProductImageComponent {
18     @Input() product: Product;
19     @HostBinding('attr.class') cssClass = 'ui small image';
20   }
```

The one thing to note here is in the `img` tag, notice how we use the `[src]` input to `img`.

By using the `[src]` attribute, we're telling Angular that we want to use the `[src]` *input* on this `img` tag. Angular will then replace the value of the `src` attribute once the expression is resolved.

We could also have written this tag this way:

```
1   <img src="{{ product.imageUrl }}">
```

Both styles do essentially the same thing, so feel free to pick the style that works best for your team.

The `PriceDisplayComponent` Component

Next, let's look at `PriceDisplayComponent`:

code/how-angular-works/inventory-app/src/app/price-display/price-display.component.ts

```
1   import {
2     Component,
3     Input
4   } from '@angular/core';
5
6   /**
7    * @PriceDisplay: A component to show the price of a
8    * Product
9    */
10  @Component({
11    selector: 'price-display',
12    template: `
13    <div class="price-display">\${{ price }}</div>
14    `
15  })
16  export class PriceDisplayComponent {
17    @Input() price: number;
18  }
```

One thing to note is that we're escaping the dollar sign $ because this is a backtick string and the dollar sign is used for template variables (in ES6).

The ProductDepartmentComponent

Here is our ProductDepartmentComponent:

code/how-angular-works/inventory-app/src/app/product-department/product-department.component.ts

```
1   import {
2     Component,
3     Input
4   } from '@angular/core';
5   import { Product } from '../product.model';
6
7   /**
8    * @ProductDepartment: A component to show the breadcrumbs to a
9    * Product's department
10   */
11  @Component({
12    selector: 'product-department',
```

```
13    templateUrl: './product-department.component.html'
14  })
15  export class ProductDepartmentComponent {
16    @Input() product: Product;
17  }
```

and template:

code/how-angular-works/inventory-app/src/app/product-department/product-department.component.html

```
1  <div class="product-department">
2    <span *ngFor="let name of product.department; let i=index">
3      <a href="#">{{ name }}</a>
4      <span>{{i < (product.department.length-1) ? '>' : ''}}</span>
5    </span>
6  </div>
```

The thing to note about the ProductDepartmentComponent Component is the ngFor and the span tag.

Our ngFor loops over product.department and assigns each department string to name. The new part is the second expression that says: let i=index. This is how you get the iteration number out of ngFor.

In the span tag, we use the i variable to determine if we should show the greater-than > symbol.

The idea is that given a department, we want to show the department string like:

```
1  Women > Apparel > Jackets & Vests
```

The expression {{i < (product.department.length-1) ? '>' : ''}} says that we only want to use the '>' character if we're not the last department. On the last department just show an empty string ''.

> ℹ️ This format: test ? valueIfTrue : valueIfFalse is called the *ternary operator*.

NgModule **and Booting the App**

The final thing we have to do is ensure we have a NgModule for this app and boot it up:

code/how-angular-works/inventory-app/src/app/app.module.ts

```
1   import { BrowserModule } from '@angular/platform-browser';
2   import { NgModule } from '@angular/core';
3   import { FormsModule } from '@angular/forms';
4   import { HttpModule } from '@angular/http';
5
6   import { AppComponent } from './app.component';
7   import { ProductImageComponent } from './product-image/product-image.component';
8   import { ProductDepartmentComponent } from './product-department/product-departm\
9   ent.component';
10  import { PriceDisplayComponent } from './price-display/price-display.component';
11  import { ProductRowComponent } from './product-row/product-row.component';
12  import { ProductsListComponent } from './products-list/products-list.component';
13
14  @NgModule({
15    declarations: [
16      AppComponent,
17      ProductImageComponent,
18      ProductDepartmentComponent,
19      PriceDisplayComponent,
20      ProductRowComponent,
21      ProductsListComponent
22    ],
23    imports: [
24      BrowserModule,
25      FormsModule,
26      HttpModule
27    ],
28    providers: [],
29    bootstrap: [AppComponent]
30  })
31  export class AppModule { }
```

Angular provides a *module* system that helps organize our code. Unlike AngularJS 1.x, where all directives are essentially globals, in Angular you must specify exactly *which components* you're going to be using in your app.

While it is a bit more configuration to do it this way, it's a lifesaver for larger apps.

When you create new components in Angular, in order to use them they must be *accessible* from the current module. That is, if we want to use the ProductsListComponent component with the products-list selector in the AppComponent template, then we need to make sure that the AppComponent's module either:

1. is in the same module as the `ProductsListComponent` component or
2. The `AppComponent`'s module `imports` the module that contains `ProductsListComponent`

> Remember **every** component you write must be declared in one `NgModule` before it can be used in a template.

In this case, we're putting `AppComponent`, `ProductsListComponent`, and **all** the other components for this app in one module. This is easy and it means they can all "see" each other.

Notice that we tell `NgModule` that we want to `bootstrap` with `AppComponent`. This says that `AppComponent` will be the top-level component.

Because we are writing a browser app, we also put `BrowserModule` in the `imports` of the `NgModule`.

Booting the app

To bootstrap this app we write this in our `main.ts`:

code/how-angular-works/inventory-app/src/main.ts

```
1  import { enableProdMode } from '@angular/core';
2  import { platformBrowserDynamic } from '@angular/platform-browser-dynamic';
3
4  import { AppModule } from './app/app.module';
5  import { environment } from './environments/environment';
6
7  if (environment.production) {
8    enableProdMode();
9  }
10
11 platformBrowserDynamic().bootstrapModule(AppModule);
```

The last line in this file is what boots our `AppModule` and subsequently boots our Angular app.

Because this app was written with `angular-cli`, we can use the `ng` tool to run the app by running `ng serve`.

That said, it can be tricky to understand what's going on there. When we run our app with `ng serve` this is what happens:

- `ng serve` looks at `.angular-cli.json` which specifies `main.ts` as our entry point (and `index.html` as our index file)
- `main.ts` bootstraps `AppModule`
- `AppModule` specifies that `AppComponent` is the top level component
- ... and then `AppComponent` renders the rest of our app!

The Completed Project

To try it out, change into the project directory and type:

```
1   npm install
2   ng serve
```

Now we have all the pieces we need for the working project!

Here's what it will look like when we're done:

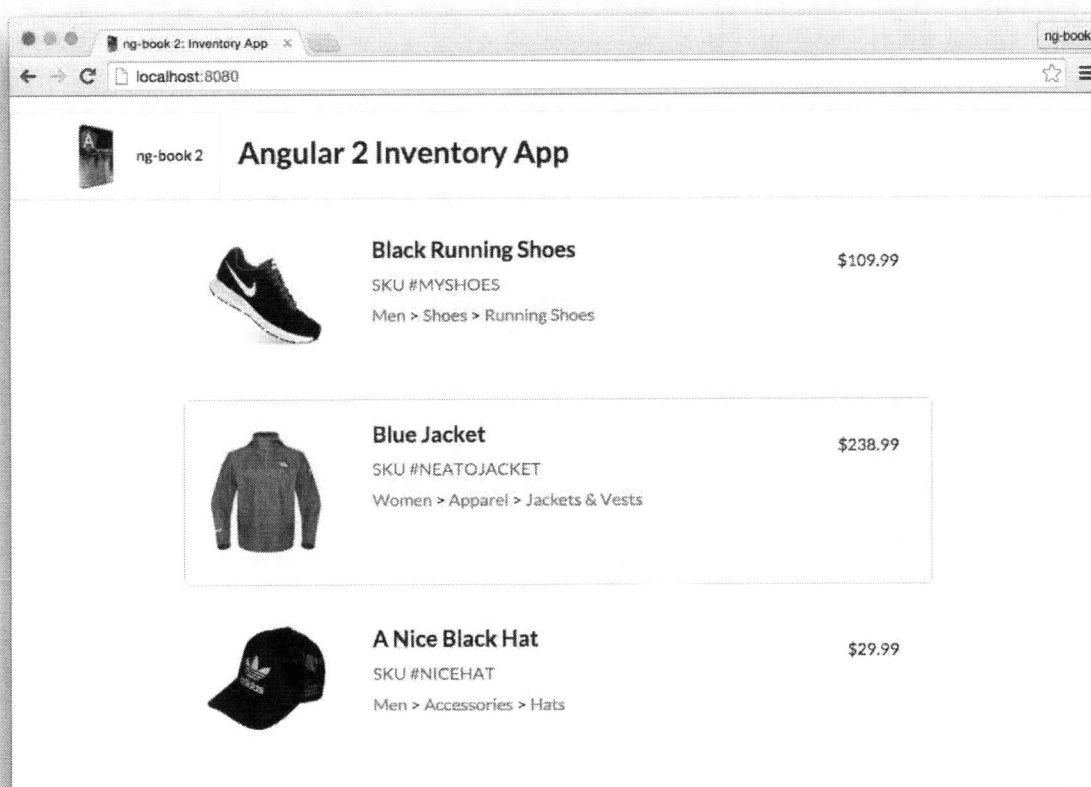

Completed Inventory App

Now you can click to select a particular product and have it render a nice purple outline when selected. If you add new Products in your code, you'll see them rendered.

Deploying the App

We can deploy this app in the same way we deployed the app in the first chapter:

```
1   ng build --target=production --base-href /
```

And then push the files in `dist` to our server!

A Word on Data Architecture

You might be wondering at this point how we would manage the data flow if we started adding more functionality to this app.

For instance, say we wanted to add a shopping cart view and then we would add items to our cart. How could we implement this?

The only tools we've talked about are emitting output events. When we click add-to-cart do we simply bubble up an `addedToCart` event and handle at the root component? That feels a bit awkward.

Data architecture is a large topic with many opinions. Thankfully, Angular is flexible enough to handle a wide variety of data architectures, but that means that you have to decide for yourself which to use.

In Angular 1, the default option was two-way data binding. Two-way data binding is super easy to get started: your controllers have data, your forms manipulate that data directly, and your views show the data.

The problem with two-way data binding is that it often causes cascading effects throughout your application and makes it really difficult to trace data flow as your project grows.

Another problem with two-way data binding is that because you're passing data down through components it often forces your "data layout tree" to match your "dom view tree". In practice, these two things should really be separate.

One way you might handle this scenario would be to create a `ShoppingCartService`, which would be a singleton that would hold the list of the current items in the cart. This service could notify any interested objects when an item in the cart changes.

The idea is easy enough, but in practice there are a lot of details to be worked out.

The recommended way in Angular, and in many modern web frameworks (such as React), is to adopt a pattern of **one-way data binding**. That is, your data flows only **down** through components. If you need to make changes, you emit events that cause changes to happen "at the top" which then trickle down.

One-way data binding can seem like it adds some overhead in the beginning but it saves *a lot* of complication around change detection and it makes your systems easier to reason about.

Thankfully there are two major contenders for managing your data architecture:

  1. Use an Observables-based architecture like RxJS

2. Use a Flux-based architecture

Later in this book we'll talk about how to implement a scalable data architecture for your app. For now, bask in the joy of your new Component-based application!

Built-in Directives

Introduction

Angular provides a number of built-in *directives*, which are attributes we add to our HTML elements that give us dynamic behavior. In this chapter, we're going to cover each built-in directive and show you examples of how to use them.

By the end of this chapter you'll be able to use the basic built-in directives that Angular offers.

> **How To Use This Chapter**
>
> Instead of building an app step-by-step, this chapter is a tour of the built-in directives in Angular. Since we're early in the book, we won't explain every detail, but we will provide plenty of example code.
>
> Remember: at any time you can reference the sample code for this chapter to get the complete context.
>
> If you'd like to run the examples in this chapter then see the folder `code/built-in-directives` and run:

```
1    npm install
2    npm start
```

> And then open http://localhost:4200[34] in your browser.

NgIf

The `ngIf` directive is used when you want to display or hide an element based on a condition. The condition is determined by the result of the *expression* that you pass into the directive.

If the result of the expression returns a false value, the element will be removed from the DOM.

Some examples are:

---

[34]http://localhost:4200

```
1   <div *ngIf="false"></div>           <!-- never displayed -->
2   <div *ngIf="a > b"></div>           <!-- displayed if a is more than b -->
3   <div *ngIf="str == 'yes'"></div>    <!-- displayed if str is the string "yes" -->
4   <div *ngIf="myFunc()"></div>        <!-- displayed if myFunc returns truthy -->
```

> **Note for AngularJS 1.x Users**
>
> If you've used AngularJS 1.x, you may have used the `ngIf` directive before. You can think of the Angular version as a direct substitute.
>
> On the other hand, Angular offers no built-in alternative for `ng-show`. So, if your goal is to just change the CSS visibility of an element, you should look into either the `ngStyle` or the `class` directives, described later in this chapter.

NgSwitch

Sometimes you need to render different elements depending on a given condition.

When you run into this situation, you could use `ngIf` several times like this:

```
1   <div class="container">
2     <div *ngIf="myVar == 'A'">Var is A</div>
3     <div *ngIf="myVar == 'B'">Var is B</div>
4     <div *ngIf="myVar != 'A' && myVar != 'B'">Var is something else</div>
5   </div>
```

But as you can see, the scenario where `myVar` is neither `A` nor `B` is verbose when all we're trying to express is an `else`.

To illustrate this growth in complexity, say we wanted to handle a new value `C`.

In order to do that, we'd have to not only add the new element with `ngIf`, but also change the last case:

```
1   <div class="container">
2     <div *ngIf="myVar == 'A'">Var is A</div>
3     <div *ngIf="myVar == 'B'">Var is B</div>
4     <div *ngIf="myVar == 'C'">Var is C</div>
5     <div *ngIf="myVar != 'A' && myVar != 'B' && myVar != 'C'">Var is something els\
6   e</div>
7   </div>
```

For cases like this, Angular introduces the ngSwitch directive.

If you're familiar with the switch statement then you'll feel very at home.

The idea behind this directive is the same: allow a single evaluation of an expression, and then display nested elements based on the value that resulted from that evaluation.

Once we have the result then we can:

- Describe the known results, using the ngSwitchCase directive
- Handle all the other unknown cases with ngSwitchDefault

Let's rewrite our example using this new set of directives:

```
1  <div class="container" [ngSwitch]="myVar">
2    <div *ngSwitchCase="'A'">Var is A</div>
3    <div *ngSwitchCase="'B'">Var is B</div>
4    <div *ngSwitchDefault>Var is something else</div>
5  </div>
```

Then if we want to handle the new value C we insert a single line:

```
1  <div class="container" [ngSwitch]="myVar">
2    <div *ngSwitchCase="'A'">Var is A</div>
3    <div *ngSwitchCase="'B'">Var is B</div>
4    <div *ngSwitchCase="'C'">Var is C</div>
5    <div *ngSwitchDefault>Var is something else</div>
6  </div>
```

And we don't have to touch the default (i.e. *fallback*) condition.

Having the ngSwitchDefault element is optional. If we leave it out, nothing will be rendered when myVar fails to match any of the expected values.

You can also declare the same *ngSwitchCase value for different elements, so you're not limited to matching only a single time. Here's an example:

code/built-in-directives/src/app/ng-switch-example/ng-switch-example.component.html

```
1   <h4 class="ui horizontal divider header">
2     Current choice is {{ choice }}
3   </h4>
4
5   <div class="ui raised segment">
6     <ul [ngSwitch]="choice">
7       <li *ngSwitchCase="1">First choice</li>
8       <li *ngSwitchCase="2">Second choice</li>
9       <li *ngSwitchCase="3">Third choice</li>
10      <li *ngSwitchCase="4">Fourth choice</li>
11      <li *ngSwitchCase="2">Second choice, again</li>
12      <li *ngSwitchDefault>Default choice</li>
13    </ul>
14  </div>
15
16  <div style="margin-top: 20px;">
17    <button class="ui primary button" (click)="nextChoice()">
18      Next choice
19    </button>
20  </div>
```

In the example above when the choice is 2, both the second and fifth li s will be rendered.

NgStyle

With the NgStyle directive, you can set a given DOM element CSS properties from Angular expressions.

The simplest way to use this directive is by doing [style.<cssproperty>]="value". For example:

code/built-in-directives/src/app/ng-style-example/ng-style-example.component.html

```
5   <div [style.background-color]="'yellow'">
6     Uses fixed yellow background
7   </div>
```

This snippet is using the NgStyle directive to set the background-color CSS property to the literal string 'yellow'.

Another way to set fixed values is by using the NgStyle attribute and using key value pairs for each property you want to set, like this:

code/built-in-directives/src/app/ng-style-example/ng-style-example.component.html

```
13  <div [ngStyle]="{color: 'white', 'background-color': 'blue'}">
14    Uses fixed white text on blue background
15  </div>
```

> Notice that in the ng-style specification we have single quotes around background-color but not around color. Why is that? Well, the argument to ng-style is a JavaScript object and color is a valid key, without quotes. With background-color, however, the dash character isn't allowed in an object key, unless it's a string so we have to quote it.
>
> Generally I'd leave out quoting as much as possible in object keys and only quote keys when we have to.

Here we are setting both the color and the background-color properties.

But the real power of the NgStyle directive comes with using dynamic values.

In our example, we are defining two input boxes with an apply settings button:

code/built-in-directives/src/app/ng-style-example/ng-style-example.component.html

```
56  <div class="ui input">
57    <input type="text" name="color" value="{{color}}" #colorinput>
58  </div>
59
60  <div class="ui input">
61    <input type="text" name="fontSize" value="{{fontSize}}" #fontinput>
62  </div>
63
64  <button class="ui primary button" (click)="apply(colorinput.value, fontinput.val\
65  ue)">
66    Apply settings
67  </button>
```

And then using their values to set the CSS properties for three elements.

On the first one, we're setting the font size based on the input value:

code/built-in-directives/src/app/ng-style-example/ng-style-example.component.html

```
21  <div>
22    <span [ngStyle]="{color: 'red'}" [style.font-size.px]="fontSize">
23      red text
24    </span>
25  </div>
```

It's important to note that we have to specify units where appropriate. For instance, it isn't valid CSS to set a `font-size` of `12` - we have to specify a unit such as `12px` or `1.2em`. Angular provides a handy syntax for specifying units: here we used the notation `[style.font-size.px]`.

The `.px` suffix indicates that we're setting the `font-size` property value in pixels. You could easily replace that by `[style.font-size.em]` to express the font size in ems or even in percentage using `[style.font-size.%]`.

The other two elements use the `#colorinput` to set the text and background colors:

code/built-in-directives/src/app/ng-style-example/ng-style-example.component.html

```
33  <h4 class="ui horizontal divider header">
34    ngStyle with object property from variable
35  </h4>
36
37  <div>
38    <span [ngStyle]="{color: color}">
39      {{ color }} text
40    </span>
41  </div>
42
43  <h4 class="ui horizontal divider header">
44    style from variable
45  </h4>
46
47  <div [style.background-color]="color"
48       style="color: white;">
49    {{ color }} background
50  </div>
```

This way, when we click the **Apply settings** button, we call a method that sets the new values:

code/built-in-directives/src/app/ng-style-example/ng-style-example.component.ts

```
32    apply(color: string, fontSize: number): void {
33      this.color = color;
34      this.fontSize = fontSize;
35    }
```

And with that, both the color and the font size will be applied to the elements using the `NgStyle` directive.

NgClass

The `NgClass` directive, represented by a `ngClass` attribute in your HTML template, allows you to dynamically set and change the CSS classes for a given DOM element.

The first way to use this directive is by passing in an object literal. The object is expected to have the keys as the class names and the values should be a truthy/falsy value to indicate whether the class should be applied or not.

Let's assume we have a CSS class called `bordered` that adds a dashed black border to an element:

code/built-in-directives/src/styles.css

```
8   .bordered {
9     border: 1px dashed black;
10    background-color: #eee; }
```

Let's add two `div` elements: one always having the `bordered` class (and therefore always having the border) and another one never having it:

code/built-in-directives/src/app/ng-class-example/ng-class-example.component.html

```
2    <div [ngClass]="{bordered: false}">This is never bordered</div>
3    <div [ngClass]="{bordered: true}">This is always bordered</div>
```

As expected, this is how those two `div`s would be rendered:

This is never bordered

This is always bordered

Simple class directive usage

Of course, it's a lot more useful to use the `NgClass` directive to make class assignments dynamic.

To make it dynamic we add a variable as the value for the object value, like this:

code/built-in-directives/src/app/ng-class-example/ng-class-example.component.html

```
5    <div [ngClass]="{bordered: isBordered}">
6      Using object literal. Border {{ isBordered ? "ON" : "OFF" }}
7    </div>
```

Alternatively, we can define a `classesObj` object in our component:

code/built-in-directives/src/app/ng-class-example/ng-class-example.component.ts

```
3    @Component({
4      selector: 'app-ng-class-example',
5      templateUrl: './ng-class-example.component.html'
6    })
7    export class NgClassExampleComponent implements OnInit {
8      isBordered: boolean;
9      classesObj: Object;
10     classList: string[];
11
12     constructor() {
13     }
14
15     ngOnInit() {
16       this.isBordered = true;
17       this.classList = ['blue', 'round'];
18       this.toggleBorder();
19     }
20
21     toggleBorder(): void {
22       this.isBordered = !this.isBordered;
23       this.classesObj = {
24         bordered: this.isBordered
25       };
26     }
```

And use the object directly:

code/built-in-directives/src/app/ng-class-example/ng-class-example.component.html

```
9    <div [ngClass]="classesObj">
10     Using object var. Border {{ classesObj.bordered ? "ON" : "OFF" }}
11   </div>
```

> ⚠️ Again, be careful when you have class names that contains dashes, like bordered-box. JavaScript requires that object-literal keys with dashes be quoted like a string, as in:
>
> ```
> 1   <div [ngClass]="{'bordered-box': false}">...</div>
> ```

We can also use a list of class names to specify which class names should be added to the element. For that, we can either pass in an array literal:

code/built-in-directives/src/app/ng-class-example/ng-class-example.component.html

```
31   <div class="base" [ngClass]="['blue', 'round']">
32     This will always have a blue background and
33     round corners
34   </div>
```

Or assign an array of values to a property in our component:

```
1   this.classList = ['blue', 'round'];
```

And pass it in:

code/built-in-directives/src/app/ng-class-example/ng-class-example.component.html

```
36   <div class="base" [ngClass]="classList">
37     This is {{ classList.indexOf('blue') > -1 ? "" : "NOT" }} blue
38     and {{ classList.indexOf('round') > -1 ? "" : "NOT" }} round
39   </div>
```

In this last example, the [ngClass] assignment works alongside existing values assigned by the HTML class attribute.

The resulting classes added to the element will always be the set of the classes provided by usual class HTML attribute and the result of the evaluation of the [class] directive.

In this example:

code/built-in-directives/src/app/ng-class-example/ng-class-example.component.html

```
31    <div class="base" [ngClass]="['blue', 'round']">
32      This will always have a blue background and
33      round corners
34    </div>
```

The element will have all three classes: base from the class HTML attribute and also blue and round from the [class] assignment:

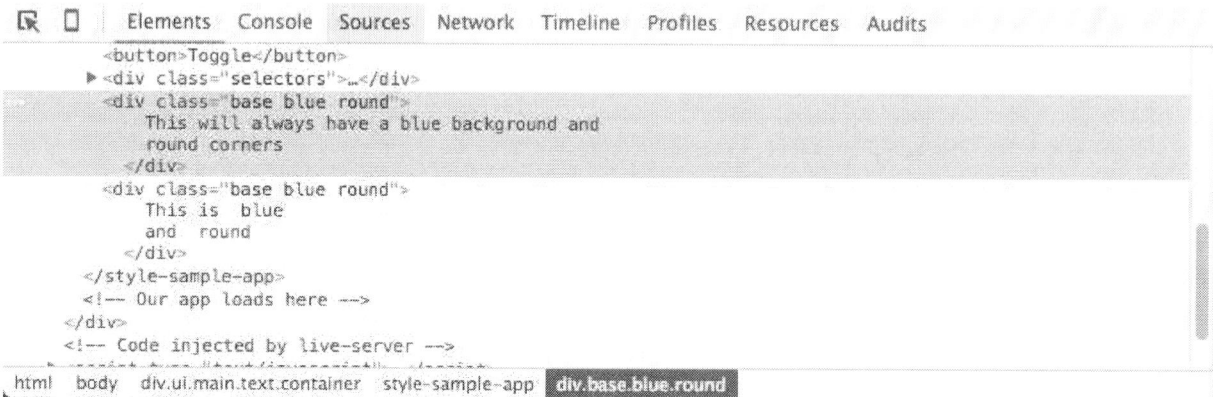

Classes from both the attribute and directive

NgFor

The role of this directive is to **repeat a given DOM element** (or a collection of DOM elements) and pass an element of the array on each iteration.

The syntax is *ngFor="let item of items".

- The let item syntax specifies a (template) variable that's receiving each element of the items array;
- The items is the collection of items from your controller.

To illustrate, we can take a look at the code example. We declare an array of cities on our component controller:

```
1  this.cities = ['Miami', 'Sao Paulo', 'New York'];
```

And then, in our template we can have the following HTML snippet:

code/built-in-directives/src/app/ng-for-example/ng-for-example.component.html

```
1   <h4 class="ui horizontal divider header">
2     Simple list of strings
3   </h4>
4
5   <div class="ui list" *ngFor="let c of cities">
6     <div class="item">{{ c }}</div>
7   </div>
```

And it will render each city inside the `div` as you would expect:

Simple list of strings

Miami

Sao Paulo

New York

Result of the ngFor directive usage

We can also iterate through an array of objects like these:

code/built-in-directives/src/app/ng-for-example/ng-for-example.component.ts

```
17      this.people = [
18        { name: 'Anderson', age: 35, city: 'Sao Paulo' },
19        { name: 'John', age: 12, city: 'Miami' },
20        { name: 'Peter', age: 22, city: 'New York' }
21      ];
```

And then render a table based on each row of data:

code/built-in-directives/src/app/ng-for-example/ng-for-example.component.html

```
9   <h4 class="ui horizontal divider header">
10    List of objects
11  </h4>
12
13  <table class="ui celled table">
14    <thead>
15      <tr>
16        <th>Name</th>
17        <th>Age</th>
```

```
18        <th>City</th>
19      </tr>
20    </thead>
21    <tr *ngFor="let p of people">
22      <td>{{ p.name }}</td>
23      <td>{{ p.age }}</td>
24      <td>{{ p.city }}</td>
25    </tr>
26  </table>
```

Getting the following result:

List of objects

Name	Age	City
Anderson	35	Sao Paulo
John	12	Miami
Peter	22	New York

Rendering array of objects

We can also work with nested arrays. If we wanted to have the same table as above, broken down by city, we could easily declare a new array of objects:

code/built-in-directives/src/app/ng-for-example/ng-for-example.component.ts

```
22      this.peopleByCity = [
23        {
24          city: 'Miami',
25          people: [
26            { name: 'John', age: 12 },
27            { name: 'Angel', age: 22 }
28          ]
29        },
30        {
31          city: 'Sao Paulo',
32          people: [
33            { name: 'Anderson', age: 35 },
34            { name: 'Felipe', age: 36 }
```

```
35            ]
36          }
37       ];
38    }
```

And then we could use `NgFor` to render one `h2` for each city:

code/built-in-directives/src/app/ng-for-example/ng-for-example.component.html

```
32  <div *ngFor="let item of peopleByCity">
33    <h2 class="ui header">{{ item.city }}</h2>
```

And use a nested directive to iterate through the people for a given city:

code/built-in-directives/src/app/ng-for-example/ng-for-example.component.html

```
13  <table class="ui celled table">
14    <thead>
15      <tr>
16        <th>Name</th>
17        <th>Age</th>
18        <th>City</th>
19      </tr>
20    </thead>
21    <tr *ngFor="let p of people">
22      <td>{{ p.name }}</td>
23      <td>{{ p.age }}</td>
24      <td>{{ p.city }}</td>
25    </tr>
26  </table>
```

Resulting in the following template code:

code/built-in-directives/src/app/ng-for-example/ng-for-example.component.html

```
28  <h4 class="ui horizontal divider header">
29    Nested data
30  </h4>
31
32  <div *ngFor="let item of peopleByCity">
33    <h2 class="ui header">{{ item.city }}</h2>
34
35    <table class="ui celled table">
36      <thead>
37        <tr>
38          <th>Name</th>
39          <th>Age</th>
40        </tr>
41      </thead>
42      <tr *ngFor="let p of item.people">
43        <td>{{ p.name }}</td>
44        <td>{{ p.age }}</td>
45      </tr>
46    </table>
47  </div>
```

And it would render one table for each city:

Miami

Name	Age
John	12
Angel	22

Sao Paulo

Name	Age
Anderson	35
Felipe	36

Rendering nested arrays

Getting an index

There are times that we need the index of each item when we're iterating an array.

We can get the index by appending the syntax `let idx = index` to the value of our `ngFor` directive, separated by a semi-colon. When we do this, ng2 will assign the current index into the variable we provide (in this case, the variable `idx`).

> ⚠️ Note that, like JavaScript, the index is always zero based. So the index for first element is 0, 1 for the second and so on...

Making some changes to our first example, adding the `let num = index` snippet like below:

code/built-in-directives/src/app/ng-for-example/ng-for-example.component.html

```
53  <div class="ui list" *ngFor="let c of cities; let num = index">
54    <div class="item">{{ num+1 }} - {{ c }}</div>
55  </div>
```

It will add the position of the city before the name, like this:

List with index

1 - Miami

2 - Sao Paulo

3 - New York

Using an index

NgNonBindable

We use ngNonBindable when we want tell Angular **not** to compile or bind a particular section of our page.

Let's say we want to render the literal text {{ content }} in our template. Normally that text will be *bound* to the value of the content variable because we're using the {{ }} template syntax.

So how can we render the exact text {{ content }}? We use the ngNonBindable directive.

Let's say we want to have a div that renders the contents of that content variable and right after we want to point that out by outputting <- *this is what {{ content }} rendered* next to the actual value of the variable.

To do that, here's the template we'd have to use:

code/built-in-directives/src/app/ng-non-bindable-example/ng-non-bindable-example.component.html

```
1  <div class='ngNonBindableDemo'>
2    <span class="bordered">{{ content }}</span>
3    <span class="pre" ngNonBindable>
4      &larr; This is what {{ content }} rendered
5    </span>
6  </div>
```

And with that ngNonBindable attribute, ng2 will not compile within that second span's context, leaving it intact:

Some text ← This is what {{ content }} rendered

Result of using ngNonBindable

Conclusion

Angular has only a few core directives, but we can combine these simple pieces to create dynamic, powerful apps. However, all of these directives help us **output** dynamic data, they don't let us **accept user interaction**.

In the next chapter we'll learn how to let our **user input data using forms**.

Forms in Angular

Forms are Crucial, Forms are Complex

Forms are probably the most crucial aspect of your web application. While we often get events from clicking on links or moving the mouse, it's through *forms* where we get the majority of our rich data input from users.

On the surface, forms seem straightforward: you make an `input` tag, the user fills it out, and hits submit. How hard could it be?

It turns out, forms can be very complex. Here's a few reasons why:

- Form inputs are meant to modify data, both on the page and the server
- Changes often need to be reflected elsewhere on the page
- Users have a lot of leeway in what they enter, so you need to validate values
- The UI needs to clearly state expectations and errors, if any
- Dependent fields can have complex logic
- We want to be able to test our forms, without relying on DOM selectors

Thankfully, Angular has tools to help with all of these things.

- `FormControls` encapsulate the inputs in our forms and give us objects to work with them
- `Validators` give us the ability to validate inputs, any way we'd like
- **Observers** let us watch our form for changes and respond accordingly

In this chapter we're going to walk through building forms, step by step. We'll start with some simple forms and build up to more complicated logic.

FormCtrl**s** and FormGroup**s**

The two fundamental objects in Angular forms are `FormControl` and `FormGroup`.

FormControl

A `FormControl` represents a single input field - it is the smallest unit of an Angular form.

`FormControls` encapsulate the field's value, and states such as being valid, dirty (changed), or has errors.

For instance, here's how we might use a `FormControl` in TypeScript:

```
1   // create a new FormControl with the value "Nate"
2   let nameControl = new FormControl("Nate");
3
4   let name = nameControl.value; // -> Nate
5
6   // now we can query this control for certain values:
7   nameControl.errors // -> StringMap<string, any> of errors
8   nameControl.dirty  // -> false
9   nameControl.valid  // -> true
10  // etc.
```

To build up forms we create FormControls (and groups of FormControls) and then attach metadata and logic to them.

Like many things in Angular, we have a class (FormControl, in this case) that we attach to the DOM with an attribute (formControl, in this case). For instance, we might have the following in our form:

```
1   <!-- part of some bigger form -->
2   <input type="text" [formControl]="name" />
```

This will create a new FormControl object within the context of our form. We'll talk more about how that works below.

FormGroup

Most forms have more than one field, so we need a way to manage multiple FormControls. If we wanted to check the validity of our form, it's cumbersome to iterate over an array of FormControls and check each FormControl for validity. FormGroups solve this issue by providing a wrapper interface around a collection of FormControls.

Here's how you create a FormGroup:

```
1   let personInfo = new FormGroup({
2       firstName: new FormControl("Nate"),
3       lastName: new FormControl("Murray"),
4       zip: new FormControl("90210")
5   })
```

FormGroup and FormControl have a common ancestor (AbstractControl[35]). That means we can check the status or value of personInfo just as easily as a single FormControl:

---

[35]https://angular.io/docs/ts/latest/api/forms/index/AbstractControl-class.html

```
1   personInfo.value; // -> {
2   //   firstName: "Nate",
3   //   lastName: "Murray",
4   //   zip: "90210"
5   // }
6
7   // now we can query this control group for certain values, which have sensible
8   // values depending on the children FormControl's values:
9   personInfo.errors  // -> StringMap<string, any> of errors
10  personInfo.dirty   // -> false
11  personInfo.valid   // -> true
12  // etc.
```

Notice that when we tried to get the value from the FormGroup we received an **object** with key-value pairs. This is a really handy way to get the full set of values from our form without having to iterate over each FormControl individually.

Our First Form

There are lots of moving pieces to create a form, and several important ones we haven't touched on. Let's jump in to a full example and I'll explain each piece as we go along.

ℹ️ You can find the full code listing for this section in the code download under forms/

Here's a screenshot of the very first form we're going to build:

Demo Form with Sku: Simple Version

In our imaginary application we're creating an e-commerce-type site where we're listing products for sale. In this app we need to store the product's SKU, so let's create a simple form that takes the SKU as the only input field.

ℹ SKU is an abbreviation for "stockkeeping unit". It's a term for a unique id for a product that is going to be tracked in inventory. When we talk about a SKU, we're talking about a human-readable item ID.

Our form is super simple: we have a single input for sku (with a label) and a submit button.

Let's turn this form into a Component. If you recall, there are three parts to defining a component:

- Configure the @Component() decorator
- Create the template
- Implement custom functionality in the component definition class

Let's take these in turn:

Loading the FormsModule

In order to use the new forms library we need to first make sure we import the forms library in our NgModule.

There are two ways of using forms in Angular and we'll talk about them both in this chapter: using FormsModule or using ReactiveFormsModule. Since we'll use both, we'll import them both into our module. To do this we do the following in our app.ts where we bootstrap the app:

```
1  import {
2    FormsModule,
3    ReactiveFormsModule
4  } from '@angular/forms';
5
6  // farther down...
7
8  @NgModule({
9    declarations: [
10     FormsDemoApp,
11     DemoFormSkuComponent,
12     // ... our declarations here
13   ],
14   imports: [
15     BrowserModule,
16     FormsModule,        // <-- add this
17     ReactiveFormsModule  // <-- and this
18   ],
19   bootstrap: [ FormsDemoApp ]
20  })
21  class FormsDemoAppModule {}
```

This ensures that we're able to use the form directives in our views. At the risk of jumping ahead, the `FormsModule` gives us *template driven* directives such as:

- `ngModel` and
- `NgForm`

Whereas `ReactiveFormsModule` gives us directives like

- `formControl` and
- `ngFormGroup`

... and several more. We haven't talked about how to use these directives or what they do, but we will shortly. For now, just know that by importing `FormsModule` and `ReactiveFormsModule` into our `NgModule` means we can *use any of the directives in that list* in our view template or *inject any of their respective providers* into our components.

Simple SKU Form: @Component Decorator

Now we can start creating our component:

code/forms/src/app/demo-form-sku/demo-form-sku.component.ts

```
1  import { Component, OnInit } from '@angular/core';
2
3  @Component({
4    selector: 'app-demo-form-sku',
5    templateUrl: './demo-form-sku.component.html',
```

Here we define a `selector` of `app-demo-form-sku`. If you recall, `selector` tells Angular what elements this component will bind to. In this case we can use this component by having a `app-demo-form-sku` tag like so:

```
1  <app-demo-form-sku></app-demo-form-sku>
```

Simple SKU Form: `template`

Let's look at our template:

code/forms/src/app/demo-form-sku/demo-form-sku.component.html

```
1   <div class="ui raised segment">
2     <h2 class="ui header">Demo Form: Sku</h2>
3     <form #f="ngForm"
4           (ngSubmit)="onSubmit(f.value)"
5           class="ui form">
6
7       <div class="field">
8         <label for="skuInput">SKU</label>
9         <input type="text"
10               id="skuInput"
11               placeholder="SKU"
12               name="sku" ngModel>
13      </div>
14
15      <button type="submit" class="ui button">Submit</button>
16    </form>
17  </div>
```

form & NgForm

Now things get interesting: because we imported FormsModule, that makes NgForm available to our view. Remember that whenever we make directives available to our view, they will **get attached to any element that matches their selector**.

NgForm does something handy but **non-obvious**: it includes the form tag in its selector (instead of requiring you to explicitly add ngForm as an attribute). What this means is that if you import FormsModule, NgForm will get *automatically* attached to any <form> tags you have in your view. This is really useful but potentially confusing because it happens behind the scenes.

There are two important pieces of functionality that NgForm gives us:

1. A FormGroup named ngForm
2. A **(ngSubmit)** output

You can see that we use both of these in the <form> tag in our view:

code/forms/src/app/demo-form-sku/demo-form-sku.component.html

```
3    <form #f="ngForm"
4          (ngSubmit)="onSubmit(f.value)"
```

First we have `#f="ngForm"`. The `#v=thing` syntax says that we want to create a local variable for this view.

Here we're creating an alias to `ngForm`, for this view, bound to the variable `#f`. Where did `ngForm` come from in the first place? It came from the `NgForm` directive.

And what type of object is `ngForm`? It is a `FormGroup`. That means we can use `f` as a `FormGroup` in our view. And that's exactly what we do in the `(ngSubmit)` output.

> Astute readers might notice that I just said above that `NgForm` is automatically attached to `<form>` tags (because of the default `NgForm` selector), which means we don't have to add an `ngForm` attribute to use `NgForm`. But here we're putting `ngForm` in an attribute (value) tag. Is this a typo?
>
> No, it's not a typo. If `ngForm` were the *key* of the attribute then we would be telling Angular that we want to use `NgForm` on this attribute. In this case, we're using `ngForm` as the *attribute* when we're assigning a *reference*. That is, we're saying the value of the evaluated expression `ngForm` should be assigned to a local template variable `f`.
>
> `ngForm` is already on this element and you can think of it as if we are "exporting" this `FormGroup` so that we can reference it elsewhere in our view.

We bind to the `ngSubmit` action of our form by using the syntax: `(ngSubmit)="onSubmit(f.value)"`.

- `(ngSubmit)` - comes from `NgForm`
- `onSubmit()` - will be implemented in our component definition class (below)
- `f.value` - `f` is the `FormGroup` that we specified above. And `.value` will return the key/value pairs of this `FormGroup`

Put it all together and that line says "when I submit the form, call `onSubmit` on my component instance, passing the value of the form as the arguments".

input & NgModel

Our `input` tag has a few things we should touch on before we talk about `NgModel`:

code/forms/src/app/demo-form-sku/demo-form-sku.component.html

```
3    <form #f="ngForm"
4          (ngSubmit)="onSubmit(f.value)"
5          class="ui form">
6
7      <div class="field">
8        <label for="skuInput">SKU</label>
9        <input type="text"
10              id="skuInput"
11              placeholder="SKU"
12              name="sku" ngModel>
13     </div>
```

- `class="ui form"` and `class="field"` - these classes are totally optional. They come from the CSS framework Semantic UI[36]. I've added them in some of our examples just to give them a nice coat of CSS but they're not part of Angular.
- The `label` "for" attribute and the `input` "id" attribute are to match, as per W3C standard[37]
- We set a `placeholder` of "SKU", which is just a hint to the user for what this `input` should say when it is blank

The `NgModel` directive specifies a `selector` of `ngModel`. This means we can attach it to our `input` tag by adding this sort of attribute: `ngModel="whatever"`. In this case, we specify `ngModel` with no attribute value.

There are a couple of different ways to specify `ngModel` in your templates and this is the first. When we use `ngModel` with no attribute value we are specifying:

1. a *one-way* data binding
2. we want to create a `FormControl` on this form with the name `sku` (because of the `name` attribute on the `input` tag)

`NgModel` **creates a new** `FormControl` that is **automatically added** to the parent `FormGroup` (in this case, on the form) and then binds a DOM element to that new `FormControl`. That is, it sets up an association between the `input` tag in our view and the `FormControl` and the association is matched by a name, in this case `"sku"`.

---

[36] http://semantic-ui.com/
[37] http://www.w3.org/TR/WCAG20-TECHS/H44.html

NgModel vs. ngModel: what's the difference? Generally, when we use PascalCase, like NgModel, we're specifying the *class* and referring to the object as it's defined in code. The lower case (CamelCase), as in ngModel, comes from the selector of the directive and it's only used in the DOM / template.

It's also worth pointing out that NgModel and FormControl are separate objects. NgModel is the *directive* that you use in your view, whereas FormControl is the object used for representing the data and validations in your form.

Sometimes we want to do *two-way* binding with ngModel like we used to do in Angular 1. We'll look at how to do that towards the end of this chapter.

Simple SKU Form: Component Definition Class

Now let's look at our class definition:

code/forms/src/app/demo-form-sku/demo-form-sku.component.ts

```
 8  export class DemoFormSkuComponent implements OnInit {
 9
10    constructor() { }
11
12    ngOnInit() {
13    }
14
15    onSubmit(form: any): void {
16      console.log('you submitted value:', form);
17    }
18
19  }
```

Here our class defines one function: onSubmit. This is the function that is called when the form is submitted. For now, we'll just console.log out the value that is passed in.

Try it out!

Putting it all together, here's what our code listing looks like:

code/forms/src/app/demo-form-sku/demo-form-sku.component.ts

```
1   import { Component, OnInit } from '@angular/core';
2
3   @Component({
4     selector: 'app-demo-form-sku',
5     templateUrl: './demo-form-sku.component.html',
6     styles: []
7   })
8   export class DemoFormSkuComponent implements OnInit {
9
10    constructor() { }
11
12    ngOnInit() {
13    }
14
15    onSubmit(form: any): void {
16      console.log('you submitted value:', form);
17    }
18
19  }
```

and the template:

code/forms/src/app/demo-form-sku/demo-form-sku.component.html

```
1   <div class="ui raised segment">
2     <h2 class="ui header">Demo Form: Sku</h2>
3     <form #f="ngForm"
4           (ngSubmit)="onSubmit(f.value)"
5           class="ui form">
6
7       <div class="field">
8         <label for="skuInput">SKU</label>
9         <input type="text"
10               id="skuInput"
11               placeholder="SKU"
12               name="sku" ngModel>
13      </div>
14
15      <button type="submit" class="ui button">Submit</button>
16    </form>
17  </div>
```

If we try this out in our browser, here's what it looks like:

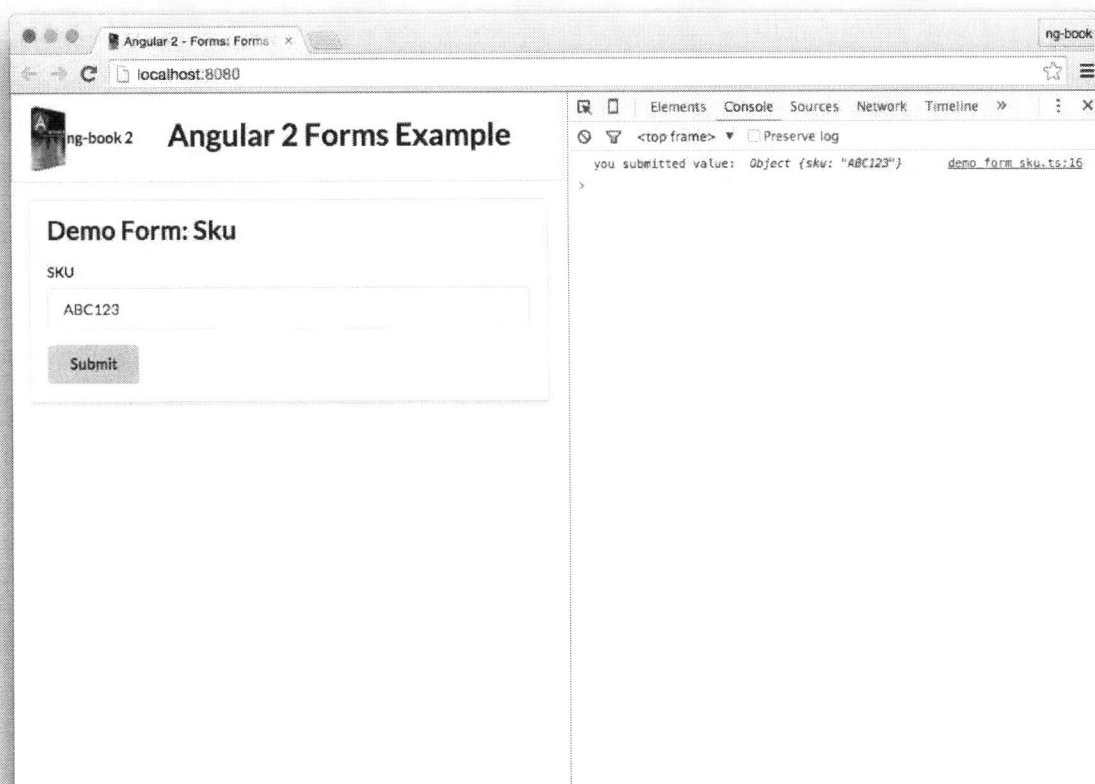

Demo Form with Sku: Simple Version, Submitted

Using FormBuilder

Building our FormControls and FormGroups implicitly using ngForm and ngControl is convenient, but doesn't give us a lot of customization options. A more flexible and common way to configure forms is to use a FormBuilder.

FormBuilder is an aptly-named helper class that helps us build forms. As you recall, forms are made up of FormControls and FormGroups and the FormBuilder helps us make them (you can think of it as a "factory" object).

Let's add a FormBuilder to our previous example. Let's look at:

- how to use the FormBuilder in our component definition class
- how to use our custom FormGroup on a form in the view

Reactive Forms with `FormBuilder`

For this component we're going to be using the `formGroup` and `formControl` directives which means we need to import the appropriate classes. We start by importing them like so:

code/forms/src/app/demo-form-sku-with-builder/demo-form-sku-with-builder.component.ts

```
1  import { Component, OnInit } from '@angular/core';
2  import {
3    FormBuilder,
4    FormGroup
5  } from '@angular/forms';
```

Using `FormBuilder`

We inject `FormBuilder` by creating an argument in the `constructor` of our component class:

> ⚠️ **What does `inject` mean?** We haven't talked much about dependency injection (DI) or how DI relates to the hierarchy tree, so that last sentence may not make a lot of sense. We talk a lot more about dependency injection in the Dependency Injection chapter, so go there if you'd like to learn more about it in depth.
>
> At a high level, Dependency Injection is a way to tell Angular what dependencies this component needs to function properly.

code/forms/src/app/demo-form-sku-with-builder/demo-form-sku-with-builder.component.ts

```
1  import { Component, OnInit } from '@angular/core';
2  import {
3    FormBuilder,
4    FormGroup
5  } from '@angular/forms';
6
7  @Component({
8    selector: 'app-demo-form-sku-with-builder',
9    templateUrl: './demo-form-sku-with-builder.component.html',
10   styles: []
11 })
12 export class DemoFormSkuWithBuilderComponent implements OnInit {
13   myForm: FormGroup;
14
15   constructor(fb: FormBuilder) {
16     this.myForm = fb.group({
```

```
17        'sku': ['ABC123']
18      });
19    }
20
21    ngOnInit() {
22    }
23
24    onSubmit(value: string): void {
25      console.log('you submitted value: ', value);
26    }
27
28 }
```

During injection an instance of `FormBuilder` will be created and we assign it to the `fb` variable (in the constructor).

There are two main functions we'll use on `FormBuilder`:

- `control` - creates a new `FormControl`
- `group` - creates a new `FormGroup`

Notice that we've setup a new *instance variable* called `myForm` on this class. (We could have just as easily called it `form`, but I want to differentiate between our `FormGroup` and the `form` we had before.)

`myForm` is typed to be a `FormGroup`. We create a `FormGroup` by calling `fb.group()`. `.group` takes an object of key-value pairs that specify the `FormControls` in this group.

In this case, we're setting up one control `sku`, and the value is `["ABC123"]` - this says that the default value of this control is `"ABC123"`. (You'll notice that is an array. That's because we'll be adding more configuration options there later.)

Now that we have `myForm` we need to use that in the view (i.e. we need to *bind* it to our `form` element).

Using `myForm` in the view

We want to change our `<form>` to use `myForm`. If you recall, in the last section we said that `ngForm` is applied for us automatically when we use `FormsModule`. We also mentioned that `ngForm` creates its own `FormGroup`. Well, in this case, we **don't** want to use an outside `FormGroup`. Instead we want to use our instance variable `myForm`, which we created with our `FormBuilder`. How can we do that?

Angular provides another directive that we use **when we have an existing `FormGroup`**: it's called `formGroup` and we use it like this:

code/forms/src/app/demo-form-sku-with-builder/demo-form-sku-with-builder.component.html

```
2    <h2 class="ui header">Demo Form: Sku with Builder</h2>
3    <form [formGroup]="myForm"
```

Here we're telling Angular that we want to use `myForm` as the `FormGroup` for this form.

> Remember how earlier we said that when using `FormsModule` that `NgForm` will be automatically applied to a `<form>` element? There is an exception: `NgForm` won't be applied to a `<form>` that has `formGroup`.
>
> If you're curious, the `selector` for `NgForm` is:
>
> ```
> 1    form:not([ngNoForm]):not([formGroup]),ngForm,[ngForm]
> ```
>
> This means you *could* have a form that doesn't get `NgForm` applied by using the `ngNoForm` attribute.

We also need to change `onSubmit` to use `myForm` instead of `f`, because now it is `myForm` that has our configuration and values.

There's one last thing we need to do to make this work: bind our `FormControl` to the `input` tag. Remember that **ngControl creates a new FormControl object**, and attaches it to the parent `FormGroup`. But in this case, we used `FormBuilder` to create our own `FormControls`.

When we want to bind an **existing FormControl** to an `input` we use `formControl`:

code/forms/src/app/demo-form-sku-with-builder/demo-form-sku-with-builder.component.html

```
8         <label for="skuInput">SKU</label>
9         <input type="text"
10               id="skuInput"
11               placeholder="SKU"
12               [formControl]="myForm.controls['sku']">
```

Here we are instructing the `formControl` directive to look at `myForm.controls` and use the existing `sku FormControl` for this `input`.

Try it out!

Here's what it looks like all together:

code/forms/src/app/demo-form-sku-with-builder/demo-form-sku-with-builder.component.ts

```
1   import { Component, OnInit } from '@angular/core';
2   import {
3     FormBuilder,
4     FormGroup
5   } from '@angular/forms';
6
7   @Component({
8     selector: 'app-demo-form-sku-with-builder',
9     templateUrl: './demo-form-sku-with-builder.component.html',
10    styles: []
11  })
12  export class DemoFormSkuWithBuilderComponent implements OnInit {
13    myForm: FormGroup;
14
15    constructor(fb: FormBuilder) {
16      this.myForm = fb.group({
17        'sku': ['ABC123']
18      });
19    }
20
21    ngOnInit() {
22    }
23
24    onSubmit(value: string): void {
25      console.log('you submitted value: ', value);
26    }
27
28  }
```

and the template:

code/forms/src/app/demo-form-sku-with-builder/demo-form-sku-with-builder.component.html

```
1   <div class="ui raised segment">
2     <h2 class="ui header">Demo Form: Sku with Builder</h2>
3     <form [formGroup]="myForm"
4           (ngSubmit)="onSubmit(myForm.value)"
5           class="ui form">
6
7       <div class="field">
8         <label for="skuInput">SKU</label>
```

```
 9        <input type="text"
10                id="skuInput"
11                placeholder="SKU"
12                [formControl]="myForm.controls['sku']">
13      </div>
14
15    <button type="submit" class="ui button">Submit</button>
16    </form>
17  </div>
```

Remember:

To create a new `FormGroup` and `FormControls` implicitly use:

- `ngForm` and
- `ngModel`

But to bind to an existing `FormGroup` and `FormControls` use:

- `formGroup` and
- `formControl`

Adding Validations

Our users aren't always going to enter data in exactly the right format. If someone enters data in the wrong format, we want to give them feedback and not allow the form to be submitted. For this we use *validators*.

Validators are provided by the `Validators` module and the simplest validator is `Validators.required` which simply says that the designated field is required or else the `FormControl` will be considered invalid.

To use validators we need to do two things:

1. Assign a validator to the `FormControl` object
2. Check the status of the validator in the view and take action accordingly

To assign a validator to a `FormControl` object we simply pass it as the second argument to our `FormControl` constructor:

```
1   let control = new FormControl('sku', Validators.required);
```

Or in our case, because we're using `FormBuilder` we will use the following syntax:

code/forms/src/app/demo-form-with-validations-explicit/demo-form-with-validations-explicit.component.ts

```
18    constructor(fb: FormBuilder) {
19      this.myForm = fb.group({
20        'sku':  ['', Validators.required]
21      });
22
23      this.sku = this.myForm.controls['sku'];
24    }
```

Now we need to use our validation in the view. There are two ways we can access the validation value in the view:

1. We can explicitly assign the `FormControl` sku to an instance variable of the class - which is more verbose, but gives us easy access to the `FormControl` in the view.
2. We can lookup the `FormControl` sku from `myForm` in the view. This requires less work in the component definition class, but is slightly more verbose in the view.

To make this difference clearer, let's look at this example both ways:

Explicitly setting the sku FormControl as an instance variable

Here's a screenshot of what our form is going to look like with validations:

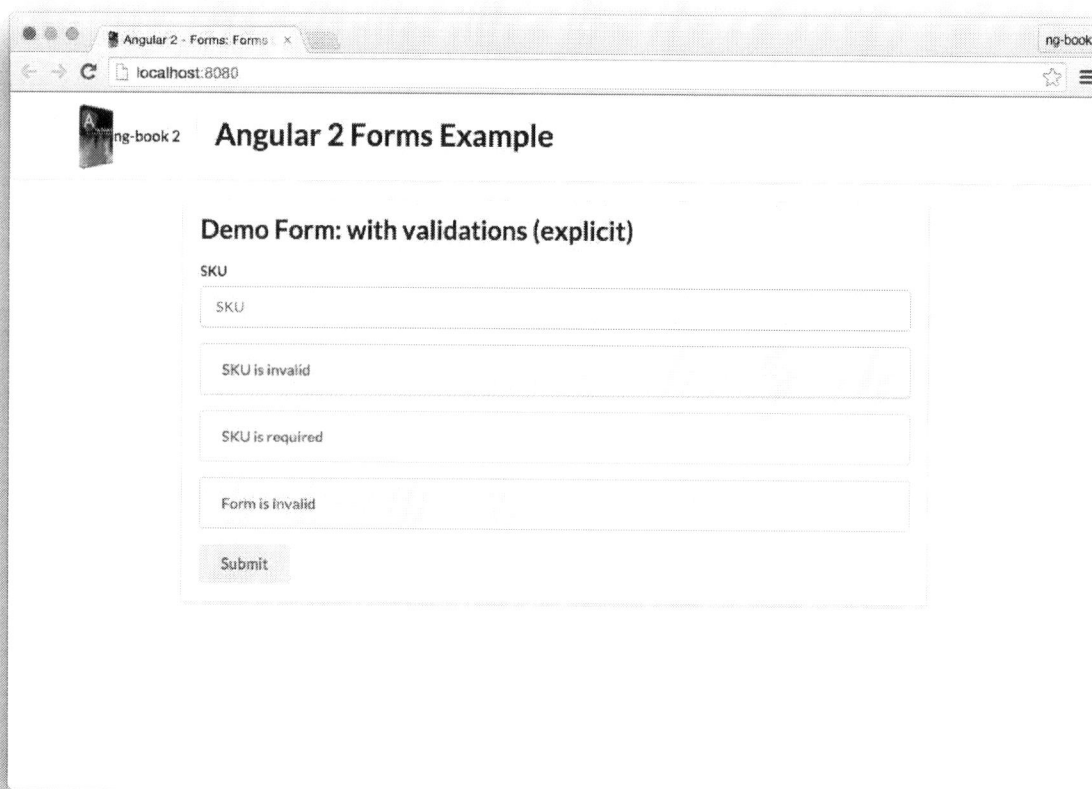

Demo Form with Validations

The most flexible way to deal with individual `FormControls` in your view is to set each `FormControl` up as an instance variable in your component definition class. Here's how we could setup `sku` in our class:

code/forms/src/app/demo-form-with-validations-explicit/demo-form-with-validations-explicit.component.ts

```
14   export class DemoFormWithValidationsExplicitComponent {
15     myForm: FormGroup;
16     sku: AbstractControl;
17
18     constructor(fb: FormBuilder) {
19       this.myForm = fb.group({
20         'sku': ['', Validators.required]
21       });
22
23       this.sku = this.myForm.controls['sku'];
24     }
25
```

```
26    onSubmit(value: string): void {
27      console.log('you submitted value: ', value);
28    }
29
30  }
```

Notice that:

1. We setup `sku: AbstractControl` at the top of the class and
2. We assign `this.sku` after we've created `myForm` with the `FormBuilder`

This is great because it means we can reference `sku` anywhere in our component view. The downside is that by doing it this way, we'd have to setup an instance variable **for every field in our form**. For large forms, this can get pretty verbose.

Now that we have our `sku` being validated, I want to look at four different ways we can use it in our view:

1. Checking the validity of our whole form and displaying a message
2. Checking the validity of our individual field and displaying a message
3. Checking the validity of our individual field and coloring the field red if it's invalid
4. Checking the validity of our individual field on a particular requirement and displaying a message

Form message

We can check the validity of our whole form by looking at `myForm.valid`:

code/forms/src/app/demo-form-with-validations-explicit/demo-form-with-validations-explicit.component.html

```
20      <div *ngIf="!myForm.valid"
```

Remember, `myForm` is a `FormGroup` and a `FormGroup` is valid if all of the children `FormControls` are also valid.

Field message

We can also display a message for the specific field if that field's `FormControl` is invalid:

code/forms/src/app/demo-form-with-validations-explicit/demo-form-with-validations-explicit.component.html

```
14              [formControl]="sku">
15         <div *ngIf="!sku.valid"
16           class="ui error message">SKU is invalid</div>
17         <div *ngIf="sku.hasError('required')"
```

Field coloring

I'm using the Semantic UI CSS Framework's CSS class .error, which means if I add the class error to the <div class= "field"> it will show the input tag with a red border.

To do this, we can use the property syntax to set conditional classes:

code/forms/src/app/demo-form-with-validations-explicit/demo-form-with-validations-explicit.component.html

```
7     <div class="field"
8       [class.error]="!sku.valid && sku.touched">
```

Notice here that we have two conditions for setting the .error class: We're checking for !sku.valid and sku.touched. The idea here is that we only want to show the error state if the user has tried editing the form ("touched" it) and it's now invalid.

To try this out, enter some data into the input tag and then delete the contents of the field.

Specific validation

A form field can be invalid for many reasons. We often want to show a different message depending on the reason for a failed validation.

To look up a specific validation failure we use the hasError method:

code/forms/src/app/demo-form-with-validations-explicit/demo-form-with-validations-explicit.component.html

```
17         <div *ngIf="sku.hasError('required')"
18           class="ui error message">SKU is required</div>
```

Note that hasError is defined on both FormControl and FormGroup. This means you can pass a second argument of path to lookup a specific field from FormGroup. For example, we could have written the previous example as:

```
1    <div *ngIf="myForm.hasError('required', 'sku')"
2      class="error">SKU is required</div>
```

Putting it together

Here's the full code listing of our form with validations with the FormControl set as an instance variable:

code/forms/src/app/demo-form-with-validations-explicit/demo-form-with-validations-explicit.component.ts

```
1    import { Component } from '@angular/core';
2    import {
3      FormBuilder,
4      FormGroup,
5      Validators,
6      AbstractControl
7    } from '@angular/forms';
8
9    @Component({
10     selector: 'app-demo-form-with-validations-explicit',
11     templateUrl: './demo-form-with-validations-explicit.component.html',
12     styles: []
13   })
14   export class DemoFormWithValidationsExplicitComponent {
15     myForm: FormGroup;
16     sku: AbstractControl;
17
18     constructor(fb: FormBuilder) {
19       this.myForm = fb.group({
20         'sku': ['', Validators.required]
21       });
22
23       this.sku = this.myForm.controls['sku'];
24     }
25
26     onSubmit(value: string): void {
27       console.log('you submitted value: ', value);
28     }
29
30   }
```

And the template:

code/forms/src/app/demo-form-with-validations-explicit/demo-form-with-validations-explicit.component.html

```html
1  <div class="ui raised segment">
2    <h2 class="ui header">Demo Form: with validations (explicit)</h2>
3    <form [formGroup]="myForm"
4          (ngSubmit)="onSubmit(myForm.value)"
5          class="ui form"
6          [class.error]="!myForm.valid && myForm.touched">
7
8      <div class="field"
9           [class.error]="!sku.valid && sku.touched">
10       <label for="skuInput">SKU</label>
11       <input type="text"
12              id="skuInput"
13              placeholder="SKU"
14              [formControl]="sku">
15       <div *ngIf="!sku.valid"
16          class="ui error message">SKU is invalid</div>
17       <div *ngIf="sku.hasError('required')"
18          class="ui error message">SKU is required</div>
19     </div>
20
21     <div *ngIf="!myForm.valid"
22        class="ui error message">Form is invalid</div>
23
24     <button type="submit" class="ui button">Submit</button>
25   </form>
26 </div>
```

Removing the sku instance variable

In the example above we set sku: AbstractControl as an instance variable. We often won't want to create an instance variable for each AbstractControl, so how would we reference this FormControl in our view without an instance variable?

Instead we can use the myForm.controls property as in:

code/forms/src/app/demo-form-with-validations-shorthand/demo-form-with-validations-short-hand.component.html

```
10        <label for="skuInput">SKU</label>
11        <input type="text"
12               id="skuInput"
13               placeholder="SKU"
14               [formControl]="myForm.controls['sku']">
15        <div *ngIf="!myForm.controls['sku'].valid"
16          class="ui error message">SKU is invalid</div>
17        <div *ngIf="myForm.controls['sku'].hasError('required')"
```

In this way we can access the sku control without being forced to explicitly add it as an instance variable on the component class.

> We used bracket-notation, e.g. myForm.controls['sku']. We could also use the dot-notation, e.g myForm.controls.sku. In general, be aware that TypeScript may give a warning if you use the dot-notation and the object is not properly typed (but that is not a problem here).

Custom Validations

We often are going to want to write our own custom validations. Let's take a look at how to do that.

To see how validators are implemented, let's look at Validators.required from the Angular core source:

```
1  export class Validators {
2    static required(c: FormControl): StringMap<string, boolean> {
3      return isBlank(c.value) || c.value == "" ? {"required": true} : null;
4    }
```

A validator: - Takes a FormControl as its input and - Returns a StringMap<string, boolean> where the key is "error code" and the value is true if it fails

Writing the Validator

Let's say we have specific requirements for our sku. For example, say our sku needs to begin with 123. We could write a validator like so:

code/forms/src/app/demo-form-with-custom-validation/demo-form-with-custom-validation.component.ts

```
18   function skuValidator(control: FormControl): { [s: string]: boolean } {
19     if (!control.value.match(/^123/)) {
20       return {invalidSku: true};
21     }
22   }
```

This validator will return an error code `invalidSku` if the input (the `control.value`) does not begin with `123`.

Assigning the Validator to the `FormControl`

Now we need to add the validator to our `FormControl`. However, there's one small problem: we already have a validator on `sku`. How can we add multiple validators to a single field?

For that, we use `Validators.compose`:

code/forms/src/app/demo-form-with-custom-validation/demo-form-with-custom-validation.component.ts

```
33     constructor(fb: FormBuilder) {
34       this.myForm = fb.group({
35         'sku':  ['', Validators.compose([
36           Validators.required, skuValidator])]
37       });
```

`Validators.compose` wraps our two validators and lets us assign them both to the `FormControl`. The `FormControl` is not `valid` unless both validations are valid.

Now we can use our new validator in the view:

code/forms/src/app/demo-form-with-custom-validation/demo-form-with-custom-validation.component.html

```
19         <div *ngIf="sku.hasError('invalidSku')"
20           class="ui error message">SKU must begin with <span>123</span></div>
```

> **ⓘ** Note that in this section, I'm using "explicit" notation of adding an instance variable for each `FormControl`. That means that in the view in this section, `sku` refers to a `FormControl`.

If you run the sample code, one neat thing you'll notice is that if you type something in to the field, the `required` validation will be fulfilled, but the `invalidSku` validation may not. This is great - it means we can partially-validate our fields and show the appropriate messages.

Watching For Changes

So far we've only extracted the value from our form by calling onSubmit when the form is submitted. But often we want to watch for any value changes on a control.

Both FormGroup and FormControl have an EventEmitter that we can use to observe changes.

> ℹ️ EventEmitter is an *Observable*, which means it conforms to a defined specification for watching for changes. If you're interested in the Observable spec, you can find it here[38]

To watch for changes on a control we:

1. get access to the EventEmitter by calling control.valueChanges. Then we
2. add an *observer* using the .subscribe method

Here's an example:

code/forms/src/app/demo-form-with-events/demo-form-with-events.component.ts

```
21  constructor(fb: FormBuilder) {
22    this.myForm = fb.group({
23      'sku':  ['', Validators.required]
24    });
25
26    this.sku = this.myForm.controls['sku'];
27
28    this.sku.valueChanges.subscribe(
29      (value: string) => {
30        console.log('sku changed to:', value);
31      }
32    );
33
34    this.myForm.valueChanges.subscribe(
35      (form: any) => {
36        console.log('form changed to:', form);
37      }
38    );
39
40  }
```

---

[38] https://github.com/jhusain/observable-spec

Here we're observing two separate events: changes on the sku field and changes on the form as a whole.

The observable that we pass in is an object with a single key: next (there are other keys you can pass in, but we're not going to worry about those now). next is the function we want to call with the new value whenever the value changes.

If we type 'kj' into the text box we will see in our console:

```
1  sku changed to:  k
2  form changed to:  Object {sku: "k"}
3  sku changed to:  kj
4  form changed to:  Object {sku: "kj"}
```

As you can see each keystroke causes the control to change, so our observable is triggered. When we observe the individual FormControl we receive a value (e.g. kj), but when we observe the whole form, we get an object of key-value pairs (e.g. {sku: "kj"}).

ngModel

NgModel is a special directive: it binds a model to a form. ngModel is special in that it **implements two-way data binding**. Two-way data binding is almost always more complicated and difficult to reason about vs. one-way data binding. Angular is built to generally have data flow one-way: top-down. However, when it comes to forms, there are times where it is easier to opt-in to a two-way bind.

> ⚠ Just because you've used ng-model in Angular 1 in the past, don't rush to use ngModel right away. There are good reasons to avoid two-way data binding[39]. Of course, ngModel can be really handy, but know that we don't necessarily rely on two-way data binding as much as we did in Angular 1.

Let's change our form a little bit and say we want to input productName. We're going to use ngModel to keep the component instance variable in sync with the view.

First, here's our component definition class:

---

[39]https://www.quora.com/Why-is-the-two-way-data-binding-being-dropped-in-Angular-2

code/forms/src/app/demo-form-ng-model/demo-form-ng-model.component.ts

```
12  export class DemoFormNgModelComponent {
13    myForm: FormGroup;
14    productName: string;
15
16    constructor(fb: FormBuilder) {
17      this.myForm = fb.group({
18        'productName': ['', Validators.required]
19      });
20    }
21
22    onSubmit(value: string): void {
23      console.log('you submitted value: ', value);
24    }
25  }
```

Notice that we're simply storing `productName: string` as an instance variable.

Next, let's use `ngModel` on our `input` tag:

code/forms/src/app/demo-form-ng-model/demo-form-ng-model.component.html

```
13        <label for="productNameInput">Product Name</label>
14        <input type="text"
15               id="productNameInput"
16               placeholder="Product Name"
17               [formControl]="myForm.get('productName')"
18               [(ngModel)]="productName">
```

Now notice something - the syntax for `ngModel` is funny: we are using both brackets and parentheses around the `ngModel` attribute! The idea this is intended to invoke is that we're using both the *input* `[]` brackets and the *output* `()` parentheses. It's an indication of the two-way bind.

Notice something else here: we're still using `formControl` to specify that this `input` should be bound to the `FormControl` on our form. We do this because `ngModel` is only binding the `input` to the instance variable - the `FormControl` is completely separate. But because we still want to validate this value and submit it as part of the form, we keep the `formControl` directive.

Last, let's display our `productName` value in the view:

code/forms/src/app/demo-form-ng-model/demo-form-ng-model.component.html

```
4    <div class="ui info message">
5      The product name is: {{productName}}
6    </div>
```

Here's what it looks like:

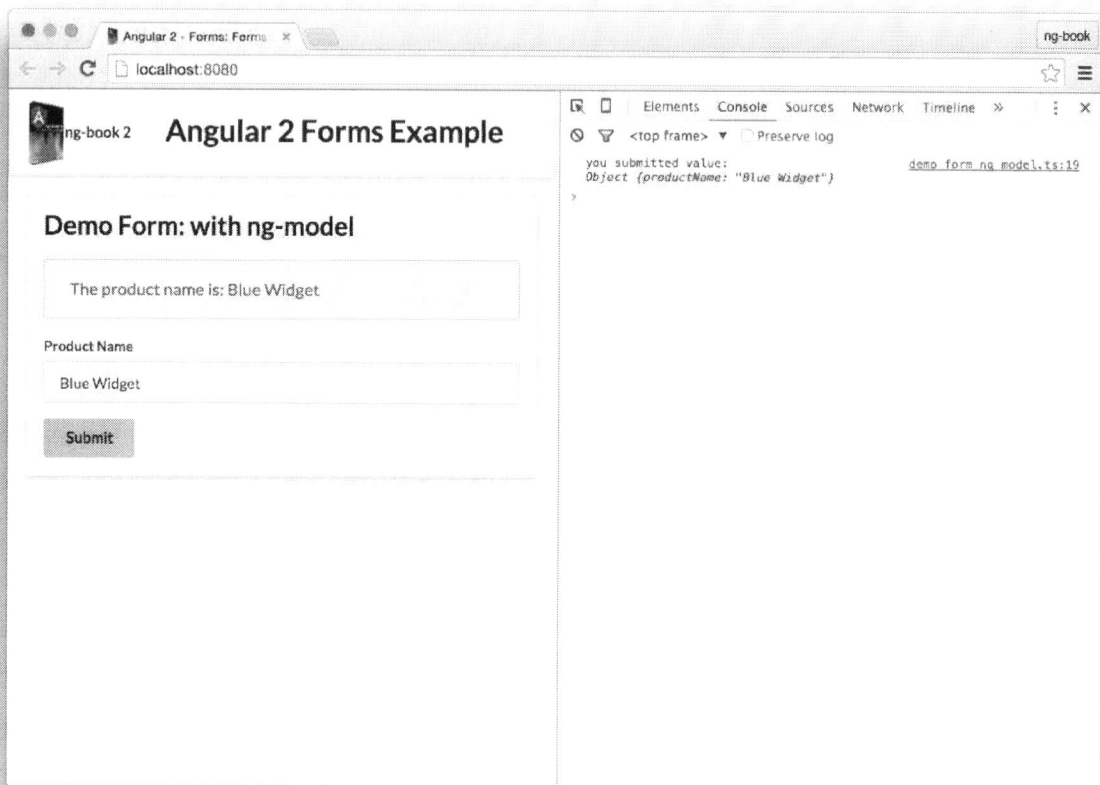

Demo Form with ngModel

Easy!

Wrapping Up

Forms have a lot of moving pieces, but Angular makes it fairly straightforward. Once you get a handle on how to use FormGroups, FormControls, and Validations, it's pretty easy going from there!

HTTP

Introduction

Angular comes with its own HTTP library which we can use to call out to external APIs.

When we make calls to an external server, we want our user to continue to be able to interact with the page. That is, we don't want our page to freeze until the HTTP request returns from the external server. To achieve this effect, our HTTP requests are *asynchronous*.

Dealing with *asynchronous* code is, historically, more tricky than dealing with synchronous code. In JavaScript, there are generally three approaches to dealing with async code:

1. Callbacks
2. Promises
3. Observables

In Angular, the preferred method of dealing with async code is using Observables, and so that's what we'll cover in this chapter.

> **There's a whole chapter on RxJS and Observables:** In this chapter we're going to be using Observables and not explaining them much. If you're just starting to read this book at this chapter, you should know that there's a whole chapter on Observables that goes into RxJS in more detail.

In this chapter we're going to:

1. show a basic example of `HttpClient`
2. create a YouTube search-as-you-type component
3. discuss API details about the `HttpClient` library

> **Sample Code** The complete code for the examples in this chapter can be found in the `http` folder of the sample code. That folder contains a `README.md` which gives instructions for building and running the project.
>
> Try running the code while reading the chapter and feel free play around to get a deeper insight about how it all works.

Using @angular/common/http

HTTP has been split into a separate module in Angular. This means that to use it you need to import constants from @angular/common/http. For instance, we might import constants from @angular/common/http like this:

```
1  import {
2    // The NgModule for using @angular/common/http
3    HttpClientModule,
4
5    // the class constants
6    HttpClient
7  } from '@angular/common/http';
```

import from @angular/common/http

In our app.module.ts we're going to import HttpClientModule which is a convenience collection of modules.

code/http/src/app/app.module.ts

```
1  import { BrowserModule } from '@angular/platform-browser';
2  import { NgModule } from '@angular/core';
3  import { FormsModule } from '@angular/forms';
4  import { HttpClientModule } from '@angular/common/http';
```

In our NgModule we will add HttpClientModule to the list of imports. The effect is that we will be able to inject Http (and a few other modules) into our components.

code/http/src/app/app.module.ts

```
14  @NgModule({
15    declarations: [
16      AppComponent,
17      SimpleHttpComponent,
18      MoreHttpRequestsComponent,
19      YouTubeSearchComponent,
20      SearchResultComponent,
21      SearchBoxComponent
22    ],
23    imports: [
24      BrowserModule,
```

```
25      FormsModule,
26      HttpClientModule // <-- right here
27    ],
28    providers: [youTubeSearchInjectables],
29    bootstrap: [AppComponent]
30  })
31  export class AppModule {}
```

> ℹ️ Notice that we have custom components in declarations as well as a custom provider. We'll talk about these later in the chapter.

Now we can inject the HttpClient service into our components (or anywhere we use dependency injection).

```
1  class MyFooComponent {
2    constructor(public http: HttpClient) {
3    }
4
5    makeRequest(): void {
6      // do something with this.http ...
7    }
8  }
```

A Basic Request

The first thing we're going to do is make a simple GET request to the jsonplaceholder API[40].

What we're going to do is:

1. Have a button that calls makeRequest
2. makeRequest will call the http library to perform a GET request on our API
3. When the request returns, we'll update this.data with the results of the data, which will be rendered in the view.

Here's a screenshot of our example:

---

[40] https://jsonplaceholder.typicode.com

Basic Request

Make Request

```
{
  "userId": 1,
  "id": 1,
  "title": "sunt aut facere repellat provident occaecati excepturi optio reprehenderit",
  "body": "quia et suscipit\nsuscipit recusandae consequuntur expedita et cum\nreprehende
rit molestiae ut ut quas totam\nnostrum rerum est autem sunt rem eveniet architecto"
}
```

Basic Request

Building the SimpleHttpComponent **Component Definition**

The first thing we're going to do is import a few modules and then specify a selector for our @Component:

code/http/src/app/simple-http/simple-http.component.ts

```
1  import { Component, OnInit } from '@angular/core';
2  import { HttpClient } from '@angular/common/http';
3
4  @Component({
5    selector: 'app-simple-http',
6    templateUrl: './simple-http.component.html'
7  })
8  export class SimpleHttpComponent implements OnInit {
9    data: Object;
10   loading: boolean;
11
12   constructor(private http: HttpClient) {}
```

Building the SimpleHttpComponent template

Next we build our view:

code/http/src/app/simple-http/simple-http.component.html

```
1  <h2>Basic Request</h2>
2  <button type="button" (click)="makeRequest()">Make Request</button>
3  <div *ngIf="loading">loading...</div>
4  <pre>{{data | json}}</pre>
```

Our template has three interesting parts:

1. The `button`
2. The loading indicator
3. The `data`

On the `button` we bind to (`click`) to call the `makeRequest` function in our controller, which we'll define in a minute.

We want to indicate to the user that our request is loading, so to do that we will show `loading...` if the instance variable `loading` is true, using `ngIf`.

The `data` is an `Object`. A great way to debug objects is to use the `json` pipe as we do here. We've put this in a `pre` tag to give us nice, easy to read formatting.

Building the `SimpleHttpComponent` Controller

We start by defining a new `class` for our `SimpleHttpComponent`:

code/http/src/app/simple-http/simple-http.component.ts

```
8   export class SimpleHttpComponent implements OnInit {
9     data: Object;
10    loading: boolean;
```

We have two instance variables: `data` and `loading`. This will be used for our API return value and loading indicator respectively.

Next we define our constructor:

code/http/src/app/simple-http/simple-http.component.ts

```
12    constructor(private http: HttpClient) {}
```

The `constructor` body is empty, but we inject one key module: `HttpClient`.

> 🔑 Remember that when we use the `public` keyword in `public http: HttpClient` TypeScript will assign `http` to `this.http`. It's a shorthand for:

```
1        // other instance variables here
2        http: HttpClient;
3
4        constructor(http: HttpClient) {
5          this.http = http;
6        }
```

Now let's make our first HTTP request by implementing the `makeRequest` function:

code/http/src/app/simple-http/simple-http.component.ts

```
16    makeRequest(): void {
17      this.loading = true;
18      this.http
19        .get('https://jsonplaceholder.typicode.com/posts/1')
20        .subscribe(data => {
21          this.data = data;
22          this.loading = false;
23        });
24    }
```

When we call `makeRequest`, the first thing we do is set `this.loading = true`. This will turn on the loading indicator in our view.

To make an HTTP request is straightforward: we call `this.http.get` and pass the URL to which we want to make a `GET` request.

`http.get` returns an `Observable`. We can subscribe to changes (akin to using `then` from a Promise) using `subscribe`.

code/http/src/app/simple-http/simple-http.component.ts

```
18    this.http
19      .get('https://jsonplaceholder.typicode.com/posts/1')
20      .subscribe(data => {
```

When our `http.request` returns (from the server) the stream will emit a `Response` object. We extract the body of the response as an `Object` by using `json` and then we set `this.data` to that `Object`.

Since we have a response, we're not loading anymore so we set `this.loading = false`

> `.subscribe` can also handle failures and stream completion by passing a function to the second and third arguments respectively. In a production app it would be a good idea to handle those cases, too. That is, `this.loading` should also be set to `false` if the request fails (i.e. the stream emits an error).

Full `SimpleHttpComponent`

Here's what our `SimpleHttpComponent` looks like altogether:

code/http/src/app/simple-http/simple-http.component.ts

```
1   import { Component, OnInit } from '@angular/core';
2   import { HttpClient } from '@angular/common/http';
3
4   @Component({
5     selector: 'app-simple-http',
6     templateUrl: './simple-http.component.html'
7   })
8   export class SimpleHttpComponent implements OnInit {
9     data: Object;
10    loading: boolean;
11
12    constructor(private http: HttpClient) {}
13
14    ngOnInit() {}
15
16    makeRequest(): void {
17      this.loading = true;
18      this.http
19        .get('https://jsonplaceholder.typicode.com/posts/1')
20        .subscribe(data => {
21          this.data = data;
22          this.loading = false;
23        });
24    }
25  }
```

Writing a `YouTubeSearchComponent`

The last example was a minimal way to get the data from an API server into your code. Now let's try to build a more involved example.

In this section, we're going to build a way to search YouTube as you type. When the search returns we'll show a list of video thumbnail results, along with a description and link to each video.

Here's a screenshot of what happens when I search for "cats playing ipads":

Can I get my cat to write Angular?

For this example we're going to write several things:

1. A `SearchResult` object that will hold the data we want from each result

2. A `YouTubeSearchService` which will manage the API request to YouTube and convert the results to a stream of `SearchResult[]`

3. A `SearchBoxComponent` which will call out to the `YouTube` service as the user types

4. A `SearchResultComponent` which will render a specific `SearchResult`

5. A `YouTubeSearchComponent` which will encapsulate our whole YouTube searching app and render the list of results

Let's handle each part one at a time.

> Patrick Stapleton has an excellent repository named angular2-webpack-starter[41]. This repo has an RxJS example which autocompletes Github repositories. Some of the ideas in this section are inspired from that example. It's a fantastic project with lots of examples and you should check it out.

Writing a `SearchResult`

First let's start with writing a basic `SearchResult` class. This class is just a convenient way to store the specific fields we're interested in from our search results.

code/http/src/app/you-tube-search/search-result.model.ts

```
1   /**
2    * SearchResult is a data-structure that holds an individual
3    * record from a YouTube video search
4    */
5   export class SearchResult {
6     id: string;
7     title: string;
8     description: string;
9     thumbnailUrl: string;
10    videoUrl: string;
11
12    constructor(obj?: any) {
13      this.id           = obj && obj.id           || null;
14      this.title        = obj && obj.title        || null;
15      this.description  = obj && obj.description   || null;
16      this.thumbnailUrl = obj && obj.thumbnailUrl || null;
17      this.videoUrl     = obj && obj.videoUrl     ||
18                             `https://www.youtube.com/watch?v=${this.id}`;
19    }
20  }
```

---

[41] https://github.com/angular-class/angular2-webpack-starter

This pattern of taking an `obj?: any` lets us simulate keyword arguments. The idea is that we can create a new `SearchResult` and just pass in an object containing the keys we want to specify.

The only thing to point out here is that we're constructing the `videoUrl` using a hard-coded URL format. You're welcome to change this to a function which takes more arguments, or use the video `id` directly in your view to build this URL if you need to.

Writing the `YouTubeSearchService`

The API

For this example we're going to be using the YouTube v3 search API[42].

> In order to use this API you need to have an API key. I've included an API key in the sample code which you can use. However, by the time you read this, you may find it's over the rate limits. If that happens, you'll need to issue your own key.
>
> To issue your own key see this documentation[43]. For the sake of simplicity, I've registered a server key, but you should probably use a browser key if you're going to put your javascript code online.

We're going to setup two constants for our `YouTubeSearchService` mapping to our API key and the API URL:

```
1  let YOUTUBE_API_KEY: string = "XXX_YOUR_KEY_HERE_XXX";
2  let YOUTUBE_API_URL: string = "https://www.googleapis.com/youtube/v3/search";
```

Eventually we're going to want to test our app. One of the things we find when testing is that we don't always want to test against production - we often want to test against staging or a development API.

To help with this environment configuration, one of the things we can do is **make these constants injectable**.

Why should we inject these constants instead of just using them in the normal way? Because if we make them injectable we can

1. have code that injects the right constants for a given environment at deploy time and
2. replace the injected value easily at test-time

By injecting these values, we have a lot more flexibility about their values down the line.

In order to make these values injectable, we use the `{ provide: ... , useValue: ... }` syntax like this:

---

[42] https://developers.google.com/youtube/v3/docs/search/list

[43] https://developers.google.com/youtube/registering_an_application#Create_API_Keys

code/http/src/app/you-tube-search/you-tube-search.injectables.ts

```
1  import {
2    YouTubeSearchService,
3    YOUTUBE_API_KEY,
4    YOUTUBE_API_URL
5  } from './you-tube-search.service';
6
7  export const youTubeSearchInjectables: Array<any> = [
8    {provide: YouTubeSearchService, useClass: YouTubeSearchService},
9    {provide: YOUTUBE_API_KEY, useValue: YOUTUBE_API_KEY},
10   {provide: YOUTUBE_API_URL, useValue: YOUTUBE_API_URL}
11 ];
```

Here we're specifying that we want to bind YOUTUBE_API_KEY "injectably" to the value of YOUTUBE_-
API_KEY. (Same for YOUTUBE_API_URL, and we'll define YouTubeSearchService in a minute.)

> To get a refresher on the different ways to create 'injectables', checkout the chapter on dependency injection

If you recall, to make something available to be injected throughout our application, we need to put it in providers for our NgModule. Since we're exporting youTubeServiceInjectables here we can use it in our app.module.ts

```
1  // http/app.ts
2  import { HttpClientModule } from '@angular/common/http';
3  import { youTubeServiceInjectables } from "components/YouTubeSearchComponent";
4
5  // ...
6  // further down
7  // ...
8
9  @NgModule({
10   declarations: [
11     HttpApp,
12     // others ....
13   ],
14   imports: [ BrowserModule, HttpClientModule ],
15   bootstrap: [ HttpApp ],
16   providers: [
17     youTubeServiceInjectables // <--- right here
```

```
18    ]
19  })
20  class HttpAppModule {}
```

Now we can inject YOUTUBE_API_KEY (from the youTubeServiceInjectables) instead of using the variable directly.

YouTubeSearchService constructor

We create our YouTubeSearchService by making a service class:

code/http/src/app/you-tube-search/you-tube-search.service.ts

```
26  /**
27   * YouTubeService connects to the YouTube API
28   * See: * https://developers.google.com/youtube/v3/docs/search/list
29   */
30  @Injectable()
31  export class YouTubeSearchService {
32    constructor(
33      private http: HttpClient,
34      @Inject(YOUTUBE_API_KEY) private apiKey: string,
35      @Inject(YOUTUBE_API_URL) private apiUrl: string
36    ) {}
```

> The @Injectable annotation allows us to inject things into this classes constructor.

In the constructor we inject three things:

1. HttpClient
2. YOUTUBE_API_KEY
3. YOUTUBE_API_URL

Notice that we make instance variables from all three arguments, meaning we can access them as this.http, this.apiKey, and this.apiUrl respectively.

Notice that we explicitly inject using the @Inject(YOUTUBE_API_KEY) notation.

YouTubeSearchService search

Next let's implement the search function. search takes a query string and returns an Observable which will emit a stream of SearchResult[]. That is, each item emitted is an *array* of SearchResults.

code/http/src/app/you-tube-search/you-tube-search.service.ts

```
38    search(query: string): Observable<SearchResult[]> {
39      const params: string = [
40        `q=${query}`,
41        `key=${this.apiKey}`,
42        `part=snippet`,
43        `type=video`,
44        `maxResults=10`
45      ].join('&');
46      const queryUrl = `${this.apiUrl}?${params}`;
```

We're building the `queryUrl` in a manual way here. We start by simply putting the query params in the `params` variable. (You can find the meaning of each of those values by reading the search API docs[44].)

Then we build the `queryUrl` by concatenating the `apiUrl` and the `params`.

Now that we have a `queryUrl` we can make our request. In this case we are going to use `http.get`, although `HttpClient` can make any kind of request (POST, DELETE, GET, etc.):

code/http/src/app/you-tube-search/you-tube-search.service.ts

```
38    search(query: string): Observable<SearchResult[]> {
39      const params: string = [
40        `q=${query}`,
41        `key=${this.apiKey}`,
42        `part=snippet`,
43        `type=video`,
44        `maxResults=10`
45      ].join('&');
46      const queryUrl = `${this.apiUrl}?${params}`;
47      return this.http.get(queryUrl).map(response => {
48        return <any>response['items'].map(item => {
49          // console.log("raw item", item); // uncomment if you want to debug
50          return new SearchResult({
51            id: item.id.videoId,
52            title: item.snippet.title,
53            description: item.snippet.description,
54            thumbnailUrl: item.snippet.thumbnails.high.url
55          });
56        });
```

---

[44]https://developers.google.com/youtube/v3/docs/search/list

```
57      });
58    }
```

Here we take the return value of `http.get` and use `map` to get the `Response` from the request. From that `response` we extract the body as an object using `.json()` and then we iterate over each item and convert it to a `SearchResult`.

> If you'd like to see what the raw `item` looks like, just uncomment the `console.log` and inspect it in your browsers developer console.

> Notice that we're calling `(<any>response.json()).items`. What's going on here? We're telling TypeScript that we're not interested in doing strict type checking.
>
> When working with a JSON API, we don't generally have typing definitions for the API responses, and so TypeScript won't know that the `Object` returned even has an `items` key, so the compiler will complain.
>
> We could call `response.json()["items"]` and then cast that to an `Array` etc., but in this case (and in creating the `SearchResult`, it's just cleaner to use an `any` type, at the expense of strict type checking

`YouTubeSearchService` Full Listing

Here's the full listing of our `YouTubeSearchService`.

> In this chapter we are adding some style using the CSS framework Bootstrap[45]

code/http/src/app/you-tube-search/you-tube-search.service.ts

```
26  /**
27   * YouTubeService connects to the YouTube API
28   * See: * https://developers.google.com/youtube/v3/docs/search/list
29   */
30  @Injectable()
31  export class YouTubeSearchService {
32    constructor(
33      private http: HttpClient,
34      @Inject(YOUTUBE_API_KEY) private apiKey: string,
```

---

[45]http://getbootstrap.com

```
35        @Inject(YOUTUBE_API_URL) private apiUrl: string
36    ) {}
37
38    search(query: string): Observable<SearchResult[]> {
39      const params: string = [
40        `q=${query}`,
41        `key=${this.apiKey}`,
42        `part=snippet`,
43        `type=video`,
44        `maxResults=10`
45      ].join('&');
46      const queryUrl = `${this.apiUrl}?${params}`;
47      return this.http.get(queryUrl).map(response => {
48        return <any>response['items'].map(item => {
49          // console.log("raw item", item); // uncomment if you want to debug
50          return new SearchResult({
51            id: item.id.videoId,
52            title: item.snippet.title,
53            description: item.snippet.description,
54            thumbnailUrl: item.snippet.thumbnails.high.url
55          });
56        });
57      });
58    }
59 }
```

Writing the SearchBoxComponent

The SearchBoxComponent plays a key role in our app: it is the mediator between our UI and the YouTubeSearchService.

The SearchBoxComponent will :

1. Watch for keyup on an input and submit a search to the YouTubeSearchService
2. Emit a loading event when we're loading (or not)
3. Emit a results event when we have new results

SearchBoxComponent @Component Definition

Let's define our SearchBoxComponent @Component:

code/http/src/app/you-tube-search/search-box.component.ts

```
22  @Component({
23    selector: 'app-search-box',
24    template: `
25      <input type="text" class="form-control" placeholder="Search" autofocus>
26    `
27  })
28  export class SearchBoxComponent implements OnInit {
29    @Output() loading: EventEmitter<boolean> = new EventEmitter<boolean>();
30    @Output() results: EventEmitter<SearchResult[]> = new EventEmitter<SearchResul\
31  t[]>();
32
33    constructor(private youtube: YouTubeSearchService,
34                private el: ElementRef) {
35    }
```

The `selector` we've seen many times before: this allows us to create a `<app-search-box>` tag.

The two `@Outputs` specify that events will be emitted from this component. That is, we can use the `(output)="callback()"` syntax in our view to listen to events on this component. For example, here's how we will use the `app-search-box` tag in our view later on:

```
1  <app-search-box
2    (loading)="loading = $event"
3    (results)="updateResults($event)"
4    ></app-search-box>
```

In this example, when the `SearchBoxComponent` emits a `loading` event, we will set the variable `loading` in the parent context. Likewise, when the `SearchBoxComponent` emits a `results` event, we will call the `updateResults()` function, with the value, in the parent's context.

In the `@Component` class we're specifying the properties of the events with the names `loading` and `results`. In this example, each event will have a corresponding `EventEmitter` as an *instance variable of the controller class*. We'll implement that in a few minutes.

For now, remember that `@Component` is like the public API for our component, so here we're just specifying the name of the events, and we'll worry about implementing the `EventEmitter`s later.

SearchBoxComponent template Definition

Our template is straightforward. We have one `input` tag:

code/http/src/app/you-tube-search/search-box.component.ts

```
24    template: `
25      <input type="text" class="form-control" placeholder="Search" autofocus>
26    `
```

SearchBoxComponent Controller Definition

Our SearchBoxComponent controller is a new class:

code/http/src/app/you-tube-search/search-box.component.ts

```
28  export class SearchBoxComponent implements OnInit {
29    @Output() loading: EventEmitter<boolean> = new EventEmitter<boolean>();
30    @Output() results: EventEmitter<SearchResult[]> = new EventEmitter<SearchResul\
31  t[]>();
```

We say that this class implements OnInit because we want to use the ngOnInit lifecycle callback. If a class implements OnInit then the ngOnInit function will be called after the first change detection check.

ngOnInit is a good place to do initialization (vs. the constructor) because inputs set on a component are not available in the constructor.

Here we create the EventEmitters for both loading and the results. loading will emit a boolean when this search is loading and results will emit an array of SearchResults when the search is finished.

SearchBoxComponent Controller Definition constructor

Let's talk about the SearchBoxComponent constructor:

code/http/src/app/you-tube-search/search-box.component.ts

```
32    constructor(private youtube: YouTubeSearchService,
33                private el: ElementRef) {
34    }
```

In our constructor we inject :

1. Our YouTubeSearchService and
2. The element el that this component is attached to. el is an object of type ElementRef, which is an Angular wrapper around a native element.

We set both injections as instance variables.

SearchBoxComponent `Controller Definition` `ngOnInit`

On this input box we want to watch for `keyup` events. The thing is, if we simply did a search after every `keyup` that wouldn't work very well. There are three things we can do to improve the user experience:

1. Filter out any empty or short queries
2. "debounce" the input, that is, don't search on every character but only after the user has stopped typing after a short amount of time
3. discard any old searches, if the user has made a new search

We could manually bind to `keyup` and call a function on each `keyup` event and then implement filtering and debouncing from there. However, there is a better way: turn the `keyup` events into an observable stream.

RxJS provides a way to listen to events on an element using `Rx.Observable.fromEvent`. We can use it like so:

code/http/src/app/you-tube-search/search-box.component.ts

```
36    ngOnInit(): void {
37      // convert the `keyup` event into an observable stream
38      Observable.fromEvent(this.el.nativeElement, 'keyup')
```

Notice that in `fromEvent`:

- the first argument is `this.el.nativeElement` (the native DOM element this component is attached to)
- the second argument is the string `'keyup'`, which is the name of the event we want to turn into a stream

We can now perform some RxJS magic over this stream to turn it into `SearchResults`. Let's walk through step by step.

Given the stream of `keyup` events we can chain on more methods. In the next few paragraphs we're going to chain several functions on to our stream which will transform the stream. Then at the end we'll show the whole example together.

First, let's extract the value of the input tag:

```
1    .map((e: any) => e.target.value) // extract the value of the input
```

Above says, map over each `keyup` event, then find the event target (`e.target`, that is, our `input` element) and extract the `value` of that element. This means our stream is now a stream of strings.

Next:

```
1   .filter((text: string) => text.length > 1)
```

This `filter` means the stream will not emit any search strings for which the length is less than one. You could set this to a higher number if you want to ignore short searches.

```
1   .debounceTime(250)
```

`debounceTime` means we will throttle requests that come in faster than 250ms. That is, we won't search on every keystroke, but rather after the user has paused a small amount.

```
1   .do(() => this.loading.emit(true))        // enable loading
```

Using `do` on a stream is a way to perform a function mid-stream for each event, but it does not change anything in the stream. The idea here is that we've got our search, it has enough characters, and we've debounced, so now we're about to search, so we turn on `loading`.

`this.loading` is an `EventEmitter`. We "turn on" `loading` by emitting `true` as the next event. We emit something on an `EventEmitter` by calling `next`. Writing `this.loading.emit(true)` means, emit a `true` event on the `loading` `EventEmitter`. When we listen to the `loading` event on this component, the `$event` value will now be `true` (we'll look more closely at using `$event` below).

```
1   .map((query: string) => this.youtube.search(query))
2   .switch()
```

We use `.map` to call perform a search for each query that is emitted. By using `switch` we're, essentially, saying "ignore all search events but the most recent". That is, if a new search comes in, we want to use the most recent and discard the rest.

> Reactive experts will note that I'm handwaving here. `switch` has a more specific technical definition which you can read about in the RxJS docs here[46].

For each `query` that comes in, we're going to perform a `search` on our `YouTubeSearchService`.

Putting the chain together we have this:

---

[46] https://github.com/Reactive-Extensions/RxJS/blob/master/doc/api/core/operators/switch.md

code/http/src/app/you-tube-search/search-box.component.ts

```
36    ngOnInit(): void {
37      // convert the `keyup` event into an observable stream
38      Observable.fromEvent(this.el.nativeElement, 'keyup')
39        .map((e: any) => e.target.value) // extract the value of the input
40        .filter((text: string) => text.length > 1) // filter out if empty
41        .debounceTime(250)                 // only once every 250ms
42        .do(() => this.loading.emit(true))      // enable loading
43        // search, discarding old events if new input comes in
44        .map((query: string) => this.youtube.search(query))
45        .switch()
46        // act on the return of the search
47        .subscribe(
```

The API of RxJS can be a little intimidating because the API surface area is large. That said, we've implemented a sophisticated event-handling stream in very few lines of code!

Because we are calling out to our YouTubeSearchService our stream is now a stream of SearchResult[]. We can subscribe to this stream and perform actions accordingly.

subscribe takes three arguments: onSuccess, onError, onCompletion.

code/http/src/app/you-tube-search/search-box.component.ts

```
47        .subscribe(
48          (results: SearchResult[]) => { // on sucesss
49            this.loading.emit(false);
50            this.results.emit(results);
51          },
52          (err: any) => { // on error
53            console.log(err);
54            this.loading.emit(false);
55          },
56          () => { // on completion
57            this.loading.emit(false);
58          }
59        );
60    }
```

The first argument specifies what we want to do when the stream emits a regular event. Here we emit an event on both of our EventEmitters:

1. We call this.loading.emit(false), indicating we've stopped loading

2. We call `this.results.emit(results)`, which will emit an event containing the list of results

The second argument specifies what should happen when the stream has an error event. Here we set `this.loading.emit(false)` and log out the error.

The third argument specifies what should happen when the stream completes. Here we also emit that we're done loading.

`SearchBoxComponent`: **Full Listing**

All together, here's the full listing of our `SearchBoxComponent` Component:

code/http/src/app/you-tube-search/search-box.component.ts

```
22  @Component({
23    selector: 'app-search-box',
24    template: `
25      <input type="text" class="form-control" placeholder="Search" autofocus>
26      `
27  })
28  export class SearchBoxComponent implements OnInit {
29    @Output() loading: EventEmitter<boolean> = new EventEmitter<boolean>();
30    @Output() results: EventEmitter<SearchResult[]> = new EventEmitter<SearchResul\
31  t[]>();
32
33    constructor(private youtube: YouTubeSearchService,
34                private el: ElementRef) {
35    }
36
37    ngOnInit(): void {
38      // convert the `keyup` event into an observable stream
39      Observable.fromEvent(this.el.nativeElement, 'keyup')
40        .map((e: any) => e.target.value) // extract the value of the input
41        .filter((text: string) => text.length > 1) // filter out if empty
42        .debounceTime(250)                // only once every 250ms
43        .do(() => this.loading.emit(true))       // enable loading
44        // search, discarding old events if new input comes in
45        .map((query: string) => this.youtube.search(query))
46        .switch()
47        // act on the return of the search
48        .subscribe(
49          (results: SearchResult[]) => { // on sucesss
50            this.loading.emit(false);
51            this.results.emit(results);
```

```
52        },
53        (err: any) => { // on error
54          console.log(err);
55          this.loading.emit(false);
56        },
57        () => { // on completion
58          this.loading.emit(false);
59        }
60      );
61    }
62 }
```

Writing SearchResultComponent

The SearchBoxComponent was fairly complicated . Let's handle a **much** easier component now: the SearchResultComponent. The SearchResultComponent's job is to render a single SearchResult.

Given what we've already covered there aren't any new ideas here, so let's take it all at once:

code/http/src/app/you-tube-search/search-result.component.ts

```
1  import {
2    Component,
3    OnInit,
4    Input
5  } from '@angular/core';
6  import { SearchResult } from './search-result.model';
7
8
9  @Component({
10   selector: 'app-search-result',
11   templateUrl: './search-result.component.html'
12 })
13 export class SearchResultComponent implements OnInit {
14   @Input() result: SearchResult;
15
16   constructor() { }
17
18   ngOnInit() {
19   }
```

Charlie The Cat - Kitten Playing iPad 2 !!! Game For Cats Cute Funny Clever Pets Bloopers

HELLO REDDIT, Thanks for the support! More Charlie the Cat Videos - http://youtu.be/xZHwYNrfWd0 Check My Other Videos Kitten HArlem Shake ...

Watch

Single Search Result Component

```
20
21   }
```

A few things:

The @Component takes a single input result, on which we will put the SearchResult assigned to this component.

The template shows the title, description, and thumbnail of the video and then links to the video via a button.

code/http/src/app/you-tube-search/search-result.component.html

```
1    <div class="col-sm-6 col-md-3">
2      <div class="thumbnail">
3        <img src="{{result.thumbnailUrl}}">
4        <div class="caption">
5          <h3>{{result.title}}</h3>
6          <p>{{result.description}}</p>
7          <p><a href="{{result.videoUrl}}"
8               class="btn btn-default" role="button">
9               Watch</a></p>
10       </div>
11     </div>
12   </div>
```

The SearchResultComponent simply stores the SearchResult in the instance variable result.

Writing YouTubeSearchComponent

The last component we have to implement is the YouTubeSearch-Component. This is the component that ties everything together.

YouTubeSearchComponent @Component

code/http/src/app/you-tube-search/you-tube-search.component.ts

```
4   @Component({
5     selector: 'app-you-tube-search',
6     templateUrl: './you-tube-search.component.html'
7   })
8   export class YouTubeSearchComponent implements OnInit {
9     results: SearchResult[];
10    loading: boolean;
```

Our @Component decorator is straightforward: use the selector
app-you-tube-search.

YouTubeSearchComponent Controller

Before we look at the template, let's take a look at the YouTubeSearchComponent controller:

code/http/src/app/you-tube-search/you-tube-search.component.ts

```
8   export class YouTubeSearchComponent implements OnInit {
9     results: SearchResult[];
10    loading: boolean;
11
12    constructor() { }
13    ngOnInit() { }
14
15    updateResults(results: SearchResult[]): void {
16      this.results = results;
17      // console.log("results:", this.results); // uncomment to take a look
18    }
19  }
```

This component holds one instance variable: results which is an array of SearchResults.

We also define one function: updateResults. updateResults simply takes whatever new SearchResult[] it's given and sets this.results to the new value.

We'll use both results and updateResults in our template.

YouTubeSearchComponent template

Our view needs to do three things:

1. Show the loading indicator, if we're loading

2. Listen to events on the search-box

3. Show the search results

Next lets look at our template. Let's build some basic structure and show the loading gif next to the header:

code/http/src/app/you-tube-search/you-tube-search.component.html

```
1  <div class='container'>
2      <div class="page-header">
3        <h1>YouTube Search
4          <img
5            style="float: right;"
6            *ngIf="loading"
7            src='assets/images/loading.gif' />
8        </h1>
9      </div>
```

We only want to show this loading image if `loading` is true, so we use `ngIf` to implement that functionality.

Next, let's look at the markup where we use our `search-box`:

code/http/src/app/you-tube-search/you-tube-search.component.html

```
10      <div class="row">
11        <div class="input-group input-group-lg col-md-12">
12          <app-search-box
13            (loading)="loading = $event"
14            (results)="updateResults($event)"
15            ></app-search-box>
16        </div>
```

The interesting part here is how we bind to the `loading` and `results` outputs. Notice, that we use the `(output)="action()"` syntax here.

For the `loading` output, we run the expression `loading = $event`. `$event` will be substituted with the value of the event that is emitted from the `EventEmitter`. That is, in our `SearchBoxComponent`, when we call `this.loading.emit(true)` then `$event` will be `true`.

Similarly, for the `results` output, we call the `updateResults()` function whenever a new set of results are emitted. This has the effect of updating our components `results` instance variable.

Lastly, we want to take the list of `results` in this component and render a `search-result` for each one:

code/http/src/app/you-tube-search/you-tube-search.component.html

```
19    <div class="row">
20      <app-search-result
21        *ngFor="let result of results"
22        [result]="result">
23      </app-search-result>
24    </div>
25  </div>
```

`YouTubeSearchComponent` **Full Listing**

Here's the full listing for the `YouTubeSearchComponent`:

code/http/src/app/you-tube-search/you-tube-search.component.ts

```
4   @Component({
5     selector: 'app-you-tube-search',
6     templateUrl: './you-tube-search.component.html'
7   })
8   export class YouTubeSearchComponent implements OnInit {
9     results: SearchResult[];
10    loading: boolean;
11
12    constructor() { }
13    ngOnInit() { }
14
15    updateResults(results: SearchResult[]): void {
16      this.results = results;
17      // console.log("results:", this.results); // uncomment to take a look
18    }
19  }
```

and the template:

code/http/src/app/you-tube-search/you-tube-search.component.html

```
1   <div class='container'>
2       <div class="page-header">
3         <h1>YouTube Search
4           <img
5             style="float: right;"
6             *ngIf="loading"
7             src='assets/images/loading.gif' />
8         </h1>
9       </div>
10
11      <div class="row">
12        <div class="input-group input-group-lg col-md-12">
13          <app-search-box
14              (loading)="loading = $event"
15              (results)="updateResults($event)"
16                ></app-search-box>
17        </div>
18      </div>
19
20      <div class="row">
21        <app-search-result
22          *ngFor="let result of results"
23          [result]="result">
24        </app-search-result>
25      </div>
26  </div>
```

There we have it! A functional search-as-you-type implemented for YouTube video search! Try running it from the code examples if you haven't already.

@angular/common/http API

Of course, all of the HTTP requests we've made so far have simply been GET requests. It's important that we know how we can make other requests too.

Making a POST request

Making POST request with @angular/common/http is very much like making a GET request except that we have one additional parameter: a body.

jsonplaceholder API[47] also provides a convent URL for testing our POST requests, so let's use it for a POST:

code/http/src/app/more-http-requests/more-http-requests.component.ts

```
20    makePost(): void {
21      this.loading = true;
22      this.http
23        .post(
24          'https://jsonplaceholder.typicode.com/posts',
25          JSON.stringify({
26            body: 'bar',
27            title: 'foo',
28            userId: 1
29          })
30        )
31        .subscribe(data => {
32          this.data = data;
33          this.loading = false;
34        });
35    }
```

Notice in the second argument we're taking an `Object` and converting it to a JSON string using `JSON.stringify`.

PUT / PATCH / DELETE / HEAD

There are a few other fairly common HTTP requests and we call them in much the same way.

- `http.put` and `http.patch` map to PUT and PATCH respectively and both take a URL and a body
- `http.delete` and `http.head` map to DELETE and HEAD respectively and both take a URL (no body)

Here's how we might make a DELETE request:

---

[47] http://jsonplaceholder.typicode.com

code/http/src/app/more-http-requests/more-http-requests.component.ts

```
37    makeDelete(): void {
38      this.loading = true;
39      this.http
40        .delete('https://jsonplaceholder.typicode.com/posts/1')
41        .subscribe(data => {
42          this.data = data;
43          this.loading = false;
44        });
45    }
```

Custom HTTP Headers

Let's say we want to craft a GET request that uses a special X-API-TOKEN header. We can create a request with this header like so:

code/http/src/app/more-http-requests/more-http-requests.component.ts

```
47    makeHeaders(): void {
48      const headers: HttpHeaders = new HttpHeaders({
49        'X-API-TOKEN': 'ng-book'
50      });
51
52      const req = new HttpRequest(
53        'GET',
54        'https://jsonplaceholder.typicode.com/posts/1',
55        {
56          headers: headers
57        }
58      );
59
60      this.http.request(req).subscribe(data => {
61        this.data = data['body'];
62      });
63    }
```

Summary

@angular/common/http is flexible and suitable for a wide variety of APIs.

One of the great things about @angular/common/http is that it has support for mocking the backend which is very useful in testing. To learn about testing HTTP, flip on over to the testing chapter.

Routing

In web development, *routing* means splitting the application into different areas usually based on rules that are derived from the current URL in the browser.

For instance, if we visit the / path of a website, we may be visiting the **home route** of that website. Or if we visit /about we want to render the "about page", and so on.

Why Do We Need Routing?

Defining routes in our application is useful because we can:

- separate different areas of the app;
- maintain the state in the app;
- protect areas of the app based on certain rules;

For example, imagine we are writing an inventory application similar to the one we described in previous chapters.

When we first visit the application, we might see a search form where we can enter a search term and get a list of products that match that term.

After that, we might click a given product to visit that product's details page.

Because our app is client-side, it's not technically required that we change the URL when we change "pages". But it's worth thinking about for a minute: what would be the consequences of using the same URL for all pages?

- You wouldn't be able to refresh the page and keep your location within the app
- You wouldn't be able to bookmark a page and come back to it later
- You wouldn't be able to share the URL of that page with others

Or put in a positive light, routing lets us define a URL string that specifies where within our app a user should be.

In our inventory example we could determine a series of different routes for each activity, for instance:

The initial root URL could be represented by http://our-app/. When we visit this page, we could be redirected to our "home" route at http://our-app/home.

When accessing the 'About Us' area, the URL could become http://our-app/about. This way if we sent the URL http://our-app/about to another user they would see same page.

How client-side routing works

Perhaps you've written server-side routing code before (though, it isn't necessary to complete this chapter). Generally with server-side routing, the HTTP request comes in and the server will render a different controller depending on the incoming URL.

For instance, with Express.js[48] you might write something like this:

```
1  var express = require('express');
2  var router = express.Router();
3
4  // define the about route
5  router.get('/about', function(req, res) {
6    res.send('About us');
7  });
```

Or with Ruby on Rails[49] you might have:

```
1  # routes.rb
2  get '/about', to: 'pages#about'
3
4  # PagesController.rb
5  class PagesController < ActionController::Base
6    def about
7      render
8    end
9  end
```

The pattern varies per framework, but in both of these cases you have a **server** that accepts a request and *routes* to a **controller** and the controller runs a specific **action**, depending on the path and parameters.

Client-side routing is very similar in concept but different in implementation. With client-side routing **we're not necessarily making a request to the server** on every URL change. With our Angular apps, we refer to them as "Single Page Apps" (SPA) because our server only gives us a single page and it's our JavaScript that renders the different pages.

So how can we have different routes in our JavaScript code?

---

[48]http://expressjs.com/guide/routing.html

[49]http://rubyonrails.org/

The beginning: using anchor tags

Client-side routing started out with a clever hack: Instead of using a normal server-side URL for a page in our SPA, we use the *anchor tag* as the client-side URL.

As you may already know, anchor tags were traditionally used to link directly to a place *within* the webpage and make the browser scroll all the way to where that anchor was defined. For instance, if we define an anchor tag in an HTML page:

```
1  <!-- ... lots of page content here ... -->
2  <a name="about"><h1>About</h1></a>
```

And we visited the URL `http://something/#about`, the browser would jump straight to that H1 tag that identified by the `about` anchor.

The clever move for client-side frameworks used for SPAs was to take the anchor tags and use them represent the routes within the app by formatting them as paths.

For example, the `about` route for an SPA would be something like `http://something/#/about`. This is what is known as **hash-based routing**.

What's neat about this trick is that it looks like a "normal" URL because we're starting our anchor with a slash (`/about`).

The evolution: HTML5 client-side routing

With the introduction of HTML5, browsers acquired the ability to programmatically create new browser history entries that change the displayed URL *without the need for a new request.*

This is achieved using the `history.pushState` method that exposes the browser's navigational history to JavaScript.

So now, instead of relying on the anchor hack to navigate routes, modern frameworks can rely on `pushState` to perform history manipulation without reloads.

> **Angular 1 Note:** This way of routing already works in Angular 1, but it needs to be explicitly enabled using `$locationProvider.html5Mode(true)`.

In Angular, however, the HTML5 is the default mode. Later in this chapter we show how to change from HTML5 mode to the old anchor tag mode.

There's two things you need to be aware of when using HTML5 mode routing, though

1. Not all browsers support HTML5 mode routing, so if you need to support older browsers you might be stuck with hash-based routing for a while.
2. **The server has to support HTML5 based routing**.

It may not be immediately clear why the server has to support HTML5 based-routing, we'll talk more about why later in this chapter.

Writing our first routes

The Angular docs recommends using HTML5 mode routing[50]. But due to the challenges mentioned in the previous section we will for simplicity be using hash based routing in our examples.

In Angular we configure routes by mapping *paths* to the component that will handle them.

Let's create a small app that has multiple routes. On this sample application we will have 3 routes:

- A main page route, using the /#/home path;
- An about page, using the /#/about path;
- A contact us page, using the /#/contact path;

And when the user visits the root path (/#/), it will redirect to the home path.

Components of Angular routing

There are three main components that we use to configure routing in Angular:

- Routes describes the routes our application supports
- RouterOutlet is a "placeholder" component that shows Angular where to put the content of each route
- RouterLink directive is used to link to routes

Let's look at each one more closely.

Imports

In order to use the router in Angular, we import constants from the @angular/router package:

---

[50]https://angular.io/docs/ts/latest/guide/router.html#!#browser-url-styles

code/routes/routing/src/app/app.module.ts

```
5   import {
6     RouterModule,
7     Routes
8   } from '@angular/router';
```

Now we can define our router configuration.

Routes

To define routes for our application, create a `Routes` configuration and then use `RouterModule.forRoot(routes)` to provide our application with the dependencies necessary to use the router. First, let's look at the routes definitions:

code/routes/routing/src/app/app.module.ts

```
26  const routes: Routes = [
27    // basic routes
28    { path: '', redirectTo: 'home', pathMatch: 'full' },
29    { path: 'home', component: HomeComponent },
30    { path: 'about', component: AboutComponent },
31    { path: 'contact', component: ContactComponent },
32    { path: 'contactus', redirectTo: 'contact' },
33
34    // authentication demo
35    { path: 'login', component: LoginComponent },
36    {
37      path: 'protected',
38      component: ProtectedComponent,
39      canActivate: [ LoggedInGuard ]
40    },
41
42    // nested
43    {
44      path: 'products',
45      component: ProductsComponent,
46      children: childRoutes
47    }
48  ];
```

Notice a few things about the routes:

- `path` specifies the URL this route will handle
- `component` is what ties a given route path to a component that will handle the route
- the optional `redirectTo` is used to redirect a given path to an existing route

We'll dive into the details of each route in this chapter, but at a high-level, the goal of routes is to specify which component will handle a given path.

Redirections

When we use `redirectTo` on a route definition, it will tell the router that when we visit the `path` of the route, we want the browser to be redirected to another route.

In our sample code above, if we visit the `root` path at http://localhost:4200/#/[51], we'll be redirected to the route `home`.

Another example is the `contactus` route:

code/routes/routing/src/app/app.module.ts

```
32    { path: 'contactus', redirectTo: 'contact' },
```

In this case, if we visit the URL http://localhost:4200/#/contactus[52], we'll see that the browser redirects to /contact.

> **Sample Code** The complete code for the examples in this section can be found in the `routes/routing` folder of the sample code. That folder contains a `README.md`, which gives instructions for building and running the project.
>
> There are many different `imports` required for routing and we don't list every single one in every code example below. However we do list the filename and line number from which almost every example is taken from. If you're having trouble figuring out how to `import` a particular class, open up the code using your editor to see the entire code listing.
>
> Try running the code while reading this section and feel free play around to get a deeper insight about how it all works.

Installing our Routes

Now that we have our `Routes` routes, we need to install it. To use the routes in our app we do two things to our `NgModule`:

1. Import the `RouterModule`
2. Install the routes using `RouterModule.forRoot(routes)` in the `imports` of our `NgModule`

Here's our routes configured into our `NgModule` for this app:

---

[51] http://localhost:4200/#/
[52] http://localhost:4200/#/contactus

code/routes/routing/src/app/app.module.ts

```
26  const routes: Routes = [
27    // basic routes
28    { path: '', redirectTo: 'home', pathMatch: 'full' },
29    { path: 'home', component: HomeComponent },
30    { path: 'about', component: AboutComponent },
31    { path: 'contact', component: ContactComponent },
32    { path: 'contactus', redirectTo: 'contact' },
```

code/routes/routing/src/app/app.module.ts

```
59    imports: [
60      BrowserModule,
61      FormsModule,
62      HttpModule,
63      RouterModule.forRoot(routes), // <-- routes
64
65      // added this for our child module
66      ProductsModule
67    ],
```

RouterOutlet using <router-outlet>

When we change routes, we want to keep our outer "layout" template and only substitute the "inner section" of the page with the route's component.

In order to describe to Angular where in our page we want to render the contents for each route, we use the RouterOutlet directive.

Our component @Component has a template which specifies some div structure, a section for Navigation, and a directive called router-outlet.

The router-outlet element indicates where the contents of each route component will be rendered.

> We are are able to use the router-outlet directive in our template because we imported the RouterModule in our NgModule.

Here's the component and template for the navigation wrapper of our app:

code/routes/routing/src/app/app.component.ts

```
6   @Component({
7     selector: 'app-root',
8     templateUrl: './app.component.html',
9     styleUrls: ['./app.component.css']
10  })
11  export class AppComponent {
12    constructor(private router: Router) {
13    };
14  }
```

and the template:

code/routes/routing/src/app/app.component.html

```
1   <div class="page-header">
2     <div class="container">
3       <h1>Router Sample</h1>
4       <div class="navLinks">
5         <a [routerLink]="['/home']">Home</a>
6         <a [routerLink]="['/about']">About Us</a>
7         <a [routerLink]="['/contact']">Contact Us</a>
8         |
9         <a [routerLink]="['/products']">Products</a>
10        <a [routerLink]="['/login']">Login</a>
11        <a [routerLink]="['/protected']">Protected</a>
12      </div>
13    </div>
14  </div>
15
16  <div id="content">
17    <div class="container">
18      <router-outlet></router-outlet>
19    </div>
20  </div>
```

If we look at the template above, you will note the router-outlet element right below the navigation menu. When we visit /home, that's where HomeComponent template will be rendered. The same happens for the other components.

RouterLink using [routerLink]

Now that we know where route templates will be rendered, how do we tell Angular to navigate to a given route?

We might try linking to the routes directly using pure HTML:

```
1  <a href="/#/home">Home</a>
```

But if we do this, we'll notice that clicking the link triggers a page reload and that's definitely not what we want when programming single page apps.

To solve this problem, Angular provides a solution that can be used to link to routes **with no page reload**: the RouterLink directive.

This directive allows you to write links using a special syntax:

code/routes/routing/src/app/app.component.html

```
3      <h1>Router Sample</h1>
4      <div class="navLinks">
5        <a [routerLink]="['/home']">Home</a>
6        <a [routerLink]="['/about']">About Us</a>
7        <a [routerLink]="['/contact']">Contact Us</a>
8        |
```

We can see on the left-hand side the [routerLink] that applies the directive to the current element (in our case a tags).

Now, on the right-hand side we have an array with the route path as the first element, like "['/home']" or "['/about']" that will indicate which route to navigate to when we click the element.

It might seem a little odd that the value of routerLink is a string with an array containing a string ("['/home']", for example). This is because there are more things you can provide when linking to routes, but we'll look at this into more detail when we talk about child routes and route parameters.

For now, we're only using routes names from the root app component.

Putting it all together

So now that we have all the basic pieces, let's make them work together to transition from one route to the other.

The first thing we need to write for our application is the index.html file.

Here's the full code for that:

code/routes/routing/src/index.html

```
 1  <!doctype html>
 2  <html>
 3  <head>
 4    <meta charset="utf-8">
 5    <title>Routing</title>
 6    <base href="/">
 7
 8    <meta name="viewport" content="width=device-width, initial-scale=1">
 9    <link rel="icon" type="image/x-icon" href="favicon.ico">
10  </head>
11  <body>
12    <app-root>Loading...</app-root>
13  </body>
14  </html>
```

The code should be familiar by now, with the exception of this line:

```
 1  <base href="/">
```

This line declares the base HTML tag. This tag is traditionally used to tell the browser where to look for images and other resources declared using relative paths.

It turns out Angular Router also relies on this tag to determine how to construct its routing information.

For instance, if we have a route with a path of /hello and our base element declares href="/app", the application will use /app/# as the concrete path.

Sometimes though, coders of an Angular application don't have access to the head section of the application HTML. This is true for instance, when reusing headers and footers of a larger, pre-existing application.

Fortunately there is a workaround for this case. You can declare the application base path programmatically, when configuring our NgModule by using the APP_BASE_HREF provider:

```
1  @NgModule({
2    declarations: [ RoutesDemoApp ],
3    imports: [
4      BrowserModule,
5      RouterModule.forRoot(routes) // <-- routes
6    ],
7    bootstrap: [ RoutesDemoApp ],
8    providers: [
9      { provide: LocationStrategy, useClass: HashLocationStrategy },
10     { provide: APP_BASE_HREF, useValue: '/' } // <--- this right here
11   ]
12 })
```

Putting { provide: APP_BASE_HREF, useValue: '/' } in the providers is the equivalent of using
<base href="/"> on our application HTML header.

> When deploying to production we can also set the value of the base-href by using the
> --base-href command-line option

Creating the Components

Before we get to the main app component, let's create 3 simple components, one for each of the
routes.

HomeComponent

The HomeComponent will just have an h1 tag that says "Welcome!". Here's the full code for our
HomeComponent:

code/routes/routing/src/app/home/home.component.ts

```
1  import { Component, OnInit } from '@angular/core';
2
3  @Component({
4    selector: 'app-home',
5    templateUrl: './home.component.html',
6    styleUrls: ['./home.component.css']
7  })
8  export class HomeComponent implements OnInit {
9
10   constructor() { }
```

```
11
12      ngOnInit() {
13      }
14
15  }
```

And template:

code/routes/routing/src/app/home/home.component.html

```
1   <h1>Welcome Home!</h1>
```

AboutComponent

Similarly, the AboutComponent will just have a basic h1:

code/routes/routing/src/app/about/about.component.ts

```
1   import { Component, OnInit } from '@angular/core';
2
3   @Component({
4     selector: 'app-about',
5     templateUrl: './about.component.html',
6     styleUrls: ['./about.component.css']
7   })
8   export class AboutComponent implements OnInit {
9
10    constructor() { }
11
12    ngOnInit() {
13    }
14
15  }
```

And template:

code/routes/routing/src/app/about/about.component.html

```
1   <h1>About Us</h1>
```

ContactComponent

And, likewise with AboutComponent:

code/routes/routing/src/app/contact/contact.component.ts

```
1  import { Component, OnInit } from '@angular/core';
2
3  @Component({
4    selector: 'app-contact',
5    templateUrl: './contact.component.html',
6    styleUrls: ['./contact.component.css']
7  })
8  export class ContactComponent implements OnInit {
9
10   constructor() { }
11
12   ngOnInit() {
13   }
14
15 }
```

And template:

code/routes/routing/src/app/contact/contact.component.html

```
1  <h1>Contact Us</h1>
```

Nothing really very interesting about those components, so let's move on to the main `app.module.ts` file.

Application Component

Now we need to create the root-level "application" component that will tie everything together.

We start with the imports we'll need, both from the core and router bundles:

code/routes/routing/src/app/app.module.ts

```
1  import { BrowserModule } from '@angular/platform-browser';
2  import { NgModule } from '@angular/core';
3  import { FormsModule } from '@angular/forms';
4  import { HttpModule } from '@angular/http';
5  import {
6    RouterModule,
7    Routes
```

Next step is to import the three components we created above:

code/routes/routing/src/app/app.module.ts

```
15  import { AppComponent } from './app.component';
16  import { HomeComponent } from './home/home.component';
17  import { ContactComponent } from './contact/contact.component';
18  import { AboutComponent } from './about/about.component';
```

For our root component, we're going to use two router directives: `RouterOutlet` and the `RouterLink`. Those directives, along with all other common router directives are imported when we put `RouterModule` in the `imports` section of our `NgModule`.

As a recap, the `RouterOutlet` directive is then used to indicate where in our template the route contents should be rendered. That's represented by the `<router-outlet></router-outlet>` snippet in our `AppComponent` template.

The `RouterLink` directive is used to create navigation links to our routes:

code/routes/routing/src/app/app.component.html

```
1   <div class="page-header">
2     <div class="container">
3       <h1>Router Sample</h1>
4       <div class="navLinks">
5         <a [routerLink]="['/home']">Home</a>
6         <a [routerLink]="['/about']">About Us</a>
7         <a [routerLink]="['/contact']">Contact Us</a>
8         |
9         <a [routerLink]="['/products']">Products</a>
10        <a [routerLink]="['/login']">Login</a>
11        <a [routerLink]="['/protected']">Protected</a>
12      </div>
13    </div>
14  </div>
15
16  <div id="content">
17    <div class="container">
18      <router-outlet></router-outlet>
19    </div>
20  </div>
```

Using `[routerLink]` will instruct Angular to take ownership of the `click` event and then initiate a route switch to the right place, based on the route definition.

Configuring the Routes

Next, we declare the routes creating an array of objects that conform to the `Routes` type:

code/routes/routing/src/app/app.module.ts

```
26  const routes: Routes = [
27    // basic routes
28    { path: '', redirectTo: 'home', pathMatch: 'full' },
29    { path: 'home', component: HomeComponent },
30    { path: 'about', component: AboutComponent },
31    { path: 'contact', component: ContactComponent },
32    { path: 'contactus', redirectTo: 'contact' },
```

code/routes/routing/src/app/app.module.ts

```
50  @NgModule({
51    declarations: [
52      AppComponent,
53      HomeComponent,
54      ContactComponent,
55      AboutComponent,
56      LoginComponent,
57      ProtectedComponent,
58    ],
59    imports: [
60      BrowserModule,
61      FormsModule,
62      HttpModule,
63      RouterModule.forRoot(routes), // <-- routes
64
65      // added this for our child module
66      ProductsModule
67    ],
68    providers: [
69      // uncomment this for "hash-bang" routing
70      // { provide: LocationStrategy, useClass: HashLocationStrategy }
71      AUTH_PROVIDERS,
72      LoggedInGuard
73    ],
74    bootstrap: [AppComponent]
75  })
76  export class AppModule { }
```

Notice that we put all necessary components in our declarations. If we're going to route to a component, then it needs to be declared in *some* NgModule (either this module or imported).

In our `imports` we have `RouterModule.forRoot(routes)`. `RouterModule.forRoot(routes)` is a function that will take our routes, configure the router, and return a list of dependencies like `RouteRegistry`, `Location`, and several other classes that are necessary to make routing work.

In our `providers` we have this:

```
1    { provide: LocationStrategy, useClass: HashLocationStrategy }
```

Let's take an in depth look of what we want to achieve with this line.

Routing Strategies

The way the Angular application parses and creates paths from and to route definitions is called *location strategy*.

> 🛈   In Angular 1 this is called *routing modes* instead

The default strategy is `PathLocationStrategy`, which is what we call HTML5 routing. While using this strategy, routes are represented by regular paths, like `/home` or `/contact`.

We can change the location strategy used for our application by binding the `LocationStrategy` class to a new, concrete strategy class.

Instead of using the default `PathLocationStrategy` we can also use the `HashLocationStrategy`.

The reason we're using the hash strategy as a default is because if we were using HTML5 routing, our URLs would end up being regular paths (that is, not using hash/anchor tags).

This way, the routes would work when you click a link and navigate on the client side, let's say from `/about` to `/contact`.

If we were to refresh the page, instead of asking the server for the root URL, which is what is being served, instead we'd be asking for `/about` or `/contact`. Because there's no known page at `/about` the server would return a 404.

This default strategy works with hash based paths, like `/#/home` or `/#/contact` that the server understands as being the `/` path. (This is also the default mode in Angular 1.)

> 🛈   Let's say you want to use HTML5 mode in production, how do you set this up?
>
> In order to use HTML5 mode routing, you have to configure your server to redirect every "missing" route to the root URL.
>
> Angular CLI supports this natively, but know that it doesn't necessarily work by default on your server. In the `routes/routing` project you can use HTML5 routes by simply doing `ng serve`

If we wanted to make our example application work with this new strategy, first we have to import `LocationStrategy` and `HashLocationStrategy` and then add that location strategy to the providers of our `NgModule`.

> **You could write your own strategy if you wanted to**. All you need to do is extend the `LocationStrategy` class and implement the methods. A good way to start is reading the Angular source for the `HashLocationStrategy` or `PathLocationStrategy` classes.

Running the application

You can now go into the application root folder (`code/routes/routing`) and run `npm start` to boot the application.

When you type http://localhost:4200/[53] into your browser you should see the home route rendered:

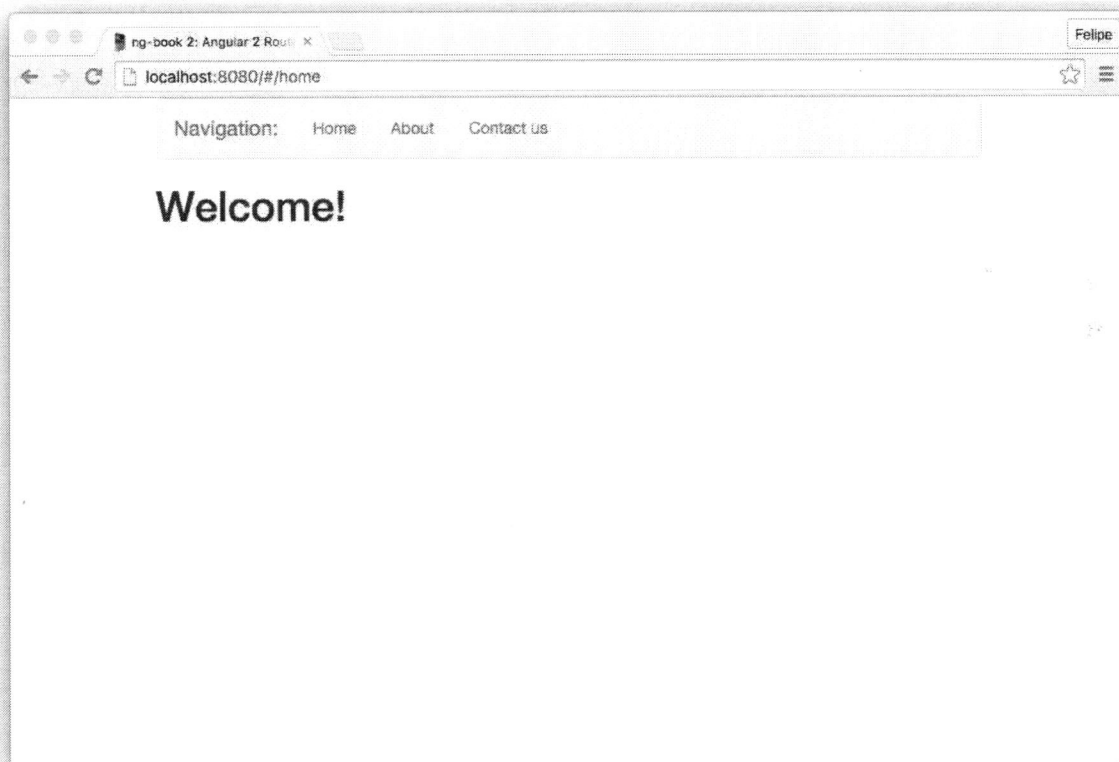

Home Route

---

[53] http://localhost:4200/

Notice that the URL in the browser was redirected to http://localhost:4200/home[54].

Now clicking each link will render the appropriate routes:

About Route

[54] http://localhost:4200/home

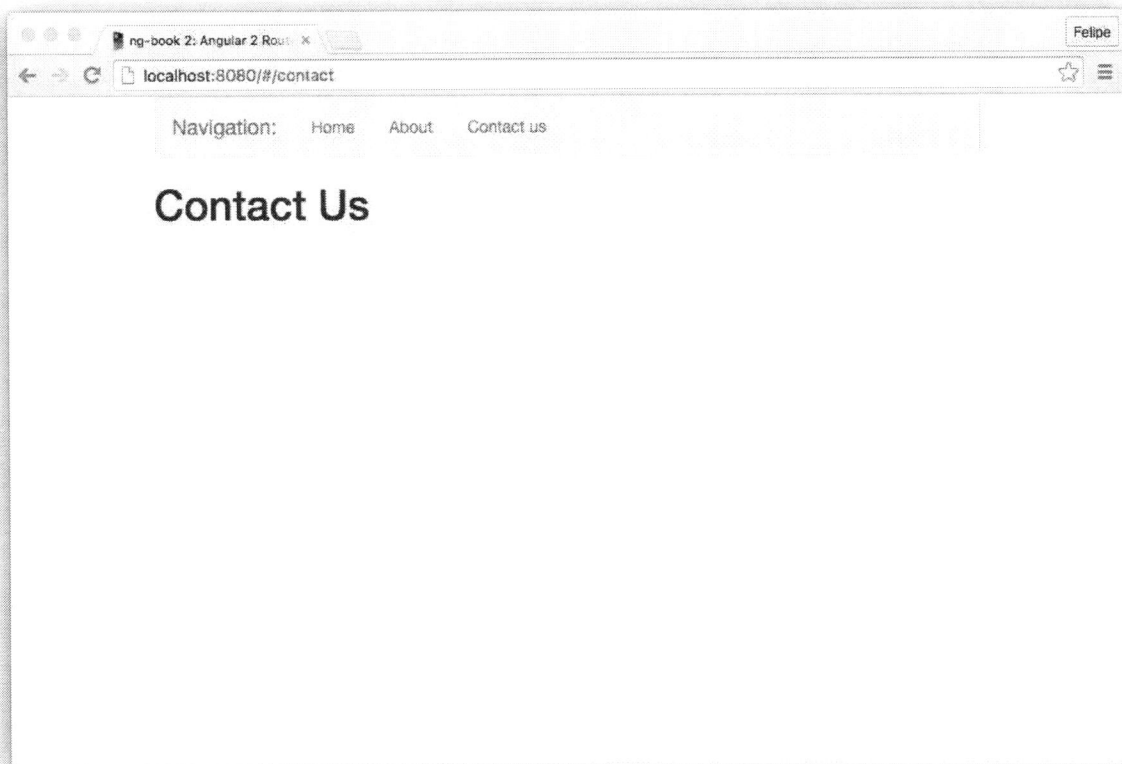

Contact Us Route

Route Parameters

In our apps we often want to navigate to a specific resource. For instance, say we had a news website and we had many articles. Each article may have an ID, and if we had an article with ID 3 then we might navigate to that article by visiting the URL:

```
/articles/3
```

And if we had an article with an ID of 4 we would access it at

```
/articles/4
```

and so on.

Obviously we're not going to want to write a route for each article, but instead we want to use a variable, or *route parameter*. We can specify that a route takes a parameter by putting a colon : in front of the path segment like this:

```
/route/:param
```

So in our example news site, we might specify our route as:

```
/product/:id
```

To add a parameter to our router configuration, we specify the route path like this:

```
1  const routes: Routes = [
2    { path: 'product/:id', component: ProductComponent },
3  ];
```

When we visit the route /product/123, the 123 part will be passed as the id route parameter to our route.

But how can we retrieve the parameter for a given route? That's where we use route parameters.

ActivatedRoute

In order to use route parameters, we need to first import ActivatedRoute:

```
1  import { ActivatedRoute } from '@angular/router';
```

Next, we inject the ActivatedRoute into the constructor of our component. For example, let's say we have a Routes that specifies the following:

```
1  const routes: Routes = [
2    { path: 'product/:id', component: ProductComponent }
3  ];
```

Then when we write the ProductComponent, we add the ActivatedRoute as one of the constructor arguments:

```
1  export class ProductComponent {
2    id: string;
3
4    constructor(private route: ActivatedRoute) {
5      route.params.subscribe(params => { this.id = params['id']; });
6    }
7  }
```

Notice that route.params is an *observable*. We can extract the value of the param into a hard value by using .subscribe. In this case, we assign the value of params['id'] to the id instance variable on the component.

Now when we visit /product/230, our component's id attribute will receive 230.

Music Search App

Let's now work on a more complex application. We will build a music search application that has the following features:

1. **Search for tracks** that match a given term
2. Show **matching tracks** in a grid
3. Show **artist details** when the artist name is clicked
4. Show **album details** and show a list of tracks when the album name is clicked
5. Show **song details** allow the user to **play a preview** when the song name is clicked

Sportify music for active people

Search

rhapsody in blue | Search

Results

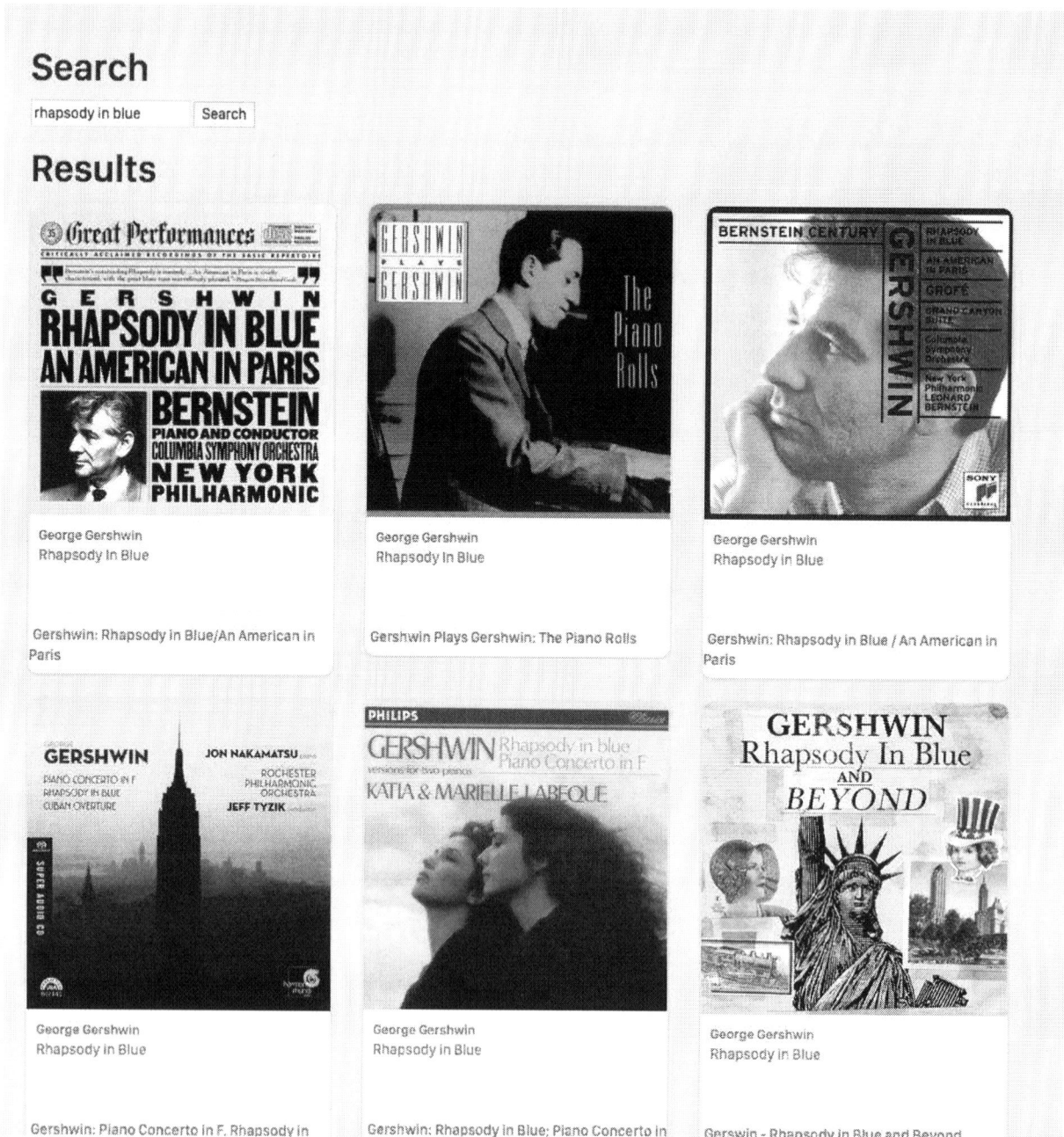

George Gershwin
Rhapsody In Blue

Gershwin: Rhapsody in Blue/An American in Paris

George Gershwin
Rhapsody In Blue

Gershwin Plays Gershwin: The Piano Rolls

George Gershwin
Rhapsody in Blue

Gershwin: Rhapsody in Blue / An American in Paris

George Gershwin
Rhapsody in Blue

Gershwin: Piano Concerto in F, Rhapsody in

George Gershwin
Rhapsody in Blue

Gershwin: Rhapsody in Blue; Piano Concerto in

George Gershwin
Rhapsody in Blue

Gerswin - Rhapsody in Blue and Beyond

The Search View of our Music App

The routes we will need for this application will be:

- /search - search form and results
- /artists/:id - artist info, represented by a Spotify ID

- /albums/:id - album info, with a list of tracks using the Spotify ID
- /tracks/:id - track info and preview, also using the Spotify ID

> **Sample Code** The complete code for the examples in this section can be found in the routes/music folder of the sample code. That folder contains a README.md, which gives instructions for building and running the project.

We will use the Spotify API[55] to get information about tracks, artists and albums.

First Steps

The first file we need work on is app.module.ts. Let's start by importing classes we'll use from Angular:

code/routes/music/src/app/app.module.ts

```
1  import { BrowserModule } from '@angular/platform-browser';
2  import { NgModule } from '@angular/core';
3  import { FormsModule } from '@angular/forms';
4  import { HttpModule } from '@angular/http';
5  import {
6    RouterModule,
7    Routes
8  } from '@angular/router';
9  import {
10   LocationStrategy,
11   HashLocationStrategy,
12   APP_BASE_HREF
13 } from '@angular/common';
14
15 import { AppComponent } from './app.component';
16 import { AlbumComponent } from './album/album.component';
17 import { ArtistComponent } from './artist/artist.component';
```

Now that we have the imports there, let's think about the components we'll use for each route.

- For the Search route, we'll create a SearchComponent. This component will talk to the Spotify API to perform the search and then display the results on a grid.

---

[55]https://developer.spotify.com/web-api

- For the `Artists` route, we'll create an `ArtistComponent` which will show the artist's information
- For the `Albums` route, we'll create an `AlbumComponent` which will show the list of tracks in the album
- For the `Tracks` route, we'll create a `TrackComponent` which will show the track and let us play a preview of the song

Since this new component will need to interact with the Spotify API, it seems like we need to build a service that uses the `http` module to call out to the API server.

Everything in our app depends on the data, so let's build the `SpotifyService` first.

The `SpotifyService`

> You can find the full code for the final version of the `SpotifyService` in the `routes/music/src/app` folder of the sample code.

The first method we'll implement is `searchTrack` which will search for a track, given a search term.

One of the endpoints documented on Spotify API docs is the Search endpoint[56].

This endpoint does exactly what we want: it takes a query (using the `q` parameter) and a `type` parameter.

Query in this case is the search term. And since we're searching for songs, we should use `type=track`.

Here's what a first version of the service could look like:

```
1  class SpotifyService {
2    constructor(public http: Http) {
3    }
4
5    searchTrack(query: string) {
6      let params: string = [
7        `q=${query}`,
8        `type=track`
9      ].join("&");
10     let queryURL: string = `https://api.spotify.com/v1/search?${params}`;
11     return this.http.request(queryURL).map(res => res.json());
12   }
13 }
```

---

[56] https://developer.spotify.com/web-api/search-item/

This code performs an HTTP GET request to the URL https://api.spotify.com/v1/search[57], passing our query as the search term and type hardcoded to track.

This http call returns an Observable. We are going one step further and using the RxJS function map to transform the result we would get (which is an http module's Response object) and parsing it as JSON, resulting on an object.

Any function that calls searchTrack will then have to use the Observable API to subscribe to the response like this:

```
1  service
2    .searchTrack('query')
3    .subscribe((res: any) => console.log('Got object', res))
```

The SearchComponent

Now that we have a service that will perform track searches, we can start coding the SearchComponent.

Again, we start with an import section:

code/routes/music/src/app/search/search.component.ts

```
1  /*
2   * Angular
3   */
4
5  import {Component, OnInit} from '@angular/core';
6  import {
7    Router,
8    ActivatedRoute,
9  } from '@angular/router';
10
11  /*
12   * Services
13   */
14  import {SpotifyService} from '../spotify.service';
```

Here we're importing, among other things, the SpotifyService class we just created.

The goal here is to render each resulting track side by side on a card like below:

---

[57]https://api.spotify.com/v1/search

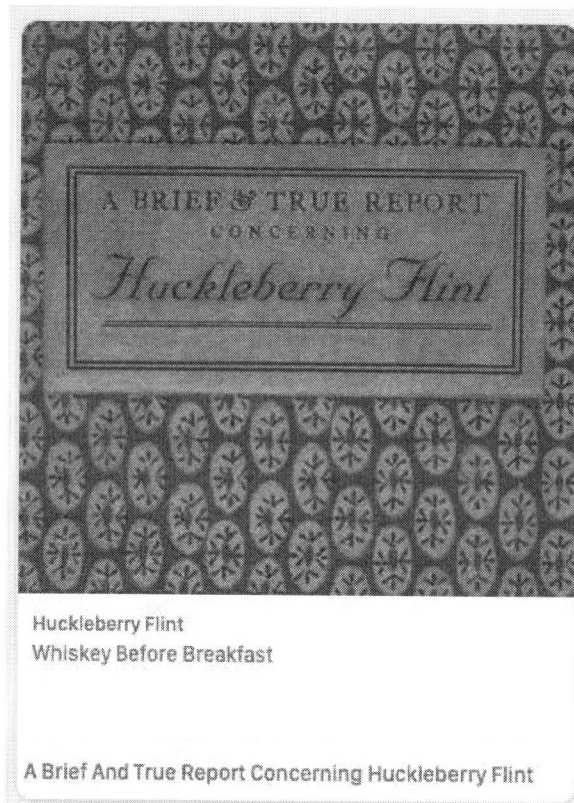

Music App Card

We then start coding the component. We're using `search` as the selector, making a few imports and using the following template. The template is a bit long because we're putting some reasonable styles on it using the CSS framework Bootstrap[58], but it isn't particularly complicated, relative to what we've done so far:

code/routes/music/src/app/search/search.component.html

```
1   <h1>Search</h1>
2
3   <p>
4     <input type="text" #newquery
5       [value]="query"
6       (keydown.enter)="submit(newquery.value)">
7     <button (click)="submit(newquery.value)">Search</button>
8   </p>
9
10  <div *ngIf="results">
11    <div *ngIf="!results.length">
12      No tracks were found with the term '{{ query }}'
```

---

[58]http://getbootstrap.com

```
13    </div>
14
15    <div *ngIf="results.length">
16      <h1>Results</h1>
17
18    <div class="row">
19      <div class="col-sm-6 col-md-4" *ngFor="let t of results">
20        <div class="thumbnail">
21          <div class="content">
22            <img src="{{ t.album.images[0].url }}" class="img-responsive">
23            <div class="caption">
24              <h3>
25                <a [routerLink]="['/artists', t.artists[0].id]">
26                  {{ t.artists[0].name }}
27                </a>
28              </h3>
29              <br>
30              <p>
31                <a [routerLink]="['/tracks', t.id]">
32                  {{ t.name }}
33                </a>
34              </p>
35            </div>
36            <div class="attribution">
37              <h4>
38                <a [routerLink]="['/albums', t.album.id]">
39                  {{ t.album.name }}
40                </a>
41              </h4>
42            </div>
43          </div>
44        </div>
45      </div>
46    </div>
47  </div>
48 </div>
```

The Search Field

Let's break down the HTML template a bit.

This first section will have the search field:

code/routes/music/src/app/search/search.component.html

```
3   <p>
4     <input type="text" #newquery
5       [value]="query"
6       (keydown.enter)="submit(newquery.value)">
7     <button (click)="submit(newquery.value)">Search</button>
8   </p>
```

Here we have the input field and we're binding its DOM element `value` property to the `query` property of our component.

We also give this element a template variable named `#newquery`. We can now access the value of this input within our template code by using `newquery.value`.

The button will trigger the `submit` method of the component, passing the value of the input field as a parameter.

We also want to trigger `submit` when the user hits "Enter" so we bind to the `keydown.enter` event on the input.

Search Results and Links

The next section displays the results. We're relying on the `NgFor` directive to iterate through each track from our results object:

code/routes/music/src/app/search/search.component.html

```
18      <div class="row">
19        <div class="col-sm-6 col-md-4" *ngFor="let t of results">
20          <div class="thumbnail">
```

For each track, we display the artist name:

code/routes/music/src/app/search/search.component.html

```
24            <h3>
25              <a [routerLink]="['/artists', t.artists[0].id]">
26                {{ t.artists[0].name }}
27              </a>
28            </h3>
```

Notice how we're using the `RouterLink` directive to redirect to `['/artists', t.artists[0].id]`.

This is how we set *route parameters* for a given route. Say we have an artist with an id `abc123`. When this link is clicked, the app would then navigate to `/artist/abc123` (where `abc123` is the `:id` parameter).

Further down we'll show how we can retrieve this value inside the component that handles this route.

Now we display the track:

code/routes/music/src/app/search/search.component.html

```
30              <p>
31                <a [routerLink]="['/tracks', t.id]">
32                  {{ t.name }}
33                </a>
34              </p>
```

And the album:

code/routes/music/src/app/search/search.component.html

```
38              <a [routerLink]="['/albums', t.album.id]">
39                {{ t.album.name }}
40              </a>
41            </h4>
```

`SearchComponent` Class

Let's take a look at the constructor first:

code/routes/music/src/app/search/search.component.ts

```
22 export class SearchComponent implements OnInit {
23   query: string;
24   results: Object;
25
26   constructor(private spotify: SpotifyService,
27               private router: Router,
28               private route: ActivatedRoute) {
29     this.route
30       .queryParams
31       .subscribe(params => { this.query = params['query'] || ''; });
32   }
```

Here we're declaring two properties:

- query for current search term and
- results for the search results

On the constructor we're injecting the SpotifyService (that we created above), Router, and the ActivatedRoute and making them properties of our class.

In our constructor we subscribe to the queryParams property - this lets us access *query parameters*, such as the search term (params['query']).

In a URL like: http://localhost/#/search?query=cats&order=ascending, queryParams gives us the parameters in an object. This means we could access the order with params['order'] (in this case, ascending).

Also note that queryParams are different than route.params. Whereas route.params match parameters in the *route* queryParams match parameters in the query string.

In this case, if there is no query param, we set this.query to the empty string.

search

In our SearchComponent we will call out to the SpotifyService and render the results. There are two cases when we want to run a search:

We want to run a search when the user:

- enters a search query and submits the form
- navigates to this page with a given URL in the query parameters (e.g. someone shared a link or bookmarked the page)

To perform the actual search for both cases, we create the search method:

code/routes/music/src/app/search/search.component.ts

```
43    search(): void {
44      console.log('this.query', this.query);
45      if (!this.query) {
46        return;
47      }
48
49      this.spotify
50        .searchTrack(this.query)
51        .subscribe((res: any) => this.renderResults(res));
52    }
```

The `search` function uses the current value of `this.query` to know what to search for. Because we subscribed to the `queryParams` in the constructor, we can be sure that `this.query` will always have the most up-to-date value.

We then subscribe to the `searchTrack Observable` and whenever new results are emitted we call `renderResults`.

code/routes/music/src/app/search/search.component.ts

```
54    renderResults(res: any): void {
55      this.results = null;
56      if (res && res.tracks && res.tracks.items) {
57        this.results = res.tracks.items;
58      }
59    }
```

We declared `results` as a component property. Whenever its value is changed, the view will be automatically updated by Angular.

Searching on Page Load

As we pointed out above, we want to be able to jump straight into the results if the URL includes a search query.

To do that, we are going to implement a hook Angular router provides for us to run whenever our component is initialized.

> But isn't that what constructors are for? Well, yes and no. Yes, constructors are used to initialize values, but if you want to write good, testable code, you want to minimize the side effects of *constructing* an object. So keep in mind that you should put your component's initialization logic always on a hook like below.

Here's the implementation of the `ngOnInit` method:

code/routes/music/src/app/search/search.component.ts

```
34    ngOnInit(): void {
35      this.search();
36    }
```

> To use `ngOnInit` we imported the `OnInit` class and declared that our component implements `OnInit`.

As you can see, we're just performing the search here. Since the term we're searching for comes from the URL, we're good.

submit

Now let's see what we do when the user submits the form.

code/routes/music/src/app/search/search.component.ts

```
38    submit(query: string): void {
39      this.router.navigate(['search'], { queryParams: { query: query } })
40        .then(_ => this.search() );
41    }
```

We're manually telling the router to navigate to the search route, and providing a `query` parameter, then performing the actual search.

Doing things this way gives us a great benefit: if we reload the browser, we're going to see the same search result rendered. We can say that we're **persisting the search term on the URL**.

Putting it all together

Here's the full listing for the `SearchComponent` class:

code/routes/music/src/app/search/search.component.ts

```
 1   /*
 2    * Angular
 3    */
 4
 5   import {Component, OnInit} from '@angular/core';
 6   import {
 7     Router,
 8     ActivatedRoute,
 9   } from '@angular/router';
10
11   /*
12    * Services
13    */
14   import {SpotifyService} from '../spotify.service';
15   ;
16
17   @Component({
18     selector: 'app-search',
19     templateUrl: './search.component.html',
20     styleUrls: ['./search.component.css']
21   })
```

```
22   export class SearchComponent implements OnInit {
23     query: string;
24     results: Object;
25
26     constructor(private spotify: SpotifyService,
27                 private router: Router,
28                 private route: ActivatedRoute) {
29       this.route
30         .queryParams
31         .subscribe(params => { this.query = params['query'] || ''; });
32     }
33
34     ngOnInit(): void {
35       this.search();
36     }
37
38     submit(query: string): void {
39       this.router.navigate(['search'], { queryParams: { query: query } })
40         .then(_ => this.search() );
41     }
42
43     search(): void {
44       console.log('this.query', this.query);
45       if (!this.query) {
46         return;
47       }
48
49       this.spotify
50         .searchTrack(this.query)
51         .subscribe((res: any) => this.renderResults(res));
52     }
53
54     renderResults(res: any): void {
55       this.results = null;
56       if (res && res.tracks && res.tracks.items) {
57         this.results = res.tracks.items;
58       }
59     }
60   }
```

Trying the search

Now that we have completed the code for the search, let's try it out:

Sportify music for active people

Home   Add

Search

andre de sapato novo   Search

Results

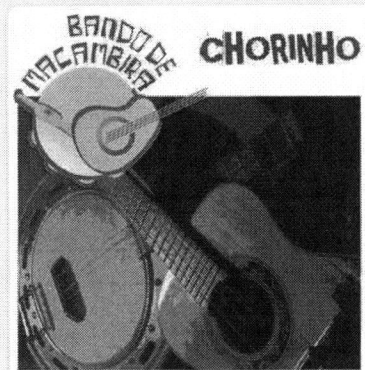

Bando De Macambira
André do Sapato Novo

Chorinho

Ordinarius
André de Sapato Novo / Tico Tico no Fubá

Rio de Choro

Evandro Do Bandolim
André De Sapato Novo

Chorinhos De Ouro

Pixinguinha
André de Sapato Novo

Benedito Lacerda E Pixinguinha

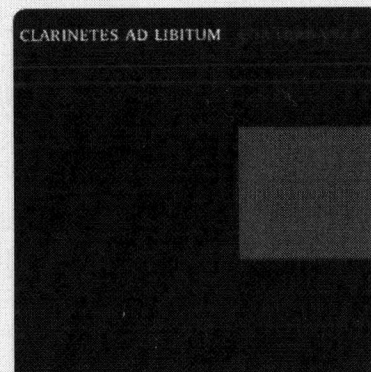

Clarinetes Ad Libitum
André de Sapato Novo

Contradanza

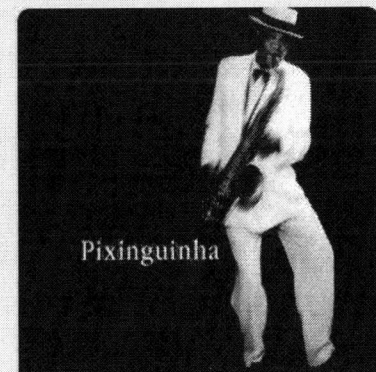

Pixinguinha
Andre De Sapato Novo

Latin Jazz Roots

Trying out Search

We can click the artist, track or album links to navigate to the proper route.

TrackComponent

For the track route, we use the TrackComponent. It basically displays the track name, the album cover image and allow the user to play a preview using an HTML5 audio tag:

code/routes/music/src/app/track/track.component.html

```
1  <div *ngIf="track">
2    <h1>{{ track.name }}</h1>
3
4    <p>
5      <img src="{{ track.album.images[1].url }}">
6    </p>
7
8    <p>
9      <audio controls src="{{ track.preview_url }}"></audio>
10   </p>
11
12   <p><a href (click)="back()">Back</a></p>
13 </div>
```

Like we did for the search before, we're going to use the Spotify API. Let's refactor the method searchTrack and extract two other useful methods we can reuse:

code/routes/music/src/app/spotify.service.ts

```
17 export class SpotifyService {
18   static BASE_URL = 'https://api.spotify.com/v1';
19
20   constructor(private http: Http) {}
21
22   query(
23     URL: string,
24     params?: Array<string>
25   ): Observable<any[]> {
26     let queryURL = `${SpotifyService.BASE_URL}${URL}`;
27     if (params) {
28       queryURL = `${queryURL}?${params.join('&')}`;
29     }
30     const apiKey = environment.spotifyApiKey;
31     const headers = new Headers({
32       Authorization: `Bearer ${apiKey}`
33     });
34     const options = new RequestOptions({
```

```
35       headers: headers
36     });
37
38     return this.http
39       .request(queryURL, options)
40       .map((res: any) => res.json());
41   }
42
43   search(query: string, type: string): Observable<any[]> {
44     return this.query(`/search`, [
45       `q=${query}`,
46       `type=${type}`
47     ]);
48   }
```

Now that we've extracted those methods into the `SpotifyService`, notice how much simpler `searchTrack` becomes:

code/routes/music/src/app/spotify.service.ts

```
50   searchTrack(query: string): Observable<any[]> {
51     return this.search(query, 'track');
52   }
```

Now let's create a method to allow the component we're building retrieve track information, based in the track ID:

code/routes/music/src/app/spotify.service.ts

```
54   getTrack(id: string): Observable<any[]> {
55     return this.query(`/tracks/${id}`);
56   }
```

And now we can use `getTrack` from a new `ngOnInit` method on the `TrackComponent`:

218   Routing

code/routes/music/src/app/track/track.component.ts

```
28    ngOnInit(): void {
29      this.spotify
30        .getTrack(this.id)
31        .subscribe((res: any) => this.renderTrack(res));
32    }
```

The other components work in a similar way and use `get*` methods from the `SpotifyService` to retrieve information about either an Artist or a Track based on their ID.

Wrapping up music search

Now we have a pretty functional music search and preview app. Try searching for a few of your favorite tunes and try it out!

It Had to Route You

Router Hooks

There are times that we may want to do some action when changing routes. A classic example of that is authentication. Let's say we have a **login** route and a **protected** route.

We want to only allow the app to go to the protected route if the correct username and password were provided on the login page.

In order to do that, we need to hook into the lifecycle of the router and ask to be notified when the protected route is being activated. We then can call an authentication service and ask whether or not the user provided the right credentials.

In order to check if a component can be activated we add a *guard class* to the key `canActivate` in our router configuration.

Let's revisit our initial application, adding login and password input fields and a new protected route that only works if we provide a certain username and password combination.

> **Sample Code** The complete code for the examples in this section build on the first section and can be found in the `routes/routing` folder of the sample code. That folder contains a `README.md`, which gives instructions for building and running the project.

AuthService

Let's create a very simple and minimal implementation of a service, responsible for authentication and authorization of resources:

code/routes/routing/src/app/auth.service.ts

```
1  import { Injectable } from '@angular/core';
2
3  @Injectable()
4  export class AuthService {
5    login(user: string, password: string): boolean {
6      if (user === 'user' && password === 'password') {
7        localStorage.setItem('username', user);
8        return true;
9      }
10
11     return false;
12   }
```

The `login` method will return true if the provided user/password pair equals `'user'` and `'password'`, respectively. Also, when it is matched, it's going to use `localStorage` to save the username. This will also serve as a flag to indicate whether or not there is an active logged user.

ℹ️ If you're not familiar, localStorage is an HTML5 provided key/value pair that allows you to persist information on the browser. The API is very simple, and basically allows the setting, retrieval and deletion of items. For more information, see the Storage interface documents on MDN[59]

The logout method just clears the username value:

code/routes/routing/src/app/auth.service.ts

```
14    logout(): any {
15      localStorage.removeItem('username');
16    }
```

And the final two methods:

- getUser returns the username or null
- isLoggedIn uses getUser() to return true if we have a user

Here's the code for those methods:

code/routes/routing/src/app/auth.service.ts

```
18    getUser(): any {
19      return localStorage.getItem('username');
20    }
21
22    isLoggedIn(): boolean {
23      return this.getUser() !== null;
24    }
```

The last thing we do is export an AUTH_PROVIDERS, so it can be injected into our app:

code/routes/routing/src/app/auth.service.ts

```
27  export const AUTH_PROVIDERS: Array<any> = [
28    { provide: AuthService, useClass: AuthService }
29  ];
```

Now that we have the AuthService we can inject it in our components to log the user in, check for the currently logged in user, log the user out, etc.

In a little bit, we'll also use it in our router to protect the ProtectedComponent. But first, let's create the component that we use to log in.

---

[59] https://developer.mozilla.org/en-US/docs/Web/API/Storage

LoginComponent

This component will either show a login form, for the case when there is no logged user, or display a little banner with user information along with a logout link.

The relevant code here is the `login` and `logout` methods:

code/routes/routing/src/app/login/login.component.ts

```
 9  export class LoginComponent {
10    message: string;
11
12    constructor(public authService: AuthService) {
13      this.message = '';
14    }
15
16    login(username: string, password: string): boolean {
17      this.message = '';
18      if (!this.authService.login(username, password)) {
19        this.message = 'Incorrect credentials.';
20        setTimeout(function() {
21          this.message = '';
22        }.bind(this), 2500);
23      }
24      return false;
25    }
26
27    logout(): boolean {
28      this.authService.logout();
29      return false;
30    }
```

Once our service validates the credentials, we log the user in.

The component template has two snippets that are displayed based on whether the user is logged in or not.

The first is a login form, protected by `*ngIf="!authService.getUser()"`:

code/routes/routing/src/app/login/login.component.html

```
5    </div>
6
7    <form class="form-inline" *ngIf="!authService.getUser()">
8      <div class="form-group">
9        <label for="username">User: (type <em>user</em>)</label>
10       <input class="form-control" name="username" #username>
11     </div>
12
13     <div class="form-group">
14       <label for="password">Password: (type <em>password</em>)</label>
15       <input class="form-control" type="password" name="password" #password>
16     </div>
17
18     <a class="btn btn-default" (click)="login(username.value, password.value)">
19       Submit
```

And the information banner, containing the logout link, protected by the inverse -
`*ngIf="authService.getUser()"`:

code/routes/routing/src/app/login/login.component.html

```
23   <div class="well" *ngIf="authService.getUser()">
24     Logged in as <b>{{ authService.getUser() }}</b>
25     <a href (click)="logout()">Log out</a>
26   </div>
```

There's another snippet of code that is displayed when we have an authentication error:

code/routes/routing/src/app/login/login.component.html

```
3    <div class="alert alert-danger" role="alert" *ngIf="message">
4      {{ message }}
5    </div>
```

Now that we can handle the user login, let's create a resource that we are going to protect behind a user login.

`ProtectedComponent` **and Route Guards**

The `ProtectedComponent`

Before we can protect the component, it needs to exist. Our `ProtectedComponent` is straightforward:

code/routes/routing/src/app/protected/protected.component.ts

```
1  import { Component, OnInit } from '@angular/core';
2
3  @Component({
4    selector: 'app-protected',
5    templateUrl: './protected.component.html',
6    styleUrls: ['./protected.component.css']
7  })
8  export class ProtectedComponent implements OnInit {
9
10   constructor() { }
11
12   ngOnInit() {
13   }
14
15 }
```

And the template will show some protected content:

code/routes/routing/src/app/protected/protected.component.html

```
1  <h1>Protected</h1>
2  <p>
3    Protected content
4  </p>
```

We want this component to only be accessible to logged in users. But how can we do that?

The answer is to use the router hook `canActivate` with a *guard class* that implements `CanActivate`.

The `LoggedInGuard`

We create a new file `logged-in.guard.ts`:

code/routes/routing/src/app/logged-in.guard.ts

```
1   /* tslint:disble max-line-length */
2   import { Injectable } from '@angular/core';
3   import {
4     CanActivate,
5     ActivatedRouteSnapshot,
6     RouterStateSnapshot
7   } from '@angular/router';
8   import { Observable } from 'rxjs/Observable';
9   import { AuthService } from './auth.service';
10
11  @Injectable()
12  export class LoggedInGuard implements CanActivate {
13    constructor(private authService: AuthService) {}
14
15    canActivate(
16      next: ActivatedRouteSnapshot,
17      state: RouterStateSnapshot): Observable<boolean> | Promise<boolean> | boolea\
18  n {
19        const isLoggedIn = this.authService.isLoggedIn();
20        console.log('canActivate', isLoggedIn);
21        return isLoggedIn;
22    }
23  }
```

> Angular CLI contains a generator for creating guards. So this file could be created with the command: `ng generate guard logged-in`

Our guard states that it implements the `CanActivate` interface. This is satisfied by implementing a method `canActive`.

We inject the `AuthService` into this class in the constructor and save it as a private variable `authService`.

In our `canActivate` function we check `this.authService` to see if the user `isLoggedIn`.

Configuring the Router

To configure the router to use this guard we need to do the following:

1. `import` the `LoggedInGuard`

2. Use the `LoggedInGuard` in a route configuration
3. Include `LoggedInGuard` in the list of providers (so that it can be injected)

We do all of these steps in our `app.ts`.

We import the `LoggedInGuard`:

code/routes/routing/src/app/app.module.ts

```
23  import { AUTH_PROVIDERS } from './auth.service';
24  import { LoggedInGuard } from './logged-in.guard';
```

We add `canActivate` with our guard to the `protected` route:

code/routes/routing/src/app/app.module.ts

```
26  const routes: Routes = [
27    // basic routes
28    { path: '', redirectTo: 'home', pathMatch: 'full' },
29    { path: 'home', component: HomeComponent },
30    { path: 'about', component: AboutComponent },
31    { path: 'contact', component: ContactComponent },
32    { path: 'contactus', redirectTo: 'contact' },
33
34    // authentication demo
35    { path: 'login', component: LoginComponent },
36    {
37      path: 'protected',
38      component: ProtectedComponent,
39      canActivate: [ LoggedInGuard ]
40    },
41
42    // nested
43    {
44      path: 'products',
45      component: ProductsComponent,
46      children: childRoutes
47    }
48  ];
```

We add `LoggedInGuard` to our list of providers:

code/routes/routing/src/app/app.module.ts

```
68    providers: [
69      // uncomment this for "hash-bang" routing
70      // { provide: LocationStrategy, useClass: HashLocationStrategy }
71      AUTH_PROVIDERS,
72      LoggedInGuard
73    ],
```

Logging in

We import the `LoginComponent`:

code/routes/routing/src/app/app.module.ts

```
19    import { LoginComponent } from './login/login.component';
```

And then to access it we have:

1. a route that links to the `LoginComponent`
2. a new link to the protected route

Now when we open the application on the browser, we can see the new login form and the new protected link:

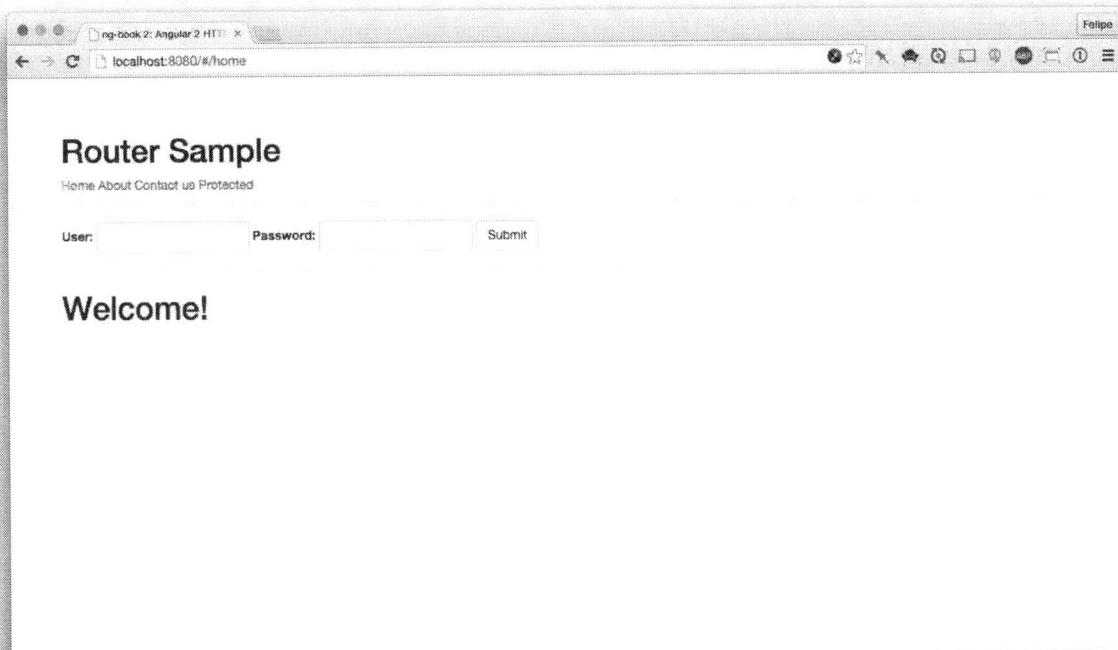

Auth App - Initial Page

If you click the Protected link, you'll see nothing happens. The same happens if you try to manually visit http://localhost:4200/protected[60].

Now enter the string user for the user and password for the password on the form and click **Submit**. You'll see that we now get the current user displayed on a banner:

---

[60]http://localhost:4200/protected

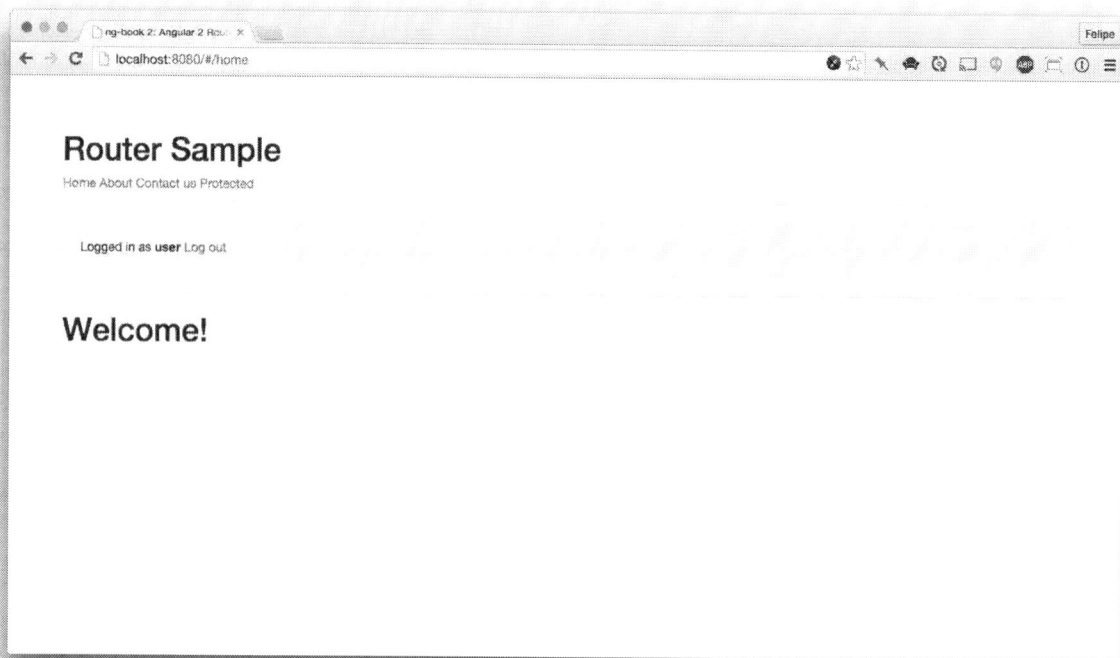

Auth App - Logged In

And, sure enough, if we click the Protected link, it gets redirected and the component is rendered:

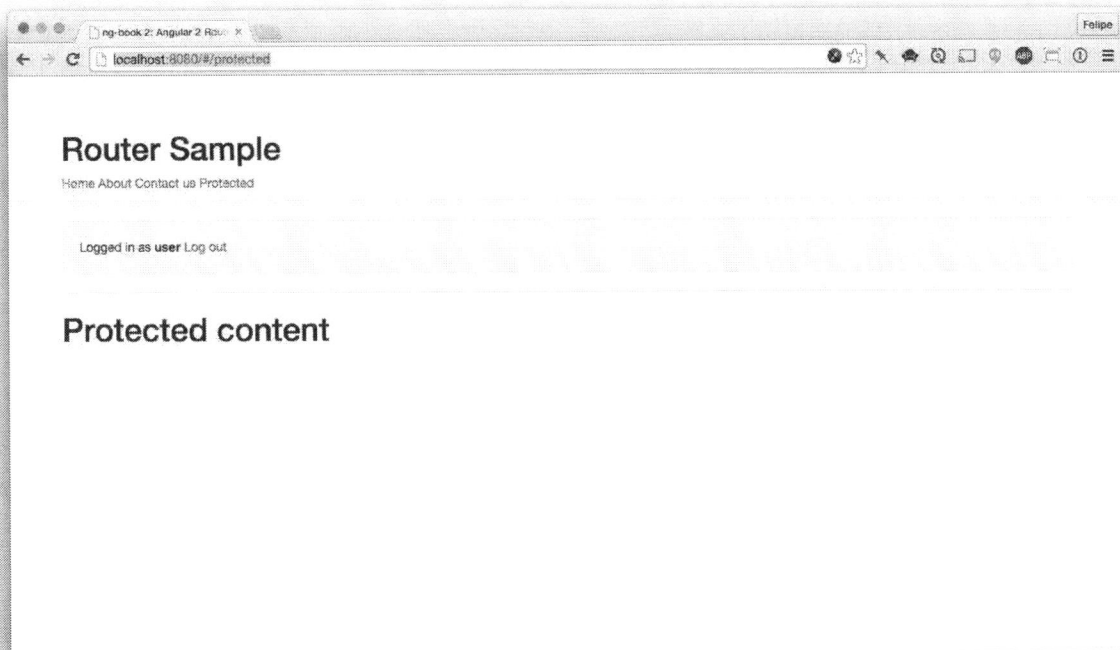

Auth App - Protected Area

⚠ **A Note on Security**: It's important to know how client-side route protection is working before you rely too heavily on it for security. That is, you should consider client-side route protection a form of *user-experience* and not one of security.

Ultimately all of the javascript in your app that gets served to the client can be inspected, whether the user is logged in or not.

So if you have sensitive data that needs to be protected, you must protect it with **server-side authentication**. That is, require an API key (or auth token) from the user which is validated by the server on every request for data.

Writing a full-stack authentication system is beyond the scope of this book. The important thing to know is that protecting routes on the client-side don't necessarily keep anyone from viewing the javascript pages behind those routes.

Nested Routes

Nested routes is the concept of containing routes within other routes. With nested routes we're able to encapsulate the functionality of parent routes and have that functionality apply to the child routes.

Let's say we have a website with one area to allow users to know our team, called **Who we are?** and another one for our **Products**.

We could think that the perfect route for **Who we are?** would be /about and for products /products.

And we're happily displaying all our team and all our products when visiting these areas.

What happens when the website grows and we now need to display individual information about each person in our team and also for each product we sell?

In order to support scenarios like these, the router allows the user to define nested routes.

To do that, you can have multiple, nested router-outlet. So each area of our application can have their own child components, that also have their own router-outlets.

Let's work on an example to clear things up.

In this example, we'll have a products section where the user will be able to view two highlighted products by visiting a nice URL. For all the other products, the routes will use the product ID.

Configuring Routes

We will start by describing the products route on the app.module.ts file:

code/routes/routing/src/app/app.module.ts

```
26  const routes: Routes = [
27    // basic routes
28    { path: '', redirectTo: 'home', pathMatch: 'full' },
29    { path: 'home', component: HomeComponent },
30    { path: 'about', component: AboutComponent },
31    { path: 'contact', component: ContactComponent },
32    { path: 'contactus', redirectTo: 'contact' },
33
34    // authentication demo
35    { path: 'login', component: LoginComponent },
36    {
37      path: 'protected',
38      component: ProtectedComponent,
39      canActivate: [ LoggedInGuard ]
40    },
41
42    // nested
43    {
44      path: 'products',
45      component: ProductsComponent,
46      children: childRoutes
47    }
48  ];
```

Notice that products has a children parameter. Where does this come from? We've defined the childRoutes **in a new module**: the ProductsModule. Let's take a look:

ProductsModule

The ProductsModule will have its own route configuration:

code/routes/routing/src/app/products/products.module.ts

```
15  export const routes: Routes = [
16    { path: '', redirectTo: 'main', pathMatch: 'full' },
17    { path: 'main', component: MainComponent },
18    { path: 'more-info', component: MoreInfoComponent },
19    { path: ':id', component: ProductComponent },
20  ];
```

Notice here that we have an empty path on the first object. We do this so that when we visit /products, we'll be redirected to the main route.

The other route we need to look at is :id. In this case, when the user visits something *that doesn't match any other route*, it will fallback to this route. Everything that is passed after / will be extracted to a parameter of the route, called id.

Now on the component template, we'll have a link to each of those static child routes:

code/routes/routing/src/app/products/products.component.html

```
3  <div class="navLinks">
4    <a [routerLink]="['./main']">Main</a> |
5    <a [routerLink]="['./more-info']">More Info</a> |
```

You can see that the route links are all in the format ['./main'], with a preceding ./. This indicates that you want to navigate the Main route *relative to the current route context*.

You could also declare the routes with the ['products', 'main'] notation. The downside is that by doing it this way, the child route is aware of the parent route and if you were to move this component around or reuse it, you would have to rewrite your route links.

After the links, we'll add an input where the user will be able to enter a product id, along with a button to navigate to it, and lastly add our router-outlet:

code/routes/routing/src/app/products/products.component.html

```
1   <h2>Products</h2>
2
3   <div class="navLinks">
4     <a [routerLink]="['./main']">Main</a> |
5     <a [routerLink]="['./more-info']">More Info</a> |
6     Enter id: <input #id size="6">
7     <button (click)="goToProduct(id.value)">Go</button>
8   </div>
9
10  <div class="products-area">
11    <router-outlet></router-outlet>
12  </div>
```

Let's look at the ProductsComponent definition:

code/routes/routing/src/app/products/products.component.ts

```
1   import { Component } from '@angular/core';
2   import {
3     ActivatedRoute,
4     Router
5   } from '@angular/router';
6
7   @Component({
8     selector: 'app-products',
9     templateUrl: './products.component.html',
10    styleUrls: ['./products.component.css']
11  })
12  export class ProductsComponent {
13    constructor(private router: Router, private route: ActivatedRoute) {
14    }
15
16    goToProduct(id: string): void {
17      this.router.navigate(['./', id], {relativeTo: this.route});
18    }
19  }
```

First on the constructor we're declaring an instance variable for the Router, since we're going to use that instance to navigate to the product by id.

When we want to go to a particular product we use the `goToProduct` method. In `goToProduct` we call the router's `navigate` method and providing the route name and an object with route parameters. In our case we're just passing the `id`.

Notice that we use the relative `./` path in the `navigate` function. In order to use this we also pass the `relativeTo` object to the options, which tells the router what that route is relative to.

Now, if we run the application we will see the main page:

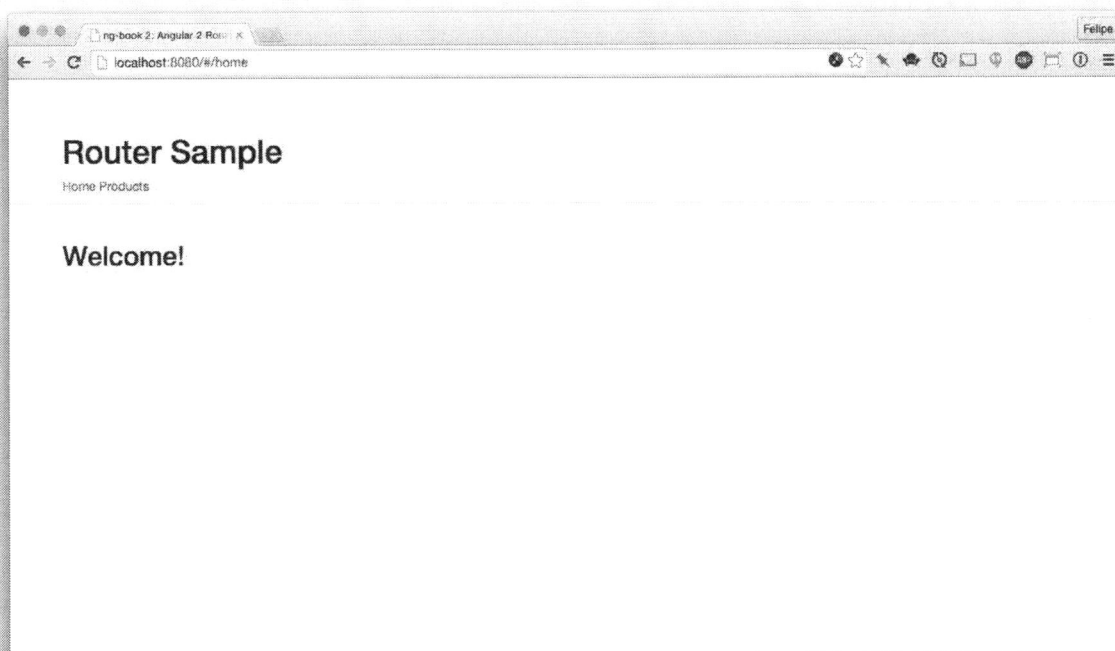

Nested Routes App

If you click on the Products link, you'll be redirected to `/products/main` that will render as follows:

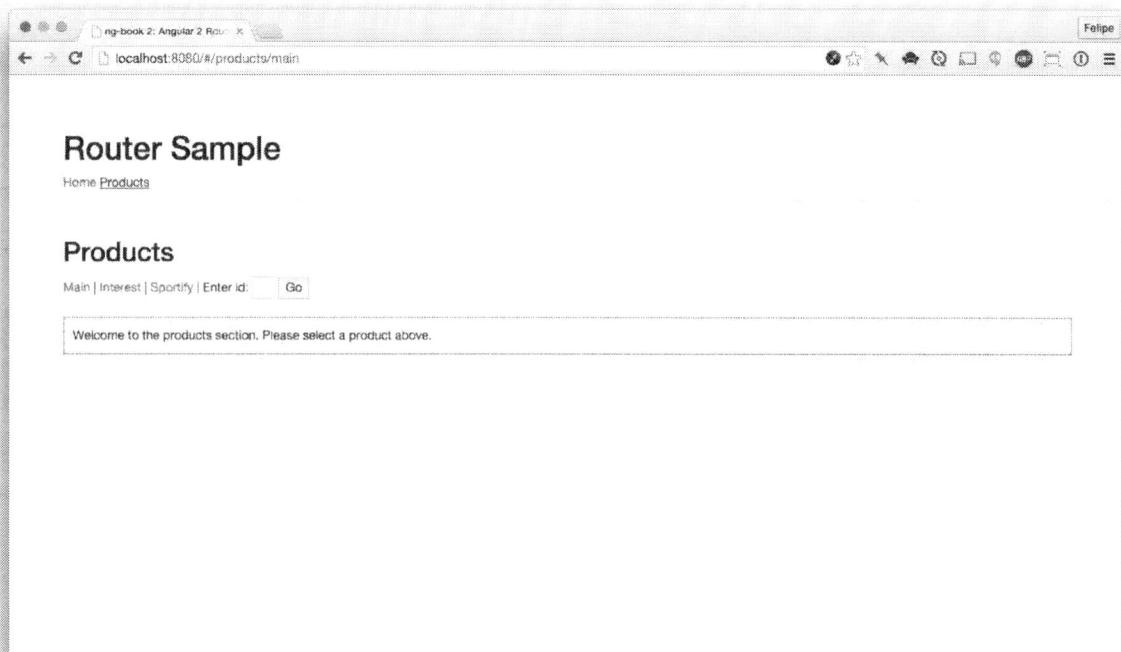

Nested Routes App - Products Section

Everything below that thin grey line is being rendered using the main application's `router-outlet`.

And the contents of the dotted red line is being rendered inside the `ProductComponent`'s `router-outlet`. That's how you indicate how the parent and child routes will be rendered.

When we visit one of the product links, or if we enter an ID on the textbox and click Go, the new content is rendered inside the `ProductComponent`'s outlet:

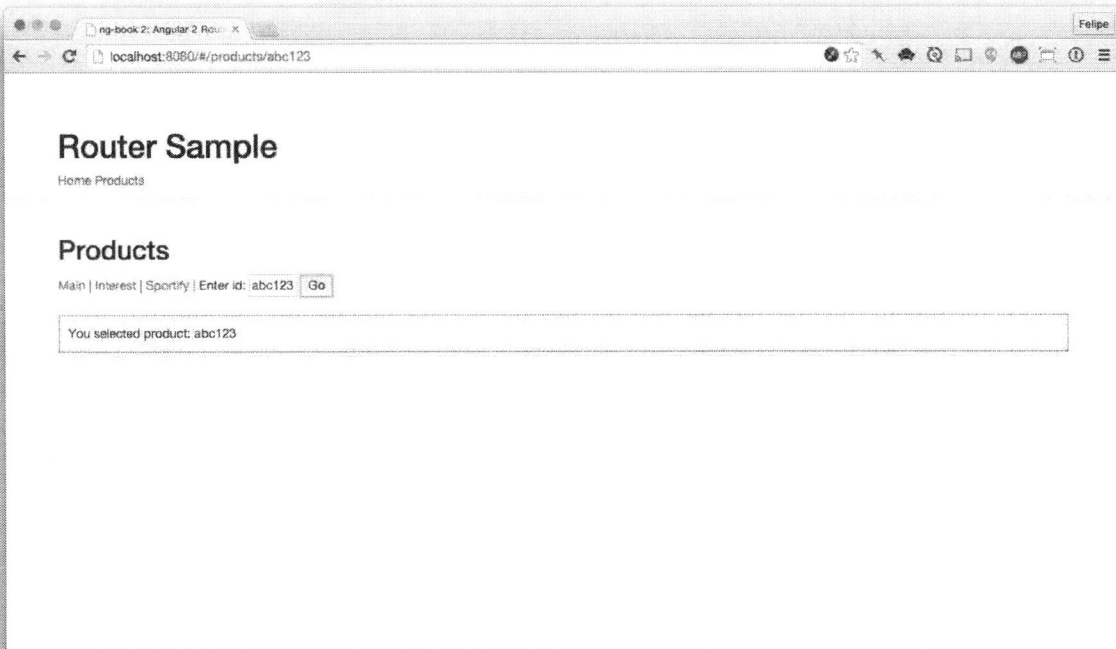

Nested Routes App - Product By Id

It's also worth noting that the Angular router is smart enough to prioritize concrete routes first (like `/products/spotify`) over the parameterized ones (like `/products/123`). This way `/products/spotify` will never be handled by the more generic, catch-all route `/products/:id`.

Redirecting and linking nested routes

Just to recap, if we want to go to a route named `MyRoute` on your top-level routing context, you use `['myRoute']`. This will only work if you're in that same top-level context.

If you are on a child component, and you try to link or redirect to `['myRoute']`, it will try to find a sibling route, and error out. In this case, you need to use `['/myRoute']` with a leading slash.

In a similar way, if we are on the top-level context and we want to link or redirect to a child route, we have to need to use multiple elements on the route definition array.

Let's say we want to visit the `Show` route, which is a child of the `Product` route. In this case, we use `['product', 'show']` as the route definition.

Summary

As we can see, the new Angular router is very powerful and flexible. Now go out and route your apps!

Dependency Injection

As our programs grow in size, parts of the app need to communicate with other modules. When module A requires module B to run, we say that B is a *dependency* of A.

One of the most common ways to get access to dependencies is to simply `import` a file. For instance, in this hypothetical module we might do the following:

```
1   // in A.ts
2   import {B} from 'B'; // a dependency!
3
4   B.foo(); // using B
```

In many cases, simply `import`ing code is sufficient, but other times we need to provide dependencies in a more sophisticated way. For instance, we may want to:

- substitute out the implementation of B for MockB during testing
- share a *single instance* of the B class across our whole app (e.g. the *Singleton* pattern)
- create a *new instance* of the B class every time it is used (e.g. the *Factory* pattern)

Dependency Injection can solve these problems.

Dependency Injection (DI) is a system to make parts of our program accessible to other parts of the program - and we can configure how that happens.

> One way to think about "the injector" is as a replacement for the `new` operator. That is, instead of using the language-provided `new` operator, Dependency Injection let's us configure *how* objects are created.

The term Dependency Injection is used to describe both a design pattern (used in many different frameworks) and also the *specific implementation* of DI that is built-in to Angular.

The major benefit of using Dependency Injection is that the client component needn't be aware of ***how* to create the dependencies**. All the client component needs to know is how to *interact* with those dependencies. This is all very abstract, so let's dive in to some code.

How to use this chapter

This chapter is a tour of Angular DI system and concepts. You can find the code for this chapter in `code/dependency-injection`.

While reading this chapter, run the demo project by changing into the project directory and running:

```
1  npm install
2  npm start
```

As a preview, to get Dependency Injection to work involves configuration in your `NgModules`. It can feel a bit confusing at first to figure out "where" things are coming from.

The example code has full, runnable examples with all of the context. So if you feel lost, we'd encourage you to checkout the sample code alongside reading this chapter.

Injections Example: `PriceService`

Let's imagine we're building a store that has `Products` and we need to calculate the final price of that product after sales tax. In order to calculate the full price for this product, we use a `PriceService` that takes as input:

- the **base price** of the `Product` and
- the **state** we're selling it to.

and then returns the final price of the `Product`, plus tax:

code/dependency-injection/src/app/price-service-demo/price.service.1.ts

```
1  export class PriceService {
2    constructor() { }
3
4    calculateTotalPrice(basePrice: number, state: string) {
5      // e.g. Imgine that in our "real" application we're
6      // accessing a real database of state sales tax amounts
7      const tax = Math.random();
8
9      return basePrice + tax;
10   }
11
12 }
```

In this service, the `calculateTotalPrice` function will take the `basePrice` of a product and the `state` and return the total price of product.

Say we want to use this service on our `Product` model. Here's how it could look without dependency injection:

code/dependency-injection/src/app/price-service-demo/product.model.1.ts

```
 1   import { PriceService } from './price.service';
 2
 3   export class Product {
 4     service: PriceService;
 5     basePrice: number;
 6
 7     constructor(basePrice: number) {
 8       this.service = new PriceService(); // <-- create directly ("hardcoded")
 9       this.basePrice = basePrice;
10     }
11
12     totalPrice(state: string) {
13       return this.service.calculateTotalPrice(this.basePrice, state);
14     }
15   }
```

Now imagine we need to write a test for this `Product` class. We could write a test like this:

```
 1   import { Product } from './product';
 2
 3   describe('Product', () => {
 4
 5     let product;
 6
 7     beforeEach(() => {
 8       product = new Product(11);
 9     });
10
11     describe('price', () => {
12       it('is calculated based on the basePrice and the state', () => {
13         expect(product.totalPrice('FL')).toBe(11.66); // <-- hmmm
14       });
15     })
16
17   });
```

The problem with this test is that we don't actually know what the exact value for tax in Florida ('FL') is going to be. Even if we implemented the PriceService the 'real' way by calling an API or calling a database, we have the problem that:

- The API needs to be available (or the database needs to be running) and
- We need to know the exact Florida tax at the time we write the test.

What should we do if we want to test the price method of the Product *without* relying on this external resource? In this case we often *mock* the PriceService. For example, if we know the *interface* of a PriceService, we could write a MockPriceService which will always give us a predictable calculation (and not be reliant on a database or API).

Here's the interface for IPriceService:

code/dependency-injection/src/app/price-service-demo/price-service.interface.ts

```
1  export interface IPriceService {
2    calculateTotalPrice(basePrice: number, state: string): number;
3  }
```

This interface defines just one function: calculateTotalPrice. Now we can write a MockPriceService that conforms to this interface, which we will use only for our tests:

code/dependency-injection/src/app/price-service-demo/price.service.mock.ts

```
1  import { IPriceService } from './price-service.interface';
2
3  export class MockPriceService implements IPriceService {
4    calculateTotalPrice(basePrice: number, state: string) {
5      if (state === 'FL') {
6        return basePrice + 0.66; // it's always 66 cents!
7      }
8
9      return basePrice;
10   }
11 }
```

Now, just because we've written a MockPriceService doesn't mean our Product will use it. In order to use this service, we need to modify our Product class:

code/dependency-injection/src/app/price-service-demo/product.model.ts

```
1  import { IPriceService } from './price-service.interface';
2
3  export class Product {
4    service: IPriceService;
5    basePrice: number;
6
7    constructor(service: IPriceService, basePrice: number) {
8      this.service = service; // <-- passed in as an argument!
9      this.basePrice = basePrice;
10   }
11
12   totalPrice(state: string) {
13     return this.service.calculateTotalPrice(this.basePrice, state);
14   }
15 }
```

Now, when creating a Product **the client using the Product class becomes responsible for deciding which concrete implementation of the PriceService is going to be given to the new instance.**

And with this change, we can tweak our test slightly and get rid of the dependency on the unpredictable PriceService:

code/dependency-injection/src/app/price-service-demo/product.spec.ts

```
1  import { Product } from './product.model';
2  import { MockPriceService } from './price.service.mock';
3
4  describe('Product', () => {
5    let product;
6
7    beforeEach(() => {
8      const service = new MockPriceService();
9      product = new Product(service, 11.00);
10   });
11
12   describe('price', () => {
13     it('is calculated based on the basePrice and the state', () => {
14       expect(product.totalPrice('FL')).toBe(11.66);
15     });
16   });
17 });
```

We also get the bonus of having confidence that we're testing the `Product` class *in isolation*. That is, we're making sure that our class works with a predictable dependency.

While the predictability is nice, it's a bit laborious to pass a concrete implementation of a service every time we want a new `Product`. Thankfully, Angular's DI library helps us deal with that problem, too. More on that below.

Within Angular's DI system, instead of directly `importing` and creating a `new` instance of a class, instead we will:

- Register the "dependency" with Angular
- Describe *how* the dependency will be *injected*
- Inject the dependency

One benefit of this model is that the dependency *implementation* can be swapped at run-time (as in our mocking example above). But another significant benefit is that we can configure **how the dependency is created**.

That is, often in the case of program-wide services, we may want to have **only one instance** - that is, a Singleton. With DI we're able to configure Singletons easily.

A third use-case for DI is for configuration or environment-specific variables. For instance, we might define a "constant" `API_URL`, but then inject a different value in production vs. development.

Let's learn how to create our own services and the different ways of injecting them.

Dependency Injection Parts

To register a dependency we have to **bind it** to something that will **identify that dependency**. This identification is called the dependency **token**. For instance, if we want to register the URL of an API, we can use the string `API_URL` as the token. Similarly, if we're registering a class, we can use the class itself as its **token** as we'll see below.

Dependency injection in Angular has three pieces:

- the **Provider** (also often referred to as a binding) maps a *token* (that can be a string or a class) to a list of dependencies. It tells Angular how to create an object, given a token.
- the **Injector** that holds a set of bindings and is responsible for resolving dependencies and injecting them when creating objects
- the **Dependency** that is what's being injected

We can think of the role of each piece as illustrated below:

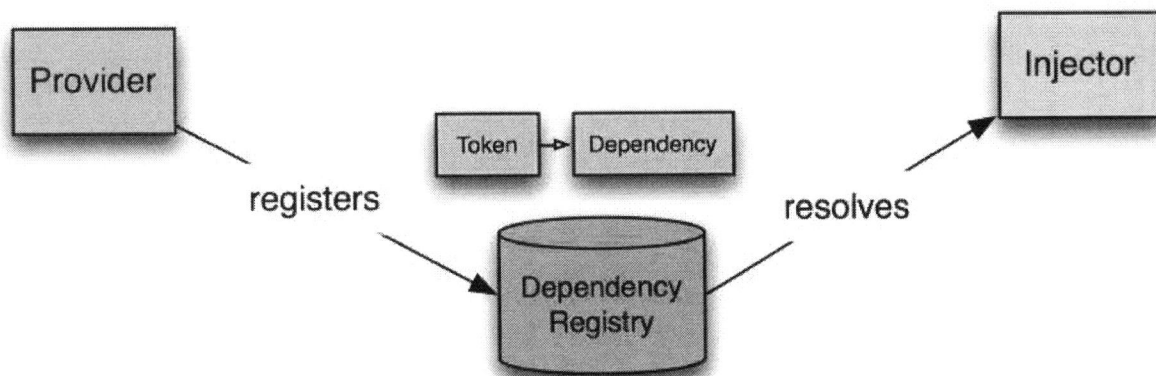

Dependency Injection

A way of thinking about this is that when we configure DI we specify **what** is being injected and **how** it will be resolved.

Playing with an Injector

Above with our `Product` and `PriceService` we **manually** created the `PriceService` using the `new` operator. This mimics what Angular itself does.

Angular uses an *injector* to **resolve** a dependency and **create the instance**. This is done for us behind the scenes, but as an exercise, it's useful to explore what's happening. It can be enlightening to use the injector manually, because we can see what Angular does for us behind the scenes.

Let's **manually use the injector** in our component to resolve and create a service. (After we've resolved a dependency manually, we'll show the typical, easy way of injecting dependencies.)

One of the common use-cases for services is to have a 'global' Singleton object. For instance, we might have a `UserService` which contains the information for the currently logged in user. Many different components will want to have logic based on the current user, so this is a good case for a service.

Here's a basic `UserService` that stores the user object as a property:

code/dependency-injection/src/app/services/user.service.ts

```
1  import { Injectable } from '@angular/core';
2
3  @Injectable()
4  export class UserService {
5    user: any;
6
7    setUser(newUser) {
8      this.user = newUser;
9    }
10
11   getUser(): any {
12     return this.user;
13   }
14 }
```

Say we want to create a toy sign-in form:

code/dependency-injection/src/app/user-demo/user-demo.component.html

```
1  <div>
2    <p
3      *ngIf="userName"
4      class="welcome">
5      Welcome: {{ userName }}!
6    </p>
7    <button
8      (click)="signIn()"
9      class="ui button"
10     >Sign In
11   </button>
12 </div>
```

Above, we click the "Sign In" button to call the signIn() function (which we'll define in a moment). If we have a userName, we'll display a greeting.

Sign In

Simple Sign In Button

Now let's implement this functionality in our component by **using the injector directly**.

code/dependency-injection/src/app/user-demo/user-demo.injector.component.ts

```
 1  import {
 2    Component,
 3    ReflectiveInjector
 4  } from '@angular/core';
 5
 6  import { UserService } from '../services/user.service';
 7
 8  @Component({
 9    selector: 'app-injector-demo',
10    templateUrl: './user-demo.component.html',
11    styleUrls: ['./user-demo.component.css']
12  })
13  export class UserDemoInjectorComponent {
14    userName: string;
15    userService: UserService;
16
17    constructor() {
18      // Create an _injector_ and ask for it to resolve and create a UserService
19      const injector: any = ReflectiveInjector.resolveAndCreate([UserService]);
20
21      // use the injector to **get the instance** of the UserService
22      this.userService = injector.get(UserService);
23    }
24
```

```
25    signIn(): void {
26      // when we sign in, set the user
27      // this mimics filling out a login form
28      this.userService.setUser({
29        name: 'Nate Murray'
30      });
31
32      // now **read** the user name from the service
33      this.userName = this.userService.getUser().name;
34      console.log('User name is: ', this.userName);
35    }
36  }
```

This starts as a basic component: we have a selector, template, and CSS. Note that we have two properties: userName, which holds the currently logged-in user's name and userService, which holds a reference to the UserService.

In our component's constructor we are using a static method from ReflectiveInjector called resolveAndCreate. That method is responsible for creating a new injector. The parameter we pass in is an array with all the *injectable things* we want this new injector to *know*. In our case, we just wanted it to know about the UserService injectable.

The ReflectiveInjector is a concrete implementation of Injector that uses *reflection* to look up the proper parameter types. While there are other injectors that are possible ReflectiveInjector is the "normal" injector we'll be using in most apps.

Welcome: Nate Murray!

Sign In

Signed In

Providing Dependencies with `NgModule`

While it's interesting to see how an `injector` is created directly, that isn't the typical way we'd use injections. Instead, what we'd normally do is

- use `NgModule` to *register* what we'll inject – these are called *providers* and
- use decorators (generally on a `constructor`) to specify **what we're injecting**

By doing these two steps **Angular** will manage creating the injector and resolving the dependencies.

Let's convert our `UserService` to be *injectable* as a singleton across our app. First, we're going to add it to the `providers` key of our `NgModule`:

code/dependency-injection/src/app/user-demo/user-demo.module.ts

```
 1  import { NgModule } from '@angular/core';
 2  import { CommonModule } from '@angular/common';
 3
 4  // imported here
 5  import { UserService } from '../services/user.service';
 6
 7  @NgModule({
 8    imports: [
 9      CommonModule
10    ],
11    providers: [
12      UserService // <-- added right here
13    ],
14    declarations: []
15  })
16  export class UserDemoModule { }
```

Now we can inject `UserService` into our component like this:

code/dependency-injection/src/app/user-demo/user-demo.component.ts

```
 1  import { Component, OnInit } from '@angular/core';
 2
 3  import { UserService } from '../services/user.service';
 4
 5  @Component({
 6    selector: 'app-user-demo',
 7    templateUrl: './user-demo.component.html',
 8    styleUrls: ['./user-demo.component.css']
 9  })
10  export class UserDemoComponent {
11    userName: string;
12    // removed `userService` because of constructor shorthand below
13
14    // Angular will inject the singleton instance of `UserService` here.
15    // We set it as a property with `private`.
16    constructor(private userService: UserService) {
17      // empty because we don't have to do anything else!
18    }
19
20    // below is the same...
21    signIn(): void {
22      // when we sign in, set the user
23      // this mimics filling out a login form
24      this.userService.setUser({
25        name: 'Nate Murray'
26      });
27
28      // now **read** the user name from the service
29      this.userName = this.userService.getUser().name;
30      console.log('User name is: ', this.userName);
31    }
32  }
```

Notice in the constructor above that we have made userService: UserService an argument to
the UserDemoComponent. When this component is created on our page **Angular will resolve and
inject the UserService singleton**. What's great about this is that because Angular is managing the
instance, we don't have to worry about doing it ourselves. Every class that injects the UserService
will receive the same singleton.

Providers are the Key

It's important to know that when we put the `UserService` on the constructor of the `UserDemoComponent`, Angular knows what to inject (and how) **because we listed `UserService` in the `providers` key of our `NgModule`.

It **does not** inject arbitrary classes. You **must** configure an `NgModule` for DI to work.

We've been talking a lot about Singleton services, but we can inject things in lots of other ways. Let's take a look.

Providers

There are several ways we can configure resolving injected dependencies in Angular. For instance we can:

- Inject a (singleton) instance of a class (as we've seen)
- Inject a **value**
- **Call any function** and inject the return value of that function

Let's look into detail at how we create each one:

Using a Class

As we've discussed, injecting a singleton instance of a class is probably the most common type of injection.

When we put the class itself into the list of `providers` like this:

```
1    providers: [ UserService ]
```

This tells Angular that we want to provide a singleton *instance* of `UserService` whenever `UserService` is injected. Because this pattern is so common, the class by itself is actually shorthand notation for the following, equivalent configuration:

```
1    providers: [
2      { provide: UserService, useClass: UserService }
3    ]
```

What's interesting to note is that the object configuration with provide takes **two** keys. provide is the *token* that we use **to identify the injection** and the second useClass is **how and what** to inject.

Here we're mapping the UserService *class* to the UserService *token*. In this case, the name of the class and the token match. This is the common case, but know that the token and the injected thing *aren't required to have the same name.*

As we've seen above, in this case the injector will create a **singleton** behind the scenes and return the same instance every time we inject it . Of course, the first time it is injected, the singleton hasn't been instantiated yet, so when creating the UserService instance for the first time, the DI system will trigger the class constructor method.

Using a Value

Another way we can use DI is to provide a value, much like we might use a global constant. For instance, we might configure an API Endpoint URL depending on the environment.

To do this, in our NgModule providers, we use the key useValue:

```
1    providers: [
2      { provide: 'API_URL', useValue: 'http://my.api.com/v1' }
3    ]
```

Above, for the provide token we're using a *string* of API_URL. If we use a string for the provide value, Angular can't infer which dependency we're resolving by the type. For instance we **can't** write:

```
1  // doesn't work - anti-example
2  export class AnalyticsDemoComponent {
3    constructor(apiUrl: 'API_URL') { // <--- this isn't a type, just a string
4                                     // if we put `string` that is ambiguous
5    }
6  }
```

So what can we do? In this case, we'll use the @Inject() decorator like this:

```
1  import { Inject } from '@angular/core';
2
3  export class AnalyticsDemoComponent {
4    constructor(@Inject('API_URL') apiUrl: string) {
5      // works! do something w/ apiUrl
6    }
7  }
```

Now that we know how to do simple values with useValue and Singleton classes with useClass, we're ready to talk about the more advanced case: writing configurable services using factories.

Configurable Services

In the case of the UserService, no arguments are required for the constructor. But what happens if a service's constructor requires arguments? We can implement this by using a *factory* which is a function that can return **any object** when injected.

For instance, let's say we're writing a library for recording user analytics (that is, keeping a record of events of actions a user took on the page). In this scenario, we want to have an AnalyticsService with a catch: the AnalyticsService should define the interface for *recording* events, **but not the implementation for handling the event**.

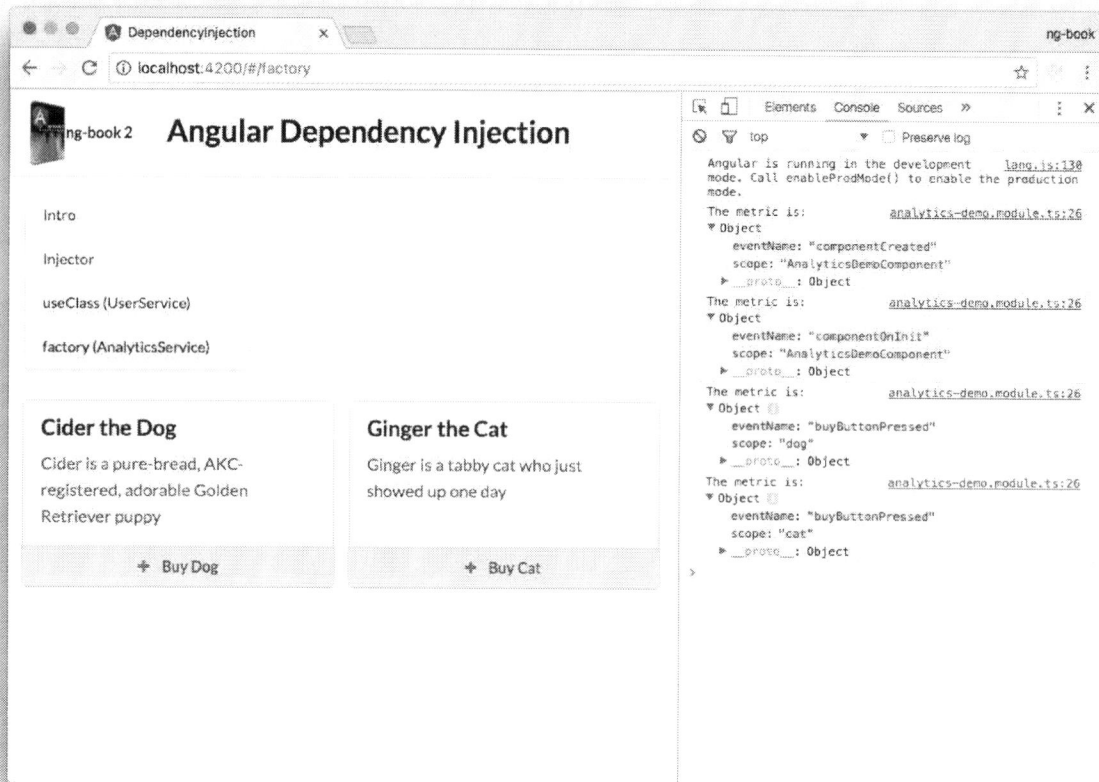

Tracking Analytics on the events

Our user may, for instance, want to record these metrics with Google Analytics or they may want to use Optimizely, or some other in-house solution. Let's write an injectable `AnalyticsService` which can take an implementation configuration.

First, a couple of definitions. Let's define a `Metric`:

code/dependency-injection/src/app/analytics-demo/analytics-demo.interface.ts

```
4   export interface Metric {
5     eventName: string;
6     scope: string;
7   }
```

A `Metric` will store an `eventName` and a `scope`. We could use this for say, when a the user `nate` logs-in the `eventName` could be `loggedIn` and the `scope` would be `nate`.

```
1   // just an example
2   let metric: Metric = {
3     eventName: 'loggedIn',
4     scope: 'nate'
5   }
```

This way we could, in theory, count the number of user logins by counting the events with eventName loggedIn and count the number of times the specific user nate logged in by counting the loggedIn events with user nate.

We also need to define what an analytics implementation would look like:

code/dependency-injection/src/app/analytics-demo/analytics-demo.interface.ts

```
12   export interface AnalyticsImplementation {
13     recordEvent(metric: Metric): void;
14   }
```

Here we define an AnalyticsImplementation interface to have one function: recordEvent which takes a Metric as an argument.

Now let's define the AnalyticsService:

code/dependency-injection/src/app/services/analytics.service.ts

```
1   import { Injectable } from '@angular/core';
2   import {
3     Metric,
4     AnalyticsImplementation
5   } from '../analytics-demo/analytics-demo.interface';
6
7   @Injectable()
8   export class AnalyticsService {
9     constructor(private implementation: AnalyticsImplementation) {
10    }
11
12    record(metric: Metric): void {
13      this.implementation.recordEvent(metric);
14    }
15  }
```

Above our AnalyticsService defines one method: record which accepts a Metric and then passes it on to the implementation.

> Of course, this `AnalyticsService` is a bit trivial and in this case, we probably wouldn't need the indirection. But this same pattern could be used in the case where you had a more advanced `AnalyticsService`. For instance, we could add middleware or broadcast to several implementations.

Notice how its constructor method takes a phrase as a parameter? If we try to use the "regular" `useClass` injection mechanism we would see an error on the browser like:

```
1  Cannot resolve all parameters for AnalyticsService.
```

This happens because we didn't provide the injector with the implementation necessary for the constructor. In order to resolve this problem, we need to configure the provider to **use a factory**.

Using a Factory

So to use our `AnalyticsService`, we need to:

- create an implementation that conforms to `AnalyticsImplementation` and
- add it to `providers` with `useFactory`

Here's how:

code/dependency-injection/src/app/analytics-demo/analytics-demo.module.1.ts

```
1  import { NgModule } from '@angular/core';
2  import { CommonModule } from '@angular/common';
3  import {
4    Metric,
5    AnalyticsImplementation
6  } from './analytics-demo.interface';
7  import { AnalyticsService } from '../services/analytics.service';
8
9  @NgModule({
10   imports: [
11     CommonModule
12   ],
13   providers: [
14     {
15       // `AnalyticsService` is the _token_ we use to inject
16       // note, the token is the class, but it's just used as an identifier!
17       provide: AnalyticsService,
18
```

```
19      // useFactory is a function - whatever is returned from this function
20      // will be injected
21      useFactory() {
22
23        // create an implementation that will log the event
24        const loggingImplementation: AnalyticsImplementation = {
25          recordEvent: (metric: Metric): void => {
26            console.log('The metric is:', metric);
27          }
28        };
29
30        // create our new `AnalyticsService` with the implementation
31        return new AnalyticsService(loggingImplementation);
32      }
33    }
34  ],
35  declarations: [ ]
36 })
37 export class AnalyticsDemoModule { }
```

Here in providers we're using the syntax:

```
1 providers: [
2   { provide: AnalyticsService, useFactory: () => ... }
3 ]
```

useFactory takes a function and **whatever this function returns** will be injected.

Also note that we provide AnalyticsService. Again, when we use provide this way, we're using the class AnalyticsService as the *identifying token* of what we're going to inject. (If you wanted to be confusing, you could use a completely separate class, or less-confusingly a string.)

In useFactory we're creating an AnalyticsImplementation object that has one function: recordEvent. recordEvent is where we could, in theory, configure **what** happens when an event is recorded. Again, in a real app this would probably send an event to Google Analytics or a custom event logging software.

Lastly, we instantiate our AnalyticsService and return it.

Factory Dependencies

Using a factory is the most powerful way to create injectables, because we can do whatever we want within the factory function. Sometimes our factory function will have dependencies of it's own.

Say that we wanted to configure our AnalyticsImplementation to make an HTTP request to a particular URL. In order to do this we'd need:

- The Angular `Http` client and
- Our `API_URL` value

Here's how we could set that up:

code/dependency-injection/src/app/analytics-demo/analytics-demo.module.ts

```
1   import { NgModule } from '@angular/core';
2   import { CommonModule } from '@angular/common';
3   import {
4     Metric,
5     AnalyticsImplementation
6   } from './analytics-demo.interface';
7   import { AnalyticsService } from '../services/analytics.service';
8
9   // added this ->
10  import {
11    HttpModule,
12    Http
13  } from '@angular/http';
14
15  @NgModule({
16    imports: [
17      CommonModule,
18      HttpModule, // <-- added
19    ],
20    providers: [
21      // add our API_URL provider
22      { provide: 'API_URL', useValue: 'http://devserver.com' },
23      {
24        provide: AnalyticsService,
25
26        // add our `deps` to specify the factory depencies
27        deps: [ Http, 'API_URL' ],
28
29        // notice we've added arguments here
30        // the order matches the deps order
31        useFactory(http: Http, apiUrl: string) {
32
33          // create an implementation that will log the event
34          const loggingImplementation: AnalyticsImplementation = {
35            recordEvent: (metric: Metric): void => {
36              console.log('The metric is:', metric);
```

```
37            console.log('Sending to: ', apiUrl);
38            // ... You'd send the metric using http here ...
39          }
40        };
41
42        // create our new `AnalyticsService` with the implementation
43        return new AnalyticsService(loggingImplementation);
44      }
45    },
46  ],
47  declarations: [ ]
48 })
49 export class AnalyticsDemoModule { }
```

Here we're importing the HttpModule, both in the ES6 import (which makes the class *constants* available) and in our NgModule imports (which makes it available for dependency injection).

We've added an API_URL provider, as we did above. And then in our AnalyticsService provider, we've added a new key: deps. deps is an array of injection tokens and these tokens will be resolved and **passed as arguments to the factory function**.

Dependency Injection in Apps

To review, when writing our apps there are three steps we need to take in order to perform an injection:

1. Create the dependency (e.g. the service class)
2. Configure the injection (i.e. register the injection with Angular in our NgModule)
3. Declare the dependencies on the **receiving component**

The first thing we do is create the service class, that is, the class that exposes some behavior we want to use. This will be called the *injectable* because it is the *thing* that our components will receive via the *injection*.

Reminder on terminology: a *provider* provides (creates, instantiates, etc.) the *injectable* (the thing you want). In Angular when you want to access an *injectable* you *inject* a dependency into a function (often a constructor) and Angular's dependency injection framework will locate it and provide it to you.

As we can see, Dependency Injection provides a powerful way to manage dependencies within our app.

More Resources

- Official Angular DI Docs[61]
- Victor Savkin Compare DI in Angular 1 vs. Angular 2[62]

---

[61]https://angular.io/docs/ts/latest/guide/dependency-injection.html

[62]http://victorsavkin.com/post/126514197956/dependency-injection-in-angular-1-and-angular-2

Data Architecture in Angular

An Overview of Data Architecture

Managing data can be one of the trickiest aspects of writing a maintainable app. There are tons of ways to get data into your application:

- AJAX HTTP Requests
- Websockets
- Indexdb
- LocalStorage
- Service Workers
- etc.

The problem of data architecture addresses questions like:

- How can we aggregate all of these different sources into a coherent system?
- How can we avoid bugs caused by unintended side-effects?
- How can we structure the code sensibly so that it's easier to maintain and on-board new team members?
- How can we make the app run as fast as possible when data changes?

For many years MVC was a standard pattern for architecting data in applications: the Models contained the domain logic, the View displayed the data, and the Controller tied it all together. The problem is, we've learned that MVC doesn't translate directly into client-side web applications very well.

There has been a renaissance in the area of data architectures and many new ideas are being explored. For instance:

- **MVW / Two-way data binding**: *Model-View-Whatever* is a term used[63] to describe Angular 1's default architecture. The $scope provides a two-way data-binding - the whole application shares the same data structures and a change in one area propagates to the rest of the app.
- **Flux**[64]: uses a unidirectional data flow. In Flux, Stores hold data, Views render what's in the Store, and Actions change the data in the Store. There is a bit more ceremony to setup Flux, but the idea is that because data only flows in one direction, it's easier to reason about.
- **Observables**: Observables give us streams of data. We subscribe to the streams and then perform operations to react to changes. RxJs[65] is the most popular reactive streams library for

---

[63] See: Model View Whatever
[64] https://facebook.github.io/flux/
[65] https://github.com/Reactive-Extensions/RxJS

JavaScript and it gives us powerful operators for composing operations on streams of data.

> There are a lot of variations on these ideas. For instance:
>
> - Flux is a pattern, and not an implementation. There are **many** different implementations of Flux (just like there are many implementations of MVC)
> - Immutability is a common variant on all of the above data architectures.
> - Falcor[66] is a powerful framework that helps bind your client-side models to the server-side data. Falcor is often used with an Observables-type data architecture.

Data Architecture in Angular

Angular is extremely flexible in what it allows for data architecture. A data strategy that works for one project doesn't necessarily work for another. So Angular doesn't prescribe a particular stack, but instead tries to make it easy to use whatever architecture we choose (while still retaining fast performance).

The benefit of this is that you have flexibility to fit Angular into almost any situation. The downside is that you have to make your own decisions about what's right for your project.

Don't worry, we're not going to leave you to make this decision on your own! In the chapters that follow, we're going to cover how to build applications using some of these patterns.

---

[66] http://netflix.github.io/falcor/

Data Architecture with Observables - Part 1: Services

Observables and RxJS

In Angular, we can structure our application to use Observables as the backbone of our data architecture. Using Observables to structure our data is called *Reactive Programming*.

But what are Observables, and Reactive Programming anyway? Reactive Programming is a way to work with asynchronous streams of data. Observables are the main data structure we use to implement Reactive Programming. But I'll admit, those terms may not be that clarifying. So we'll look at concrete examples through the rest of this chapter that should be more enlightening.

Note: Some RxJS Knowledge Required

I want to point out **this book is not primarily about Reactive Programming**. There are several other good resources that can teach you the basics of Reactive Programming and you should read them. We've listed a few below.

Consider this chapter a tutorial on how to work with RxJS and Angular rather than an exhaustive introduction to RxJS and Reactive Programming.

In this chapter, I'll **explain in detail the RxJS concepts and APIs that we encounter**. But know that you may need to supplement the content here with other resources if RxJS is still new to you.

> **ℹ️ Use of Underscore.js in this chapter**
>
> Underscore.js[67] is a popular library that provides functional operators on JavaScript data structures such as `Array` and `Object`. We use it a bunch in this chapter alongside RxJS. If you see the `_` in code, such as `_.map` or `_.sortBy` know that we're using the Underscore.js library. You can find the docs for Underscore.js here[68].

Learning Reactive Programming and RxJS

If you're just learning RxJS I recommend that you read this article first:

---

[67] http://underscorejs.org/

[68] http://underscorejs.org/

- The introduction to Reactive Programming you've been missing[69] by Andre Staltz

After you've become a bit more familiar with the concepts behind RxJS, here are a few more links that can help you along the way:

- Which static operators to use to create streams?[70]
- Which instance operators to use on streams?[71]
- RxMarbles[72] - Interactive diagrams of the various operations on streams

Throughout this chapter I'll provide links to the API documentation of RxJS. The RxJS docs have tons of great example code that shed light on how the different streams and operators work.

> **Do I have to use RxJS to use Angular?** - No, you definitely don't. Observables are just one pattern out of many that you can use with Angular. We talk more about other data patterns you can use here.

I want to give you fair warning: learning RxJS can be a bit mind-bending at first. But trust me, you'll get the hang of it and it's worth it. Here's a few big ideas about streams that you might find helpful:

1. **Promises emit a single value whereas streams emit many values.** - Streams fulfill the same role in your application as promises. If you've made the jump from callbacks to promises, you know that promises are a big improvement in readability and data maintenance vs. callbacks. In the same way, streams improve upon the promise pattern in that we can continuously respond to data changes on a stream (vs. a one-time resolve from a promise)
2. **Imperative code "pulls" data whereas reactive streams "push" data** - In Reactive Programming our code subscribes to be notified of changes and the streams "push" data to these subscribers
3. **RxJS is *functional*** - If you're a fan of functional operators like `map`, `reduce`, and `filter` then you'll feel right at home with RxJS because streams are, in some sense, lists and so the powerful functional operators all apply
4. **Streams are composable** - Think of streams like a pipeline of operations over your data. You can subscribe to any part of your stream and even combine them to create new streams

---

[69] https://gist.github.com/staltz/868e7e9bc2a7b8c1f754

[70] https://github.com/Reactive-Extensions/RxJS/blob/master/doc/gettingstarted/which-static.md

[71] https://github.com/Reactive-Extensions/RxJS/blob/master/doc/gettingstarted/which-instance.md

[72] http://rxmarbles.com

Chat App Overview

In this chapter, we're going to use RxJS to build a chat app. Here's a screenshot:

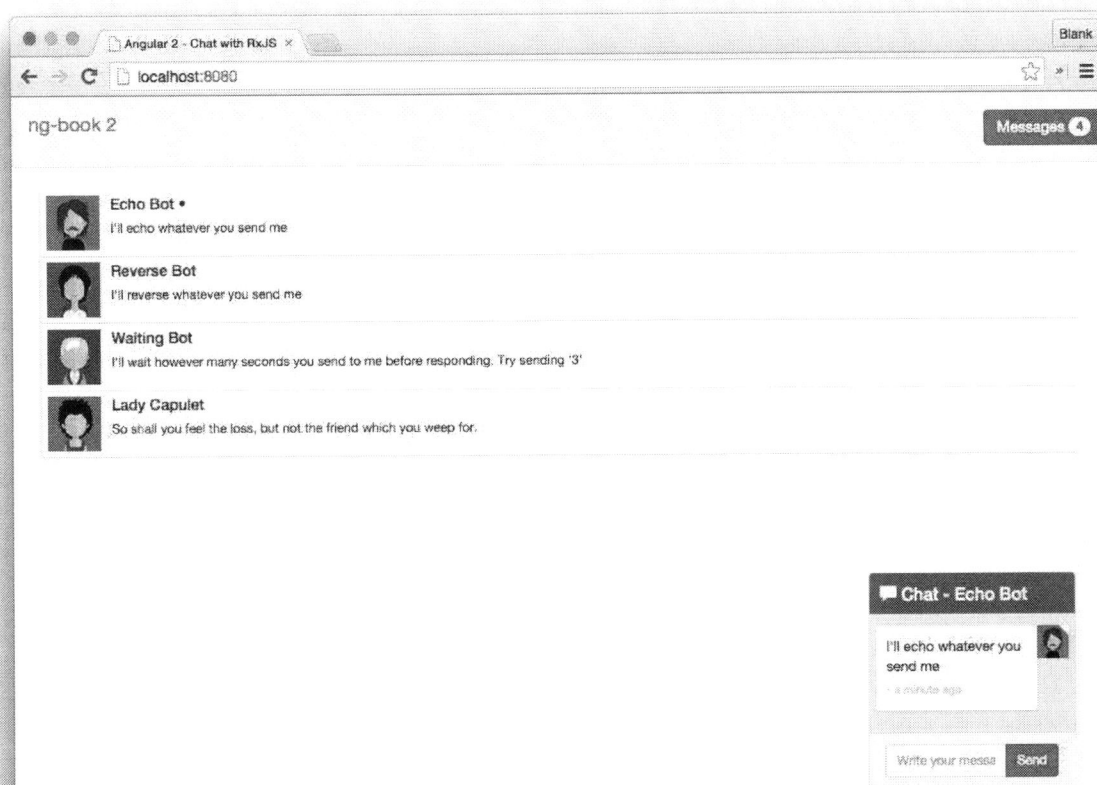

Completed Chat Application

> Usually we try to show every line of code here in the book text. However, this chat application has a lot of moving parts, so in this chapter we're not going to have every single line of code in the text. You can find the sample code for this chapter in the folder `code/rxjs/rxjs-chat`. We'll call out each filter where you can view the context, where appropriate.

In this application we've provided a few bots you can chat with. Open up the code and try it out:

```
1   cd code/rxjs/rxjs-chat
2   npm install
3   npm start
```

Now open your browser to `http://localhost:4200`.

Notice a few things about this application:

- You can click on the threads to chat with another person
- The bots will send you messages back, depending on their personality
- The unread message count in the top corner stays in sync with the number of unread messages

Let's look at an overview of how this app is constructed. We have

- 3 top-level Angular Components
- 3 models
- and 3 services

Let's look at them one at a time.

Components

The page is broken down into three top-level components:

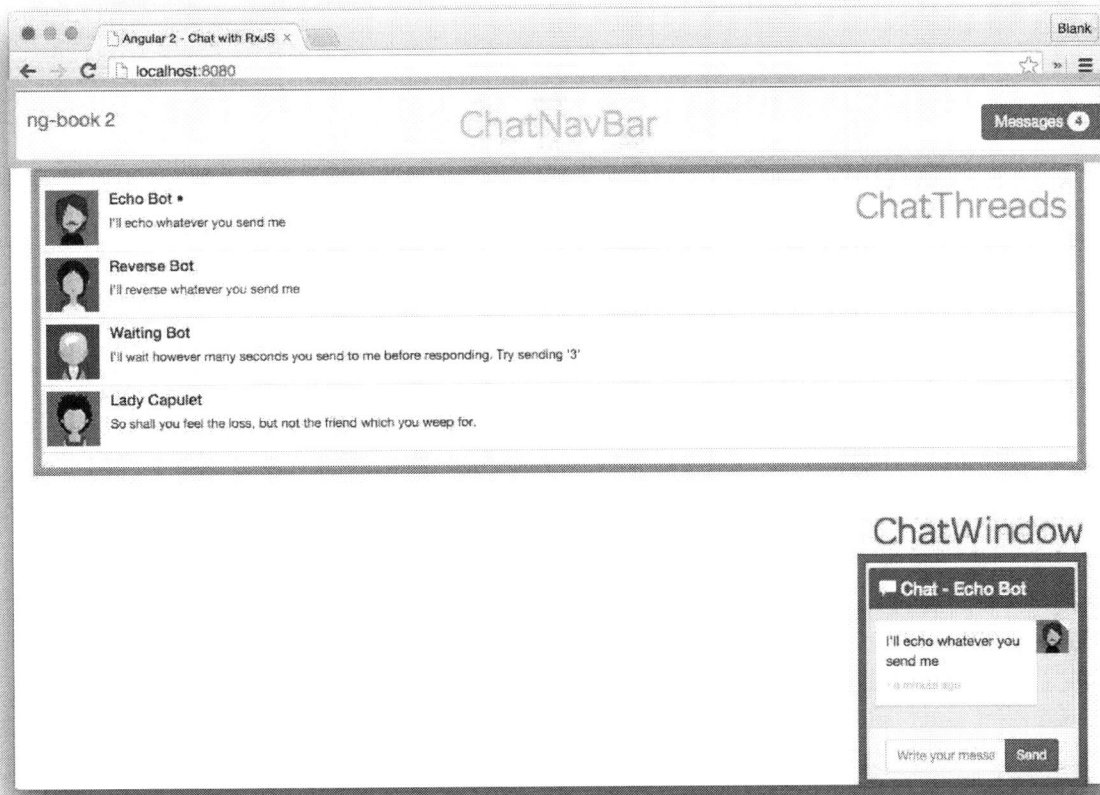

Chat Top-Level Components

- `ChatNavBarComponent` - contains the unread messages count
- `ChatThreadsComponent` - shows a clickable list of threads, along with the most recent message and the conversation avatar
- `ChatWindowComponent` - shows the messages in the current thread with an input box to send new messages

Models

This application also has three models:

Chat Models

- `User` - stores information about a chat participant
- `Message` - stores an individual message
- `Thread` - stores a collection of `Messages` as well as some data about the conversation

Services

In this app, each of our models has a corresponding *service*. The services are singleton objects that play two roles:

1. **Provide streams** of data that our application can subscribe to
2. **Provide operations** to add or modify data

For instance, the `UsersService`:

- publishes a stream that emits the current user and
- offers a `setCurrentUser` function which will set the current user (that is, emit the current user from the `currentUser` stream)

Summary

At a high level, the application data architecture is straightforward:

- The **services** maintain streams which emit models (e.g. `Messages`)
- The **components** subscribe to those streams and render according to the most recent values

For instance, the `ChatThreads` component listens for the most recent list of threads from the `ThreadService` and the `ChatWindow` subscribes for the most recent list of messages.

In the rest of this chapter, we're going to go in-depth on how we implement this using Angular and RxJS. We'll start by implementing our models, then look at how we create Services to manage our streams, and then finally implement the Components.

Implementing the Models

Let's start with the easy stuff and take a look at the models.

User

Our User class is straightforward. We have an id, name, and avatarSrc.

code/rxjs/rxjs-chat/src/app/user/user.model.ts

```
1  import { uuid } from '../util/uuid';
2
3  /**
4   * A User represents an agent that sends messages
5   */
6  export class User {
7    id: string;
8
9    constructor(public name: string,
10               public avatarSrc: string) {
11     this.id = uuid();
12   }
13 }
```

> **ⓘ** Notice above that we're using a TypeScript shorthand in the constructor. When we say
> public name: string we're telling TypeScript that 1. we want name to be a public property
> on this class and 2. assign the argument value to that property when a new instance is
> created.

Thread

Similarly, Thread is also a straightforward TypeScript class:

code/rxjs/rxjs-chat/src/app/thread/thread.model.ts

```
1   import { Message } from '../message/message.model';
2   import { uuid } from '../util/uuid';
3
4   /**
5    * Thread represents a group of Users exchanging Messages
6    */
7   export class Thread {
8     id: string;
9     lastMessage: Message;
10    name: string;
11    avatarSrc: string;
12
13    constructor(id?: string,
14                name?: string,
15                avatarSrc?: string) {
16      this.id = id || uuid();
17      this.name = name;
18      this.avatarSrc = avatarSrc;
19    }
20  }
```

Note that we store a reference to the `lastMessage` in our `Thread`. This lets us show a preview of the most recent message in the threads list.

Message

`Message` is also a simple TypeScript class, however in this case we use a slightly different form of constructor:

code/rxjs/rxjs-chat/src/app/message/message.model.ts

```
1   import { User } from '../user/user.model';
2   import { Thread } from '../thread/thread.model';
3   import { uuid } from './../util/uuid';
4
5   /**
6    * Message represents one message being sent in a Thread
7    */
8   export class Message {
9     id: string;
```

```
10      sentAt: Date;
11      isRead: boolean;
12      author: User;
13      text: string;
14      thread: Thread;
15
16      constructor(obj?: any) {
17        this.id            = obj && obj.id          || uuid();
18        this.isRead        = obj && obj.isRead      || false;
19        this.sentAt        = obj && obj.sentAt      || new Date();
20        this.author        = obj && obj.author      || null;
21        this.text          = obj && obj.text        || null;
22        this.thread        = obj && obj.thread      || null;
23      }
24    }
```

The pattern you see here in the constructor allows us to simulate using keyword arguments in the constructor. Using this pattern, we can create a new `Message` using whatever data we have available and we don't have to worry about the order of the arguments. For instance we could do this:

```
1    let msg1 = new Message();
2
3    # or this
4
5    let msg2 = new Message({
6      text: "Hello Nate Murray!"
7    })
```

Now that we've looked at our models, let's take a look at our first service: the `UsersService`.

Implementing UsersService

The point of the `UsersService` is to provide a place where our application can learn about the current user and also notify the rest of the application if the current user changes.

The first thing we need to do is create a TypeScript class and add the `@Injectable` decorator.

code/rxjs/rxjs-chat/src/app/user/users.service.ts

```
10  export class UsersService {
11    // `currentUser` contains the current user
12    currentUser: Subject<User> = new BehaviorSubject<User>(null);
13
14    public setCurrentUser(newUser: User): void {
15      this.currentUser.next(newUser);
16    }
17  }
```

We make a class that we will be able to use as a dependency to other components in our application. Briefly, two benefits of dependency-injection are:

1. we let Angular handle the lifecycle of the object and
2. it's easier to test injected components.

We talk more about `@Injectable` in the chapter on dependency injection, but the result is that we can now inject other dependencies into our constructor like so:

```
1  class UsersService {
2    constructor(public someOtherService: SomeOtherService) {
3      // do something with `someOtherService` here
4    }
5  }
```

currentUser **stream**

Next we setup a stream which we will use to manage our current user:

code/rxjs/rxjs-chat/src/app/user/users.service.ts

```
12  currentUser: Subject<User> = new BehaviorSubject<User>(null);
```

There's a lot going on here, so let's break it down:

- We're defining an instance variable `currentUser` which is a `Subject` stream.
- Concretely, `currentUser` is a `BehaviorSubject` which will contain `User`.

- However, the first value of this stream is `null` (the constructor argument).

If you haven't worked with RxJS much, then you may not know what `Subject` or `BehaviorSubject` are. You can think of a `Subject` as a "read/write" stream.

> **ⓘ** Technically a `Subject`[73] inherits from both `Observable`[74] and `Observer`[75]

One consequence of streams is that, because messages are published immediately, a new subscriber risks missing the latest value of the stream. BehaviourSubject compensates for this.

`BehaviourSubject`[76] has a special property in that it **stores the last value**. Meaning that any subscriber to the stream will receive the latest value. This is great for us because it means that any part of our application can subscribe to the `UsersService.currentUser` stream and immediately know who the current user is.

Setting a new user

We need a way to publish a new user to the stream whenever the current user changes (e.g. logging in).

There's two ways we can expose an API for doing this:

1. Add new users to the stream directly:

The most straightforward way to update the current user is to have clients of the `UsersService` simply publish a new `User` directly to the stream like this:

```
1  UsersService.currentUser.subscribe((newUser) => {
2    console.log('New User is: ', newUser.name);
3  })
4
5  // => New User is: originalUserName
6
7  let u = new User('Nate', 'anImgSrc');
8  UsersService.currentUser.next(u);
9
10 // => New User is: Nate
```

---

[73] https://github.com/Reactive-Extensions/RxJS/blob/master/doc/api/subjects/subject.md
[74] https://github.com/Reactive-Extensions/RxJS/blob/master/doc/api/core/observable.md
[75] https://github.com/Reactive-Extensions/RxJS/blob/master/doc/api/core/observer.md
[76] https://github.com/Reactive-Extensions/RxJS/blob/master/doc/api/subjects/behaviorsubject.md

ⓘ   Note here that we use the next method on a Subject to push a new value to the stream

The pro here is that we're able to reuse the existing API from the stream, so we're not introducing any new code or APIs

2. Create a setCurrentUser(newUser: User) method

The other way we could update the current user is to create a helper method on the UsersService like this:

code/rxjs/rxjs-chat/src/app/user/users.service.ts

```
14    public setCurrentUser(newUser: User): void {
15      this.currentUser.next(newUser);
16    }
```

You'll notice that we're still using the next method on the currentUser stream, so why bother doing this?

Because there is value in decoupling the implementation of the currentUser from the implementation of the stream. By wrapping the next in the setCurrentUser call we give ourselves room to change the implementation of the UsersService without breaking our clients.

In this case, I wouldn't recommend one method very strongly over the other, but it can make a big difference on the maintainability of larger projects.

ⓘ   A third option could be to have the updates expose streams of their own (that is, a stream where we place the action of changing the current user). We explore this pattern in the MessagesService below.

UsersService.ts

Putting it together, our UsersService looks like this:

code/rxjs/rxjs-chat/src/app/user/users.service.ts

```
1   import { Injectable } from '@angular/core';
2   import { Subject, BehaviorSubject } from 'rxjs';
3   import { User } from './user.model';
4
5
6   /**
7    * UserService manages our current user
8    */
9   @Injectable()
10  export class UsersService {
11    // `currentUser` contains the current user
12    currentUser: Subject<User> = new BehaviorSubject<User>(null);
13
14    public setCurrentUser(newUser: User): void {
15      this.currentUser.next(newUser);
16    }
17  }
18
19  export const userServiceInjectables: Array<any> = [
20    UsersService
21  ];
```

The MessagesService

The MessagesService is the backbone of this application. In our app, all messages flow through the MessagesService.

Our MessagesService has much more sophisticated streams compared to our UsersService. There are five streams that make up our MessagesService: 3 "data management" streams and 2 "action" streams.

The three data management streams are:

- newMessages - emits each new Message only once
- messages - emits **an array** of the current Messages
- updates - performs operations on messages

the newMessages stream

newMessages is a Subject that will publish each new Message only once.

code/rxjs/rxjs-chat/src/app/message/messages.service.ts

```
14  export class MessagesService {
15    // a stream that publishes new messages only once
16    newMessages: Subject<Message> = new Subject<Message>();
```

If we want, we can define a helper method to add Messages to this stream:

code/rxjs/rxjs-chat/src/app/message/messages.service.ts

```
90    addMessage(message: Message): void {
91      this.newMessages.next(message);
92    }
```

It would also be helpful to have a stream that will get all of the messages from a thread that are not from a particular user. For instance, consider the Echo Bot:

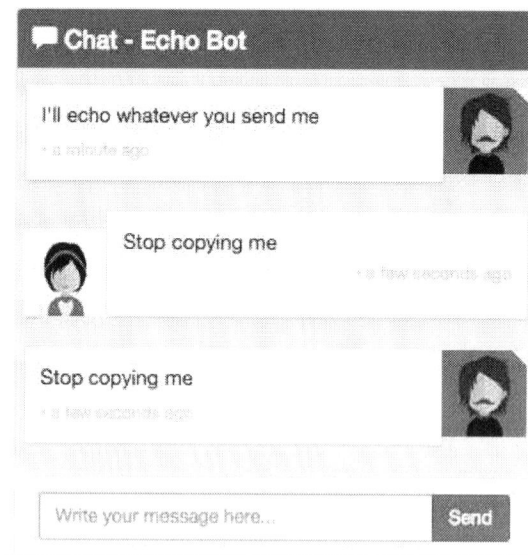

Real mature, Echo Bot

When we are implementing the Echo Bot, we don't want to enter an infinite loop and repeat back the bot's messages to itself.

To implement this we can subscribe to the newMessages stream and filter out all messages that are

1. part of this thread and
2. not written by the bot.

You can think of this as saying, for a given Thread I want a stream of the messages that are "for" this User.

```
94    messagesForThreadUser(thread: Thread, user: User): Observable<Message> {
95      return this.newMessages
96        .filter((message: Message) => {
97                // belongs to this thread
98          return (message.thread.id === thread.id) &&
99                // and isn't authored by this user
100               (message.author.id !== user.id);
101       });
102    }
```

messagesForThreadUser takes a Thread and a User and returns a new stream of Messages that are filtered on that Thread and not authored by the User. That is, it is a stream of "everyone else's" messages in this Thread.

the messages stream

Whereas newMessages emits individual Messages, the messages stream emits **an Array of the most recent Messages**.

```
19    messages: Observable<Message[]>;
```

> **ℹ** The type Message[] is the same as Array<Message>. Another way of writing the same thing would be: Observable<Array<Message>>. When we define the type of messages to be Observable<Message[]> we mean that this stream emits an **Array** (of Messages), not individual Messages.

So how does messages get populated? For that we need to talk about the updates stream and a new pattern: the Operation stream.

The Operation Stream Pattern

Here's the idea:

- We'll maintain state in messages which will hold an Array of the most current Messages
- We use an updates stream which is a **stream of functions** to apply to messages

You can think of it this way: any function that is put on the updates stream will change the list of the current messages. A function that is put on the updates stream should **accept a list of Messages** and then **return a list of Messages**. Let's formalize this idea by creating an interface in code:

code/rxjs/rxjs-chat/src/app/message/messages.service.ts

```
 9   interface IMessagesOperation extends Function {
10     (messages: Message[]): Message[];
11   }
```

Let's define our `updates` stream:

code/rxjs/rxjs-chat/src/app/message/messages.service.ts

```
21     // `updates` receives _operations_ to be applied to our `messages`
22     // it's a way we can perform changes on *all* messages (that are currently
23     // stored in `messages`)
24     updates: Subject<any> = new Subject<any>();
```

Remember, `updates` receives *operations* that will be applied to our list of messages. But how do we make that connection? We do (in the `constructor` of our `MessagesService`) like this:

code/rxjs/rxjs-chat/src/app/message/messages.service.ts

```
30     constructor() {
31       this.messages = this.updates
32         // watch the updates and accumulate operations on the messages
33         .scan((messages: Message[],
34                operation: IMessagesOperation) => {
35                  return operation(messages);
36                },
37                initialMessages)
38         // make sure we can share the most recent list of messages across anyone
```

This code introduces a new stream function: `scan`[77]. If you're familiar with functional programming, `scan` is a lot like `reduce`: it runs the function for each element in the incoming stream and **accumulates a value**. What's special about `scan` is that it will **emit a value for each intermediate result**. That is, it doesn't wait for the stream to complete before emitting a result, which is exactly what we want.

When we call `this.updates.scan`, we are creating a new stream that is subscribed to the `updates` stream. On each pass, we're given:

1. the `messages` we're accumulating and
2. the new `operation` to apply.

and then we return the new `Message[]`.

---

[77]https://github.com/Reactive-Extensions/RxJS/blob/master/doc/api/core/operators/scan.md

Sharing the Stream

One thing to know about streams is that they aren't shareable by default. That is, if one subscriber reads a value from a stream, it can be gone forever. In the case of our messages, we want to 1. share the same stream among many subscribers and 2. replay the last value for any subscribers who come "late".

To do that, we use two operators: `publishReplay` and `refCount`.

- `publishReplay` let's us share a subscription between multiple subscribers and replay *n* number of values to future subscribers. (see `publish`[78] and `replay`[79])
- `refCount`[80] - makes it easier to use the return value of publish, by managing when the observable will emit values

> **Wait, so what does `refCount` do?**
>
> `refCount` can be a little tricky to understand because it relates to how one manages "hot" and "cold" observables. We're not going to dive deep into explaining how this works and we direct the reader to:
>
> - RxJS docs on `refCount`[81]
> - Introduction to Rx: Hot and Cold observables[82]
> - RefCount Marble Diagram[83]

code/rxjs/rxjs-chat/src/app/message/messages.service.ts

```
32    // watch the updates and accumulate operations on the messages
33    .scan((messages: Message[],
34        operation: IMessagesOperation) => {
35            return operation(messages);
36        },
37        initialMessages)
38    // make sure we can share the most recent list of messages across anyone
39    // who's interested in subscribing and cache the last known list of
40    // messages
41    .publishReplay(1)
42    .refCount();
```

[78] https://github.com/Reactive-Extensions/RxJS/blob/master/doc/api/core/operators/publish.md
[79] https://github.com/Reactive-Extensions/RxJS/blob/master/doc/api/core/operators/replay.md
[80] https://github.com/Reactive-Extensions/RxJS/blob/master/doc/api/core/operators/refcount.md
[81] https://github.com/Reactive-Extensions/RxJS/blob/master/doc/api/core/operators/refcount.md
[82] http://www.introtorx.com/Content/v1.0.10621.0/14_HotAndColdObservables.html#RefCount
[83] http://reactivex.io/documentation/operators/refcount.html

Adding Messages to the messages Stream

Now we could add a Message to the messages stream like so:

```
1  var myMessage = new Message(/* params here... */);
2
3  updates.next( (messages: Message[]): Message[] => {
4    return messages.concat(myMessage);
5  })
```

Above, we're adding an operation to the updates stream. The effect is that messages is "subscribed" to that stream and so it will apply that operation which will concat our newMessage on to the accumulated list of messages.

> ℹ️ It's okay if this takes a few minutes to mull over. It can feel a little foreign if you're not used to this style of programming.

One problem with the above approach is that it's a bit verbose to use. It would be nice to not have to write that inner function every time. We could do something like this:

```
1  addMessage(newMessage: Message) {
2    updates.next( (messages: Message[]): Message[] => {
3      return messages.concat(newMessage);
4    })
5  }
6
7  // somewhere else
8
9  var myMessage = new Message(/* params here... */);
10 MessagesService.addMessage(myMessage);
```

This is a little bit better, but it's not "the reactive way". In part, because this action of creating a message isn't composable with other streams. (Also this method is circumventing our newMessages stream. More on that later.)

A reactive way of creating a new message would be **to have a stream that accepts Messages to add to the list**. Again, this can be a bit new if you're not used to thinking this way. Here's how you'd implement it:

First we make an "action stream" called create. (The term "action stream" is only meant to describe its role in our service. The stream itself is still a regular Subject):

279

code/rxjs/rxjs-chat/src/app/message/messages.service.ts

```
26    // action streams
27    create: Subject<Message> = new Subject<Message>();
```

Next, in our constructor we configure the create stream:

code/rxjs/rxjs-chat/src/app/message/messages.service.ts

```
58    this.create
59      .map( function(message: Message): IMessagesOperation {
60        return (messages: Message[]) => {
61          return messages.concat(message);
62        };
63      })
```

The map[84] operator is a lot like the built-in Array.map function in JavaScript except that it works on streams. That is, it runs the function once for each item in the stream and emits the return value of the function.

In this case, we're saying "for each Message we receive as input, return an IMessagesOperation that adds this message to the list". Put another way, this stream will emit a **function** which accepts the list of Messages and adds this Message to our list of messages.

Now that we have the create stream, we still have one thing left to do: we need to actually hook it up to the updates stream. We do that by using subscribe[85].

code/rxjs/rxjs-chat/src/app/message/messages.service.ts

```
58    this.create
59      .map( function(message: Message): IMessagesOperation {
60        return (messages: Message[]) => {
61          return messages.concat(message);
62        };
63      })
64      .subscribe(this.updates);
```

What we're doing here is *subscribing* the updates stream to listen to the create stream. This means that if create receives a Message it will emit an IMessagesOperation that will be received by updates and then the Message will be added to messages.

Here's a diagram that shows our current situation:

---

[84]https://github.com/Reactive-Extensions/RxJS/blob/master/doc/api/core/operators/select.md

[85]https://github.com/Reactive-Extensions/RxJS/blob/master/doc/api/core/operators/subscribe.md

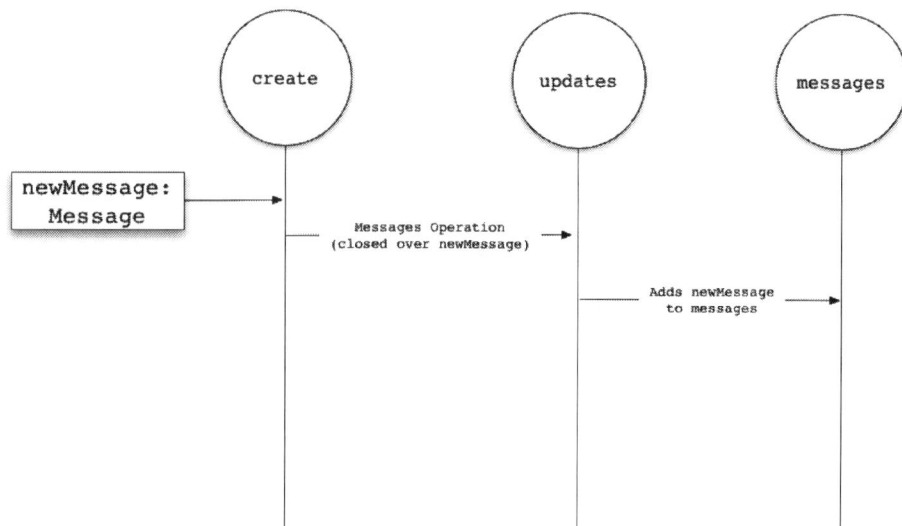

Creating a new message, starting with the `create` stream

This is great because it means we get a few things:

1. The current list of messages from `messages`
2. A way to process operations on the current list of messages (via `updates`)
3. An easy-to-use stream to put create operations on our `updates` stream (via `create`)

Anywhere in our code, if we want to get the most current list of messages, we just have to go to the `messages` stream. But we have a problem, **we still haven't connected this flow to the `newMessages` stream**.

It would be great if we had a way to easily connect this stream with any `Message` that comes from `newMessages`. It turns out, it's really easy:

`code/rxjs/rxjs-chat/src/app/message/messages.service.ts`

```
66      this.newMessages
67          .subscribe(this.create);
```

Now our diagram looks like this:

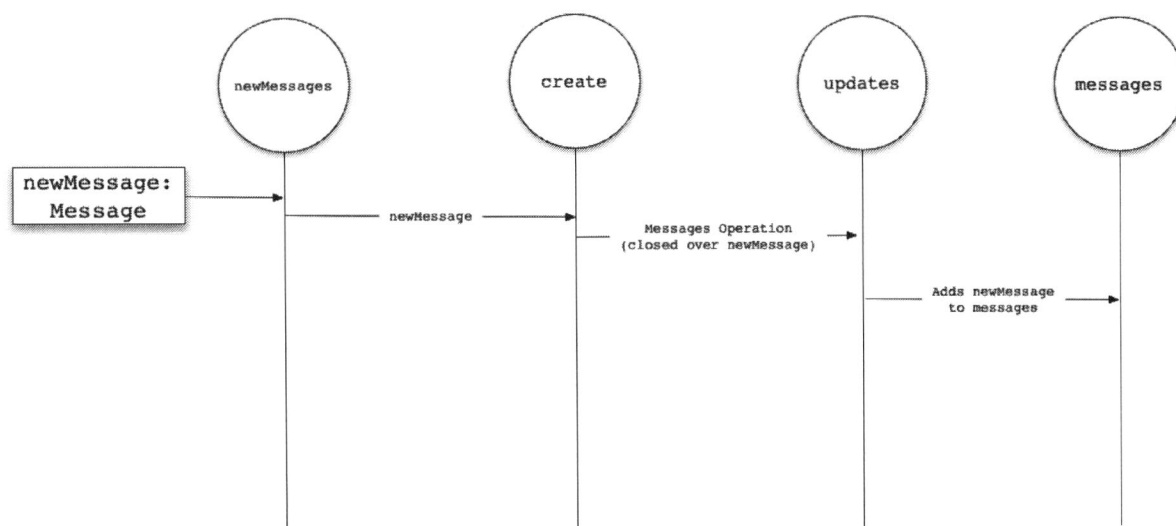

Creating a new message, starting with the newMessages stream

Now our flow is complete! It's the best of both worlds: we're able to subscribe to the stream of individual messages through newMessages, but if we just want the most up-to-date list, we can subscribe to messages.

It's worth pointing out some implications of this design: if you subscribe to newMessages directly, you have to be careful about changes that may happen downstream. Here are three things to consider:

First, you obviously won't get any downstream updates that are applied to the Messages.

Second, in this case, we have **mutable** Message objects. So if you subscribe to newMessages and store a reference to a Message, that Message's attributes may change.

Third, in the case where you want to take advantage of the mutability of our Messages you may not be able to. Consider the case where we could put an operation on the updates queue that makes a copy of each Message and then mutates the copy. (This is probably a better design than what we're doing here.) In this case, you couldn't rely on any Message emitted directly from newMessages being in its "final" state.

That said, as long as you keep these considerations in mind, you shouldn't have too much trouble.

Our completed MessagesService

Here's what the completed MessagesService looks like:

code/rxjs/rxjs-chat/src/app/message/messages.service.ts

```
1   import { Injectable } from '@angular/core';
2   import { Subject, Observable } from 'rxjs';
3   import { User } from '../user/user.model';
4   import { Thread } from '../thread/thread.model';
5   import { Message } from '../message/message.model';
6
7   const initialMessages: Message[] = [];
8
9   interface IMessagesOperation extends Function {
10    (messages: Message[]): Message[];
11  }
12
13  @Injectable()
14  export class MessagesService {
15    // a stream that publishes new messages only once
16    newMessages: Subject<Message> = new Subject<Message>();
17
18    // `messages` is a stream that emits an array of the most up to date messages
19    messages: Observable<Message[]>;
20
21    // `updates` receives _operations_ to be applied to our `messages`
22    // it's a way we can perform changes on *all* messages (that are currently
23    // stored in `messages`)
24    updates: Subject<any> = new Subject<any>();
25
26    // action streams
27    create: Subject<Message> = new Subject<Message>();
28    markThreadAsRead: Subject<any> = new Subject<any>();
29
30    constructor() {
31      this.messages = this.updates
32        // watch the updates and accumulate operations on the messages
33        .scan((messages: Message[],
34               operation: IMessagesOperation) => {
35                 return operation(messages);
36               },
37               initialMessages)
38        // make sure we can share the most recent list of messages across anyone
39        // who's interested in subscribing and cache the last known list of
40        // messages
41        .publishReplay(1)
```

```
42        .refCount();
43
44     // `create` takes a Message and then puts an operation (the inner function)
45     // on the `updates` stream to add the Message to the list of messages.
46     //
47     // That is, for each item that gets added to `create` (by using `next`)
48     // this stream emits a concat operation function.
49     //
50     // Next we subscribe `this.updates` to listen to this stream, which means
51     // that it will receive each operation that is created
52     //
53     // Note that it would be perfectly acceptable to simply modify the
54     // "addMessage" function below to simply add the inner operation function to
55     // the update stream directly and get rid of this extra action stream
56     // entirely. The pros are that it is potentially clearer. The cons are that
57     // the stream is no longer composable.
58     this.create
59       .map( function(message: Message): IMessagesOperation {
60         return (messages: Message[]) => {
61           return messages.concat(message);
62         };
63       })
64       .subscribe(this.updates);
65
66     this.newMessages
67       .subscribe(this.create);
68
69     // similarly, `markThreadAsRead` takes a Thread and then puts an operation
70     // on the `updates` stream to mark the Messages as read
71     this.markThreadAsRead
72       .map( (thread: Thread) => {
73         return (messages: Message[]) => {
74           return messages.map( (message: Message) => {
75             // note that we're manipulating `message` directly here. Mutability
76             // can be confusing and there are lots of reasons why you might want
77             // to, say, copy the Message object or some other 'immutable' here
78             if (message.thread.id === thread.id) {
79               message.isRead = true;
80             }
81             return message;
82           });
83         };
```

```
84          })
85        .subscribe(this.updates);
86
87    }
88
89    // an imperative function call to this action stream
90    addMessage(message: Message): void {
91      this.newMessages.next(message);
92    }
93
94    messagesForThreadUser(thread: Thread, user: User): Observable<Message> {
95      return this.newMessages
96        .filter((message: Message) => {
97                  // belongs to this thread
98          return (message.thread.id === thread.id) &&
99                  // and isn't authored by this user
100                 (message.author.id !== user.id);
101      });
102    }
103 }
104
105 export const messagesServiceInjectables: Array<any> = [
106   MessagesService
107 ];
```

Trying out MessagesService

If you haven't already, this would be a good time to open up the code and play around with the MessagesService to get a feel for how it works. We've got an example you can start with in code/rxjs/rxjs-chat/src/app/message/messages.service.spec.ts.

> ⓘ   To run the tests in this project, open up your terminal then:
>
> ```
> 1   cd /path/to/code/rxjs/rxjs-chat // <-- your path will vary
> 2   npm install
> 3   npm run test
> ```

Let's start by creating a few instances of our models to use:

code/rxjs/rxjs-chat/src/app/message/messages.service.spec.ts

```
1   import { MessagesService } from './messages.service';
2
3   import { Message } from './message.model';
4   import { Thread } from './../thread/thread.model';
5   import { User } from './../user/user.model';
6
7   describe('MessagesService', () => {
8     it('should test', () => {
9
10      const user: User = new User('Nate', '');
11      const thread: Thread = new Thread('t1', 'Nate', '');
12      const m1: Message = new Message({
13        author: user,
14        text: 'Hi!',
15        thread: thread
16      });
17
18      const m2: Message = new Message({
19        author: user,
20        text: 'Bye!',
21        thread: thread
22      });
```

Next let's subscribe to a couple of our streams:

code/rxjs/rxjs-chat/src/app/message/messages.service.spec.ts

```
24      const messagesService: MessagesService = new MessagesService();
25
26      // listen to each message indivdually as it comes in
27      messagesService.newMessages
28        .subscribe( (message: Message) => {
29          console.log('=> newMessages: ' + message.text);
30        });
31
32      // listen to the stream of most current messages
33      messagesService.messages
34        .subscribe( (messages: Message[]) => {
35          console.log('=> messages: ' + messages.length);
36        });
37
```

```
38        messagesService.addMessage(m1);
39        messagesService.addMessage(m2);
40
41        // => messages: 1
42        // => newMessages: Hi!
43        // => messages: 2
44        // => newMessages: Bye!
45    });
46
47
48  });
```

Notice that even though we subscribed to newMessages first and newMessages is called directly by addMessage, our messages subscription is logged first. The reason for this is because messages subscribed to newMessages earlier than our subscription in this test (when MessagesService was instantiated). (You shouldn't be relying on the ordering of independent streams in your code, but why it works this way is worth thinking about.)

Play around with the MessagesService and get a feel for the streams there. We're going to be using them in the next section where we build the ThreadsService.

The ThreadsService

On our ThreadsService were going to define four streams that emit respectively:

1. A map of the current set of Threads (in threads)
2. A chronological list of Threads, newest-first (in orderedthreads)
3. The currently selected Thread (in currentThread)
4. The list of Messages for the currently selected Thread (in currentThreadMessages)

Let's walk through how to build each of these streams, and we'll learn a little more about RxJS along the way.

A map of the current set of Threads (in threads)

Let's start by defining our ThreadsService class and the instance variable that will emit the Threads:

code/rxjs/rxjs-chat/src/app/thread/threads.service.ts

```
1  import { Injectable } from '@angular/core';
2  import { Subject, BehaviorSubject, Observable } from 'rxjs/Rx';
3  import { Thread } from './thread.model';
4  import { Message } from '../message/message.model';
5  import { MessagesService } from '../message/messages.service';
6  import * as _ from 'lodash';
7
8  @Injectable()
9  export class ThreadsService {
10
11    // `threads` is a observable that contains the most up to date list of threads
12    threads: Observable<{ [key: string]: Thread }>;
```

Notice that this stream will emit a map (an object) with the id of the Thread being the string key and the Thread itself will be the value.

To create a stream that maintains the current list of threads, we start by attaching to the messagesService.messages stream:

code/rxjs/rxjs-chat/src/app/thread/threads.service.ts

```
12    threads: Observable<{ [key: string]: Thread }>;
```

Recall that each time a new Message is added to the steam, messages will emit an array of the current Messages. We're going to look at each Message and we want to return a unique list of the Threads.

code/rxjs/rxjs-chat/src/app/thread/threads.service.ts

```
27      this.threads = messagesService.messages
28        .map( (messages: Message[]) => {
29          const threads: {[key: string]: Thread} = {};
30          // Store the message's thread in our accumulator `threads`
31          messages.map((message: Message) => {
32            threads[message.thread.id] = threads[message.thread.id] ||
33              message.thread;
```

Notice above that each time we will create a new list of threads. The reason for this is because we might delete some messages down the line (e.g. leave the conversation). Because we're recalculating the list of threads each time, we naturally will "delete" a thread if it has no messages.

In the threads list, we want to show a preview of the chat by using the text of the most recent Message in that Thread.

List of Threads with Chat Preview

In order to do that, we'll store the most recent Message for each Thread. We know which Message is newest by comparing the sentAt times:

code/rxjs/rxjs-chat/src/app/thread/threads.service.ts

```
34            // Cache the most recent message for each thread
35            const messagesThread: Thread = threads[message.thread.id];
36            if (!messagesThread.lastMessage ||
37                messagesThread.lastMessage.sentAt < message.sentAt) {
38              messagesThread.lastMessage = message;
39            }
40          });
41        return threads;
42      });
```

Putting it all together, threads looks like this:

code/rxjs/rxjs-chat/src/app/thread/threads.service.ts

```
27    this.threads = messagesService.messages
28      .map( (messages: Message[]) => {
29        const threads: {[key: string]: Thread} = {};
30        // Store the message's thread in our accumulator `threads`
31        messages.map((message: Message) => {
32          threads[message.thread.id] = threads[message.thread.id] ||
33            message.thread;
34
35            // Cache the most recent message for each thread
```

```
36            const messagesThread: Thread = threads[message.thread.id];
37            if (!messagesThread.lastMessage ||
38                messagesThread.lastMessage.sentAt < message.sentAt) {
39              messagesThread.lastMessage = message;
40            }
41          });
42          return threads;
43        });
```

Trying out the ThreadsService

Let's try out our ThreadsService. First we'll create a few models to work with:

code/rxjs/rxjs-chat/src/app/thread/threads.service.spec.ts

```
1   import { Message } from './../message/message.model';
2   import { Thread } from './thread.model';
3   import { User } from './../user/user.model';
4
5   import { ThreadsService } from './threads.service';
6   import { MessagesService } from './../message/messages.service';
7   import * as _ from 'lodash';
8
9   describe('ThreadsService', () => {
10    it('should collect the Threads from Messages', () => {
11
12      const nate: User = new User('Nate Murray', '');
13      const felipe: User = new User('Felipe Coury', '');
14
15      const t1: Thread = new Thread('t1', 'Thread 1', '');
16      const t2: Thread = new Thread('t2', 'Thread 2', '');
17
18      const m1: Message = new Message({
19        author: nate,
20        text: 'Hi!',
21        thread: t1
22      });
23
24      const m2: Message = new Message({
25        author: felipe,
26        text: 'Where did you get that hat?',
27        thread: t1
28      });
```

```
29
30     const m3: Message = new Message({
31       author: nate,
32       text: 'Did you bring the briefcase?',
33       thread: t2
34     });
```

Now let's create an instance of our services:

code/rxjs/rxjs-chat/src/app/thread/threads.service.spec.ts

```
36     const messagesService: MessagesService = new MessagesService();
37     const threadsService: ThreadsService = new ThreadsService(messagesService);
```

> Notice here that we're passing `messagesService` as an argument to the constructor of our
> `ThreadsService`. Normally we let the Dependency Injection system handle this for us. But
> in our test, we can provide the dependencies ourselves.

Let's subscribe to `threads` and log out what comes through:

code/rxjs/rxjs-chat/src/app/thread/threads.service.spec.ts

```
37     const threadsService: ThreadsService = new ThreadsService(messagesService);
38
39     threadsService.threads
40       .subscribe( (threadIdx: { [key: string]: Thread }) => {
41         const threads: Thread[] = _.values(threadIdx);
42         const threadNames: string = _.map(threads, (t: Thread) => t.name)
43                                       .join(', ');
44         console.log(`=> threads (${threads.length}): ${threadNames} `);
45       });
46
47     messagesService.addMessage(m1);
48     messagesService.addMessage(m2);
49     messagesService.addMessage(m3);
50
51     // => threads (1): Thread 1
52     // => threads (1): Thread 1
53     // => threads (2): Thread 1, Thread 2
54
55   });
56 });
```

A chronological list of Thread**s, newest-first (in** orderedthreads**)**

threads gives us a map which acts as an "index" of our list of threads. But we want the threads view to be ordered according to the most recent message.

Echo Bot •
I'll echo whatever you send me

Reverse Bot
I'll reverse whatever you send me

Waiting Bot
I'll wait however many seconds you send
to me before responding. Try sending '3'

Lady Capulet
So shall you feel the loss, but not the
friend which you weep for.

Time Ordered List of Threads

Let's create a new stream that returns an Array of Threads ordered by the most recent Message time: We'll start by defining orderedThreads as an instance property:

code/rxjs/rxjs-chat/src/app/thread/threads.service.ts

```
14    // `orderedThreads` contains a newest-first chronological list of threads
15    orderedThreads: Observable<Thread[]>;
```

Next, in the constructor we'll define orderedThreads by subscribing to threads and ordered by the most recent message:

code/rxjs/rxjs-chat/src/app/thread/threads.service.ts

```
45    this.orderedThreads = this.threads
46      .map((threadGroups: { [key: string]: Thread }) => {
47        const threads: Thread[] = _.values(threadGroups);
48        return _.sortBy(threads, (t: Thread) => t.lastMessage.sentAt).reverse();
49      });
```

The currently selected Thread **(in** currentThread**)**

Our application needs to know which Thread is the currently selected thread. This lets us know:

1. which thread should be shown in the messages window
2. which thread should be marked as the current thread in the list of threads

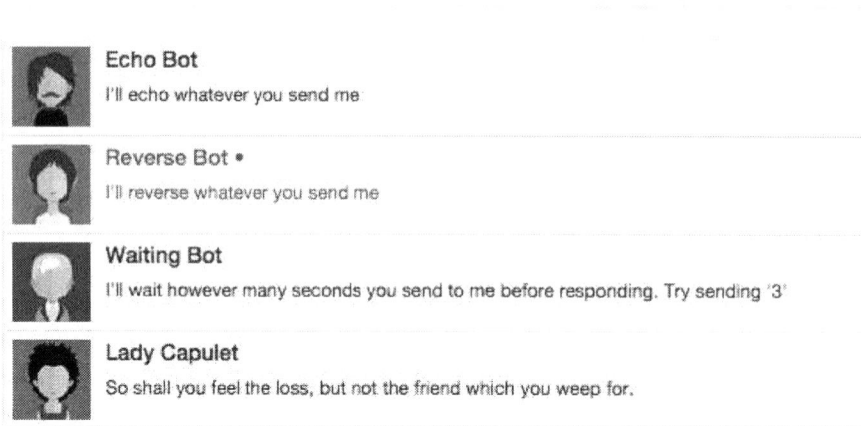

Echo Bot
I'll echo whatever you send me

Reverse Bot •
I'll reverse whatever you send me

Waiting Bot
I'll wait however many seconds you send to me before responding. Try sending '3'

Lady Capulet
So shall you feel the loss, but not the friend which you weep for.

The current thread is marked by a dot symbol

Let's create a BehaviorSubject that will store the currentThread:

code/rxjs/rxjs-chat/src/app/thread/threads.service.ts

```
17    // `currentThread` contains the currently selected thread
18    currentThread: Subject<Thread> =
19      new BehaviorSubject<Thread>(new Thread());
```

Notice that we're issuing an empty Thread as the default value. We don't need to configure the currentThread any further.

Setting the Current Thread

To set the current thread we can have clients either

1. submit new threads via next directly or
2. add a helper method to do it.

Let's define a helper method setCurrentThread that we can use to set the next thread:

code/rxjs/rxjs-chat/src/app/thread/threads.service.ts

```
70    setCurrentThread(newThread: Thread): void {
71      this.currentThread.next(newThread);
72    }
```

Marking the Current Thread as Read

We want to keep track of the number of unread messages. If we switch to a new Thread then we want to mark all of the Messages in that Thread as read. We have the parts we need to do this:

1. The messagesService.markThreadAsRead accepts a Thread and then will mark all Messages in that Thread as read
2. Our currentThread emits a single Thread that represents the current Thread

So all we need to do is hook them together:

code/rxjs/rxjs-chat/src/app/thread/threads.service.ts

```
67      this.currentThread.subscribe(this.messagesService.markThreadAsRead);
```

The list of Messages for the currently selected Thread (in currentThreadMessages)

Now that we have the currently selected thread, we need to make sure we can show the list of Messages in that Thread.

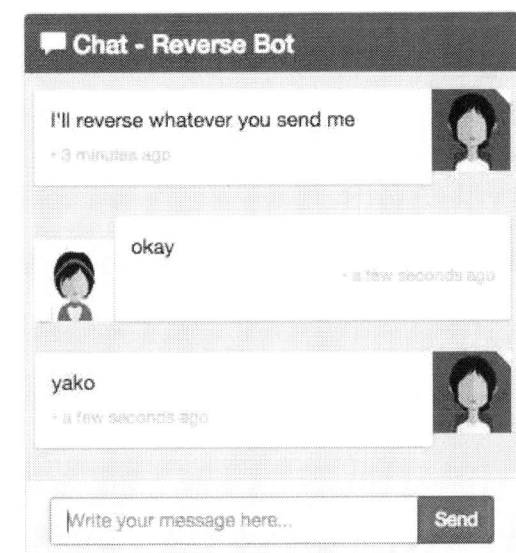

The current list of messages is for the Reverse Bot

Implementing this is a little bit more complicated than it may seem at the surface. Say we implemented it like this:

```
1   var theCurrentThread: Thread;
2
3   this.currentThread.subscribe((thread: Thread) => {
4     theCurrentThread = thread;
5   })
6
7   this.currentThreadMessages.map(
8     (messages: Message[]) => {
9       return _.filter(messages,
10        (message: Message) => {
11          return message.thread.id == theCurrentThread.id;
12        })
13    })
```

What's wrong with this approach? Well, if the currentThread changes, currentThreadMessages won't know about it and so we'll have an outdated list of currentThreadMessages!

What if we reversed it, and stored the current list of messages in a variable and subscribed to the changing of currentThread? We'd have the same problem only this time we would know when the thread changes but not when a new message came in.

How can we solve this problem?

It turns out, RxJS has a set of operators that we can use to **combine multiple streams**. In this case we want to say "if *either* currentThread **or** messagesService.messages changes, then we want to emit something." For this we use the combineLatest[86] operator.

code/rxjs/rxjs-chat/src/app/thread/threads.service.ts

```
51      this.currentThreadMessages = this.currentThread
52        .combineLatest(messagesService.messages,
53                  (currentThread: Thread, messages: Message[]) => {
```

When we're combining two streams one or the other will arrive first and there's no guarantee that we'll have a value on both streams, so we need to check to make sure we have what we need otherwise we'll just return an empty list.

Now that we have both the current thread and messages, we can filter out just the messages we're interested in:

---

[86]https://github.com/Reactive-Extensions/RxJS/blob/master/doc/api/core/operators/combinelatestproto.md

code/rxjs/rxjs-chat/src/app/thread/threads.service.ts

```
51      this.currentThreadMessages = this.currentThread
52        .combineLatest(messagesService.messages,
53                      (currentThread: Thread, messages: Message[]) => {
54        if (currentThread && messages.length > 0) {
55          return _.chain(messages)
56            .filter((message: Message) =>
57                    (message.thread.id === currentThread.id))
```

One other detail, since we're already looking at the messages for the current thread, this is a convenient area to mark these messages as read.

code/rxjs/rxjs-chat/src/app/thread/threads.service.ts

```
55          return _.chain(messages)
56            .filter((message: Message) =>
57                    (message.thread.id === currentThread.id))
58            .map((message: Message) => {
59              message.isRead = true;
60              return message; })
61            .value();
```

⚠️ Whether or not we should be marking messages as read here is debatable. The biggest drawback is that we're mutating objects in what is, essentially, a "read" thread. i.e. this is a read operation with a side effect, which is generally a Bad Idea. That said, in this application the `currentThreadMessages` only applies to the `currentThread` and the `currentThread` should always have its messages marked as read. That said, the "read with side-effects" is not a pattern I recommend in general.

Putting it together, here's what `currentThreadMessages` looks like:

code/rxjs/rxjs-chat/src/app/thread/threads.service.ts

```
51      this.currentThreadMessages = this.currentThread
52        .combineLatest(messagesService.messages,
53                      (currentThread: Thread, messages: Message[]) => {
54        if (currentThread && messages.length > 0) {
55          return _.chain(messages)
56            .filter((message: Message) =>
57                    (message.thread.id === currentThread.id))
58            .map((message: Message) => {
```

```
59              message.isRead = true;
60               return message; })
61           .value();
62       } else {
63         return [];
64       }
65     });
```

Our Completed ThreadsService

Here's what our ThreadsService looks like:

code/rxjs/rxjs-chat/src/app/thread/threads.service.ts

```
1  import { Injectable } from '@angular/core';
2  import { Subject, BehaviorSubject, Observable } from 'rxjs/Rx';
3  import { Thread } from './thread.model';
4  import { Message } from '../message/message.model';
5  import { MessagesService } from '../message/messages.service';
6  import * as _ from 'lodash';
7
8  @Injectable()
9  export class ThreadsService {
10
11   // `threads` is a observable that contains the most up to date list of threads
12   threads: Observable<{ [key: string]: Thread }>;
13
14   // `orderedThreads` contains a newest-first chronological list of threads
15   orderedThreads: Observable<Thread[]>;
16
17   // `currentThread` contains the currently selected thread
18   currentThread: Subject<Thread> =
19     new BehaviorSubject<Thread>(new Thread());
20
21   // `currentThreadMessages` contains the set of messages for the currently
     // selected thread
     currentThreadMessages: Observable<Message[]>;

     constructor(public messagesService: MessagesService) {

       this.threads = messagesService.messages
         .map( (messages: Message[]) => {
           const threads: {[key: string]: Thread} = {};
```

```
30        // Store the message's thread in our accumulator `threads`
31        messages.map((message: Message) => {
32          threads[message.thread.id] = threads[message.thread.id] ||
33            message.thread;
34
35          // Cache the most recent message for each thread
36          const messagesThread: Thread = threads[message.thread.id];
37          if (!messagesThread.lastMessage ||
38              messagesThread.lastMessage.sentAt < message.sentAt) {
39            messagesThread.lastMessage = message;
40          }
41        });
42        return threads;
43      });
44
45    this.orderedThreads = this.threads
46      .map((threadGroups: { [key: string]: Thread }) => {
47        const threads: Thread[] = _.values(threadGroups);
48        return _.sortBy(threads, (t: Thread) => t.lastMessage.sentAt).reverse();
49      });
50
51    this.currentThreadMessages = this.currentThread
52      .combineLatest(messagesService.messages,
53                     (currentThread: Thread, messages: Message[]) => {
54        if (currentThread && messages.length > 0) {
55          return _.chain(messages)
56            .filter((message: Message) =>
57                    (message.thread.id === currentThread.id))
58            .map((message: Message) => {
59              message.isRead = true;
60              return message; })
61            .value();
62        } else {
63          return [];
64        }
65      });
66
67    this.currentThread.subscribe(this.messagesService.markThreadAsRead);
68  }
69
70  setCurrentThread(newThread: Thread): void {
71    this.currentThread.next(newThread);
```

```
72      }
73
74   }
75
76   export const threadsServiceInjectables: Array<any> = [
77     ThreadsService
78   ];
```

Data Model Summary

Our data model and services are complete! Now we have everything we need now to start hooking it up to our view components! In the next chapter we'll build out our 3 major components to render and interact with these streams.

Data Architecture with Observables - Part 2: View Components

Building Our Views: The AppComponent Top-Level Component

Let's turn our attention to our app and implement our view components.

> **ⓘ** For the sake of clarity and space, in the following sections I'll be leaving out some import statements, CSS, and a few other similar lines of code. If you're curious about each line of those details, open up the sample code because it contains everything we need to run this app.

The first thing we're going to do is create our top-level component chat-app

As we talked about earlier, the page is broken down into three top-level components:

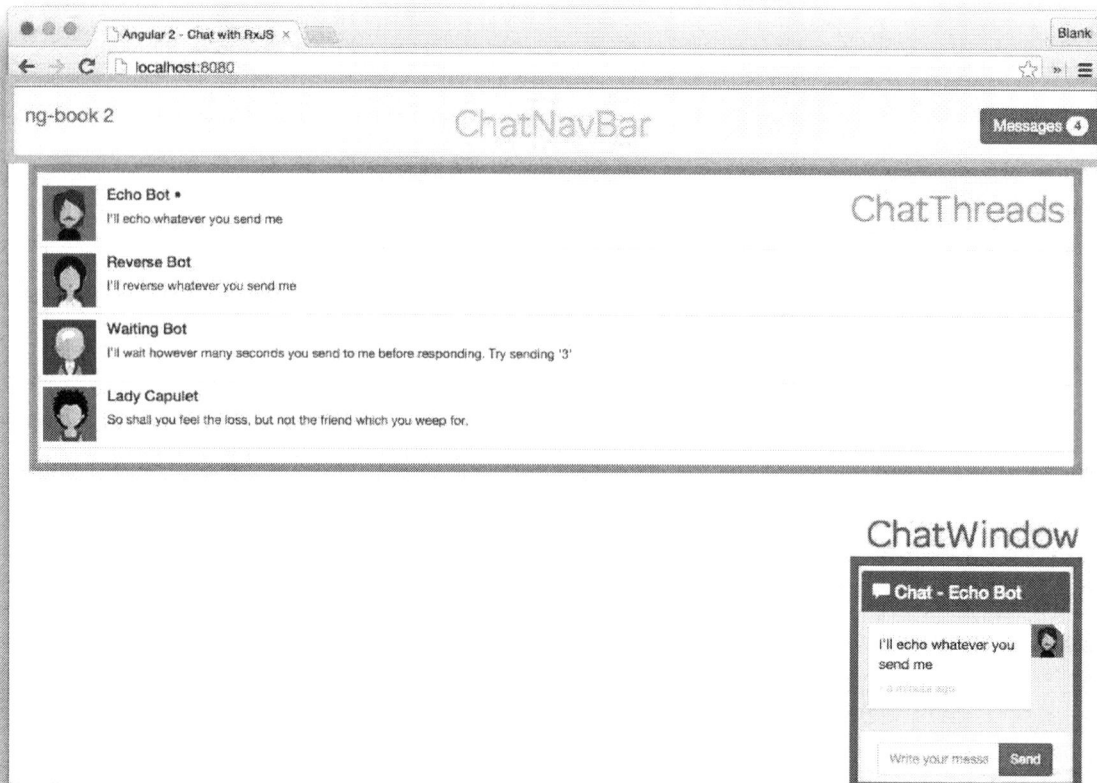

Chat Top-Level Components

- `ChatNavBarComponent` - contains the unread messages count
- `ChatThreadsComponent` - shows a clickable list of threads, along with the most recent message and the conversation avatar
- `ChatWindowComponent` - shows the messages in the current thread with an input box to send new messages

Here's what our top-level component looks like in code:

code/rxjs/rxjs-chat/src/app/app.component.ts

```
1   import { Component, Inject } from '@angular/core';
2   import { ChatExampleData } from './data/chat-example-data';
3
4   import { UsersService } from './user/users.service';
5   import { ThreadsService } from './thread/threads.service';
6   import { MessagesService } from './message/messages.service';
7
8   @Component({
9     selector: 'app-root',
10    templateUrl: './app.component.html',
11    styleUrls: ['./app.component.css']
12  })
13  export class AppComponent {
14      constructor(public messagesService: MessagesService,
15                  public threadsService: ThreadsService,
16                  public usersService: UsersService) {
17      ChatExampleData.init(messagesService, threadsService, usersService);
18    }
19  }
```

and the template:

code/rxjs/rxjs-chat/src/app/app.component.html

```
1   <div>
2     <chat-page></chat-page>
3   </div>
```

ℹ In this chapter we are adding some style using the CSS framework Bootstrap[87]

Take a look at the constructor. Here we're injecting our three services: the `MessagesService`, `ThreadsService`, and `UsersService`. We're using those services to initialize our example data.

ℹ If you're interested in the example data you can find it in `code/rxjs/rxjs-chat/src/app/data/chat-example-data.ts`.

We'll build our `chat-page` in a moment, but first let's build our thread list in the `ChatThreadsComponent`.

---

[87]http://getbootstrap.com

The `ChatThreadsComponent`

Echo Bot •
I'll echo whatever you send me

Reverse Bot
I'll reverse whatever you send me

Waiting Bot
I'll wait however many seconds you send
to me before responding. Try sending '3'

Lady Capulet
So shall you feel the loss, but not the
friend which you weep for.

Time Ordered List of Threads

code/rxjs/rxjs-chat/src/app/chat-threads/chat-threads.component.ts

```
1    import {
2      Component,
3      OnInit,
4      Inject
5    } from '@angular/core';
6    import { Observable } from 'rxjs';
7    import { Thread } from '../thread/thread.model';
8    import { ThreadsService } from './../thread/threads.service';
9
10   @Component({
11     selector: 'chat-threads',
12     templateUrl: './chat-threads.component.html',
13     styleUrls: ['./chat-threads.component.css']
14   })
15   export class ChatThreadsComponent {
16     threads: Observable<any>;
17
18     constructor(public threadsService: ThreadsService) {
19       this.threads = threadsService.orderedThreads;
20     }
21   }
```

Here we're injecting `ThreadsService` and then we're keeping a reference to the `orderedThreads`.

ChatThreadsComponent `template`

Lastly, let's look at the `template` and its configuration:

code/rxjs/rxjs-chat/src/app/chat-threads/chat-threads.component.html

```
1   <!-- conversations -->
2   <div class="row">
3     <div class="conversation-wrap">
4
5       <chat-thread
6           *ngFor="let thread of threads | async"
7           [thread]="thread">
8       </chat-thread>
9
10    </div>
11  </div>
```

There's three things to look at here: `NgFor` with the `async` pipe, the `ChangeDetectionStrategy` and `ChatThreadComponent`.

The `ChatThreadComponent` directive component (which matches `chat-thread` in the markup) will show the view for the `Threads`. We'll define that in a moment.

The `NgFor` iterates over our `threads`, and passes the input `[thread]` to our `ChatThreadComponent` directive. But you probably notice something new in our `*ngFor`: the pipe to `async`.

`async` is implemented by `AsyncPipe` and it lets us use an RxJS `Observable` here in our view. What's great about `async` is that it lets us use our async observable as if it was a sync collection. This is super convenient and really cool.

On this component we specify a custom `changeDetection`. Angular has a flexible and efficient change detection system. One of the benefits is that if we have a component which has immutable or observable bindings, then we're able to give the change detection system hints that will make our application run very efficiently.

> We talk more about various change-detection strategies in the Advanced Components Chapter

In this case, instead of watching for changes on an array of `Threads`, Angular will subscribe for changes to the `threads` observable - and trigger an update when a new event is emitted.

The Single `ChatThreadComponent`

Let's look at our `ChatThreadComponent`. This is the component that will be used to display a **single thread**. Starting with the `@Component`:

code/rxjs/rxjs-chat/src/app/chat-thread/chat-thread.component.ts

```
 1  import {
 2    Component,
 3    OnInit,
 4    Input,
 5    Output,
 6    EventEmitter
 7  } from '@angular/core';
 8  import { Observable } from 'rxjs';
 9  import { ThreadsService } from './../thread/threads.service';
10  import { Thread } from '../thread/thread.model';
11
12  @Component({
13    selector: 'chat-thread',
14    templateUrl: './chat-thread.component.html',
15    styleUrls: ['./chat-thread.component.css']
16  })
17  export class ChatThreadComponent implements OnInit {
18    @Input() thread: Thread;
19    selected = false;
20
21    constructor(public threadsService: ThreadsService) {
22    }
23
24    ngOnInit(): void {
25      this.threadsService.currentThread
26        .subscribe( (currentThread: Thread) => {
27          this.selected = currentThread &&
28            this.thread &&
29            (currentThread.id === this.thread.id);
30        });
31    }
32
33    clicked(event: any): void {
34      this.threadsService.setCurrentThread(this.thread);
35      event.preventDefault();
36    }
37  }
```

We'll come back and look at the template in a minute, but first let's look at the component definition controller.

ChatThreadComponent **Controller and** ngOnInit

Notice that we're implementing a new interface here: OnInit. Angular components can declare that they listen for certain lifecycle events. We talk more about lifecycle events here in the Advanced Components chapter.

In this case, because we declared that we implement OnInit, the method ngOnInit will be called on our component after the component has been checked for changes the first time.

A key reason we will use ngOnInit is because **our thread property won't be available in the constructor**.

Above you can see that in ngOnInit we subscribe to threadsService.currentThread and if the currentThread matches the thread property of this component, we set selected to true (conversely, if the Thread doesn't match, we set selected to false).

We also setup an event handler clicked. This is how we handle selecting the current thread. In our template (below), we will bind clicked() to clicking on the thread view. If we receive clicked() then we tell the threadsService we want to set the current thread to the Thread of this component.

ChatThreadComponent **template**

Here's the code for our template:

code/rxjs/rxjs-chat/src/app/chat-thread/chat-thread.component.html

```
1   <div class="media conversation">
2     <div class="pull-left">
3       <img class="media-object avatar"
4            src="{{thread.avatarSrc}}">
5     </div>
6     <div class="media-body">
7       <h5 class="media-heading contact-name">{{thread.name}}
8         <span *ngIf="selected">&bull;</span>
9       </h5>
10      <small class="message-preview">{{thread.lastMessage.text}}</small>
11    </div>
12    <a (click)="clicked($event)" class="div-link">Select</a>
13  </div>
```

Notice we've got some straight-forward bindings like {{thread.avatarSrc}}, {{thread.name}}, and {{thread.lastMessage.text}}.

We've got an *ngIf which will show the • symbol only if this is the selected thread.

Lastly, we're binding to the `(click)` event to call our `clicked()` handler. Notice that when we call `clicked` we're passing the argument $event. This is a special variable provided by Angular that describes the event. We use that in our `clicked` handler by calling `event.preventDefault();`. This makes sure that we don't navigate to a different page.

The `ChatWindowComponent`

The `ChatWindowComponent` is the most complicated component in our app. Let's take it one section at a time:

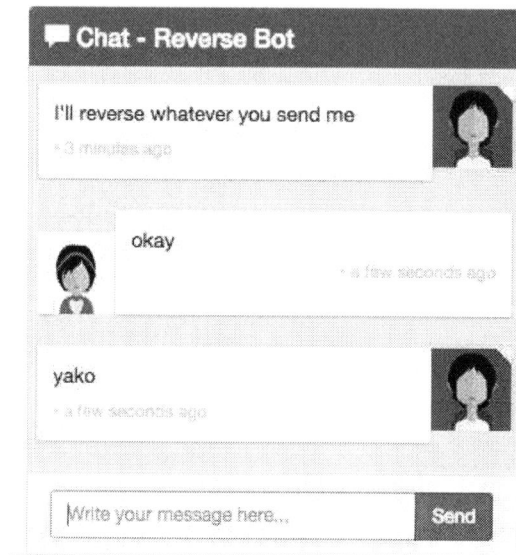

The Chat Window

We start by defining our `@Component`:

code/rxjs/rxjs-chat/src/app/chat-window/chat-window.component.ts

```
17   @Component({
18     selector: 'chat-window',
19     templateUrl: './chat-window.component.html',
20     styleUrls: ['./chat-window.component.css'],
21     changeDetection: ChangeDetectionStrategy.OnPush
```

`ChatWindowComponent` Class Properties

Our `ChatWindowComponent` class has four properties :

code/rxjs/rxjs-chat/src/app/chat-window/chat-window.component.ts

```
23  export class ChatWindowComponent implements OnInit {
24    messages: Observable<any>;
25    currentThread: Thread;
26    draftMessage: Message;
27    currentUser: User;
```

Here's a diagram of where each one is used:

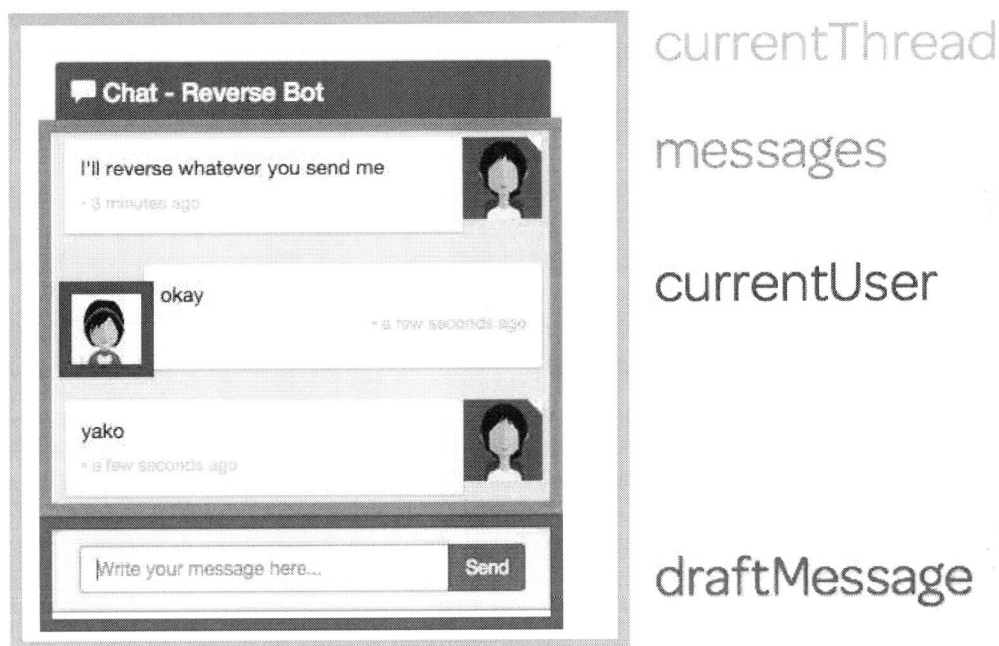

Chat Window Properties

In our constructor we're going to inject four things:

code/rxjs/rxjs-chat/src/app/chat-window/chat-window.component.ts

```
29    constructor(public messagesService: MessagesService,
30                public threadsService: ThreadsService,
31                public UsersService: UsersService,
32                public el: ElementRef) {
33    }
```

The first three are our services. The fourth, el is an ElementRef which we can use to get access to the host DOM element. We'll use that when we scroll to the bottom of the chat window when we create and receive new messages.

> **ⓘ** Remember: by using `public messagesService: MessagesService` in the constructor, we
> are not only injecting the `MessagesService` but setting up an instance variable that we can
> use later in our class via `this.messagesService`

ChatWindowComponent `ngOnInit`

We're going to put the initialization of this component in `ngOnInit`. The main thing we're going to be
doing here is setting up the subscriptions on our observables which will then change our component
properties.

code/rxjs/rxjs-chat/src/app/chat-window/chat-window.component.ts

```
35    ngOnInit(): void {
36      this.messages = this.threadsService.currentThreadMessages;
37
38      this.draftMessage = new Message();
```

First, we'll save the `currentThreadMessages` into `messages`. Next we create an empty `Message` for
the default `draftMessage`.

When we send a new message we need to make sure that `Message` stores a reference to the sending
`Thread`. The sending thread is always going to be the current thread, so let's store a reference to the
currently selected thread:

code/rxjs/rxjs-chat/src/app/chat-window/chat-window.component.ts

```
40      this.threadsService.currentThread.subscribe(
41        (thread: Thread) => {
42          this.currentThread = thread;
43        });
```

We also want new messages to be sent from the current user, so let's do the same with `currentUser`:

code/rxjs/rxjs-chat/src/app/chat-window/chat-window.component.ts

```
45      this.UsersService.currentUser
46        .subscribe(
47        (user: User) => {
48          this.currentUser = user;
49        });
```

ChatWindowComponent `sendMessage`

Since we're talking about it, let's implement a `sendMessage` function that will send a new message:

code/rxjs/rxjs-chat/src/app/chat-window/chat-window.component.ts

```
65    sendMessage(): void {
66      const m: Message = this.draftMessage;
67      m.author = this.currentUser;
68      m.thread = this.currentThread;
69      m.isRead = true;
70      this.messagesService.addMessage(m);
71      this.draftMessage = new Message();
72    }
```

The sendMessage function above takes the draftMessage, sets the author and thread using our component properties. Every message we send has "been read" already (we wrote it) so we mark it as read.

Notice here that we're not updating the draftMessage text. That's because we're going to bind the value of the messages text in the view in a few minutes.

After we've updated the draftMessage properties we send it off to the messagesService and then **create a new Message** and set that new Message to this.draftMessage. We do this to make sure we don't mutate an already sent message.

ChatWindowComponent onEnter

In our view, we want to send the message in two scenarios

1. the user hits the "Send" button or
2. the user hits the Enter (or Return) key.

Let's define a function that will handle that event:

code/rxjs/rxjs-chat/src/app/chat-window/chat-window.component.ts

```
60    onEnter(event: any): void {
61      this.sendMessage();
62      event.preventDefault();
63    }
```

ChatWindowComponent scrollToBottom

When we send a message, or when a new message comes in, we want to scroll to the bottom of the chat window. To do that, we're going to set the scrollTop property of our host element:

code/rxjs/rxjs-chat/src/app/chat-window/chat-window.component.ts

```
74    scrollToBottom(): void {
75      const scrollPane: any = this.el
76        .nativeElement.querySelector('.msg-container-base');
77      scrollPane.scrollTop = scrollPane.scrollHeight;
78    }
```

Now that we have a function that will scroll to the bottom, we have to make sure that we call it at the right time. Back in `ngOnInit` let's subscribe to the list of `currentThreadMessages` and scroll to the bottom anytime we get a new message:

code/rxjs/rxjs-chat/src/app/chat-window/chat-window.component.ts

```
50      this.messages
51        .subscribe(
52          (messages: Array<Message>) => {
53            setTimeout(() => {
54              this.scrollToBottom();
55            });
56          });
57    }
```

? **Why do we have the `setTimeout`?**

If we call `scrollToBottom` immediately when we get a new message then what happens is we scroll to the bottom before the new message is rendered. By using a `setTimeout` we're telling JavaScript that we want to run this function when it is finished with the current execution queue. This happens **after** the component is rendered, so it does what we want.

ChatWindowComponent template

The opening of our `template` should look familiar, we start by defining some markup and the panel header:

code/rxjs/rxjs-chat/src/app/chat-window/chat-window.component.html

```
1   <div class="chat-window-container">
2     <div class="chat-window">
3       <div class="panel-container">
4         <div class="panel panel-default">
5
6           <div class="panel-heading top-bar">
7             <div class="panel-title-container">
8               <h3 class="panel-title">
9                 <span class="glyphicon glyphicon-comment"></span>
10                Chat - {{currentThread.name}}
11              </h3>
12            </div>
13            <div class="panel-buttons-container">
14              <!-- you could put minimize or close buttons here -->
15            </div>
16          </div>
```

Next we show the list of messages. Here we use ngFor along with the async pipe to iterate over our list of messages. We'll describe the individual chat-message component in a minute.

code/rxjs/rxjs-chat/src/app/chat-window/chat-window.component.html

```
18          <div class="panel-body msg-container-base">
19            <chat-message
20            *ngFor="let message of messages | async"
21            [message]="message">
22            </chat-message>
23          </div>
```

Lastly we have the message input box and closing tags :

code/rxjs/rxjs-chat/src/app/chat-window/chat-window.component.html

```
24          <div class="panel-footer">
25            <div class="input-group">
26              <input type="text"
27              class="chat-input"
28              placeholder="Write your message here..."
29              (keydown.enter)="onEnter($event)"
30              [(ngModel)]="draftMessage.text" />
31              <span class="input-group-btn">
```

```
32                  <button class="btn-chat"
33                  (click)="onEnter($event)"
34                  >Send</button>
35              </span>
36            </div>
37          </div>
38
39        </div>
40      </div>
41    </div>
```

The message `input` box is the most interesting part of this view, so let's talk about two interesting properties: 1. (`keydown.enter`) and 2. [(`ngModel`)].

Handling keystrokes

Angular provides a straightforward way to handle keyboard actions: we bind to the event on an element. In this case, on the `input` tag above, we're binding to `keydown.enter` which says if "Enter" is pressed, call the function in the expression, which in this case is `onEnter($event)`.

Using ngModel

As we've talked about before, Angular doesn't have a general model for two-way binding. However it can be very useful to have a two-way binding between a component and its view. As long as the side-effects are kept local to the component, it can be a very convenient way to keep a component property in sync with the view.

In this case, we're establishing a two-way bind **between the value of the input tag and `draftMessage.text`**. That is, if we type into the `input` tag, `draftMessage.text` will automatically be set to the value of that `input`. Likewise, if we were to update `draftMessage.text` in our code, the value in the `input` tag would change in the view.

code/rxjs/rxjs-chat/src/app/chat-window/chat-window.component.html

```
27                  <input type="text"
28                  class="chat-input"
29                  placeholder="Write your message here..."
30                  (keydown.enter)="onEnter($event)"
31                  [(ngModel)]="draftMessage.text" />
```

Clicking "Send"

On our "Send" button we bind the (`click`) property to the `onEnter` function of our component:

code/rxjs/rxjs-chat/src/app/chat-window/chat-window.component.html

```
32        <span class="input-group-btn">
33          <button class="btn-chat"
34          (click)="onEnter($event)"
35          >Send</button>
36        </span>
```

The Entire ChatWindowComponent

We broke that up into a lot of tiny pieces. So that we can get a view of the whole thing, here's the code listing for the entire ChatWindowComponent:

code/rxjs/rxjs-chat/src/app/chat-window/chat-window.component.ts

```
1  import {
2    Component,
3    Inject,
4    ElementRef,
5    OnInit,
6    ChangeDetectionStrategy
7  } from '@angular/core';
8  import { Observable } from 'rxjs';
9
10 import { User } from '../user/user.model';
11 import { UsersService } from '../user/users.service';
12 import { Thread } from '../thread/thread.model';
13 import { ThreadsService } from '../thread/threads.service';
14 import { Message } from '../message/message.model';
15 import { MessagesService } from '../message/messages.service';
16
17 @Component({
18   selector: 'chat-window',
19   templateUrl: './chat-window.component.html',
20   styleUrls: ['./chat-window.component.css'],
21   changeDetection: ChangeDetectionStrategy.OnPush
22 })
23 export class ChatWindowComponent implements OnInit {
24   messages: Observable<any>;
25   currentThread: Thread;
26   draftMessage: Message;
27   currentUser: User;
28
```

```
29    constructor(public messagesService: MessagesService,
30                public threadsService: ThreadsService,
31                public UsersService: UsersService,
32                public el: ElementRef) {
33    }
34
35    ngOnInit(): void {
36      this.messages = this.threadsService.currentThreadMessages;
37
38      this.draftMessage = new Message();
39
40      this.threadsService.currentThread.subscribe(
41        (thread: Thread) => {
42          this.currentThread = thread;
43        });
44
45      this.UsersService.currentUser
46        .subscribe(
47          (user: User) => {
48            this.currentUser = user;
49          });
50
51      this.messages
52        .subscribe(
53          (messages: Array<Message>) => {
54            setTimeout(() => {
55              this.scrollToBottom();
56            });
57          });
58    }
59
60    onEnter(event: any): void {
61      this.sendMessage();
62      event.preventDefault();
63    }
64
65    sendMessage(): void {
66      const m: Message = this.draftMessage;
67      m.author = this.currentUser;
68      m.thread = this.currentThread;
69      m.isRead = true;
70      this.messagesService.addMessage(m);
```

```
71       this.draftMessage = new Message();
72     }
73
74     scrollToBottom(): void {
75       const scrollPane: any = this.el
76         .nativeElement.querySelector('.msg-container-base');
77       scrollPane.scrollTop = scrollPane.scrollHeight;
78     }
79   }
```

and template:

code/rxjs/rxjs-chat/src/app/chat-window/chat-window.component.html

```html
1  <div class="chat-window-container">
2    <div class="chat-window">
3      <div class="panel-container">
4        <div class="panel panel-default">
5
6          <div class="panel-heading top-bar">
7            <div class="panel-title-container">
8              <h3 class="panel-title">
9                <span class="glyphicon glyphicon-comment"></span>
10               Chat - {{currentThread.name}}
11             </h3>
12           </div>
13           <div class="panel-buttons-container">
14             <!-- you could put minimize or close buttons here -->
15           </div>
16         </div>
17
18         <div class="panel-body msg-container-base">
19           <chat-message
20           *ngFor="let message of messages | async"
21           [message]="message">
22           </chat-message>
23         </div>
24
25         <div class="panel-footer">
26           <div class="input-group">
27             <input type="text"
28             class="chat-input"
29             placeholder="Write your message here..."
```

```
30              (keydown.enter)="onEnter($event)"
31              [(ngModel)]="draftMessage.text" />
32              <span class="input-group-btn">
33                <button class="btn-chat"
34                (click)="onEnter($event)"
35                >Send</button>
36              </span>
37            </div>
38          </div>
39
40        </div>
41      </div>
42  </div>
```

The ChatMessageComponent

Each Message is rendered by the ChatMessageComponent.

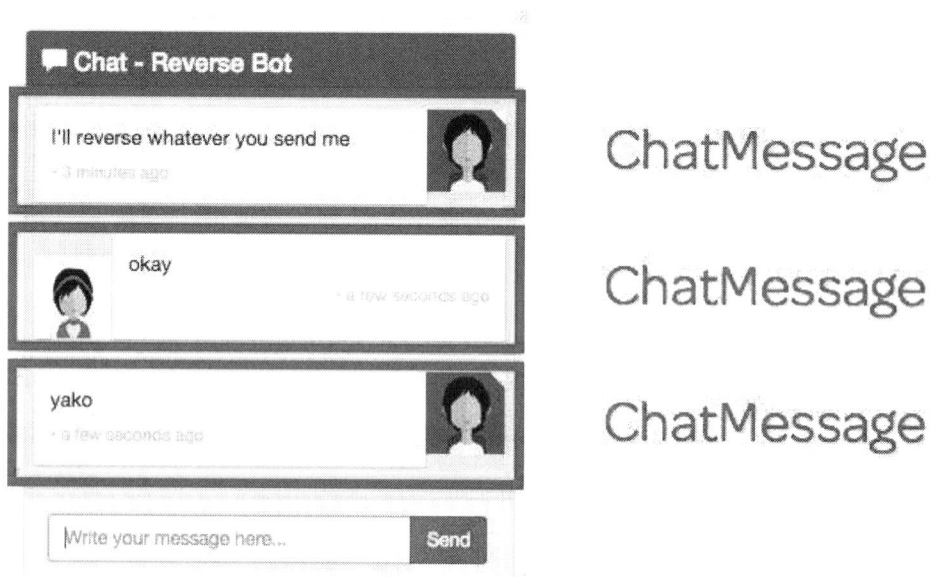

The ChatMessageComponent

This component is relatively straightforward. The main logic here is rendering a slightly different view depending on if the message was authored by the current user. If the Message was **not** written by the current user, then we consider the message incoming.

Remember that each `ChatMessageComponent` belongs to one `Message`. So in `ngOnInit` we will subscribe to the `currentUser` stream and set `incoming` depending on if this `Message` was written by the current user:

We start by defining the `@Component`

code/rxjs/rxjs-chat/src/app/chat-message/chat-message.component.ts

```
 1  import {
 2    Component,
 3    OnInit,
 4    Input
 5  } from '@angular/core';
 6  import { Observable } from 'rxjs';
 7
 8  import { UsersService } from './../user/users.service';
 9  import { ThreadsService } from './../thread/threads.service';
10  import { MessagesService } from './../message/messages.service';
11
12  import { Message } from './../message/message.model';
13  import { Thread } from './../thread/thread.model';
14  import { User } from './../user/user.model';
15
16  @Component({
17    selector: 'chat-message',
18    templateUrl: './chat-message.component.html',
19    styleUrls: ['./chat-message.component.css']
20  })
21  export class ChatMessageComponent implements OnInit {
22    @Input() message: Message;
23    currentUser: User;
24    incoming: boolean;
25
26    constructor(public UsersService: UsersService) {
27    }
28
29    ngOnInit(): void {
30      this.UsersService.currentUser
31        .subscribe(
32          (user: User) => {
33            this.currentUser = user;
34            if (this.message.author && user) {
35              this.incoming = this.message.author.id !== user.id;
36            }
```

```
37            });
38        }
39    }
```

The ChatMessageComponent template

In our template we have two interesting ideas:

1. the FromNowPipe
2. [ngClass]

First, here's the code:

code/rxjs/rxjs-chat/src/app/chat-message/chat-message.component.html
```
1   <div class="msg-container"
2       [ngClass]="{'base-sent': !incoming, 'base-receive': incoming}">
3
4     <div class="avatar"
5         *ngIf="!incoming">
6       <img src="{{message.author.avatarSrc}}">
7     </div>
8
9     <div class="messages"
10      [ngClass]="{'msg-sent': !incoming, 'msg-receive': incoming}">
11      <p>{{message.text}}</p>
12      <p class="time">{{message.sender}} • {{message.sentAt | fromNow}}</p>
13    </div>
14
15    <div class="avatar"
16        *ngIf="incoming">
17      <img src="{{message.author.avatarSrc}}">
18    </div>
19  </div>
```

The FromNowPipe is a pipe that casts our Messages sent-at time to a human-readable "x seconds ago" message. You can see that we use it by: {{message.sentAt | fromNow}}

> ℹ FromNowPipe uses the excellent moment.js[88] library. If you'd like to learn about creating your own custom pipes read the source of the FromNowPipe in code/rxjs/rxjs-chat/src/app/pipes/from-now.pipe.ts

We also make extensive use of ngClass in this view. The idea is, when we say:

---
[88]http://momentjs.com/

```
1    [ngClass]="{'msg-sent': !incoming, 'msg-receive': incoming}"
```

We're asking Angular to apply the `msg-receive` class if `incoming` is truthy (and apply `msg-sent` if `incoming` is falsey).

By using the `incoming` property, we're able to display incoming and outgoing messages differently.

The `ChatNavBarComponent`

The last component we have to talk about is the `ChatNavBarComponent`. In the nav-bar we'll show an unread messages count to the user.

The Unread Count in the `ChatNavBarComponent`

> The best way to try out the unread messages count is to use the "Waiting Bot". If you haven't already, try sending the message '3' to the Waiting Bot and then switch to another window. The Waiting Bot will then wait 3 seconds before sending you a message and you will see the unread messages counter increment.

The `ChatNavBarComponent` `@Component`

The only thing the `ChatNavBarComponent` controller needs to keep track of is the `unreadMessagesCount`. This is slightly more complicated than it seems on the surface.

The most straightforward way would be to simply listen to `messagesService.messages` and sum the number of `Messages` where `isRead` is false. This works fine for all messages outside of the current thread. However new messages in the current thread aren't guaranteed to be marked as read by the time `messages` emits new values.

The safest way to handle this is to combine the `messages` and `currentThread` streams and make sure we don't count any messages that are part of the current thread.

We do this using the `combineLatest` operator, which we've already used earlier in the chapter:

code/rxjs/rxjs-chat/src/app/chat-nav-bar/chat-nav-bar.component.ts

```
1   import {
2     Component,
3     Inject,
4     OnInit
5   } from '@angular/core';
6   import * as _ from 'lodash';
7
8   import { ThreadsService } from './../thread/threads.service';
9   import { MessagesService } from './../message/messages.service';
10
11  import { Thread } from './../thread/thread.model';
12  import { Message } from './../message/message.model';
13
14  @Component({
15    selector: 'chat-nav-bar',
16    templateUrl: './chat-nav-bar.component.html',
17    styleUrls: ['./chat-nav-bar.component.css']
18  })
19  export class ChatNavBarComponent implements OnInit {
20    unreadMessagesCount: number;
21
22    constructor(public messagesService: MessagesService,
23                public threadsService: ThreadsService) {
24    }
25
26    ngOnInit(): void {
27      this.messagesService.messages
28        .combineLatest(
29          this.threadsService.currentThread,
30          (messages: Message[], currentThread: Thread) =>
31            [currentThread, messages] )
32
33        .subscribe(([currentThread, messages]: [Thread, Message[]]) => {
34          this.unreadMessagesCount =
35            _.reduce(
36              messages,
37              (sum: number, m: Message) => {
38                const messageIsInCurrentThread: boolean = m.thread &&
39                  currentThread &&
40                  (currentThread.id === m.thread.id);
41                // note: in a "real" app you should also exclude
```

```
42            // messages that were authored by the current user b/c they've
43            // already been "read"
44            if (m && !m.isRead && !messageIsInCurrentThread) {
45              sum = sum + 1;
46            }
47            return sum;
48          },
49        0);
50      });
51    }
52  }
```

If you're not an expert in TypeScript you might find the above syntax a little bit hard to parse. In the combineLatest callback function we're returning an array with currentThread and messages as its two elements.

Then we subscribe to that stream and we're *destructuring* those objects in the function call. Next we reduce over the messages and count the number of messages that are unread and not in the current thread.

The ChatNavBarComponent template

In our view, the only thing we have left to do is display our unreadMessagesCount:

code/rxjs/rxjs-chat/src/app/chat-nav-bar/chat-nav-bar.component.html

```html
1  <nav class="navbar navbar-default">
2    <div class="container-fluid">
3      <div class="navbar-header">
4        <a class="navbar-brand" href="https://ng-book.com/2">
5          <img src="assets/images/logos/ng-book-2-minibook.png"/>
6          ng-book 2
7        </a>
8      </div>
9      <p class="navbar-text navbar-right">
10        <button class="btn btn-primary" type="button">
11          Messages <span class="badge">{{ unreadMessagesCount }}</span>
12        </button>
13      </p>
14    </div>
15  </nav>
```

Summary

There we go, if we put them all together we've got a fully functional chat app!

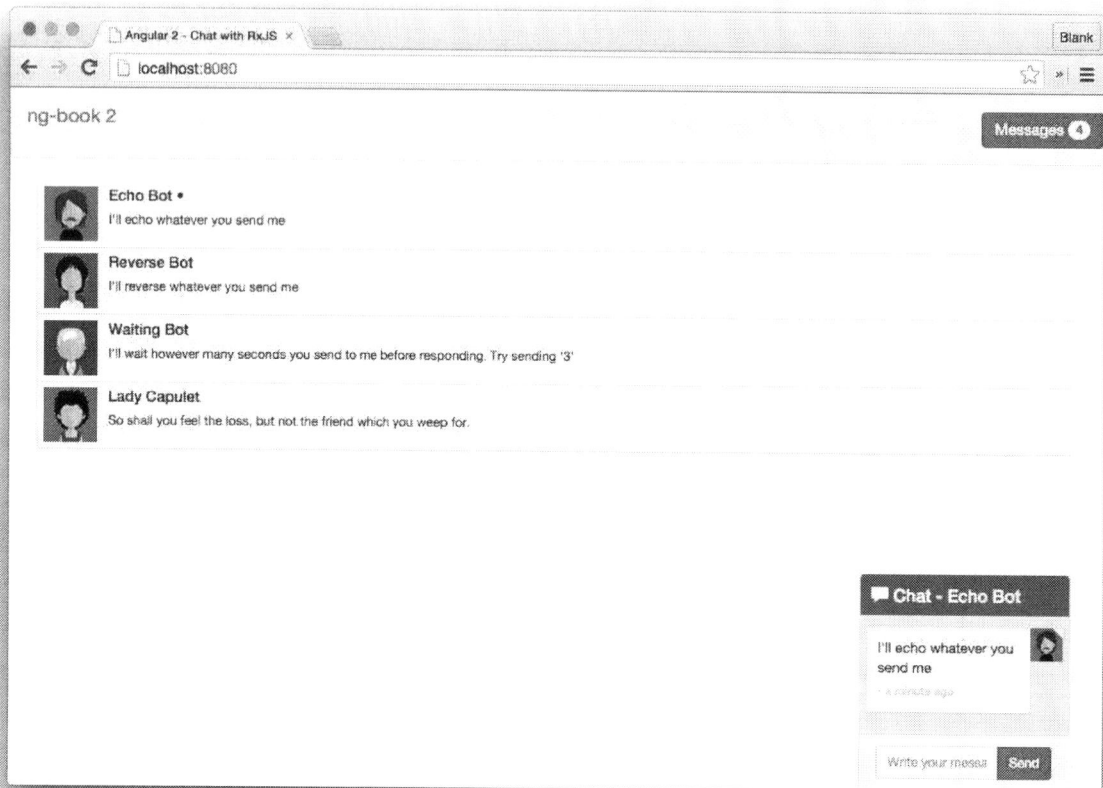

Completed Chat Application

If you checkout `code/rxjs/rxjs-chat/src/app/data/chat-example-data.ts` you'll see we've written a handful of bots for you that you can chat with. Here's a code excerpt from the Reverse Bot:

```
1 let rev: User = new User("Reverse Bot", require("images/avatars/female-avatar-4.\
2 png"));
3 let tRev: Thread = new Thread("tRev", rev.name, rev.avatarSrc);
```

code/rxjs/rxjs-chat/src/app/data/chat-example-data.ts

```
91      messagesService.messagesForThreadUser(tRev, rev)
92        .forEach( (message: Message): void => {
93          messagesService.addMessage(
94            new Message({
95              author: rev,
96              text: message.text.split('').reverse().join(''),
97              thread: tRev
98            })
99          );
100       },
```

Above you can see that we've subscribed to the messages for the "Reverse Bot" by using `messages-ForThreadUser`. Try writing a few bots of your own.

Introduction to Redux with TypeScript

In this chapter and the next we'll be looking at a data-architecture pattern called Redux. In this chapter we're going to discuss the ideas behind Redux, build our own mini version, and then hook it up to Angular. In the next chapter we'll use Redux to build a bigger application.

In most of our projects so far, we've managed state in a fairly direct way: We tend to grab data from services and render them in components, passing values down the component tree along the way.

Managing our apps in this way works fine for smaller apps, but as our apps grow, having multiple components manage different parts of the state becomes cumbersome. For instance, passing all of our values down our component tree suffers from the following downsides:

Intermediate property passing - In order to get state to any component we have to pass the values down through `inputs`. This means we have many intermediate components passing state that it isn't directly using or concerned about

Inflexible refactoring - Because we're passing `inputs` down through the component tree, we're introducing a coupling between parent and child components that often isn't necessary. This makes it more difficult to put a child component somewhere else in the hierarchy because we have to change all of the new parents to pass the state

State tree and DOM tree don't match - The "shape" of our state often doesn't match the "shape" of our view/component hierarchy. By passing all data through the component tree via `props` we run into difficulties when we need to reference data in a far branch of the tree

State throughout our app - If we manage state via components, it's difficult to get a snapshot of the total state of our app. This can make it hard to know which component "owns" a particular bit of data, and which components are concerned about changes

Pulling data out of our components and into services helps a lot. At least if services are the "owners" of our data, we have a better idea of where to put things. But this opens a new question: what are the best practices for "service-owned" data? Are there any patterns we can follow? In fact, there are.

In this chapter, we're going to discuss a data-architecture pattern called *Redux* which was designed to help with these issues. We'll implement our own version of Redux which will store **all of our state in a single place**. This idea of holding **all** of our application's state in one place might sound a little crazy, but the results are surprisingly delightful.

Redux

If you haven't heard of Redux yet you can read a bit about it on the official website[89]. Web application data architecture is evolving and the traditional ways of structuring data aren't quite adequate for large web apps. Redux has been extremely popular because it's both powerful and easy to understand.

Data architecture can be a complex topic and so Redux's best feature is probably its simplicity. If you strip Redux down to the essential core, Redux is fewer than 100 lines of code.

We can build rich, easy to understand, web apps by using Redux as the backbone of our application. But first, let's walk through how to write a minimal Redux and later we'll work out patterns that emerge as we work out these ideas in a larger app.

> There are several attempts to use Redux or create a Redux-inspired system that works with Angular. Two notable examples are:
>
> - ngrx/store[90] and
> - angular2-redux[91]
>
> ngrx is a Redux-inspired architecture that is heavily observables-based. angular2-redux uses Redux itself as a dependency, and adds some Angular helpers (dependency-injection, observable wrappers).
>
> Here we're not going to use either. Instead, we're going to use Redux directly in order to show the concepts without introducing a new dependency. That said, both of these libraries may be helpful to you when writing your apps.

Redux: Key Ideas

The key ideas of Redux are this:

- All of your application's data is in a single data structure called the *state* which is held in the *store*
- Your app reads the **state** from this **store**
- This **store** is never mutated directly
- User interaction (and other code) fires *actions* which describe what happened
- A *new state* is created by combining the **old state** and the **action** by a function called the *reducer*.

---

[89] http://redux.js.org/
[90] https://github.com/ngrx/store
[91] https://github.com/InfomediaLtd/angular2-redux

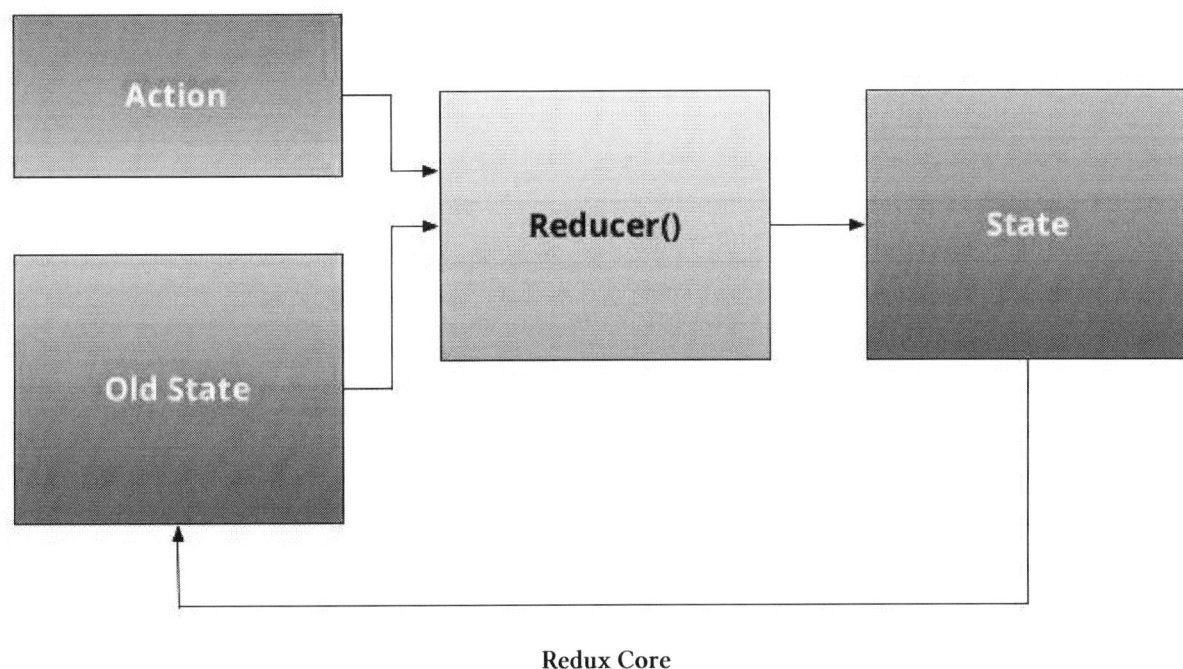

Redux Core

If the above bullet list isn't clear yet, don't worry about it - putting these ideas into practice is the goal of the rest of this chapter.

Core Redux Ideas

What's a *reducer*?

Let's talk about the *reducer* first. Here's the idea of a *reducer*: it takes the *old state* and an *action* and returns a *new state*.

A reducer must be a **pure function**[92]. That is:

1. It must not mutate the current state directly
2. It must not use any data outside of its arguments

Put another way, a pure function will always **return the same value, given the same set of arguments**. And a pure function won't call any functions which have an effect on the outside world, e.g. no database calls, no HTTP calls, and no mutating outside data structures.

Reducers should always treat the current state as **read-only**. A reducer **does not change the state** instead, it **returns a new state**. (Often this new state will start with a copy of old state, but let's not get ahead of ourselves.)

Let's define our very first reducer. Remember, there are three things involved:

---

[92]https://en.wikipedia.org/wiki/Pure_function

1. An `Action`, which defines what to do (with optional arguments)
2. The `state`, which stores *all* of the data in our application
3. The `Reducer` which takes the `state` and the `Action` and returns a new state.

Defining `Action` and `Reducer` Interfaces

Since we're using TypeScript we want to make sure this whole process is typed, so let's set up an interface for our `Action` and our `Reducer`:

The `Action` Interface

Our `Action` interface looks like this:

code/redux/redux-chat/tutorial/01-identity-reducer.ts
```
1  interface Action {
2    type: string;
3    payload?: any;
4  }
```

Notice that our `Action` has two fields:

1. type and
2. payload

The `type` will be an identifying string that describes the action like `INCREMENT` or `ADD_USER`. The `payload` can be an object of any kind. The `?` on `payload?` means that this field is optional.

The `Reducer` Interface

Our `Reducer` interface looks like this:

code/redux/redux-chat/tutorial/01-identity-reducer.ts
```
6  interface Reducer<T> {
7    (state: T, action: Action): T;
8  }
```

Our `Reducer` is using a feature of TypeScript called *generics*. In this case type `T` is the type of the state. Notice that we're saying that a valid `Reducer` has a function which takes a `state` (of type `T`) and an `action` and returns a new `state` (also of type `T`).

Creating Our First `Reducer`

The simplest possible reducer returns the state itself. (You might call this the *identity* reducer because it applies the identity function[93] on the state. This is the default case for all reducers, as we will soon

---

[93]https://en.wikipedia.org/wiki/Identity_function

see).

code/redux/redux-chat/tutorial/01-identity-reducer.ts

```
10  let reducer: Reducer<number> = (state: number, action: Action) => {
11    return state;
12  };
```

Notice that this Reducer makes the generic type concrete to number by the syntax Reducer<number>. We'll define more sophisticated states beyond a single number soon.

We're not using the Action yet, but let's try this Reducer just the same.

Running the examples in this section

You can find the code for this chapter in the folder code/redux. If the example is runnable you will see the filename the code is from above each code box.

In this first section, these examples are run **outside of the browser and run by node.js**. Because we're using TypeScript in these examples, you should run them using the commandline tool ts-node, (instead of node directly).

You can install ts-node by running:

```
1   npm install -g ts-node
```

Or by doing an npm install in the code/redux/redux-chat directory and then calling ./node_modules/.bin/ts-node [filename]

For instance, to run the example above you might type (not including the $):

```
1   $ cd code/redux/redux-chat/tutorial
2   $ npm install
3   $ ./node_modules/.bin/ts-node 01-identity-reducer.ts
```

Use this same procedure for the rest of the code in this chapter until we instruct you to switch to your browser.

Running Our First Reducer

Let's put it all together and run this reducer:

code/redux/redux-chat/tutorial/01-identity-reducer.ts

```
1  interface Action {
2    type: string;
3    payload?: any;
4  }
5
6  interface Reducer<T> {
7    (state: T, action: Action): T;
8  }
9
10 let reducer: Reducer<number> = (state: number, action: Action) => {
11   return state;
12 };
13
14 console.log( reducer(0, null) ); // -> 0
```

And run it:

```
1  $ cd code/redux/redux-chat/tutorial
2  $ ./node_modules/.bin/ts-node 01-identity-reducer.ts
3  0
```

It seems almost silly to have that as a code example, but it teaches us our first principle of reducers:

By default, reducers return the original state.

In this case, we passed a state of the number 0 and a `null` action. The result from this reducer is the state 0.

But let's do something more interesting and make our state change.

Adjusting the Counter With *actions*

Eventually our state is going to be **much more** sophisticated than a single number. We're going to be holding **all** of the data for our app in the state, so we'll need a better data structure for the state eventually.

That said, using a single number for the state lets us focus on other issues for now. So let's continue with the idea that our state is simply a single number that is storing a counter.

Let's say we want to be able to change the state number. Remember that in Redux we do not modify the state. Instead, we create *actions* which instruct the *reducer* on how to generate a *new state*.

Let's create an `Action` to change our counter. Remember that the only required property is a type. We might define our first action like this:

```
1   let incrementAction: Action = { type: 'INCREMENT' }
```

We should also create a second action that instructs our reducer to make the counter smaller with:

```
1   let decrementAction: Action = { type: 'DECREMENT' }
```

Now that we have these actions, let's try using them in our reducer:

code/redux/redux-chat/tutorial/02-adjusting-reducer.ts

```
10  let reducer: Reducer<number> = (state: number, action: Action) => {
11    if (action.type === 'INCREMENT') {
12      return state + 1;
13    }
14    if (action.type === 'DECREMENT') {
15      return state - 1;
16    }
17    return state;
18  };
```

And now we can try out the whole reducer:

code/redux/redux-chat/tutorial/02-adjusting-reducer.ts

```
20  let incrementAction: Action = { type: 'INCREMENT' };
21
22  console.log( reducer(0, incrementAction )); // -> 1
23  console.log( reducer(1, incrementAction )); // -> 2
24
25  let decrementAction: Action = { type: 'DECREMENT' };
26
27  console.log( reducer(100, decrementAction )); // -> 99
```

Neat! Now the new value of the state is returned according to which action we pass into the reducer.

Reducer `switch`

Instead of having so many `if` statements, the common practice is to convert the reducer body to a `switch` statement:

```
10  let reducer: Reducer<number> = (state: number, action: Action) => {
11    switch (action.type) {
12    case 'INCREMENT':
13      return state + 1;
14    case 'DECREMENT':
15      return state - 1;
16    default:
17      return state; // <-- dont forget!
18    }
19  };
20
21  let incrementAction: Action = { type: 'INCREMENT' };
22  console.log(reducer(0, incrementAction)); // -> 1
23  console.log(reducer(1, incrementAction)); // -> 2
24
25  let decrementAction: Action = { type: 'DECREMENT' };
26  console.log(reducer(100, decrementAction)); // -> 99
27
28  // any other action just returns the input state
29  let unknownAction: Action = { type: 'UNKNOWN' };
30  console.log(reducer(100, unknownAction)); // -> 100
```

Notice that the default case of the switch returns the original state. This ensures that if an unknown action is passed in, there's no error and we get the original state unchanged.

> Q: **Wait, all of my application state is in one giant switch statement?**
>
> A: Yes and no.
>
> If this is your first exposure to Redux reducers it might feel a little weird to have all of your application state changes be the result of a giant switch. There are two things you should know:
>
> 1. Having your state changes centralized in one place can help a **ton** in maintaining your program, particularly because it's easy to track down where the changes are happening when they're all together. (Furthermore, you can easily locate what state changes as the result of any action because you can search your code for the token specified for that action's type)
> 2. You can (and often do) break your reducers down into several sub-reducers which each manage a different branch of the state tree. We'll talk about this later.

Action "Arguments"

In the last example our actions contained only a type which told our reducer either to increment or decrement the state.

But often changes in our app can't be described by a single value - instead we need parameters to describe the change. This is why we have the payload field in our Action.

In this counter example, say we wanted to add 9 to the counter. One way to do this would be to send 9 INCREMENT actions, but that wouldn't be very efficient, especially if we wanted to add, say, 9000.

Instead, let's add a PLUS action that will use the payload parameter to send a number which specifies how much we want to add to the counter. Defining this action is easy enough:

```
1  let plusSevenAction = { type: 'PLUS', payload: 7 };
```

Next, to support this action, we add a new case to our reducer that will handle a 'PLUS' action:

code/redux/redux-chat/tutorial/04-plus-action.ts

```
10  let reducer: Reducer<number> = (state: number, action: Action) => {
11    switch (action.type) {
12    case 'INCREMENT':
13      return state + 1;
14    case 'DECREMENT':
15      return state - 1;
16    case 'PLUS':
17      return state + action.payload;
18    default:
19      return state;
20    }
21  };
```

PLUS will add whatever number is in the action.payload to the state. We can try it out:

code/redux/redux-chat/tutorial/04-plus-action.ts

```
23  console.log( reducer(3, { type: 'PLUS', payload: 7}) );     // -> 10
24  console.log( reducer(3, { type: 'PLUS', payload: 9000}) ); // -> 9003
25  console.log( reducer(3, { type: 'PLUS', payload: -2}) );    // -> 1
```

In the first line we take the state 3 and PLUS a payload of 7, which results in 10. Neat! However, notice that while we're passing in a state, it doesn't really ever *change*. That is, we're not storing the result of our reducer's changes and reusing it for future actions.

Storing Our State

Our reducers are pure functions, and do not change the world around them. The problem is, in our app, things *do* change. Specifically, our state changes and we need to keep the new state somewhere.

In Redux, we keep our state in the *store*. The store has the responsibility of **running the reducer and then keeping the new state.** Let's take a look at a minimal store:

code/redux/redux-chat/tutorial/05-minimal-store.ts

```
10  class Store<T> {
11    private _state: T;
12
13    constructor(
14      private reducer: Reducer<T>,
15      initialState: T
16    ) {
17      this._state = initialState;
18    }
19
20    getState(): T {
21      return this._state;
22    }
23
24    dispatch(action: Action): void {
25      this._state = this.reducer(this._state, action);
26    }
27  }
```

Notice that our Store is generically typed - we specify the type of the *state* with generic type T. We store the state in the private variable _state.

We also give our Store a Reducer, which is also typed to operate on T, the state type this is because **each store is tied to a specific reducer**. We store the Reducer in the private variable reducer.

> In Redux, we generally have 1 store and 1 top-level reducer per application.

Let's take a closer look at each method of our State:

- In our constructor we set the _state to the initial state.
- getState() simply returns the current _state

- `dispatch` takes an action, sends it to the reducer and then **updates the value of _state** with the return value

Notice that **dispatch doesn't return anything**. It's only *updating* the store's state (once the result returns). This is an important principle of Redux: dispatching actions is a "fire-and-forget" maneuver. **Dispatching actions is not a direct manipulation of the state, and it doesn't return the new state**.

When we dispatch actions, we're sending off a notification of what happened. If we want to know what the current state of the system is, we have to check the state of the store.

Using the Store

Let's try using our store:

code/redux/redux-chat/tutorial/05-minimal-store.ts

```
43  // create a new store
44  let store = new Store<number>(reducer, 0);
45  console.log(store.getState()); // -> 0
46
47  store.dispatch({ type: 'INCREMENT' });
48  console.log(store.getState()); // -> 1
49
50  store.dispatch({ type: 'INCREMENT' });
51  console.log(store.getState()); // -> 2
52
53  store.dispatch({ type: 'DECREMENT' });
54  console.log(store.getState()); // -> 1
```

We start by creating a new `Store` and we save this in `store`, which we can use to get the current state and dispatch actions.

The state is set to `0` initially, and then we `INCREMENT` twice and `DECREMENT` once and our final state is `1`.

Being Notified with `subscribe`

It's great that our `Store` keeps track of what changed, but in the above example we have to *ask* for the state changes with `store.getState()`. It would be nice for us to know immediately when a new action was dispatched so that we could respond. To do this we can implement the Observer pattern - that is, we'll register a callback function that will *subscribe* to all changes.

Here's how we want it to work:

1. We will register a *listener* function using `subscribe`
2. When `dispatch` is called, we will iterate over all listeners and call them, which is the notification that the state has changed.

Registering Listeners

Our listener callbacks are going to be a function that takes *no arguments*. Let's define an interface that makes it easy to describe this:

code/redux/redux-chat/tutorial/06-store-w-subscribe.ts

```
10  interface ListenerCallback {
11    (): void;
12  }
```

After we subscribe a listener, we might want to unsubscribe as well, so lets define the interface for an *unsubscribe* function as well:

code/redux/redux-chat/tutorial/06-store-w-subscribe.ts

```
14  interface UnsubscribeCallback {
15    (): void;
16  }
```

Not much going on here - it's another function that takes no arguments and has no return value. But by defining these types it makes our code clearer to read.

Our store is going to keep a list of ListenerCallbacks let's add that to our Store:

code/redux/redux-chat/tutorial/06-store-w-subscribe.ts

```
18  class Store<T> {
19    private _state: T;
20    private _listeners: ListenerCallback[] = [];
```

Now we want to be able to add to that list of _listeners with a subscribe function:

code/redux/redux-chat/tutorial/06-store-w-subscribe.ts

```
38    subscribe(listener: ListenerCallback): UnsubscribeCallback {
39      this._listeners.push(listener);
40      return () => { // returns an "unsubscribe" function
41        this._listeners = this._listeners.filter(l => l !== listener);
42      };
43    }
```

subscribe accepts a ListenerCallback (i.e. a function with no arguments and no return value) and returns an UnsubscribeCallback (the same signature). Adding the new listener is easy: we push it on to the _listeners array.

The return value is a function which will update the list of _listeners to be the list of _listeners without the listener we just added. That is, it returns the UnsubscribeCallback that we can use to remove this listener from the list.

Notifying Our Listeners

Whenever our state changes, we want to call these listener functions. What this means is, whenever we `dispatch` a new action, whenever the state changes, we want to call all of the listeners:

code/redux/redux-chat/tutorial/06-store-w-subscribe.ts

```
33    dispatch(action: Action): void {
34      this._state = this.reducer(this._state, action);
35      this._listeners.forEach((listener: ListenerCallback) => listener());
36    }
```

The Complete Store

We'll try this out below, but before we do that, here's the complete code listing for our new `Store`:

code/redux/redux-chat/tutorial/06-store-w-subscribe.ts

```
18  class Store<T> {
19    private _state: T;
20    private _listeners: ListenerCallback[] = [];
21
22    constructor(
23      private reducer: Reducer<T>,
24      initialState: T
25    ) {
26      this._state = initialState;
27    }
28
29    getState(): T {
30      return this._state;
31    }
32
33    dispatch(action: Action): void {
34      this._state = this.reducer(this._state, action);
35      this._listeners.forEach((listener: ListenerCallback) => listener());
36    }
37
38    subscribe(listener: ListenerCallback): UnsubscribeCallback {
39      this._listeners.push(listener);
40      return () => { // returns an "unsubscribe" function
41        this._listeners = this._listeners.filter(l => l !== listener);
42      };
43    }
44  }
```

Trying Out subscribe

Now that we can subscribe to changes in our store, let's try it out:

code/redux/redux-chat/tutorial/06-store-w-subscribe.ts

```
61  let store = new Store<number>(reducer, 0);
62  console.log(store.getState()); // -> 0
63
64  // subscribe
65  let unsubscribe = store.subscribe(() => {
66    console.log('subscribed: ', store.getState());
67  });
68
69  store.dispatch({ type: 'INCREMENT' }); // -> subscribed: 1
70  store.dispatch({ type: 'INCREMENT' }); // -> subscribed: 2
71
72  unsubscribe();
73  store.dispatch({ type: 'DECREMENT' }); // (nothing logged)
74
75  // decrement happened, even though we weren't listening for it
76  console.log(store.getState()); // -> 1
```

Above we subscribe to our store and in the callback function we'll log subscribed: and then the current store state.

> **ℹ** Notice that the listener function is **not** given the current state as an argument. This might seem like an odd choice, but because there are some nuances to deal with, it's easier to think of *the notification of state changed* as separate from *the current state*. Without digging too much into the weeds, you can read more about this choice here[94], here[95], and here[96].

We store the unsubscribe callback and then notice that after we call unsubscribe() our log message isn't called. We can still dispatch actions, we just won't see the results until we ask the store for them.

---

[94] https://github.com/reactjs/redux/issues/1707

[95] https://github.com/reactjs/redux/issues/1513

[96] https://github.com/reactjs/redux/issues/303

If you're the type of person who likes RxJS and Observables, you might notice that implementing our own subscription listeners could also be implemented using RxJS. You could rewrite our `Store` to use Observables instead of our own subscriptions.

In fact, we've already done this for you and you can find the sample code in the file `code/redux/redux-chat/tutorial/06b-rx-store.ts`.

Using RxJS for the `Store` is an interesting and powerful pattern if you're willing to use RxJS for the backbone of our application data.

Here we're not going to use Observables very heavily, particularly because we want to discuss Redux itself and how to think about data architecture with a single state tree. Redux itself is powerful enough to use in our applications without Observables.

Once you get the concepts of using "straight" Redux, adding in Observables isn't difficult (if you already understand RxJS, that is). For now, we're going to use "straight" Redux and we'll give you some guidance on some Observable-based Redux-wrappers at the end.

The Core of Redux

The above store is the essential core of Redux. Our reducer takes the current state and action and returns a new state, which is held by the store.

There are obviously many more things that we need to add to build a large, production web app. However, all of the new ideas that we'll cover are patterns that flow from building on this simple idea of an immutable, central store of state. If you understand the ideas presented above, you would be likely to invent many of the patterns (and libraries) you find in more advanced Redux apps.

There's still a lot for us to cover about day-to-day use of Redux though. For instance, we need to know:

- How to carefully handle more complex data structures in our state
- How to be notified when our state changes without having to poll the state (with subscriptions)
- How to intercept our dispatch for debugging (a.k.a. middleware)
- How to compute derived values (with *selectors*)
- How to split up large reducers into more manageable, smaller ones (and recombine them)
- How to deal with asynchronous data

We'll explain each of these issues and describe common patterns over the rest of this chapter and the next.

Let's first deal with handling more complex data structures in our state. To do that, we're going to need an example that's more interesting than a counter. Let's start building a chat app where users can send each other messages.

A Messaging App

In our messaging app, as in all Redux apps, there are three main parts to the data model:

1. The state
2. The actions
3. The reducer

Messaging App `state`

The `state` in our counter app was a single number. However in our messaging app, the `state` is going to be **an object**.

This state object will have a single property, `messages`. `messages` will be an array of strings, with each string representing an individual message in the application. For example:

```
1  // an example `state` value
2  {
3    messages: [
4      'here is message one',
5      'here is message two'
6    ]
7  }
```

We can define the type for the app's state like this:

code/redux/redux-chat/tutorial/07-messages-reducer.ts

```
7  interface AppState {
8    messages: string[];
9  }
```

Messaging App `actions`

Our app will process two actions: `ADD_MESSAGE` and `DELETE_MESSAGE`.

The `ADD_MESSAGE` action object will always have the property `message`, the message to be added to the state. The `ADD_MESSAGE` action object has this shape:

```
1  {
2    type: 'ADD_MESSAGE',
3    message: 'Whatever message we want here'
4  }
```

The DELETE_MESSAGE action object will delete a specified message from the state. A challenge here is that we have to be able to specify *which message* we want to delete.

If our messages were objects, we could assign each message an id property when it is created. However, to simplify this example, our messages are just simple strings, so we'll have to get a handle to the message another way. The easiest way for now is to just use the index of the message in the array (as a proxy for the ID).

With that in mind, the DELETE_MESSAGE action object has this shape:

```
1  {
2    type: 'DELETE_MESSAGE',
3    index: 2                    // <- or whatever index is appropriate
4  }
```

We can define the types for these actions by using the interface ... extends syntax in TypeScript:

code/redux/redux-chat/tutorial/07-messages-reducer.ts

```
11  interface AddMessageAction extends Action {
12    message: string;
13  }
14
15  interface DeleteMessageAction extends Action {
16    index: number;
17  }
```

In this way our AddMessageAction is able to specify a message and the DeleteMessageAction will specify an index.

Messaging App reducer

Remember that our reducer needs to handle two actions: ADD_MESSAGE and DELETE_MESSAGE. Let's talk about these individually.

Reducing ADD_MESSAGE

code/redux/redux-chat/tutorial/07-messages-reducer.ts

```
19  let reducer: Reducer<AppState> =
20    (state: AppState, action: Action): AppState => {
21    switch (action.type) {
22    case 'ADD_MESSAGE':
23      return {
24        messages: state.messages.concat(
25          (<AddMessageAction>action).message
26        ),
27      };
```

We start by switching on the action.type and handling the ADD_MESSAGE case.

> ℹ **TypeScript objects already have a type, so why are we adding a type field?**
>
> There are many different ways we might choose to handle this sort of "polymorphic dispatch". Keeping a string in a type field (where type means "action-type") is a straightforward, portable way we can use to distinguish different types of actions and handle them in one reducer. In part, it means that you don't *have* to create a new interface for every action.
>
> That said, it would be more satisfying to be able to use reflection to switch on the concrete type. While this might become possible with more advanced type guards[97], this isn't currently possible in today's TypeScript.
>
> Broadly speaking, types are a compile-time construct and this code is compiled down to JavaScript and we can lose some of the typing metadata.
>
> That said, if switching on a type field bothers you and you'd like to use language features directly, you could use the decoration reflection metadata[98]. For now, a simple type field will suffice.

Adding an Item Without Mutation

When we handle an ADD_MESSAGE action, we need to add the given message to the state. As will all reducer handlers, we need to **return a new state**. Remember that our reducers must be *pure* and not mutate the old state.

What would be the problem with the following code?

---

[97] https://basarat.gitbooks.io/typescript/content/docs/types/typeGuard.html

[98] http://blog.wolksoftware.com/decorators-metadata-reflection-in-typescript-from-novice-to-expert-part-4

```
1   case 'ADD_MESSAGE':
2     state.messages.push( action.message );
3     return { messages: messages };
4     // ...
```

The problem is that this code **mutates** the state.messages array, which changes our old state! Instead what we want to do is create a *copy* of the state.messages array and add our new message to the copy.

code/redux/redux-chat/tutorial/07-messages-reducer.ts

```
22    case 'ADD_MESSAGE':
23      return {
24        messages: state.messages.concat(
25          (<AddMessageAction>action).message
26        ),
27      };
```

> The syntax <AddMessageAction>action will cast our action to the more specific type. That is, notice that our reducer takes the more general type Action, which does not have the message field. If we leave off the cast, then the compiler will complain that Action does not have a field message.
>
> Instead, we know that we have an ADD_MESSAGE action so we cast it to an AddMessageAction. We use parentheses to make sure the compiler knows that we want to cast action and not action.message.

Remember that the reducer **must return a new AppState**. When we return an object from our reducer it must match the format of the AppState that was input. In this case we only have to keep the key messages, but in more complicated states we have more fields to worry about.

Deleting an Item Without Mutation

Remember that when we handle the DELETE_MESSAGE action we are passing the index of the item in the array as the faux ID. (Another common way of handling the same idea would be to pass a real item ID.) Again, because we do not want to mutate the old messages array, we need to handle this case with care:

code/redux/redux-chat/tutorial/07-messages-reducer.ts

```
28    case 'DELETE_MESSAGE':
29      let idx = (<DeleteMessageAction>action).index;
30      return {
31        messages: [
32          ...state.messages.slice(0, idx),
33          ...state.messages.slice(idx + 1, state.messages.length)
34        ]
```

Here we use the slice operator twice. First we take all of the items up until the item we are removing. And we concatenate the items that come after.

> There are four common non-mutating operations:
>
> - Adding an item to an array
> - Removing an item from an array
> - Adding / changing a key in an object
> - Removing a key from an object
>
> The first two (array) operations we just covered. We'll talk more about the object operations further down, but for now know that a common way to do this is to use Object.assign. As in:
>
> ```
> 1    Object.assign({}, oldObject, newObject)
> 2              // <-------<--------------
> ```
>
> You can think of Object.assign as merging objects in from the right into the object on the left. newObject is merged into oldObject which is merged into {}. This way all of the fields in oldObject will be kept, except for where the field exists in newObject. Neither oldObject nor newObject will be mutated.
>
> Of course, handling all of this on your own takes great care and it is easy to make a mistake. This is one of the reasons many people use Immutable.js[99], which is a set of data structures that help enforce immutability.

Trying Out Our Actions

Now let's try running our actions:

---

[99] https://facebook.github.io/immutable-js/

code/redux/redux-chat/tutorial/07-messages-reducer.ts

```
42  let store = new Store<AppState>(reducer, { messages: [] });
43  console.log(store.getState()); // -> { messages: [] }
44
45  store.dispatch({
46    type: 'ADD_MESSAGE',
47    message: 'Would you say the fringe was made of silk?'
48  } as AddMessageAction);
49
50  store.dispatch({
51    type: 'ADD_MESSAGE',
52    message: 'Wouldnt have no other kind but silk'
53  } as AddMessageAction);
54
55  store.dispatch({
56    type: 'ADD_MESSAGE',
57    message: 'Has it really got a team of snow white horses?'
58  } as AddMessageAction);
59
60  console.log(store.getState());
61  // ->
62  // { messages:
63  //    [ 'Would you say the fringe was made of silk?',
64  //      'Wouldnt have no other kind but silk',
65  //      'Has it really got a team of snow white horses?' ] }
```

Here we start with a new store and we call `store.getState()` and see that we have an empty `messages` array.

Next we add three messages[100] to our store. For each message we specify the `type` as `ADD_MESSAGE` and we cast each object to an `AddMessageAction`.

Finally we log the new state and we can see that `messages` contains all three messages.

Our three `dispatch` statements are a bit ugly for two reasons:

1. we manually have to specify the `type` string each time. We could use a constant, but it would be nice if we didn't have to do this and
2. we're manually casting to an `AddMessageAction`

Instead of creating these objects as an object directly we should create a *function* that will create these objects. This idea of writing a function to create actions is so common in Redux that the pattern has a name: *Action Creators*.

---

[100]https://en.wikipedia.org/wiki/The_Surrey_with_the_Fringe_on_Top

Action Creators

Instead of creating the ADD_MESSAGE actions directly as objects, let's create a function to do this for us:

code/redux/redux-chat/tutorial/08-action-creators.ts

```
19  class MessageActions {
20    static addMessage(message: string): AddMessageAction {
21      return {
22        type: 'ADD_MESSAGE',
23        message: message
24      };
25    }
26    static deleteMessage(index: number): DeleteMessageAction {
27      return {
28        type: 'DELETE_MESSAGE',
29        index: index
30      };
31    }
32  }
```

Here we've created a class with two static methods addMessage and deleteMessage. They return an AddMessageAction and a DeleteMessageAction respectively.

> You definitely don't *have* to use static methods for your action creators. You could use plain functions, functions in a namespace, even instance methods on an object, etc. The key idea is to keep them organized in a way that makes them easy to use.

Now let's use our new action creators:

code/redux/redux-chat/tutorial/08-action-creators.ts

```
55  let store = new Store<AppState>(reducer, { messages: [] });
56  console.log(store.getState()); // -> { messages: [] }
57
58  store.dispatch(
59    MessageActions.addMessage('Would you say the fringe was made of silk?'));
60
61  store.dispatch(
62    MessageActions.addMessage('Wouldnt have no other kind but silk'));
63
64  store.dispatch(
```

```
65    MessageActions.addMessage('Has it really got a team of snow white horses?'));
66
67  console.log(store.getState());
68  // ->
69  // { messages:
70  //    [ 'Would you say the fringe was made of silk?',
71  //      'Wouldnt have no other kind but silk',
72  //      'Has it really got a team of snow white horses?' ] }
```

This feels much nicer!

An added benefit is that if we eventually decided to change the format of our messages, we could do it without having to update all of our dispatch statements. For instance, say we wanted to add the time each message was created. We could add a created_at field to addMessage and now all AddMessageActions will be given a created_at field:

```
1  class MessageActions {
2    static addMessage(message: string): AddMessageAction {
3      return {
4        type: 'ADD_MESSAGE',
5        message: message,
6        // something like this
7        created_at: new Date()
8      };
9    }
10   // ....
```

Using Real Redux

Now that we've built our own mini-redux you might be asking, "What do I need to do to use the *real* Redux?" Thankfully, not very much. Let's update our code to use the real Redux now!

> **ⓘ** If you haven't already, you'll want to run `npm install` in the `code/redux/redux-chat/tutorial` directory.

The first thing we need to do is import Action, Reducer, and Store from the redux package. We're also going to import a helper method createStore while we're at it:

code/redux/redux-chat/tutorial/09-real-redux.ts

```
1  import {
2    Action,
3    Reducer,
4    Store,
5    createStore
6  } from 'redux';
```

Next, instead of specifying our initial state when we create the *store* instead we're going to let the *reducer* create the initial state. Here we'll do this as the default argument to the reducer. This way if there is no state passed in (e.g. the first time it is called at initialization) we will use the initial state:

code/redux/redux-chat/tutorial/09-real-redux.ts

```
35  let initialState: AppState = { messages: [] };
36
37  let reducer: Reducer<AppState> =
38    (state: AppState = initialState, action: Action) => {
```

What's neat about this is that the rest of our reducer stays the same!

The last thing we need to do is create the store using the `createStore` helper method from Redux:

code/redux/redux-chat/tutorial/09-real-redux.ts

```
58  let store: Store<AppState> = createStore<AppState>(reducer);
```

After that, everything else just works!

code/redux/redux-chat/tutorial/09-real-redux.ts

```
58  let store: Store<AppState> = createStore<AppState>(reducer);
59  console.log(store.getState()); // -> { messages: [] }
60
61  store.dispatch(
62    MessageActions.addMessage('Would you say the fringe was made of silk?'));
63
64  store.dispatch(
65    MessageActions.addMessage('Wouldnt have no other kind but silk'));
66
67  store.dispatch(
68    MessageActions.addMessage('Has it really got a team of snow white horses?'));
69
```

```
70  console.log(store.getState());
71  // ->
72  // { messages:
73  //     [ 'Would you say the fringe was made of silk?',
74  //        'Wouldnt have no other kind but silk',
75  //        'Has it really got a team of snow white horses?' ] }
```

Now that we have a handle on using Redux in isolation, the next step is to hook it up to our web app. Let's do that now.

Using Redux in Angular

In the last section we walked through the core of Redux and showed how to create reducers and use stores to manage our data in isolation. Now it's time to level-up and integrate Redux with our Angular components.

In this section we're going to create a minimal Angular app that contains just a counter which we can increment and decrement with a button.

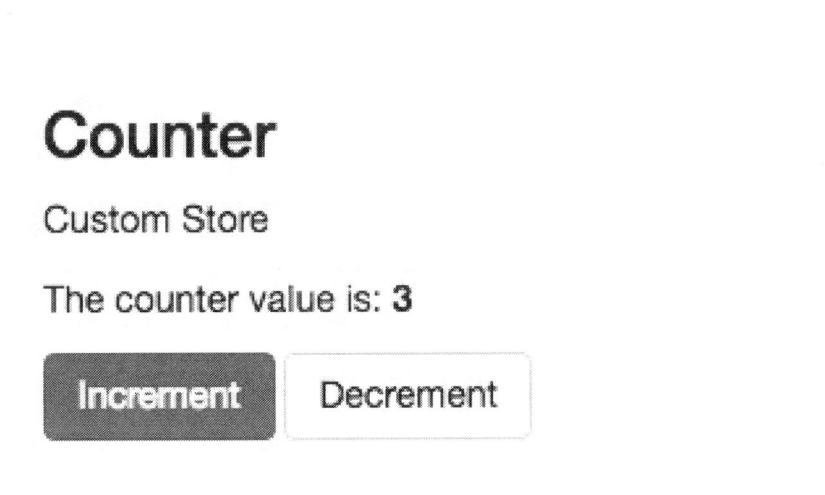

Counter

Custom Store

The counter value is: **3**

Increment   Decrement

Counter App

By using such a small app we can focus on the integration points between Redux and Angular and then we can move on to a larger app in the next section. But first, let's see how to build this counter app!

> ℹ️ Here we are going to be integrating Redux directly with Angular without any helper libraries in-between. There are several open-source libraries with the goal of making this process easier, and you can find them in the references section below.
>
> That said, it can be much easier to use those libraries once you understand what is going on underneath the hood, which is what we work through here.

Planning Our App

If you recall, the three steps to planning our Redux apps are to:

1. Define the structure of our central app state
2. Define actions that will change that state and
3. Define a reducer that takes the old state and an action and returns a new state.

For this app, we're just going to increment and decrement a counter. We did this in the last section, and so our actions, store, and reducer will all be very familiar.

The other thing we need to do when writing Angular apps is decide where we will create components. In this app, we'll have a top-level AppComponent which contains the view we see in the screenshot.

At a high level we're going to do the following:

1. Create our Store and make it accessible to our whole app via dependency injection
2. Subscribe to changes to the Store and display them in our components
3. When something changes (a button is pressed) we will dispatch an action to the Store.

Enough planning, let's look at how this works in practice!

Setting Up Redux

Defining the Application State

Let's take a look at our AppState:

code/redux/redux-chat/redux-counter/src/app/app.state.ts

```
9   export interface AppState {
10    counter: number;
11  };
```

Here we are defining our core state structure as AppState - it is an object with one key, counter which is a number. In the next example (the chat app) we'll talk about how to have more sophisticated states, but for now this will be fine.

Defining the Reducers

Next lets define the reducer which will handle incrementing and decrementing the counter in the application state:

code/redux/redux-chat/redux-counter/src/app/counter.reducer.ts

```
6   import {
7     INCREMENT,
8     DECREMENT
9   } from './counter.actions';
10
11  const initialState: AppState = { counter: 0 };
12
13  // Create our reducer that will handle changes to the state
14  export const counterReducer: Reducer<AppState> =
15    (state: AppState = initialState, action: Action): AppState => {
16      switch (action.type) {
17      case INCREMENT:
18        return Object.assign({}, state, { counter: state.counter + 1 });
19      case DECREMENT:
20        return Object.assign({}, state, { counter: state.counter - 1 });
21      default:
22        return state;
23      }
24    };
```

We start by importing the constants INCREMENT and DECREMENT, which are exported by our action creators. They're just defined as the strings 'INCREMENT' and 'DECREMENT', but it's nice to get the extra help from the compiler in case we make a typo. We'll look at those action creators in a minute.

The initialState is an AppState which sets the counter to 0.

The `counterReducer` handles two actions: `INCREMENT`, which adds `1` to the current counter and `DECREMENT`, which subtracts `1`. Both actions use `Object.assign` to ensure that we don't *mutate* the old state, but instead create a new object that gets returned as the new state.

Since we're here, let's look at the action creators

Defining Action Creators

Our action creators are functions which return objects that define the action to be taken. `increment` and `decrement` below return an object that defines the appropriate `type`.

code/redux/redux-chat/redux-counter/src/app/counter.actions.ts

```
1  import {
2    Action,
3    ActionCreator
4  } from 'redux';
5
6  export const INCREMENT: string = 'INCREMENT';
7  export const increment: ActionCreator<Action> = () => ({
8    type: INCREMENT
9  });
10
11 export const DECREMENT: string = 'DECREMENT';
12 export const decrement: ActionCreator<Action> = () => ({
13   type: DECREMENT
14 });
```

Notice that our action creator functions return the type `ActionCreator<Action>`. `ActionCreator` is a generic class defined by Redux that we use to define functions that create actions. In this case we're using the concrete class `Action`, but we could use a more specific `Action` class, such as `AddMessageAction` that we defined in the last section.

Creating the Store

Now that we have our reducer and state, we could create our store like so:

```
1  let store: Store<AppState> = createStore<AppState>(counterReducer);
```

However, one of the awesome things about Redux is that it has a robust set of developer tools. Specifically, there is a Chrome extension[101] that will let us monitor the state of our application and dispatch actions.

---

[101]https://chrome.google.com/webstore/detail/redux-devtools/lmhkpmbekcpmknklioeibfkpmmfibljd?hl=en

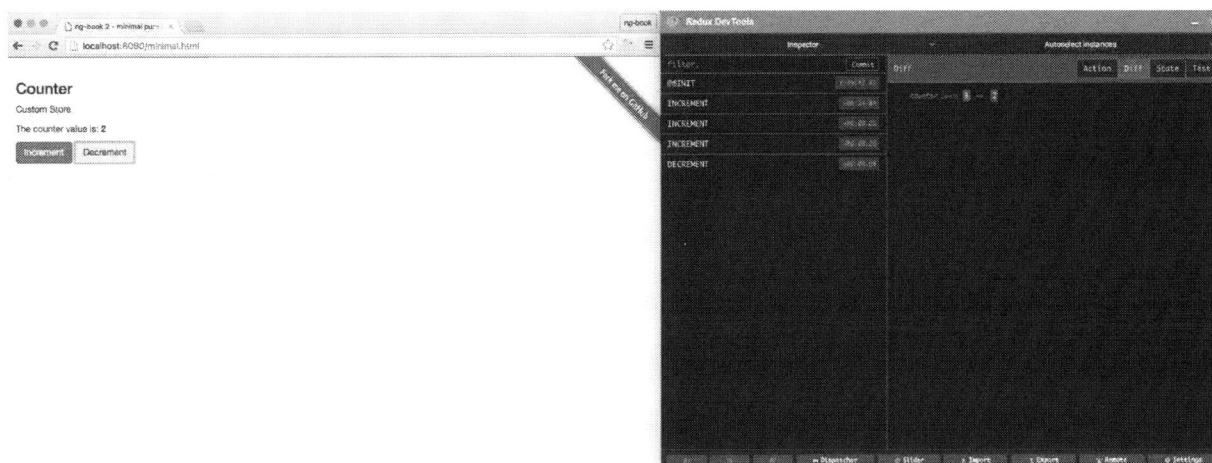

Counter App With Redux Devtools

What's really neat about the Redux Devtools is that it gives us clear insight to every action that flows through the system and it's affect on the state.

Go ahead and install the Redux Devtools Chrome extension[102] now!

In order to use the Devtools we have to do one thing: add it to our store.

code/redux/redux-chat/redux-counter/src/app/app.store.ts

```
16  const devtools: StoreEnhancer<AppState> =
17    window['devToolsExtension'] ?
18    window['devToolsExtension']() : f => f;
```

Not everyone who uses our app will necessarily have the Redux Devtools installed. The code above will check for `window.devToolsExtension`, which is defined by Redux Devtools, and if it exists, we will use it. If it doesn't exist, we're just returning an *identity function* (`f => f`) that will return whatever is passed to it.

Middleware is a term for a function that enhances the functionality of another library. The Redux Devtools is one of many possible middleware libraries for Redux. Redux supports lots of interesting middleware and it's easy to write our own.

You can read more about Redux middleware here[103]

In order to use this `devtools` we pass it as *middleware* to our Redux store:

---
[102] https://chrome.google.com/webstore/detail/redux-devtools/lmhkpmbekcpmknklioeibfkpmmfibljd?hl=en
[103] http://redux.js.org/docs/advanced/Middleware.html

code/redux/redux-chat/redux-counter/src/app/app.store.ts

```
20  export function createAppStore(): Store<AppState> {
21    return createStore<AppState>(
22      reducer,
23      compose(devtools)
24    );
25  }
```

Now whenever we dispatch an action and change our state, we can inspect it in our browser!

Providing the Store

Now that we have the Redux core setup, let's turn our attention to our Angular components. Let's create our top-level app component, AppComponent. This will be the component we use to bootstrap Angular:

We're going to use the AppComponent as the root component. Remember that since this is a Redux app, we need to make our store instance accessible everywhere in our app. How should we do this? We'll use dependency injection (DI).

If you recall from the dependency injection chapter, when we want to make something available via DI, then we use the providers configuration to add it to the list of providers in our NgModule.

When we provide something to the DI system, we specify two things:

1. the *token* to use to refer this injectable dependency
2. the *way* to inject the dependency

Oftentimes if we want to provide a singleton service we might use the useClass option as in:

```
1  { provide: SpotifyService, useClass: SpotifyService }
```

In the case above, we're using the class SpotifyService as the *token* in the DI system. The useClass option tells Angular to *create an instance* of SpotifyService and reuse that instance whenever the SpotifyService injection is requested (e.g. maintain a Singleton).

One problem with us using this method is that we don't want Angular to create our store - we did it ourselves above with createStore. We just want to use the store we've already created.

To do this we'll use the useValue option of provide. We've done this before with configurable values like API_URL:

```
1  { provide: API_URL, useValue: 'http://localhost/api' }
```

The one thing we have left to figure out is what token we want to use to inject. Our store is of type Store<AppState>:

code/redux/redux-chat/redux-counter/src/app/app.store.ts
```
20  export function createAppStore(): Store<AppState> {
21    return createStore<AppState>(
22      reducer,
23      compose(devtools)
24    );
25  }
26
27  export const appStoreProviders = [
28    { provide: AppStore, useFactory: createAppStore }
29  ];
```

Store is an *interface*, not a class and, unfortunately, we can't use interfaces as a dependency injection key.

> If you're interested in *why* we can't use an interface as a DI key, it's because TypeScript interfaces are removed after compilation and not available at runtime.
>
> If you'd like to read more, see here[104], here[105], and here[106].

This means we need to create our own token that we'll use for injecting the store. Thankfully, Angular makes this easy to do. Let's create this token in it's own file so that way we can import it from anywhere in our application;

code/redux/redux-chat/redux-counter/src/app/app.store.ts
```
14  export const AppStore = new InjectionToken('App.store');
```

Here we have created a const AppStore which uses the InjectionToken class from Angular. InjectionToken is a better choice than injecting a string directly because it helps us avoid collisions.

Now we can use this token AppStore with provide. Let's do that now.

Bootstrapping the App

Back in app.module.ts, let's create the NgModule we'll use to bootstrap our app:

[104] http://stackoverflow.com/questions/32254952/binding-a-class-to-an-interface
[105] https://github.com/angular/angular/issues/135
[106] http://victorsavkin.com/post/126514197956/dependency-injection-in-angular-1-and-angular-2

code/redux/redux-chat/redux-counter/src/app/app.module.ts

```
1   import { BrowserModule } from '@angular/platform-browser';
2   import { NgModule } from '@angular/core';
3   import { FormsModule } from '@angular/forms';
4   import { HttpModule } from '@angular/http';
5
6   import { appStoreProviders } from './app.store';
7
8   import { AppComponent } from './app.component';
9
10  @NgModule({
11    declarations: [
12      AppComponent
13    ],
14    imports: [
15      BrowserModule,
16      FormsModule,
17      HttpModule
18    ],
19    providers: [ appStoreProviders ],
20    bootstrap: [AppComponent]
21  })
22  export class AppModule { }
```

Now we are able to get a reference to our Redux store anywhere in our app by injecting `AppStore`.
The place we need it most now is our `AppComponent`.

> Notice that we exported the function `appStoreProviders` from `app.store.ts` and then
> used that function in `providers`. Why not use the `{ provide: ..., useFactory: ... }`
> syntax directly? The answer is related to AOT - if we want to ahead-of-time compile a
> provider that uses a function, we must first export is as a function from another module.

The `AppComponent`

With our setup out of the way, we can start creating our component that actually displays the counter
to the user and provides buttons for the user to change the state.

`imports`

Let's start by looking at the imports:

code/redux/redux-chat/redux-counter/src/app/app.component.ts

```
1  import { Component, Inject } from '@angular/core';
2  import { Store } from 'redux';
3  import { AppStore } from './app.store';
4  import { AppState } from './app.state';
5  import * as CounterActions from './counter.actions';
```

We import `Store` from Redux as well as our injector token `AppStore`, which will get us a reference to the singleton *instance* of our store. We also import the `AppState` type, which helps us know the structure of the central state.

Lastly, we import our action creators with `*` `as` `CounterActions`. This syntax will let us call `CounterActions.increment()` to create an `INCREMENT` action.

The template

Let's look at the template of our `AppComponent`.

In this chapter we are adding some style using the CSS framework Bootstrap[107]

Counter

Custom Store

The counter value is: **3**

Increment   Decrement

Counter App Template

---

[107]http://getbootstrap.com

code/redux/redux-chat/redux-counter/src/app/app.component.html

```
1  <div class="row">
2    <div class="col-sm-6 col-md-4">
3      <div class="thumbnail">
4        <div class="caption">
5          <h3>Counter</h3>
6          <p>Custom Store</p>
7
8          <p>
9            The counter value is:
10           <b>{{ counter }}</b>
11         </p>
12
13         <p>
14           <button (click)="increment()"
15                   class="btn btn-primary">
16             Increment
17           </button>
18           <button (click)="decrement()"
19                   class="btn btn-default">
20             Decrement
21           </button>
22         </p>
23       </div>
24     </div>
25   </div>
26 </div>
```

The three things to note here are that we're:

1. displaying the value of the counter in {{ counter }}
2. calling the increment() function in a button and
3. calling the decrement() function in a button.

The constructor

Remember that this component depends on the Store, so we need to inject it in the constructor. This is how we use our custom AppStore token to inject a dependency:

code/redux/redux-chat/redux-counter/src/app/app.component.ts

```
1  import { Component, Inject } from '@angular/core';
2  import { Store } from 'redux';
3  import { AppStore } from './app.store';
4  import { AppState } from './app.state';
5  import * as CounterActions from './counter.actions';
6
7  @Component({
8    selector: 'app-root',
9    templateUrl: './app.component.html',
10   styleUrls: ['./app.component.css']
11  })
12  export class AppComponent {
13    counter: number;
14
15    constructor(@Inject(AppStore) private store: Store<AppState>) {
16      store.subscribe(() => this.readState());
17      this.readState();
18    }
19
20    readState() {
21      const state: AppState = this.store.getState() as AppState;
22      this.counter = state.counter;
23    }
24
25    increment() {
26      this.store.dispatch(CounterActions.increment());
27    }
28
29    decrement() {
30      this.store.dispatch(CounterActions.decrement());
31    }
32  }
```

We use the `@Inject` decorator to inject `AppStore` - notice that we define the type of the variable `store` to `Store<AppState>`. Having a different injection token than the type of the dependency injected is a little different than when we use the class as the injection token (and Angular infers what to inject).

We set the `store` to an instance variable (with `private store`). Now that we have the store we can listen for changes. Here we call `store.subscribe` and call `this.readState()`, which we define below.

The store will call subscribe only when a new action is dispatched, so in this case we need to make sure we manually call readState at least once to ensure that our component gets the initial data.

The method readState reads from our store and updates this.counter to the current value. Because this.counter is a property on this class and bound in the view, Angular will detect when it changes and re-render this component.

We define two helper methods: increment and decrement, each of which dispatch their respective actions to the store.

Putting It All Together

Try it out!

```
1  cd code/redux/redux-chat/redux-counter
2  npm install
3  npm start
4  open http://localhost:4200
```

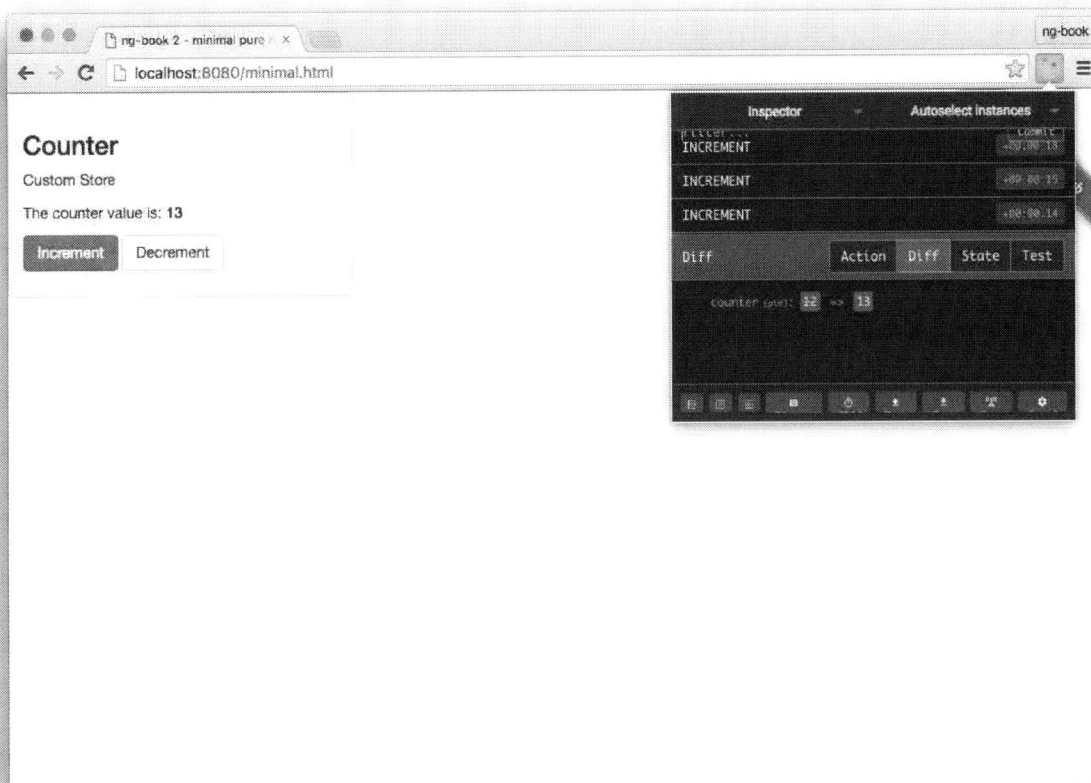

Working Counter App

Congratulations! You've created your first Angular and Redux app!

What's Next

Now that we've built a basic app using Redux and Angular, we should try building a more complicated app. When we build bigger apps we encounter new challenges like:

- How do we combine reducers?
- How do we extract data from different branches of the state?
- How should we organize our Redux code?

In the next chapter, we'll build a chat app which will tackle all of these questions!

References

If you want to learn more about Redux, here are some good resources:

- Official Redux Website[108]
- This Video Tutorial by Redux's Creator[109]
- Real World Redux[110] (presentation slides)
- The power of higher-order reducers[111]

To learn more about Redux and Angular checkout:

- angular2-redux[112]
- ng2-redux[113]
- ngrx/store[114]

Onward!

---

[108] http://redux.js.org/

[109] https://egghead.io/courses/getting-started-with-redux

[110] https://speakerdeck.com/chrisui/real-world-redux

[111] http://slides.com/omnidan/hor

[112] https://github.com/InfomediaLtd/angular2-redux

[113] https://github.com/angular-redux/ng2-redux

[114] https://github.com/ngrx/store

Intermediate Redux in Angular

In the last chapter we learned about Redux, the popular and elegant data architecture. In that chapter, we built an extremely basic app that tied our Angular components and the Redux store together.

In this chapter we're going to take on those ideas and build on them to create a more sophisticated chat app.

Here's a screenshot of the app we're going to build:

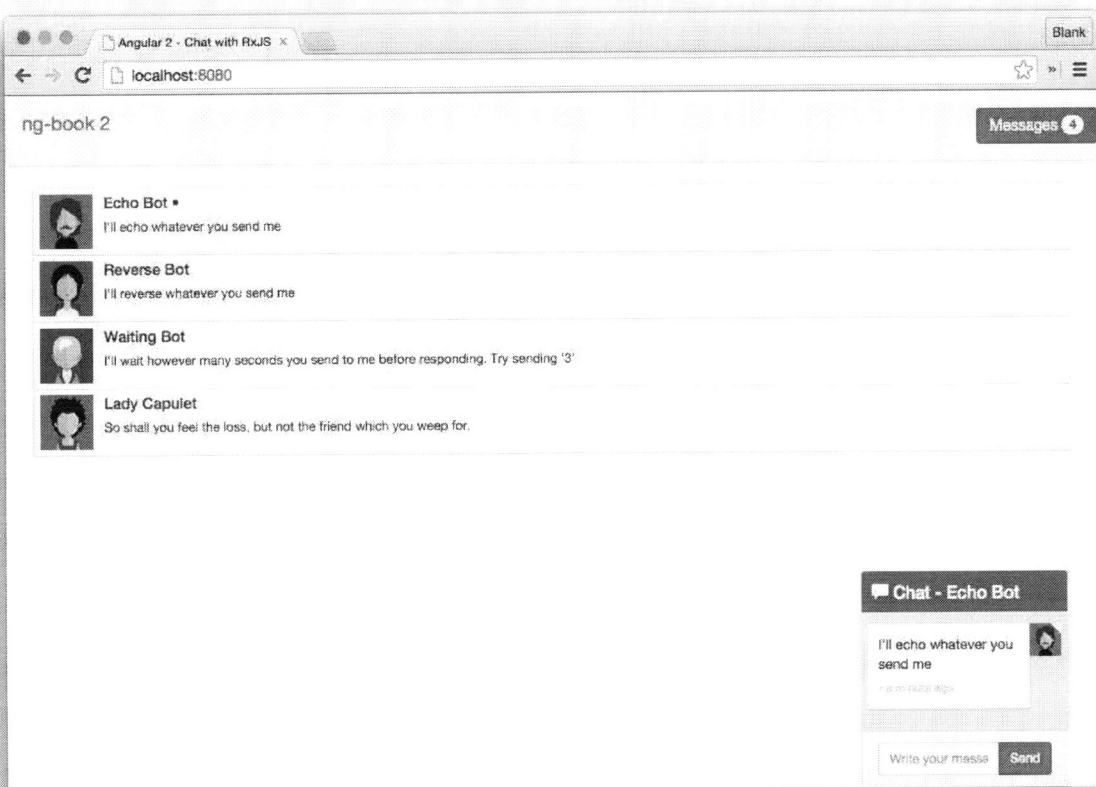

Completed Chat Application

Context For This Chapter

Earlier in this book we built a chat app using RxJS. We're going to be building that same app again only this time with Redux. The point is for you to be able to compare and contrast how the same app works with different data architecture strategies.

You are not required to have read the RxJS chapter in order to work through this one. This chapter stands on its own with regard to the RxJS chapters. If you have read that chapter, you'll be able to skim through some of the sections here where the code is largely the same (for instance, the data models themselves don't change much).

We *do* expect that you've read through the previous Redux chapter or at least have some familiarity with Redux.

Chat App Overview

In this application we've provided a few bots you can chat with. Open up the code and try it out:

```
1    cd code/redux/redux-chat
2    npm install
3    npm start
```

Now open your browser to `http://localhost:4200`.

Notice a few things about this application:

- You can click on the threads to chat with another person
- The bots will send you messages back, depending on their personality
- The unread message count in the top corner stays in sync with the number of unread messages

Let's look at an overview of how this app is constructed. We have

- 3 top-level Angular Components
- 3 models
- and 2 reducers, with their respective action creators

Let's look at them one at a time.

Components

The page is broken down into three top-level components:

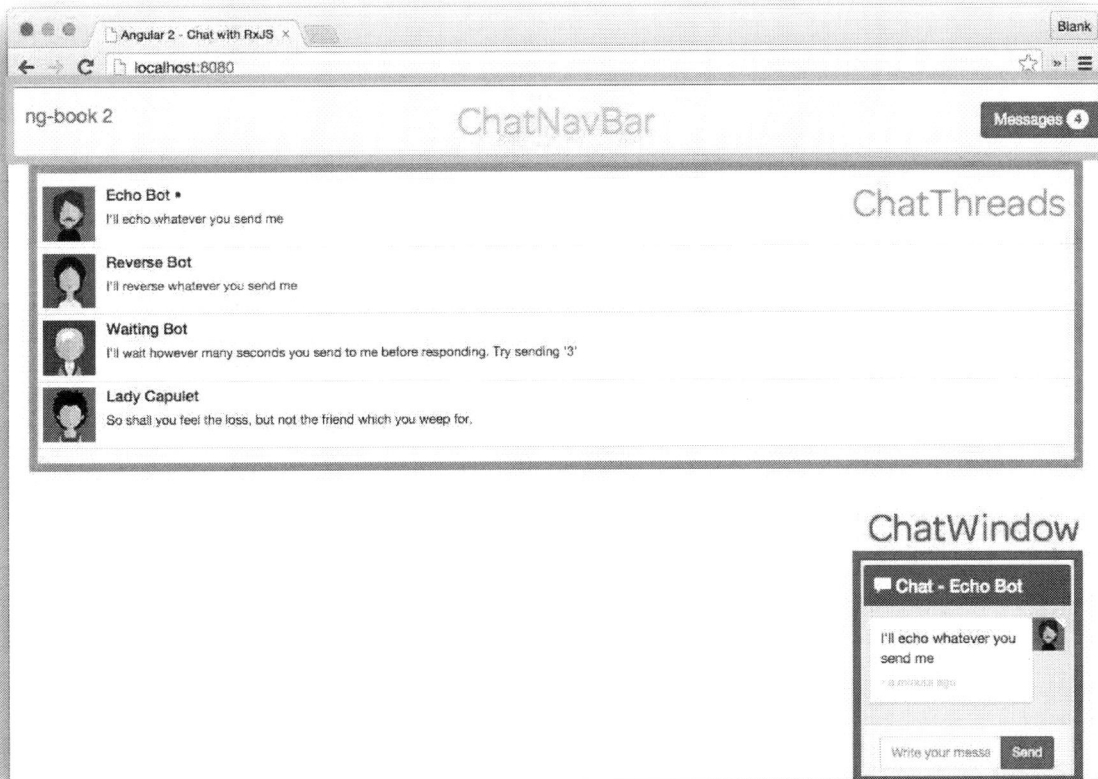

Redux Chat Top-Level Components

- `ChatNavBarComponent` - contains the unread messages count
- `ChatThreadsComponent` - shows a clickable list of threads, along with the most recent message and the conversation avatar
- `ChatWindowComponent` - shows the messages in the current thread with an input box to send new messages

Models

This application also has three models:

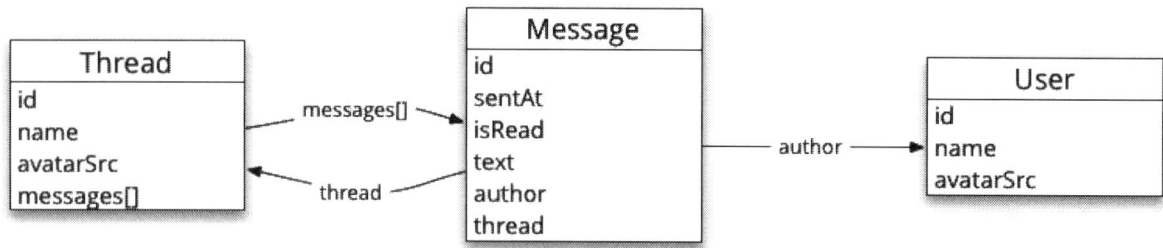

Redux Chat Models

- `User` - stores information about a chat participant
- `Message` - stores an individual message
- `Thread` - stores a collection of `Messages` as well as some data about the conversation

Reducers

In this app, we have two reducers:

- `UsersReducer` - handles information about the current user
- `ThreadsReducer` - handles threads and their messages

Summary

At a high level our data architecture looks like this:

- All information about the users and threads (which hold messages) are contained in our central store
- Components subscribe to changes in that store and display the appropriate data (unread count, list of threads, the messages themselves
- When the user sends a message, our components dispatch an action to the store

In the rest of this chapter, we're going to go in-depth on how we implement this using Angular and Redux. We'll start by implementing our models, then look at how we create our app state and reducers, and then finally we'll implement the Components.

Implementing the Models

Let's start with the easy stuff and take a look at the models.

We're going to be specifying each of our model definitions as interfaces. This isn't a requirement and you're free to use more elaborate objects if you wish. That said, objects with methods that mutate their internal state can break the functional model that we're striving for.

That is, all mutations to our app state should only be made by the reducers - the objects in the state should be immutable themselves.

So by defining an interface for our models,

1. we're able to ensure that the objects we're working with conform to an expected format at compile time and
2. we don't run the risk of someone accidentally adding a method to the model object that would work in an unexpected way.

User

Our User interface has an id, name, and avatarSrc.

code/redux/redux-chat/src/app/user/user.model.ts

```
1   /**
2    * A User represents an agent that sends messages
3    */
4   export interface User {
5     id: string;
6     name: string;
7     avatarSrc: string;
8     isClient?: boolean;
9   }
```

We also have a boolean isClient (the question mark indicates that this field is optional). We will set this value to true for the User that represents the client, the person using the app.

Thread

Similarly, Thread is also a TypeScript interface:

code/redux/redux-chat/src/app/thread/thread.model.ts

```
1  import { Message } from '../message/message.model';
2
3  /**
4   * Thread represents a group of Users exchanging Messages
5   */
6  export interface Thread {
7    id: string;
8    name: string;
9    avatarSrc: string;
10   messages: Message[];
11 }
```

We store the id of the Thread, the name, and the current avatarSrc. We also expect an array of Messages in the messages field.

Message

Message is our third and final model interface:

code/redux/redux-chat/src/app/message/message.model.ts

```
1  import { User } from '../user/user.model';
2  import { Thread } from '../thread/thread.model';
3
4  /**
5   * Message represents one message being sent in a Thread
6   */
7  export interface Message {
8    id?: string;
9    sentAt?: Date;
10   isRead?: boolean;
11   thread?: Thread;
12   author: User;
13   text: string;
14 }
```

Each message has:

  • id - the id of the message

- `sentAt` - when the message was sent
- `isRead` - a boolean indicating that the message was read
- `author` - the `User` who wrote this message
- `text` - the text of the message
- `thread` - a reference to the containing `Thread`

App State

Now that we have our models, let's talk about the shape of our central state. In the previous chapter, our central state was a single object with the key `counter` which had the value of a `number`. This app, however, is more complicated.

Here's the first part of our app state:

code/redux/redux-chat/src/app/app.reducer.ts

```
18  export interface AppState {
19    users: UsersState;
20    threads: ThreadsState;
21  }
```

Our `AppState` is also an `interface` and it has two top level keys: `users` and `threads` - these are defined by two more interfaces `UsersState` and `ThreadsState`, which are defined in their respective reducers.

A Word on Code Layout

This is a common pattern we use in Redux apps: the top level state has a top-level key for each reducer. In our app we're going to keep this top-level reducer in `app.reducer.ts`.

Each reducer will have it's own file. In that file we'll store:

- The `interface` that describes that branch of the state tree
- The value of the initial state, for that branch of the state tree
- The reducer itself
- Any *selectors* that query that branch of the state tree - we haven't talked about *selectors* yet, but we will soon.

The reason we keep all of these different things together is because they all deal with the structure of this branch of the state tree. By putting these things in the same file it's very easy to refactor everything at the same time.

You're free to have multiple layers of nesting, if you so desire. It's a nice way to break up large modules in your app.

The Root Reducer

Since we're talking about how to split up reducers, let's look at our root reducer now:

code/redux/redux-chat/src/app/app.reducer.ts

```
18  export interface AppState {
19   users: UsersState;
20   threads: ThreadsState;
21  }
22
23  const rootReducer: Reducer<AppState> = combineReducers<AppState>({
24   users: UsersReducer,
25   threads: ThreadsReducer
26  });
27
28  export default rootReducer;
```

Notice the symmetry here - our `UsersReducer` will operate on the `users` key, which is of type `UsersState` and our `ThreadsReducer` will operate on the `threads` key, which is of type `ThreadsState`.

This is made possible by the `combineReducers` function which takes a map of keys and reducers and returns a new reducer that operates appropriately on those keys.

Of course we haven't finished looking at the structure of our `AppState` yet, so let's do that now.

The `UsersState`

Our `UsersState` holds a reference to the `currentUser`.

code/redux/redux-chat/src/app/user/users.reducer.ts

```
18  export interface UsersState {
19    currentUser: User;
20  };
21
22  const initialState: UsersState = {
23    currentUser: null
24  };
```

You could imagine that this branch of the state tree could hold information about all of the users, when they were last seen, their idle time, etc. But for now this will suffice.

We'll use `initialState` in our reducer when we define it below, but for now we're just going to set the current user to `null`.

The `ThreadsState`

Let's look at the `ThreadsState`:

code/redux/redux-chat/src/app/thread/threads.reducer.ts

```
25  export interface ThreadsEntities {
26    [id: string]: Thread;
27  }
28
29  export interface ThreadsState {
30    ids: string[];
31    entities: ThreadsEntities;
32    currentThreadId?: string;
33  };
34
35  const initialState: ThreadsState = {
36    ids: [],
37    currentThreadId: null,
38    entities: {}
39  };
```

We start by defining an interface called `ThreadsEntities` which is a map of thread `ids` to `Threads`. The idea is that we'll be able to look up any thread by id in this map.

In the `ThreadsState` we're also storing an array of the `ids`. This will store the list of possible ids that we might find in `entities`.

> This strategy is used by the commonly-used library normalizr[115]. The idea is that when we standardize how we store entities in our Redux state, we're able to build helper libraries and it's clearer to work with. Instead of wondering what the format is for each tree of the state, when we use `normalizr` a lot of the choices have been made for us and we're able to work more quickly.
>
> I've opted not to teach `normalizr` in this chapter because we're learning so many other things. That said, I would be very likely to use `normalizr` in my production applications.
>
> That said, `normalizr` is totally optional - nothing major changes in our app by not using it.
>
> If you'd like to learn how to use `normalizr`, checkout the official docs[116], this blog post[117], and the thread referenced by Redux creator Dan Abramov here[118]

---

[115] https://github.com/paularmstrong/normalizr

[116] https://github.com/paularmstrong/normalizr

[117] https://medium.com/@mcowpercoles/using-normalizr-js-in-a-redux-store-96ab33991369#.l8ur7ipu6

[118] https://twitter.com/dan_abramov/status/663032263702106112

We store the currently viewed thread in `currentThreadId` - the idea here is that we want to know which thread the user is currently looking at.

We set our `initialState` to "empty" values.

Visualizing Our `AppState`

Redux Devtools provides us with a "Chart" view that lets us inspect the state of our app. Here's what mine looks like after being booted with all of the demo data:

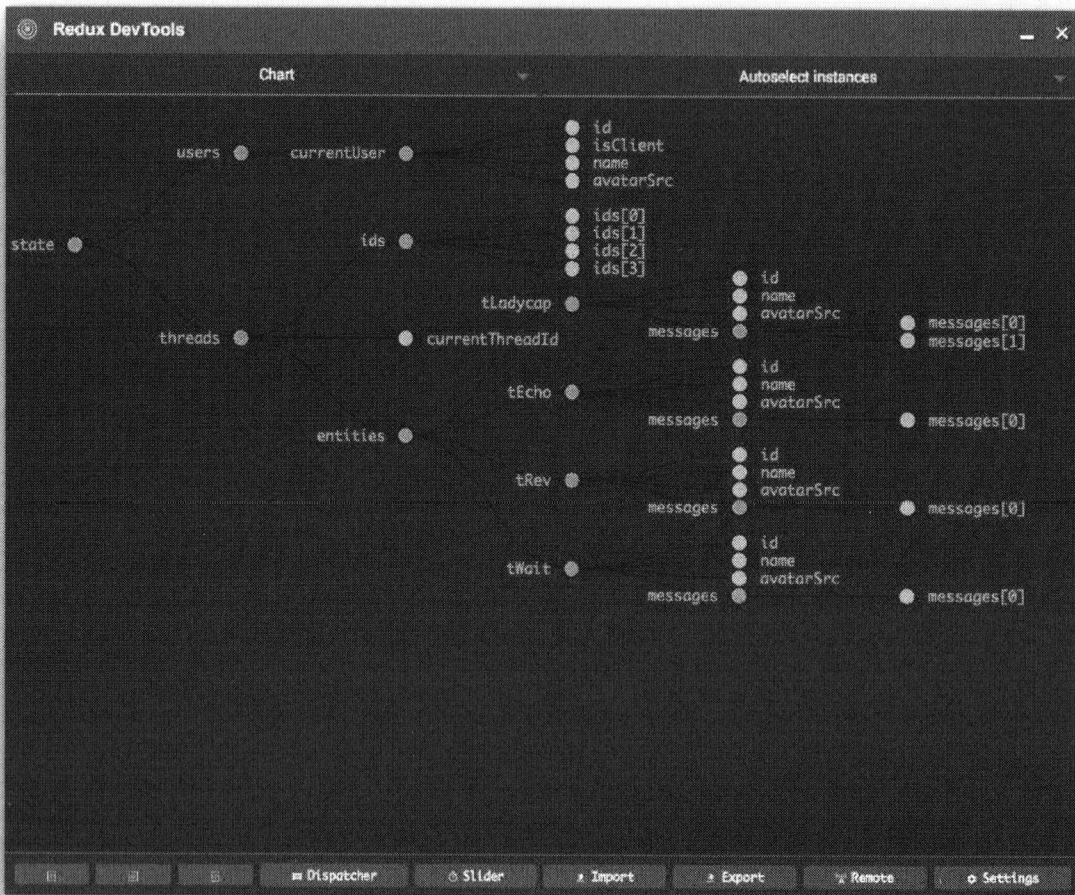

Redux Chat State Chart

What's neat is that we can hover over an individual node and see the attributes of that piece of data:

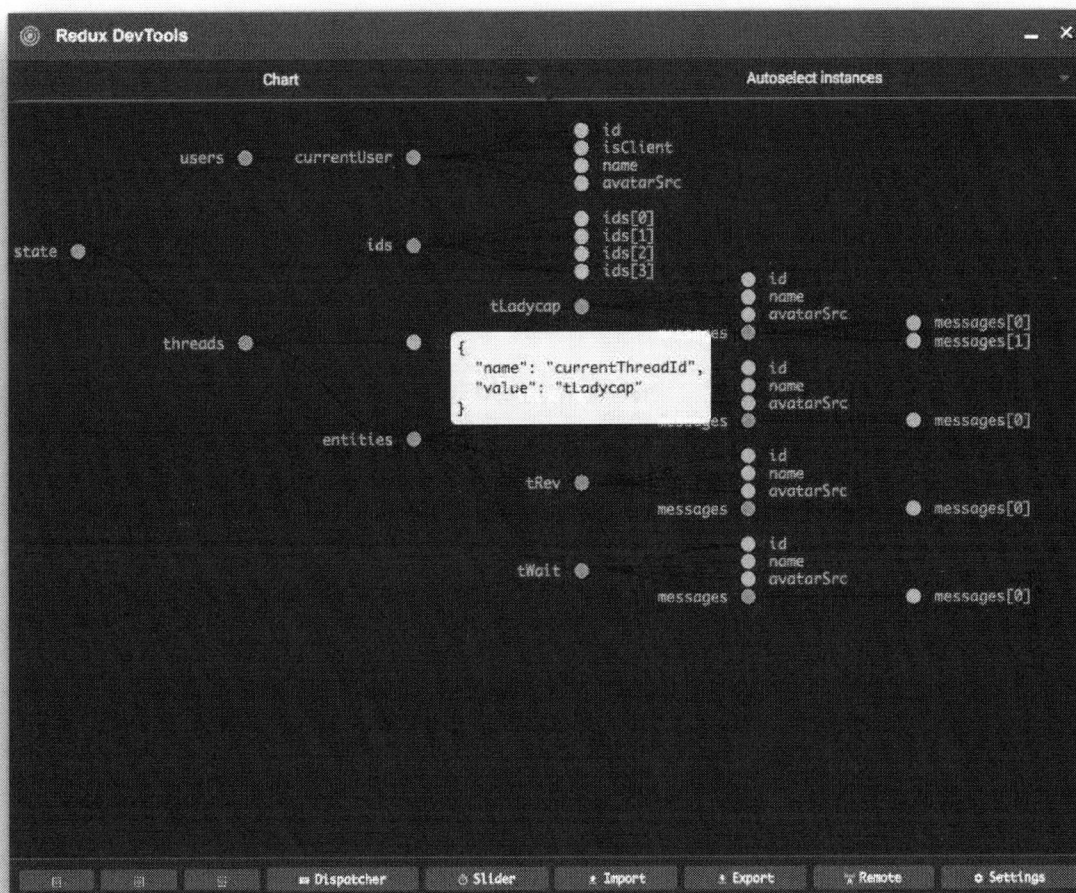

Inspecting the current thread

Building the Reducers (and Action Creators)

Now that we have our central state, we can start changing it using our reducers!

Since reducers handle actions, we need to know the format of our actions in our reducer. So let's build our action creators at the same time we build our reducers

Set Current User Action Creators

The UsersState stores the current user. This means we need an action to set the current user. We're going to keep our actions in the actions folder and name the actions to match their corresponding reducer, in this case UserActions.

code/redux/redux-chat/src/app/user/user.actions.ts

```
20  export const SET_CURRENT_USER = '[User] Set Current';
21  export interface SetCurrentUserAction extends Action {
22    user: User;
23  }
24  export const setCurrentUser: ActionCreator<SetCurrentUserAction> =
25    (user) => ({
26      type: SET_CURRENT_USER,
27      user: user
28    });
```

Here we define the const SET_CURRENT_USER, which we'll use to switch on in our reducer.

We also define a new subinterface SetCurrentUserAction which extends Action to add a user property. We'll use the user property to indicate *which user* we want to make the current user.

The function setCurrentUser is our proper action creator function. It takes user as an argument, and returns a SetCurrentUserAction which we can give to our reducer.

UsersReducer **- Set Current User**

Now we turn our attention to our UsersReducer:

code/redux/redux-chat/src/app/user/users.reducer.ts

```
26  export const UsersReducer =
27    function(state: UsersState = initialState, action: Action): UsersState {
28    switch (action.type) {
29      case UserActions.SET_CURRENT_USER:
30      const user: User = (<UserActions.SetCurrentUserAction>action).user;
31        return {
32          currentUser: user
33        };
34      default:
35        return state;
36    }
37  };
```

Our UsersReducer takes a UsersState as the first argument. Notice that this isn't the AppState! Our "child reducer" only works with it's branch of the state tree.

Our UsersReducer, like all reducers, returns a new state, in this case it is of type UsersState.

Next we `switch` on the `action.type` and we handle the `UserActions.SET_CURRENT_USER`.

In order to set the current user, we need to get the `user` from the incoming action. To do this, we first cast the `action` to `UserActions.SetCurrentUserAction` and then we read the `.user` field.

> **ⓘ** It might seem a little weird that we originally created a `SetCurrentUserAction` but then now we switch on a `type` string instead of using the type directly.
>
> Indeed, we are fighting TypeScript a little here. We lose interface metadata when the TypeScript is compiled to JavaScript. We could instead try some sort of reflection (through decorator metadata, or looking at a constructor etc.).
>
> While down-casting our `SetCurrentUserAction` to an `Action` on `dispatch` and then re-casting is a bit ugly, it's a straightforward and portable way to handle this "polymorphic dispatch" for this app.

We need to return a new `UsersState`. Since `UsersState` only has one key, we return an object with the `currentUser` set to the incoming action's `user`.

Thread and Messages Overview

The core of our application is messages in threads. There are three actions we need to support:

1. Adding a new thread to the state
2. Adding messages to a thread
3. Selecting a thread

Let's start by creating a new thread

Adding a New Thread Action Creators

Here's the action creator for adding a new `Thread` to our state:

code/redux/redux-chat/src/app/thread/thread.actions.ts

```
22  export const ADD_THREAD = '[Thread] Add';
23  export interface AddThreadAction extends Action {
24    thread: Thread;
25  }
26  export const addThread: ActionCreator<AddThreadAction> =
27    (thread) => ({
28      type: ADD_THREAD,
29      thread: thread
30    });
```

Notice that this is structurally very similar to our previous action creator. We define a const ADD_-THREAD that we can switch on, a custom Action, and an action creator addThread which generates the Action.

Notice that we don't initialize the Thread itself here - the Thread is accepted as an argument.

Adding a New Thread Reducer

Now let's start our ThreadsReducer by handling ADD_THREAD:

code/redux/redux-chat/src/app/thread/threads.reducer.ts

```
45  export const ThreadsReducer =
46    function(state: ThreadsState = initialState, action: Action): ThreadsState {
47    switch (action.type) {
48
49      // Adds a new Thread to the list of entities
50      case ThreadActions.ADD_THREAD: {
51        const thread = (<ThreadActions.AddThreadAction>action).thread;
52
53        if (state.ids.includes(thread.id)) {
54          return state;
55        }
56
57        return {
58          ids: [ ...state.ids, thread.id ],
59          currentThreadId: state.currentThreadId,
60          entities: Object.assign({}, state.entities, {
61            [thread.id]: thread
62          })
63        };
64      }
65
66      // Adds a new Message to a particular Thread
```

Our ThreadsReducer handles the ThreadsState. When we handle the ADD_THREAD action, we cast the action object back into a ThreadActions.AddThreadAction and then pull the Thread out.

Next we check to see if this new thread.id already appears in the list of state.ids. If it does, then we don't make any changes, but instead return the current state.

However if this thread is new, then we need to add it to our current state.

Remember when we create a new ThreadsState we need to take care to not mutate our old state. This looks more complicated than any state we've done so far, but it's not very different in principle.

We start by adding our `thread.id` to the `ids` array. Here we're using the ES6 spread operator (...) to indicate that we want to put all of the existing `state.ids` into this new array and then append `thread.id` to the end.

`currentThreadId` does not change when we add a new thread, so we return the *old* `state.currentThreadId` for this field.

For `entities`, remember that it is an object where the key is the `string` id of each thread and the value is the thread itself. We're using `Object.assign` here to create a new object that merges the old `state.entities` with our newly added `thread` into a new object.

> You might be kind of tired of meticulously copying these objects when we need to make changes. That's a common response! In fact, it's easy to make mutations here by accident.
>
> This is why Immutable.js[119] was written. Immutable.js is often used with Redux for this purpose. When we use Immutable, these careful updates are handled for us.
>
> I'd encourage you to take a look at Immutable.js and see if it is a good fit for your reducers.

Now we can add new threads to our central state!

Adding New Messages Action Creators

Now that we have threads we can start adding messages to them.

Let's define a new action for adding messages:

code/redux/redux-chat/src/app/thread/thread.actions.ts

```
32  export const ADD_MESSAGE = '[Thread] Add Message';
33  export interface AddMessageAction extends Action {
34    thread: Thread;
35    message: Message;
36  }
```

The `AddMessageAction` adds a `Message` to a `Thread`.

Here's the action creator for adding a message:

---

[119] https://facebook.github.io/immutable-js/

code/redux/redux-chat/src/app/thread/thread.actions.ts

```
37  export const addMessage: ActionCreator<AddMessageAction> =
38    (thread: Thread, messageArgs: Message): AddMessageAction => {
39      const defaults = {
40        id: uuid(),
41        sentAt: new Date(),
42        isRead: false,
43        thread: thread
44      };
45      const message: Message = Object.assign({}, defaults, messageArgs);
46
47      return {
48        type: ADD_MESSAGE,
49        thread: thread,
50        message: message
51      };
52    };
```

The `addMessage` action creator accepts a `thread` and an object we use for crafting the message. Notice here that we keep a list of `defaults`. The idea here is that we want to encapsulate creating an id, setting the timestamp, and setting the `isRead` status. Someone who wants to send a message shouldn't have to worry about how the UUIDs are formed, for instance.

That said, maybe the client using this library crafted the message beforehand and if they send a message with an existing id, we want to keep it. To enable this default behavior we merge the `messageArgs` into the `defaults` and copy those values to a new object.

Lastly we return the `ADD_MESSAGE` action with the `thread` and new `message`.

Adding A New Message Reducer

Now we will add our `ADD_MESSAGE` handler to our `ThreadsReducer`. When a new message is added, we need to take the thread and add the message to it.

There is one tricky thing we need to handle that may not be obvious at this point: if the `thread` is the "current thread" we need to *mark this message as read*.

The user will always have one thread that is the "current thread" that they're looking at. We're going to say that if a new message is added to the current thread, then it's automatically marked as read.

code/redux/redux-chat/src/app/thread/threads.reducer.ts

```
67      case ThreadActions.ADD_MESSAGE: {
68        const thread = (<ThreadActions.AddMessageAction>action).thread;
69        const message = (<ThreadActions.AddMessageAction>action).message;
70
71        // special case: if the message being added is in the current thread, then
72        // mark it as read
73        const isRead = message.thread.id === state.currentThreadId ?
74                          true : message.isRead;
75        const newMessage = Object.assign({}, message, { isRead: isRead });
76
77        // grab the old thread from entities
78        const oldThread = state.entities[thread.id];
79
80        // create a new thread which has our newMessage
81        const newThread = Object.assign({}, oldThread, {
82          messages: [...oldThread.messages, newMessage]
83        });
84
85        return {
86          ids: state.ids, // unchanged
87          currentThreadId: state.currentThreadId, // unchanged
88          entities: Object.assign({}, state.entities, {
89            [thread.id]: newThread
90          })
91        };
92      }
93
94      // Select a particular thread in the UI
```

The code is a bit long because we're being careful not to mutate the original thread, but it is not much different than what we've done so far in principle.

We start by extracting the thread and message.

Next we mark the message as read, if its part of the "current thread" (we'll look at how to set the current thread next).

Then we grab the oldThread and create a newThread which has the newMessage appended on to the old messages.

Finally we return the new ThreadsState. The current list of thread ids and the currentThreadId are unchanged by adding a message, so we pass the old values here. The only thing we change is that we update entities with our newThread.

Now let's implement the last part of our data backbone: selecting a thread.

Selecting A Thread Action Creators

Our user can have multiple chat sessions in progress at the same time. However, we only have one chat window (where the user can read and send messages). When the user clicks on a thread, we want to show that thread's messages in the chat window.

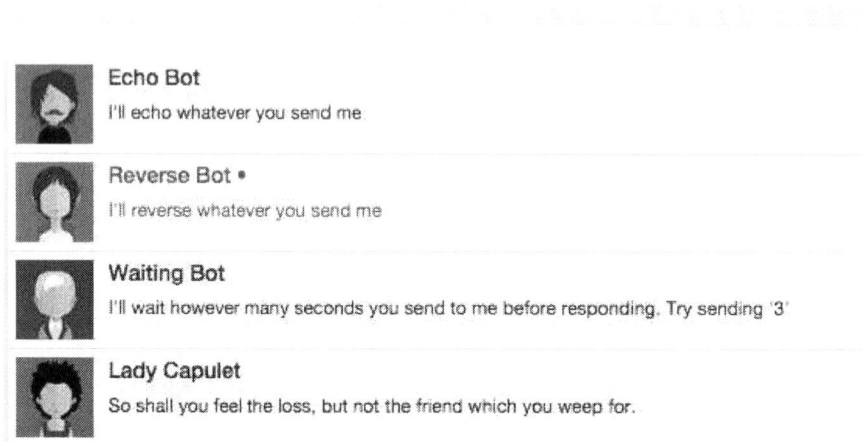

Echo Bot
I'll echo whatever you send me

Reverse Bot •
I'll reverse whatever you send me

Waiting Bot
I'll wait however many seconds you send to me before responding. Try sending '3'

Lady Capulet
So shall you feel the loss, but not the friend which you weep for.

Selecting A Thread

We need to keep track of which thread is the currently selected thread. To do that, we'll use the `currentThreadId` property in the `ThreadsState`.

Let's create the actions for this:

code/redux/redux-chat/src/app/thread/thread.actions.ts

```
54  export const SELECT_THREAD = '[Thread] Select';
55  export interface SelectThreadAction extends Action {
56    thread: Thread;
57  }
58  export const selectThread: ActionCreator<SelectThreadAction> =
59    (thread) => ({
60      type: SELECT_THREAD,
61      thread: thread
62    });
```

There's nothing conceptually new in this action: we've got a new type of SELECT_THREAD and we pass the Thread that we're selecting as an argument.

Selecting A Thread Reducer

To select a thread we need to do two things:

1. set currentThreadId to the selected thread's id
2. mark all messages in that thread as read

Here's the code for that reducer:

code/redux/redux-chat/src/app/thread/threads.reducer.ts

```
95      case ThreadActions.SELECT_THREAD: {
96        const thread = (<ThreadActions.SelectThreadAction>action).thread;
97        const oldThread = state.entities[thread.id];
98
99        // mark the messages as read
100       const newMessages = oldThread.messages.map(
101         (message) => Object.assign({}, message, { isRead: true }));
102
103       // give them to this new thread
104       const newThread = Object.assign({}, oldThread, {
105         messages: newMessages
106       });
107
108       return {
109         ids: state.ids,
110         currentThreadId: thread.id,
111         entities: Object.assign({}, state.entities, {
112           [thread.id]: newThread
113         })
114       };
115     }
116
117     default:
118       return state;
119   }
120 };
```

We start by getting the thread-to-select and then using that thread.id to get the current Thread that exists in state to get the values.

> This maneuver is a bit defensive. Why not just use the thread that is passed in? That might be the right design decision for some apps. In this case we protect against some external mutation of thread by reading the last known values of that thread in state.entities.

Next we create a copy of all of the old messages and set them as `isRead: true`. Then we assign those new read messages to `newThread`.

Finally we return our new `ThreadsState`.

Reducers Summary

We did it! Above is everything we need for the backbone of our data architecture.

To recap, we have a `UsersReducer` which maintains the current user. We have a `ThreadsReducer` which manages:

- The list of threads
- The messages in those threads
- The currently selected thread

We can derive everything else that we need (e.g. the unread count) from these pieces of data.

Now we need to hook them up to our components!

Building the Angular Chat App

As we mentioned earlier in the chapter, the page is broken down into three top-level components:

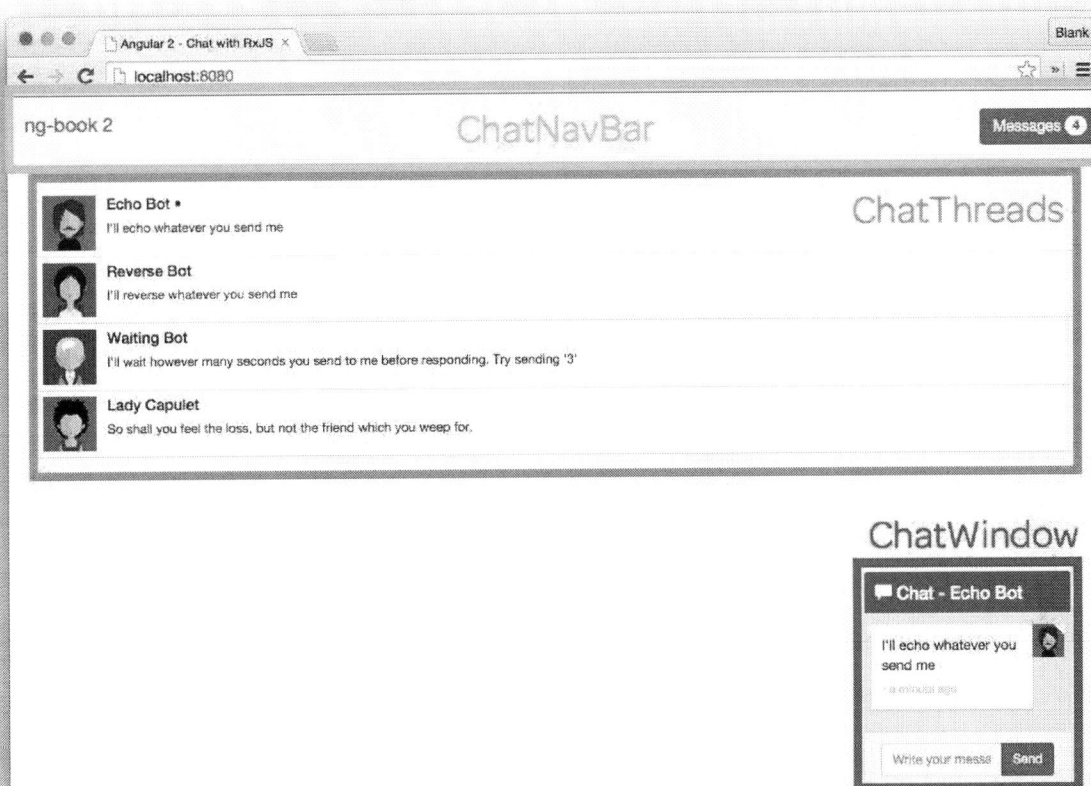

Redux Chat Top-Level Components

- `ChatNavBarComponent` - contains the unread messages count
- `ChatThreadsComponent` - shows a clickable list of threads, along with the most recent message and the conversation avatar
- `ChatWindowComponent` - shows the messages in the current thread with an input box to send new messages

We're going to bootstrap our app much like we did in the last chapter. We're going to initialize our Redux store at the top of the app and provide it via Angular's dependency injection system (take a look at the previous chapter if this looks unfamiliar):

code/redux/redux-chat/src/app/app.store.ts

```
1  import { InjectionToken } from '@angular/core';
2  import {
3    createStore,
4    Store,
5    compose,
6    StoreEnhancer
7  } from 'redux';
8
9  import {
10   AppState,
11   default as reducer
12 } from './app.reducer';
13
14 export const AppStore = new InjectionToken('App.store');
15
16 const devtools: StoreEnhancer<AppState> =
17   window['devToolsExtension'] ?
18   window['devToolsExtension']() : f => f;
19
20 export function createAppStore(): Store<AppState> {
21   return createStore<AppState>(
22     reducer,
23     compose(devtools)
24   );
25 }
26
27 export const appStoreProviders = [
28     { provide: AppStore, useFactory: createAppStore }
29 ];
```

The top-level AppComponent

Our AppComponent component is the top-level component. It doesn't do much other than render the
ChatPage.

code/redux/redux-chat/src/app/app.component.ts

```
1   import { Component, Inject } from '@angular/core';
2   import * as Redux from 'redux';
3
4   import { AppStore } from './app.store';
5   import { AppState } from './app.reducer';
6   import { ChatExampleData } from './data/chat-example-data';
7
8   @Component({
9     selector: 'app-root',
10    templateUrl: './app.component.html',
11    styleUrls: ['./app.component.css']
12  })
13  export class AppComponent {
14    constructor(@Inject(AppStore) private store: Redux.Store<AppState>) {
15      ChatExampleData(store);
16    }
17  }
```

and the template:

code/redux/redux-chat/src/app/app.component.html

```
1   <div>
2     <chat-page></chat-page>
3   </div>
```

> For this app the bots operate on data on the client and are not connected to a server. The function ChatExampleData() sets up the initial data for the app. We won't be covering this code in detail in the book, so feel free to look at the code on disk if you want to learn more about how it works.

We're not using a router in this app, but if we were, we would put it here at the top level of the app. For now, we're going to create a ChatPage which will render the bulk of our app.

We don't have any other pages in this app, but it's a good idea to give each page it's own component in case we add some in the future.

The ChatPage

Our chat page renders our three main components:

- ChatNavBarComponent
- ChatThreadsComponent and
- ChatWindowComponent

Here it is in code:

code/redux/redux-chat/src/app/chat-page/chat-page.component.ts

```
1  import { Component, OnInit } from '@angular/core';
2
3  @Component({
4    selector: 'chat-page',
5    templateUrl: './chat-page.component.html',
6    styleUrls: ['./chat-page.component.css']
7  })
8  export class ChatPageComponent implements OnInit {
9    constructor() { }
10   ngOnInit() { }
11 }
```

and the template:

code/redux/redux-chat/src/app/chat-page/chat-page.component.html

```
1  <div>
2    <chat-nav-bar></chat-nav-bar>
3    <div class="container">
4      <chat-threads></chat-threads>
5      <chat-window></chat-window>
6    </div>
7  </div>
```

For this app we are using a design pattern called *container components* and these three components are all container components. Let's talk about what that means.

Container vs. Presentational Components

It is hard to reason about our apps if there is data spread throughout all of our components. However, our apps are dynamic - they need to be populated with runtime data and they need to be responsive to user interaction.

One of the patterns that has emerged in managing this tension is the idea of presentational vs. container components. The idea is this:

1. You want to minimize the number of components which interact with outside data sources. (e.g. APIs, the Redux Store, Cookies etc.)
2. Therefore deliberately put data access into "container" components and
3. Require purely 'functional' presentation components to have all of their properties (inputs and outputs) managed by container components.

The great thing about this design is that presentational components are predictable. They're reusable because they don't make assumptions about your overall data-architecture, they only give requirements for their own use.

But even beyond reuse, they're predictable. Given the same inputs, they always return the same outputs (e.g. render the same way).

> If you squint, you can see that the philosophy that requires reducers to be pure functions is the same that requires presentational components be 'pure components'

It would be great if our entire app could be all presentational components, but of course, the real world has messy, changing data. So we try to put this complexity of adapting our real-world data into our container components.

> If you're an advanced programmer you may see that there is a loose analogy between MVC and container/presentation components. That is, the presentational component is sort of a "view" of data that is passed in. A container component is sort of a "controller" in that it takes the "model" (the data from the rest of the app) and adapts it for the presentational components.
>
> That said, if you haven't been programming very long, take this analogy with a grain of salt as Angular components are already a view and a controller themselves.

In our app the container components are going to be the components which interact with the store. This means our container components will be anything that:

1. Reads data from the store

2. Subscribes to the store for changes

3. Dispatches actions to the store

Our three main components are container components and anything below them will be presentational (i.e. functional / pure / not interact with the store).

Let's build our first container component, the nav bar.

Building the ChatNavBarComponent

In the nav bar we'll show an unread messages count to the user.

ng-book 2   Messages 4

Echo Bot •

The Unread Count in the ChatNavBarComponent

The best way to try out the unread messages count is to use the "Waiting Bot". If you haven't already, try sending the message '3' to the Waiting Bot and then switch to another window. The Waiting Bot will then wait 3 seconds before sending you a message and you will see the unread messages counter increment.

Let's look at the component code first:

code/redux/redux-chat/src/app/chat-nav-bar/chat-nav-bar.component.ts

```
1  import { Component, Inject } from '@angular/core';
2  import { AppStore } from '../app.store';
3  import * as Redux from 'redux';
4  import {
5    AppState,
6    getUnreadMessagesCount
7  } from '../app.reducer';
8
9  @Component({
10    selector: 'chat-nav-bar',
11    templateUrl: './chat-nav-bar.component.html',
12    styleUrls: ['./chat-nav-bar.component.css']
13  })
14  export class ChatNavBarComponent {
15    unreadMessagesCount: number;
16
```

```
17    constructor(@Inject(AppStore) private store: Redux.Store<AppState>) {
18      store.subscribe(() => this.updateState());
19      this.updateState();
20    }
21
22    updateState() {
23      this.unreadMessagesCount = getUnreadMessagesCount(this.store.getState());
24    }
25  }
```

and the template:

code/redux/redux-chat/src/app/chat-nav-bar/chat-nav-bar.component.html

```
1   <nav class="navbar navbar-default">
2     <div class="container-fluid">
3       <div class="navbar-header">
4         <a class="navbar-brand" href="https://ng-book.com/2">
5           <img src="assets/images/logos/ng-book-2-minibook.png"/>
6           ng-book 2
7         </a>
8       </div>
9       <p class="navbar-text navbar-right">
10        <button class="btn btn-primary" type="button">
11          Messages <span class="badge">{{ unreadMessagesCount }}</span>
12        </button>
13      </p>
14    </div>
15  </nav>
```

Our template gives us the DOM structure and CSS necessary for rendering a nav bar (these CSS-classes come from the CSS framework Bootstrap).

The only variable we're showing in this template is unreadMessagesCount.

Our ChatNavBarComponent has unreadMessagesCount as an instance variable. This number will be set to the sum of unread messages in all threads.

Notice in our constructor we do three things:

1. Inject our store
2. Subscribe to any changes in the store
3. Call this.updateState()

We call `this.updateState()` after `subscribe` because we want to make sure this component is initialized with the most recent data. `subscribe` will only be called if something changes *after* this component is initialized.

`updateState()` is the most interesting function - we set `unreadMessagesCount` to the value of the function `getUnreadMessagesCount`. What is `getUnreadMessagesCount` and where did it come from?

`getUnreadMessagesCount` is a new concept called *selectors*.

Redux Selectors

Thinking about our `AppState`, how might we go about getting the unread messages count? How about something like this:

```
 1   // get the state
 2   let state = this.store.getState();
 3
 4   // get the threads state
 5   let threadsState = state.threads;
 6
 7   // get the entities from the threads
 8   let threadsEntities = threadsState.entities;
 9
10   // get all of the threads from state
11   let allThreads = Object.keys(threadsEntities)
12                 .map((threadId) => entities[threadId]);
13
14   // iterate over all threads and ...
15   let unreadCount = allThreads.reduce(
16       (unreadCount: number, thread: Thread) => {
17         // foreach message in that thread
18         thread.messages.forEach((message: Message) => {
19           if (!message.isRead) {
20             // if it's unread, increment unread count
21             ++unreadCount;
22           }
23         });
24         return unreadCount;
25       },
26       0);
```

Should we put this logic in the `ChatNavBarComponent`? There's two problems with that approach:

1. This chunk of code reaches deep into our AppState. A better approach would be to co-locate this logic next to where the state itself is written.

2. What if we need the unread count somewhere else in the app? How could we share this logic?

Solving these problems is the idea behind *selectors*.

Selectors are functions that take a part of the state and return a value.

Let's take a look at how to make a few selectors.

Threads Selectors

Let's start with an easy one. Say we have our AppState and we want to get the ThreadsState:

code/redux/redux-chat/src/app/thread/threads.reducer.ts

```
122  export const getThreadsState = (state): ThreadsState => state.threads;
```

Pretty easy, right? Here we're saying, given the top-level AppState, we can find the ThreadsState at state.threads.

Let's say that we want to get the current thread. We could do it like this:

```
1  const getCurrentThread = (state: AppState): Thread => {
2    let currentThreadId = state.threads.currentThreadId;
3    return state.threads.entities[currentThreadId];
4  }
```

For this small example, this selector works fine. But it's worth thinking about how we can make our selectors maintainable as the app grows. It would be nice if we could use selectors to query other selectors. It also would be nice to be able to specify a selector that has multiple selectors as a dependency.

This is what the reselect[120] library provides. With reselect we can create small, focused selectors and then combine them together into bigger functionality.

Let's look at how we will get the current thread using createSelector from reselect.

---

[120] https://github.com/reactjs/reselect#createselectorinputselectors--inputselectors-resultfunc

code/redux/redux-chat/src/app/thread/threads.reducer.ts

```
124  export const getThreadsEntities = createSelector(
125    getThreadsState,
126    ( state: ThreadsState ) => state.entities );
```

We start by writing getThreadsEntities. getThreadsEntities uses createSelector and passes two arguments:

1. getThreadsState, the selector we defined above and
2. A callback function which will receive *the value of the selector in #1* and return the value we want to select.

This might seem like a lot of overhead to call state.entities, but it sets us up for a much more maintainable selectors down the line. Let's look at getCurrentThread using createSelector:

code/redux/redux-chat/src/app/thread/threads.reducer.ts

```
147  export const getCurrentThread = createSelector(
148    getThreadsEntities,
149    getThreadsState,
150    ( entities: ThreadsEntities, state: ThreadsState ) =>
151      entities[state.currentThreadId] );
```

Notice here that we're citing **two** selectors as dependencies: getThreadsEntities and getThreadsState - when these selectors resolve they become the arguments to the callback function. We can then combine them together to return the selected thread.

Unread Messages Count Selector

Now that we understand how selectors work, let's create a selector that will get the number of unread messages. If you look at our first attempt at unread messages above, we can see that each variable could instead become it's own selector (getThreadsState, getThreadsEntities, etc.)

Here's a selector that will get all Threads:

code/redux/redux-chat/src/app/thread/threads.reducer.ts

```
128  export const getAllThreads = createSelector(
129    getThreadsEntities,
130    ( entities: ThreadsEntities ) => Object.keys(entities)
131                          .map((threadId) => entities[threadId]));
```

And then given all of the threads, we can get the sum of the unread messages over all threads:

code/redux/redux-chat/src/app/thread/threads.reducer.ts

```
133  export const getUnreadMessagesCount = createSelector(
134    getAllThreads,
135    ( threads: Thread[] ) => threads.reduce(
136        (unreadCount: number, thread: Thread) => {
137          thread.messages.forEach((message: Message) => {
138            if (!message.isRead) {
139              ++unreadCount;
140            }
141          });
142          return unreadCount;
143        },
144        0));
```

Now that we have this selector, we can use it to get the number of unread messages in our `ChatNavBarComponent` (and anywhere else in our app where we might need it).

Building the ChatThreadsComponent

Next let's build our thread list in the `ChatThreadsComponent`.

Echo Bot •
I'll echo whatever you send me

Reverse Bot
I'll reverse whatever you send me

Waiting Bot
I'll wait however many seconds you send
to me before responding. Try sending '3'

Lady Capulet
So shall you feel the loss, but not the
friend which you weep for.

Time Ordered List of Threads

`ChatThreadsComponent` **Controller**

Let's take a look at our component controller `ChatThreadsComponent` before we look at the template:

code/redux/redux-chat/src/app/chat-threads/chat-threads.component.ts

```
1  import {
2    Component,
3    OnInit,
4    Inject
5  } from '@angular/core';
6  import { AppStore } from '../app.store';
7  import * as Redux from 'redux';
8  import {
9    Thread
10 } from '../thread/thread.model';
11 import * as ThreadActions from '../thread/thread.actions';
12 import {
13   AppState,
14   getCurrentThread,
15   getAllThreads
16 } from '../app.reducer';
17
18 @Component({
19   selector: 'chat-threads',
20   templateUrl: './chat-threads.component.html',
21   styleUrls: ['./chat-threads.component.css']
```

```
22  })
23  export class ChatThreadsComponent {
24    threads: Thread[];
25    currentThreadId: string;
26
27    constructor(@Inject(AppStore) private store: Redux.Store<AppState>) {
28      store.subscribe(() => this.updateState());
29      this.updateState();
30    }
31
32    updateState() {
33      const state = this.store.getState();
34
35      // Store the threads list
36      this.threads = getAllThreads(state);
37
38      // We want to mark the current thread as selected,
39      // so we store the currentThreadId as a value
40      this.currentThreadId = getCurrentThread(state).id;
41    }
42
43    handleThreadClicked(thread: Thread) {
44      this.store.dispatch(ThreadActions.selectThread(thread));
45    }
46  }
```

We're storing two instance variables on this component:

- threads - the list of Threads
- currentThreadId - the current thread (conversation) that the user is participating in

In our constructor we keep a reference to the Redux store and subscribe to updates. When the store changes, we call updateState().

updateState() keeps our instance variables in sync with the Redux store. Notice that we're using two selectors:

- getAllThreads and
- getCurrentThread

which keep their respective instance variables up to date.

The one new idea we've added is an event handler: handleThreadClicked. handleThreadClicked will dispatch the selectThread action. The idea here is that when a thread is clicked on, we'll tell our store to set this new thread as the selected thread and the rest of the application should update in turn.

ChatThreadsComponent **template**

Let's look at the ChatThreadsComponent template and its configuration:

code/redux/redux-chat/src/app/chat-threads/chat-threads.component.html

```
1  <!-- conversations -->
2  <div class="row">
3    <div class="conversation-wrap">
4      <chat-thread
5          *ngFor="let thread of threads"
6          [thread]="thread"
7          [selected]="thread.id === currentThreadId"
8          (onThreadSelected)="handleThreadClicked($event)">
9      </chat-thread>
10   </div>
11 </div>
```

In our template we're using ngFor to iterate over our threads. We're using a new directive to render the individual threads called ChatThreadComponent.

ChatThreadComponent is a *presentational* component. We **won't** be able to access the store in ChatThreadComponent, neither for fetching data nor dispatching actions. Instead, we're going to pass everything we need to this component through inputs and handle any interaction through outputs.

We'll look at the implementation of ChatThreadComponent next, but look at the inputs and outputs we have in this template first.

- We're sending the input [thread] with the individual thread
- On the input [selected] we're passing a *boolean* which indicates if this thread (thread.id) is the "current" thread (currentThreadId)
- If the thread is clicked, we will emit the output event (onThreadSelected) - when this happens we'll call handleThreadClicked() (which dispatches a thread selected event to the store).

Let's dig in to the ChatThreadComponent.

The Single `ChatThreadComponent`

The `ChatThreadComponent` will be used to display a **single thread** in the list of threads. Remember that `ChatThreadComponent` is a *presentational component* - it doesn't manipulate any data that isn't given to it directly.

Here's the component controller code:

code/redux/redux-chat/src/app/chat-thread/chat-thread.component.ts

```
1  import {
2    Component,
3    OnInit,
4    Input,
5    Output,
6    EventEmitter
7  } from '@angular/core';
8  import { Thread } from '../thread/thread.model';
9
10 @Component({
11   selector: 'chat-thread',
12   templateUrl: './chat-thread.component.html',
13   styleUrls: ['./chat-thread.component.css']
14 })
15 export class ChatThreadComponent implements OnInit {
16   @Input() thread: Thread;
17   @Input() selected: boolean;
18   @Output() onThreadSelected: EventEmitter<Thread>;
19
20   constructor() {
21     this.onThreadSelected = new EventEmitter<Thread>();
22   }
23
24   ngOnInit() { }
25
26   clicked(event: any): void {
27     this.onThreadSelected.emit(this.thread);
28     event.preventDefault();
29   }
30 }
```

The main thing to look at here is the `onThreadSelected` `EventEmitter`. If you haven't used `EventEmitter`s much, the idea is that it's an implementation of the observer pattern. We use it as the "output channel" for this component - when we want to send data we call `onThreadSelected.emit` and pass whatever data we want along with it.

In this case, we want to emit the current thread as the argument to the `EventEmitter`. When this element is clicked, we will call `onThreadSelected.emit(this.thread)` which will trigger the callback in our parent (`ChatThreadsComponent`) component.

Here is where we specify our `@Input()`s of `thread` and `selected`, as well as the `@Output()` of `onThreadSelected`.

ChatThreadComponent **template**

Here's the code for our `@Component` decorator and `template`:

code/redux/redux-chat/src/app/chat-thread/chat-thread.component.html

```
1   <div class="media conversation">
2     <div class="pull-left">
3       <img class="media-object avatar"
4            src="{{thread.avatarSrc}}">
5     </div>
6     <div class="media-body">
7       <h5 class="media-heading contact-name">{{thread.name}}
8         <span *ngIf="selected">&bull;</span>
9       </h5>
10      <small class="message-preview">
11        {{thread.messages[thread.messages.length - 1].text}}
12      </small>
13    </div>
14    <a (click)="clicked($event)" class="div-link">Select</a>
15  </div>
```

Notice that in our view we've got some straight-forward bindings like `{{thread.avatarSrc}}`, `{{thread.name}}`. In the `message-preview` tag we've got the following:

```
1   {{ thread.messages[thread.messages.length - 1].text }}
```

This gets the last message in the thread and displays the text of that message. The idea is we are showing a preview of the most recent message in that thread.

We've got an `*ngIf` which will show the `&bull;` symbol only if this is the selected thread.

Lastly, we're binding to the (`click`) event to call our `clicked()` handler. Notice that when we call `clicked` we're passing the argument $event. This is a special variable provided by Angular that describes the event. We use that in our `clicked` handler by calling `event.preventDefault();`. This makes sure that we don't navigate to a different page.

Building the `ChatWindowComponent`

The `ChatWindowComponent` is the most complicated component in our app. Let's take it one section at a time:

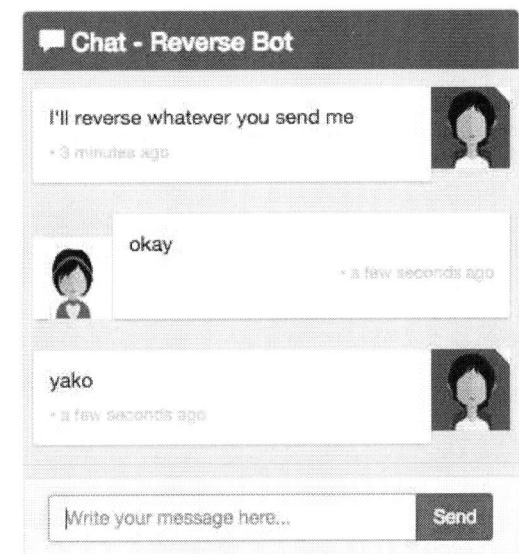

The Chat Window

Our `ChatWindowComponent` class has three properties: `currentThread` (which holds a `Thread` (that contains `Message[]` as a property), `draftMessage`, and `currentUser`:

code/redux/redux-chat/src/app/chat-window/chat-window.component.ts

```
23  export class ChatWindowComponent {
24    currentThread: Thread;
25    draftMessage: { text: string };
26    currentUser: User;
```

Here's a diagram of where each one is used:

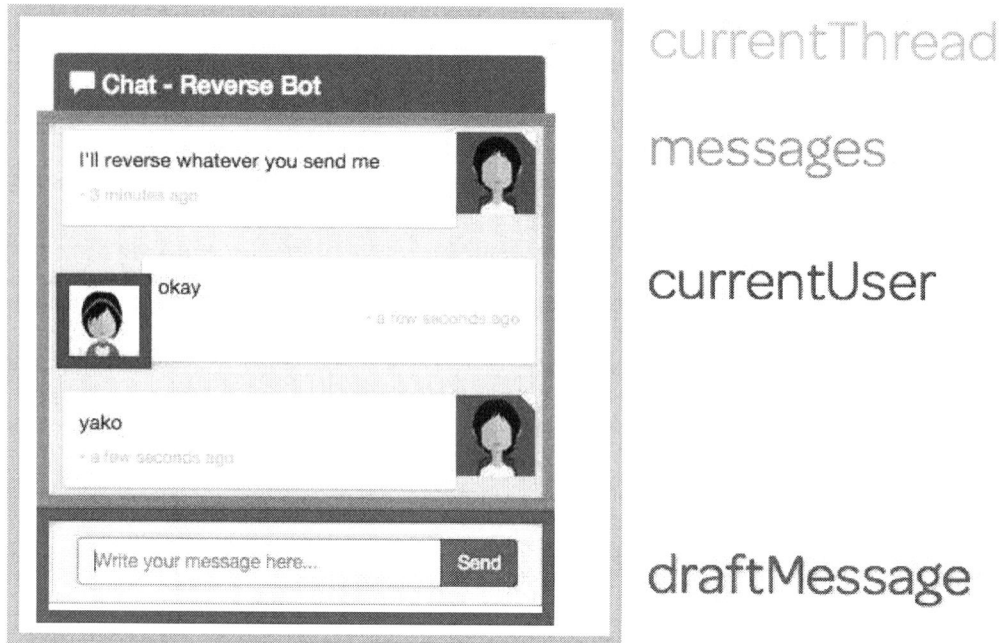

currentThread

messages

currentUser

draftMessage

Chat Window Properties

In our constructor we're going to inject two things:

code/redux/redux-chat/src/app/chat-window/chat-window.component.ts

```
28    constructor(@Inject(AppStore) private store: Redux.Store<AppState>,
29              private el: ElementRef) {
30      store.subscribe(() => this.updateState() );
31      this.updateState();
32      this.draftMessage = { text: '' };
33    }
```

The first is our Redux Store. The second, `el` is an `ElementRef` which we can use to get access to the host DOM element. We'll use that when we scroll to the bottom of the chat window when we create and receive new messages.

In our constructor we subscribe to our store, as we have in our other container components.

The next thing we do is to set a default `draftMessage` with an empty string for the `text`. We'll use the `draftMessage` to keep track of the input box as the user is typing their message.

ChatWindowComponent updateState()

When the store changes we will update the instance variables for this component:

code/redux/redux-chat/src/app/chat-window/chat-window.component.ts

```
35   updateState() {
36     const state = this.store.getState();
37     this.currentThread = getCurrentThread(state);
38     this.currentUser = getCurrentUser(state);
39     this.scrollToBottom();
40   }
```

Here we store the current thread and the current user. If a new message comes in, we also want to scroll to the bottom of the window. It's a bit coarse to call scrollToBottom here, but it's a simple way to make sure that the user doesn't have to scroll manually each time there is a new message (or they switch to a new thread).

ChatWindowComponent scrollToBottom()

To scroll to the bottom of the chat window, we're going to use the ElementRef el that we saved in the constructor. To make this element scroll, we're going to set the scrollTop property of our host element:

code/redux/redux-chat/src/app/chat-window/chat-window.component.ts

```
42   scrollToBottom(): void {
43     const scrollPane: any = this.el
44       .nativeElement.querySelector('.msg-container-base');
45     if (scrollPane) {
46       setTimeout(() => scrollPane.scrollTop = scrollPane.scrollHeight);
47     }
48   }
```

> **Why do we have the setTimeout?**
>
> If we call scrollToBottom immediately when we get a new message then what happens is we scroll to the bottom before the new message is rendered. By using a setTimeout we're telling JavaScript that we want to run this function when it is finished with the current execution queue. This happens **after** the component is rendered, so it does what we want.

ChatWindowComponent sendMessage

When we want to send a new message, we'll do it by taking:

- The current thread
- The current user
- The draft message text

And then dispatching a new `addMessage` action on the store. Here's what it looks like in code:

code/redux/redux-chat/src/app/chat-window/chat-window.component.ts

```
50    sendMessage(): void {
51      this.store.dispatch(ThreadActions.addMessage(
52        this.currentThread,
53        {
54          author: this.currentUser,
55          isRead: true,
56          text: this.draftMessage.text
57        }
58      ));
59      this.draftMessage = { text: '' };
60    }
```

The `sendMessage` function above takes the `draftMessage`, sets the `author` and `thread` using our component properties. Every message we send has "been read" already (we wrote it) so we mark it as read.

After we dispatch the message, we create a new `Message`** and set that new `Message` to `this.draftMessage`. This will clear the search box, and by creating a new object we ensure we don't mutate the message that was sent to the store.

ChatWindowComponent onEnter

In our view, we want to send the message in two scenarios

1. the user hits the "Send" button or
2. the user hits the Enter (or Return) key.

Let's define a function that will handle both events:

code/redux/redux-chat/src/app/chat-window/chat-window.component.ts

```
62    onEnter(event: any): void {
63      this.sendMessage();
64      event.preventDefault();
65    }
```

We create this `onEnter` event handler as a separate function from `sendMessage` because `onEnter` will accept an `event` as an argument and then call `event.preventDefault()`. This way we *could* call `sendMessage` in scenarios other than in response to a browser event. In this case, we're not really calling `sendMessage` in any other situation, but I find that it's nice to separate the event handler from the function that 'does the work'.

That is, a `sendMessage` function that also 1. requires an event to be passed to it and 2. handles that event feels like a function that may be handling too many concerns.

Now that we've handled the controller code, let's look at the template

ChatWindowComponent template

We start our template by opening the panel tags: and showing the chat name in the header:

code/redux/redux-chat/src/app/chat-window/chat-window.component.html

```
1    <div class="chat-window-container">
2      <div class="chat-window">
3        <div class="panel container">
4          <div class="panel panel-default">
5
6            <div class="panel-heading top-bar">
7              <div class="panel-title-container">
8                <h3 class="panel-title">
9                  <span class="glyphicon glyphicon-comment"></span>
10                 Chat - {{currentThread.name}}
11               </h3>
12             </div>
13             <div class="panel-buttons-container"  >
14               <!-- you could put minimize or close buttons here -->
15             </div>
16           </div>
17
18           <div class="panel-body msg-container-base">
19             <chat-message
```

```
20                *ngFor="let message of currentThread.messages"
21                [message]="message">
22          </chat-message>
23        </div>
24
25        <div class="panel-footer">
26          <div class="input-group">
27            <input type="text"
28                   class="chat-input"
29                   placeholder="Write your message here..."
30                   (keydown.enter)="onEnter($event)"
31                   [(ngModel)]="draftMessage.text" />
32            <span class="input-group-btn">
33              <button class="btn-chat"
34                (click)="onEnter($event)"
35                  >Send</button>
36            </span>
37          </div>
38        </div>
39
40      </div>
41    </div>
42  </div>
43 </div>
```

Next we show the list of messages. Here we use ngFor to iterate over our list of messages. We'll describe the individual chat-message component in a minute.

code/redux/redux-chat/src/app/chat-window/chat-window.component.html

```
18        <div class="panel-body msg-container-base">
19          <chat-message
20                *ngFor="let message of currentThread.messages"
21                [message]="message">
22          </chat-message>
23        </div>
```

Lastly we have the message input box and closing tags:

code/redux/redux-chat/src/app/chat-window/chat-window.component.html

```
25        <div class="panel-footer">
26          <div class="input-group">
27            <input type="text"
28                   class="chat-input"
29                   placeholder="Write your message here..."
30                   (keydown.enter)="onEnter($event)"
31                   [(ngModel)]="draftMessage.text" />
32            <span class="input-group-btn">
33              <button class="btn-chat"
34                (click)="onEnter($event)"
35                >Send</button>
36            </span>
37          </div>
38        </div>
39
40      </div>
41    </div>
42  </div>
```

The message input box is the most interesting part of this view, so let's talk about two interesting properties: 1. (keydown.enter) and 2. [(ngModel)].

Handling keystrokes

Angular provides a straightforward way to handle keyboard actions: we bind to the event on an element. In this case, we're binding to keydown.enter which says if "Enter" is pressed, call the function in the expression, which in this case is onEnter($event).

code/redux/redux-chat/src/app/chat-window/chat-window.component.html

```
27            <input type="text"
28                   class="chat-input"
29                   placeholder="Write your message here..."
30                   (keydown.enter)="onEnter($event)"
31                   [(ngModel)]="draftMessage.text" />
```

Using ngModel

As we've talked about before, we don't generally use two-way data binding as the crux of our data architecture (like we might have in Angular 1). This is particularly true when we're using Redux which is strictly a one-way data flow.

However it can be very useful to have a two-way binding between a component and its view. As long as the side-effects are kept local to the component, it can be a very convenient way to keep a component property in sync with the view.

In this case, we're establishing a two-way bind **between the value of the input tag and draftMessage.text**. That is, if we type into the `input` tag, `draftMessage.text` will automatically be set to the value of that `input`. Likewise, if we were to update `draftMessage.text` in our code, the value in the `input` tag would change in the view.

Clicking "Send"

On our "Send" button we bind the `(click)` property to the `onEnter` function of our component:

code/redux/redux-chat/src/app/chat-window/chat-window.component.html

```
33          <button class="btn-chat"
34              (click)="onEnter($event)"
35              >Send</button>
```

We're using the same `onEnter` function to handle the events which should send the draft message for both the button and hitting the enter button.

The ChatMessageComponent

Instead of putting the rendering code for each individual message in this component, instead we're going to create another *presentational component* ChatMessageComponent.

> Tip: If you're using ngFor that's a good indication you should create a new component.

Each `Message` is rendered by the `ChatMessageComponent`.

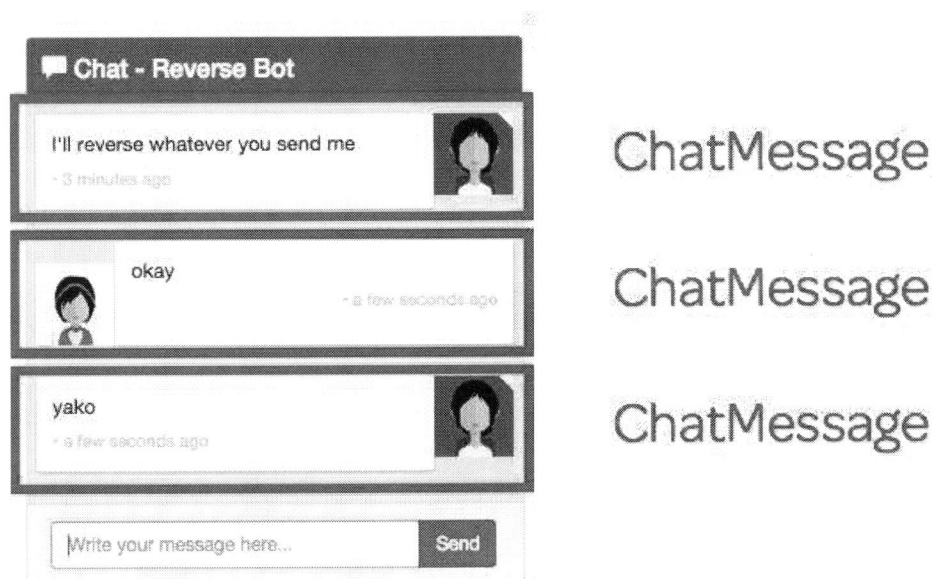

The `ChatMessageComponent`

This component is relatively straightforward. The main logic here is rendering a slightly different view depending on if the message was authored by the current user. If the `Message` was **not** written by the current user, then we consider the message `incoming`.

Setting `incoming`

Remember that each `ChatMessageComponent` belongs to one `Message`. So in `ngOnInit` we will set `incoming` depending on if this `Message` was written by the current user:

code/redux/redux-chat/src/app/chat-message/chat-message.component.ts

```
1   import {
2     Component,
3     OnInit,
4     Input
5   } from '@angular/core';
6   import { Message } from '../message/message.model';
7
8   @Component({
9     selector: 'chat-message',
10    templateUrl: './chat-message.component.html',
11    styleUrls: ['./chat-message.component.css']
12  })
```

```
13  export class ChatMessageComponent implements OnInit {
14    @Input() message: Message;
15    incoming: boolean;
16
17    ngOnInit(): void {
18      this.incoming = !this.message.author.isClient;
19    }
20  }
```

The ChatMessageComponent template

In our template we have two interesting ideas:

1. the FromNowPipe
2. [ngClass]

First, here's the code:

code/redux/redux-chat/src/app/chat-message/chat-message.component.html

```
1   <div class="msg-container"
2       [ngClass]="{'base-sent': !incoming, 'base-receive': incoming}">
3
4     <div class="avatar"
5         *ngIf="!incoming">
6       <img src="{{message.author.avatarSrc}}">
7     </div>
8
9     <div class="messages"
10        [ngClass]="{'msg-sent': !incoming, 'msg-receive': incoming}">
11      <p>{{message.text}}</p>
12      <p class="time">{{message.sender}} ● {{message.sentAt | fromNow}}</p>
13    </div>
14
15    <div class="avatar"
16        *ngIf="incoming">
17      <img src="{{message.author.avatarSrc}}">
18    </div>
19  </div>
```

The FromNowPipe is a pipe that casts our Messages sent-at time to a human-readable "x seconds ago" message. You can see that we use it by: {{message.sentAt | fromNow}} ℹ️ FromNowPipe uses the excellent `moment.js`[121] library. You can read the source of the FromNowPipe in `code/redux/redux-chat/src/app/pipes/from-now.pipe.ts`

We also make extensive use of `ngClass` in this view. The idea is, when we say:

```
1    [ngClass]="{'msg-sent': !incoming, 'msg-receive': incoming}"
```

We're asking Angular to apply the `msg-receive` class if `incoming` is truthy (and apply `msg-sent` if `incoming` is falsey).

By using the `incoming` property, we're able to display incoming and outgoing messages differently.

Summary

There we go, if we put them all together we've got a fully functional chat app!

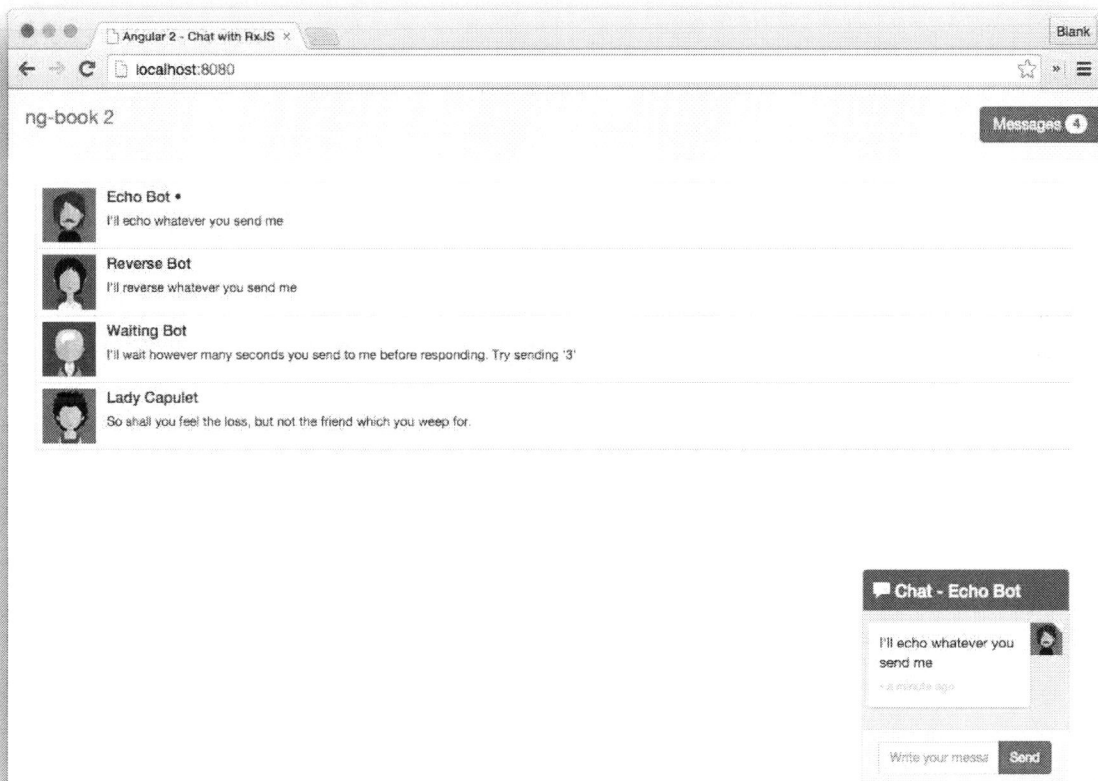

Completed Chat Application

---

[121]http://momentjs.com/

If you checkout `code/redux/redux-chat/src/app/data/chat-example-data.ts` you'll see we've written a handful of bots for you that you can chat with. Checkout the code and try writing a few bots of your own!

Advanced Components

Throughout this book, we've learned how to use Angular's built-in directives and how to create components of our own. In this chapter we'll take a deep dive into **advanced** features we can use to make components.

In this chapter we'll learn the following concepts:

- Styling components (with encapsulation)
- Modifying host DOM elements
- Modifying templates with *content projection*
- Accessing neighbor directives
- Using lifecycle hooks
- Detecting changes

How to Use This Chapter

This chapter gives a tour of advanced Angular APIs. It's assumed the reader is familiar with the basics of creating components, using built-in directives, and organizing component files.

As this is an intermediate/advanced level chapter, it's assumed the reader is able to fill in some of the basics (such as importing dependencies).

This chapter comes with runnable code, found in the `advanced-components` folder. If at any time you feel you're lacking context, checkout the example code for this chapter.

To run the demos in this chapter, change into the project folder and run:

```
1  npm install
2  npm start
```

Then open your browser to http://localhost:4200

Styling

Angular provides a mechanism for specifying component-specific styles. CSS stands for *cascading style sheet*, but sometimes we **don't** want the cascade. Instead we want to provide styles for a component that won't leak out into the rest of our page.

Angular provides two attributes that allow us to define CSS classes for our component.

To define the style for our component, we use the View attribute `styles` to define in-line styles, or `styleUrls`, to use external CSS files. We can also declare those attributes directly on the `Component` decorator.

Let's write a component that uses inline styles:

code/advanced-components/src/app/styling/inline-style/inline-style.component.ts

```
1   import { Component } from '@angular/core';
2
3   @Component({
4     selector: 'app-inline-style',
5     styles: [`
6     .highlight {
7       border: 2px solid red;
8       background-color: yellow;
9       text-align: center;
10      margin-bottom: 20px;
11    }
12    `],
13    template: `
14    <h4 class="ui horizontal divider header">
15      Inline style example
16    </h4>
17
18    <div class="highlight">
19      This uses component <code>styles</code>
20      property
21    </div>
22    `
23  })
24  export class InlineStyleComponent {
25  }
```

In this example we defined the styles we want to use by declaring the `.highlight` class as an item on the array on the `styles` parameter.

Further on in the template we reference that class on the div using `<div class="highlight">`.

And the result is exactly what we expect - a div with a red border and yellow background:

Inline style example

```
This uses component styles property
```

Example of component using styles

Another way to declare CSS classes is to use the styleUrls property. This allows us to declare our CSS in an external file and just reference them from the component.

Let's write another component that uses this, but first let's create a file called external.css with the following class:

code/advanced-components/src/app/styling/external-style/external-style.component.css

```
1  .highlight {
2    border: 2px dotted red;
3    text-align: center;
4    margin-bottom: 20px;
5  }
```

Then we can write the code that references it:

code/advanced-components/src/app/styling/external-style/external-style.component.ts

```
1  import { Component, OnInit } from '@angular/core';
2
3  @Component({
4    selector: 'app-external-style',
5    styleUrls: ['./external-style.component.css'],
6    template: `
7  <h4 class="ui horizontal divider header">
8    External style example
9  </h4>
10
11 <div class="highlight">
12   This uses component <code>styleUrls</code>
13   property
14 </div>
15 `
16 })
17 export class ExternalStyleComponent {
18 }
```

And when we load the page, we see our div with a dotted border:

External style example

```
This uses component styleUrls property
```

Example of component using styleUrls

View (Style) Encapsulation

One interesting thing about this example is that both components define a class called `highlight` with different properties, but the attributes of one didn't leak into the other.

This happens because Angular styles are **encapsulated by the component context** by default. If we inspect the page and expand the `<head>`, we'll notice that Angular injected a `<style>` tag with our style:

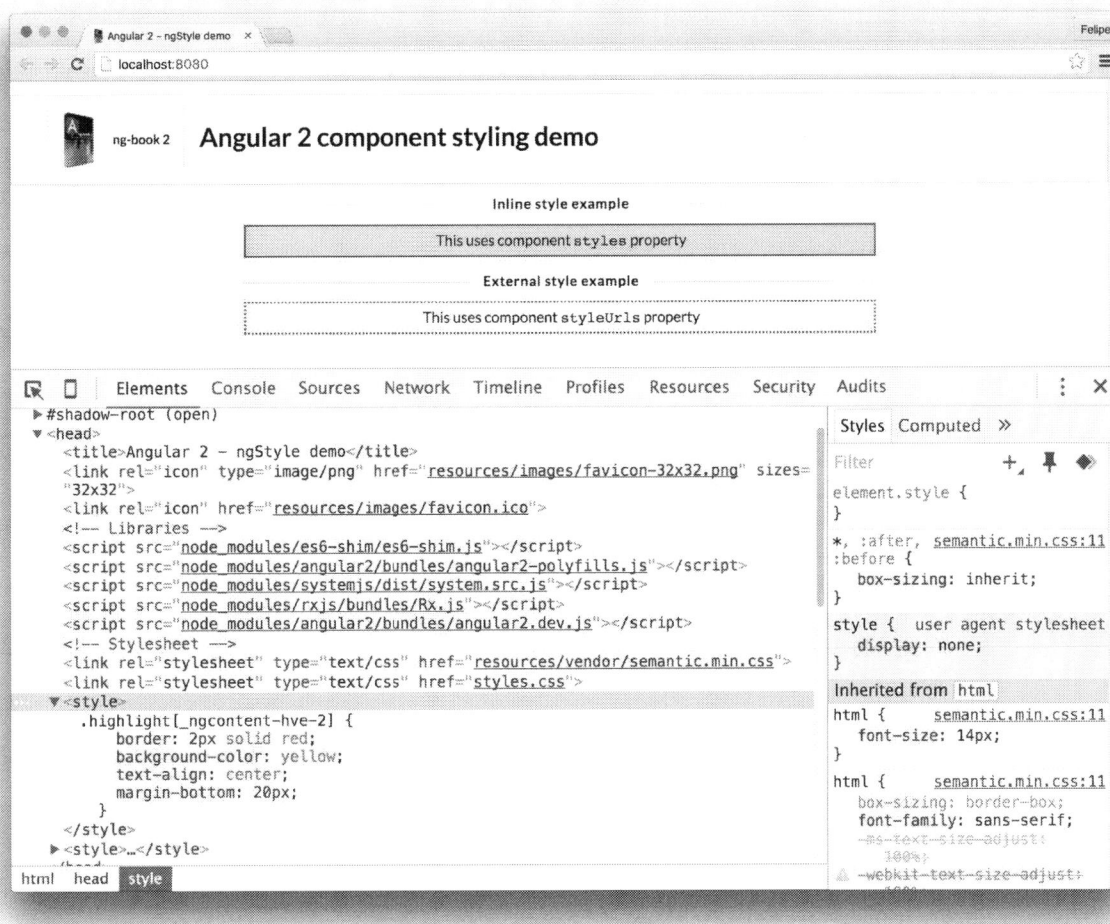

Injected style

You'll also notice that the CSS class has been scoped with _ngcontent-hve-2:

```
1  .highlight[\_ngcontent-hve-2] {
2    border: 2px solid red;
3    background-color: yellow;
4    text-align: center;
5    margin-bottom: 20px;
6  }
```

And if we check how our <div> is rendered, you'll find that _ng-content-hve-2 was added:

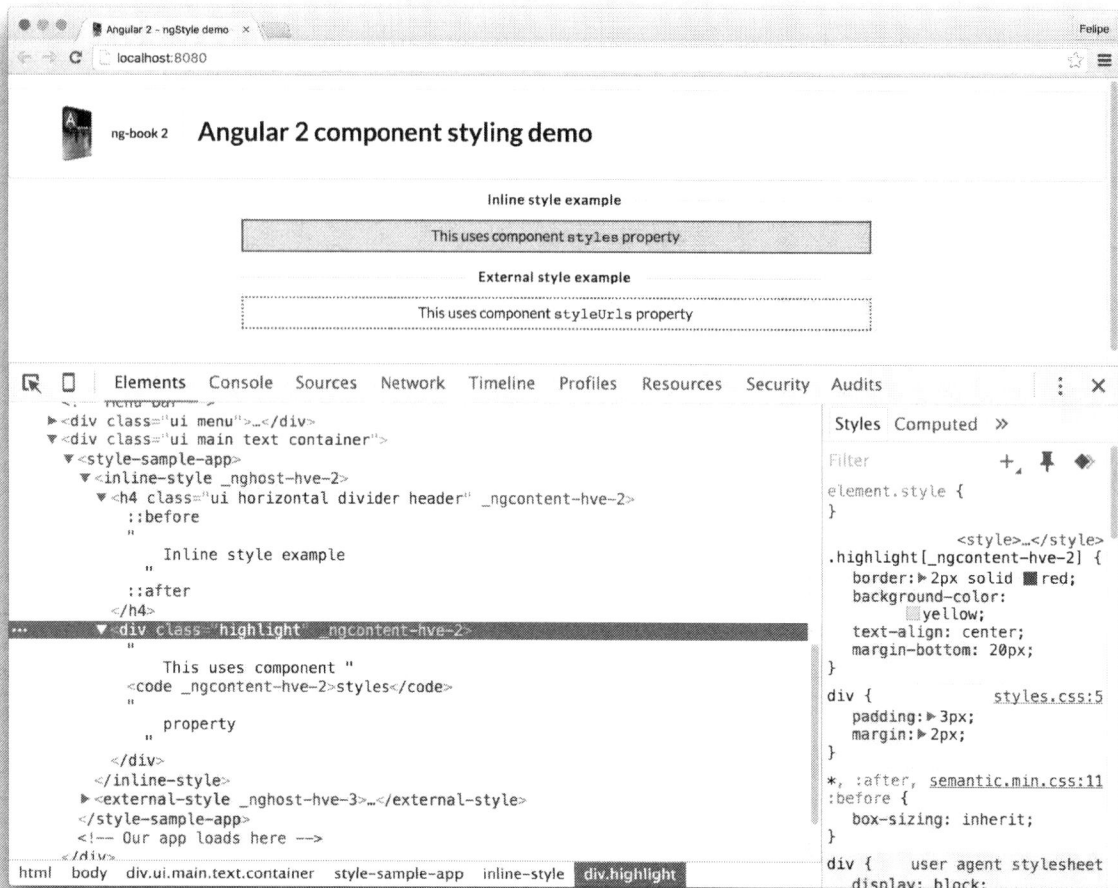

Injected style

The same thing happens for our external style:

External style

and:

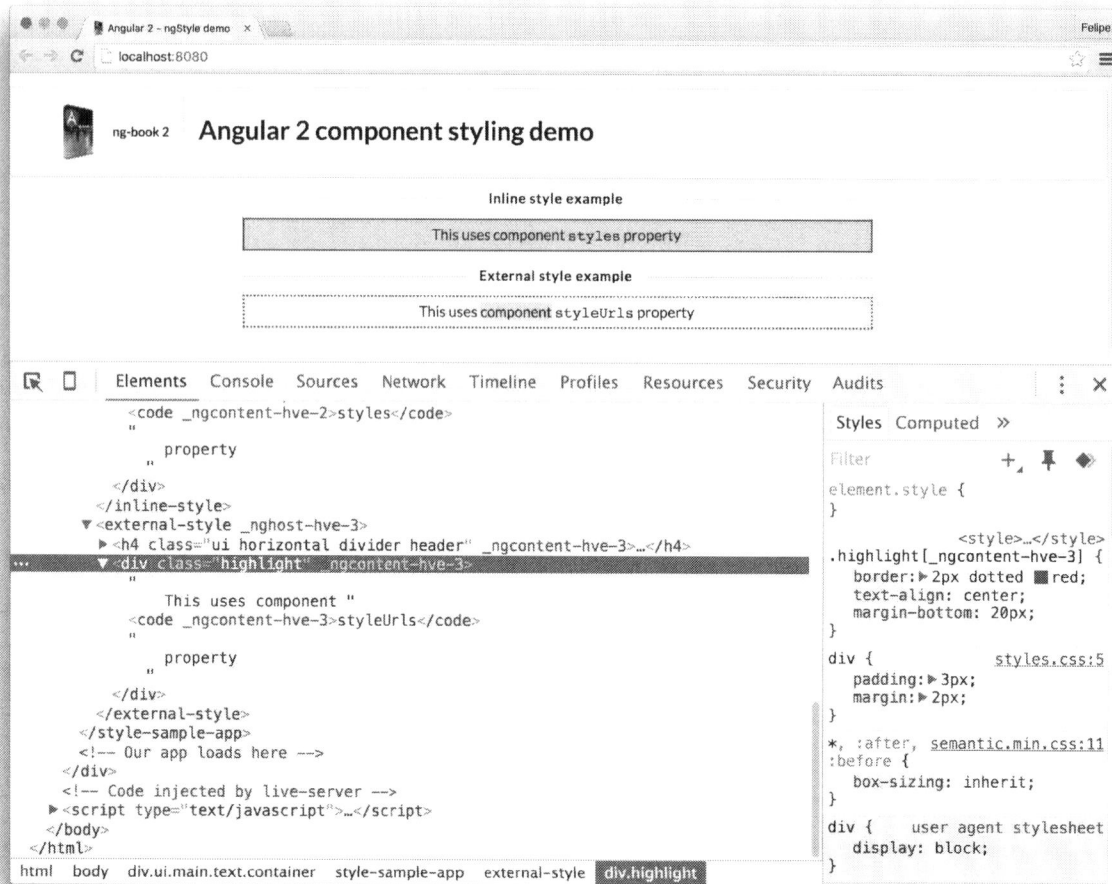

External style

Angular allows us to change this behavior, by using the `encapsulation` property.

This property can have the following values, defined by the `ViewEncapsulation` enum:

- **Emulated** - this is the default option and it will encapsulate the styles using the technique we just explained above
- **Native** - with this option, Angular will use the Shadow DOM (more on this below)
- **None** - with this option set, Angular won't encapsulate the styles at all, allowing them to leak to other elements on the page

Shadow DOM Encapsulation

You might be wondering: what is the point of using the Shadow DOM? By using the Shadow DOM the component uses **a unique DOM tree that is hidden from the other elements on the page**. This allows styles defined within that element to be invisible to the rest of the page.

For a deep dive into Shadow DOM, please check this guide by Eric Bidelman[122].

Let's create another component that uses the **Native** encapsulation (Shadow DOM) to understand how this works:

code/advanced-components/src/app/styling/native-encapsulation/native-encapsulation.component.ts

```
1   import {
2     Component,
3     ViewEncapsulation
4   } from '@angular/core';
5
6   @Component({
7     selector: 'app-native-encapsulation',
8     styles: [`
9     .highlight {
10      text-align: center;
11      border: 2px solid black;
12      border-radius: 3px;
13      margin-botton: 20px;
14    }`],
15    template: `
16    <h4 class="ui horizontal divider header">
17      Native encapsulation example
18    </h4>
19
20    <div class="highlight">
21      This component uses <code>ViewEncapsulation.Native</code>
22    </div>
23    `,
24    encapsulation: ViewEncapsulation.Native
25  })
26  export class NativeEncapsulationComponent {
27  }
```

In this case, if we inspect the source code, we'll see:

---

[122] http://www.html5rocks.com/en/tutorials/webcomponents/shadowdom/

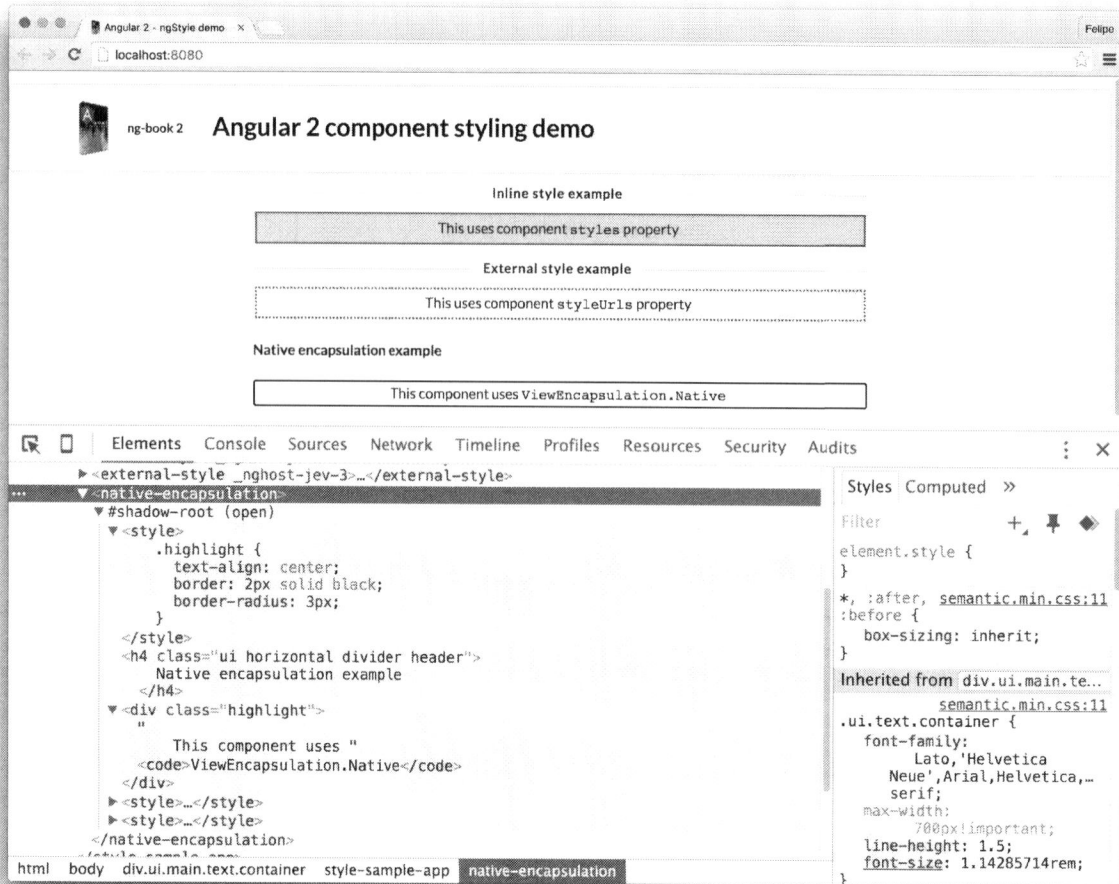

Native encapsulation

Everything inside the `#shadow-root` element has been encapsulated and isolated from the rest of the page.

No Encapsulation

Finally, if we create a component that specifies `ViewEncapsulation.None`, no style encapsulation will be added:

code/advanced-components/src/app/styling/no-encapsulation/no-encapsulation.component.ts

```
1   import {
2     Component,
3     ViewEncapsulation
4   } from '@angular/core';
5
6   @Component({
7     selector: 'app-no-encapsulation',
8     styles: [`
9     .highlight {
10      border: 2px dashed red;
11      text-align: center;
12      margin-bottom: 20px;
13    }
14    `],
15    template: `
16    <h4 class="ui horizontal divider header">
17      No encapsulation example
18    </h4>
19
20    <div class="highlight">
21      This component uses <code>ViewEncapsulation.None</code>
22    </div>
23    `,
24    encapsulation: ViewEncapsulation.None
25  })
26  export class NoEncapsulationComponent {
27  }
```

When we inspect the element:

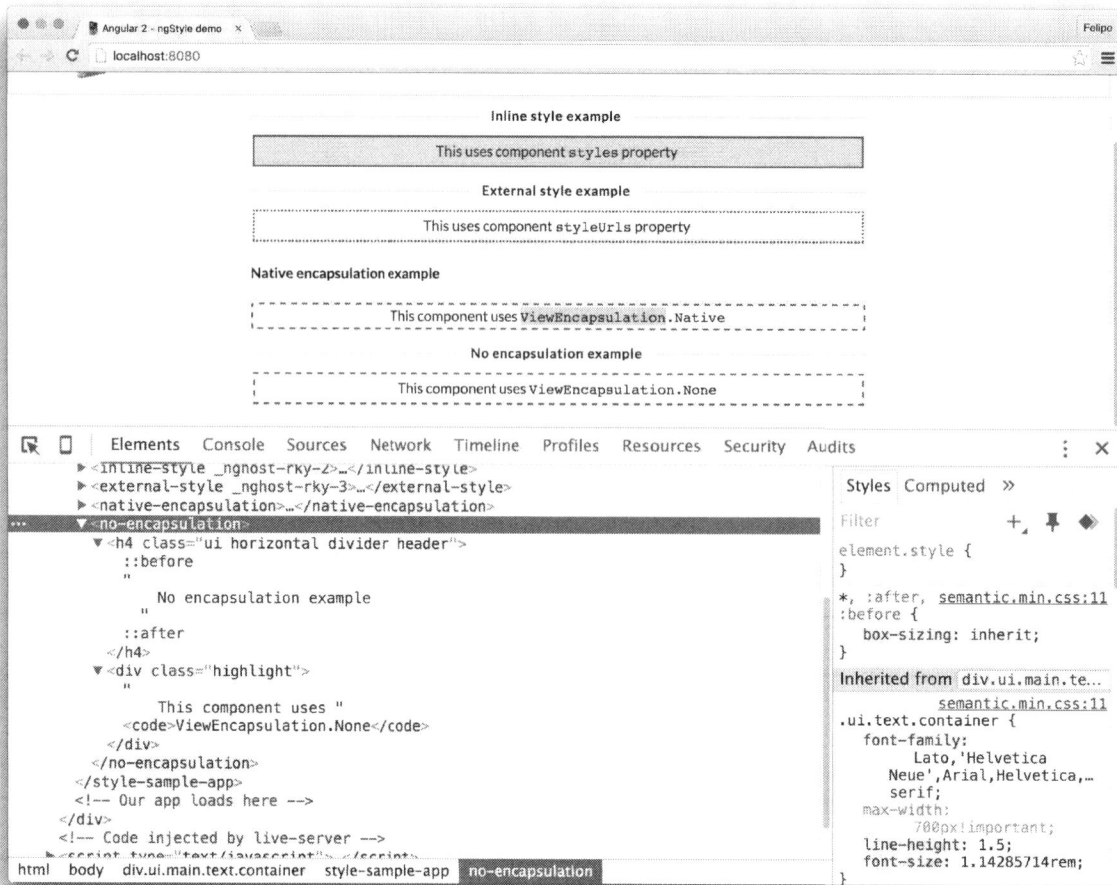

No encapsulation

We can see that nothing was injected on the HTML. Also on the header we can find that the `<style>` tag was also injected exactly like we defined on the `styles` parameter:

```
1  .highlight {
2    border: 2px dashed red;
3    text-align: center;
4    margin-bottom: 20px;
5  }
```

One side-effect of using `ViewEncapsulation.None` is that, since we don't have any encapsulation, this style "leaks" into other components. If we check the picture above, the `ViewEncapsulation.Native` component style was affected by this new component's style. But sometimes this can be exactly what you want.

You can comment out the `<app-no-encapsulation></app-no-encapsulation>` code on the `StyleSampleApp` template to see the difference.

Creating a Popup - Referencing and Modifying Host Elements

The *host element* is the element to which the directive or component is bound. Sometimes we have a component that needs to attach markup or behavior to its host element.

In this example, we're going to create a Popup directive that will attach behavior to its host element which will display a message when clicked.

⚷ Components vs. Directives - What's the difference?

Components and directives are closely related, but they are slightly different.

You may have heard that "components are directives with a view". This isn't exactly true. Components come with functionality that makes it easy to add views, but directives can have views too. In fact, **components are implemented with directives**.

One great example of a directive that renders a conditional view is NgIf.

But we can attach behaviors to an element **without a template** by using a *directive*.

Think of it this way: Components are Directives and Components always have a view. Directives may or may not have a view.

If you choose to render a view (a template) in your Directive, you can have more control over how that template is rendered. We'll talk more about how to use that control later in this chapter.

Popup Structure

Now let's write our first directive. We want this directive to **show an alert when we click a DOM element** that includes the attribute popup. The message displayed will be identified by the element's message attribute.

Here's what we want it to look like:

```
1   <element popup message="Some message"></element>
```

In order to make this directive work, there are a couple of things we need to do:

- receive the message attribute *from* the host
- be notified when the host element is clicked

Let's start coding our directive:

code/advanced-components/src/app/host/popup-demo/steps/host-1.ts

```
11   @Directive({
12     selector: '[popup]'
13   })
14   export class PopupDirective {
15     constructor() {
16       console.log('Directive bound');
17     }
18   }
```

We use the Directive decorator and set the selector option to [popup]. This will make this directive bind to any elements that define the popup attribute.

Now let's create an app that has an element that has the popup attribute:

code/advanced-components/src/app/host/popup-demo/steps/host-1.ts

```
20   @Component({
21     selector: 'app-popup-demo',
22     template: `
23     <div class="ui message" popup>
24       <div class="header">
25         Learning Directives
26       </div>
27
28       <p>
29         This should use our Popup diretive
30       </p>
31     </div>
32     `
33   })
34   export class PopupDemoComponent1 {
35   }
```

When we run this application, we expect the message Directive bound to be logged on the console, indicating we have successfully bound to the first <div> in our template:

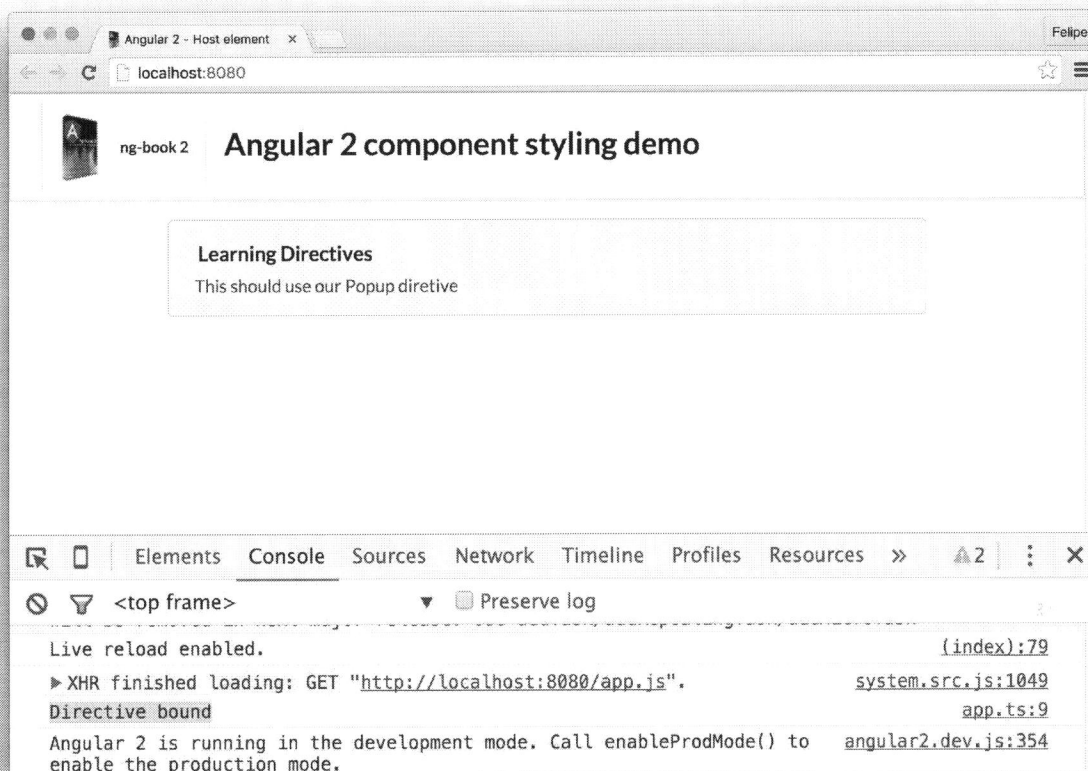

Binding to host element

Using `ElementRef`

If we want to learn more about the host element a directive is bound to, we can use the built-in `ElementRef` class.

This class holds the information about a given Angular element, including the native DOM element using the `nativeElement` property.

In order to see the elements our directive is binding to, we can change our directive constructor to receive the `ElementRef` and log it to the console:

code/advanced-components/src/app/host/popup-demo/steps/host-2.ts

```
 9  import { Component, Directive, ElementRef } from '@angular/core';
10
11  @Directive({
12    selector: '[popup]'
13  })
14  export class PopupDirective {
15    constructor(_elementRef: ElementRef) {
16      console.log(_elementRef);
17    }
18  }
```

We can also add a second element to the page that uses our directive, so we can see two different `ElementRefs` logged to the console:

code/advanced-components/src/app/host/popup-demo/steps/host-2.ts

```
20  @Component({
21    selector: 'app-pop-demo',
22    template: `
23    <div class="ui message" popup>
24      <div class="header">
25        Learning Directives
26      </div>
27
28      <p>
29        This should use our Popup diretive
30      </p>
31    </div>
32
33    <i class="alarm icon" popup></i>
34    `
35  })
36  export class PopupDemoComponent2 {
37  }
```

When we run our app now, we can see two different `ElementRefs`: one with `div.ui.message` and the other with `i.alarm.icon`. This means that the directive was successfully bound to two different host elements:

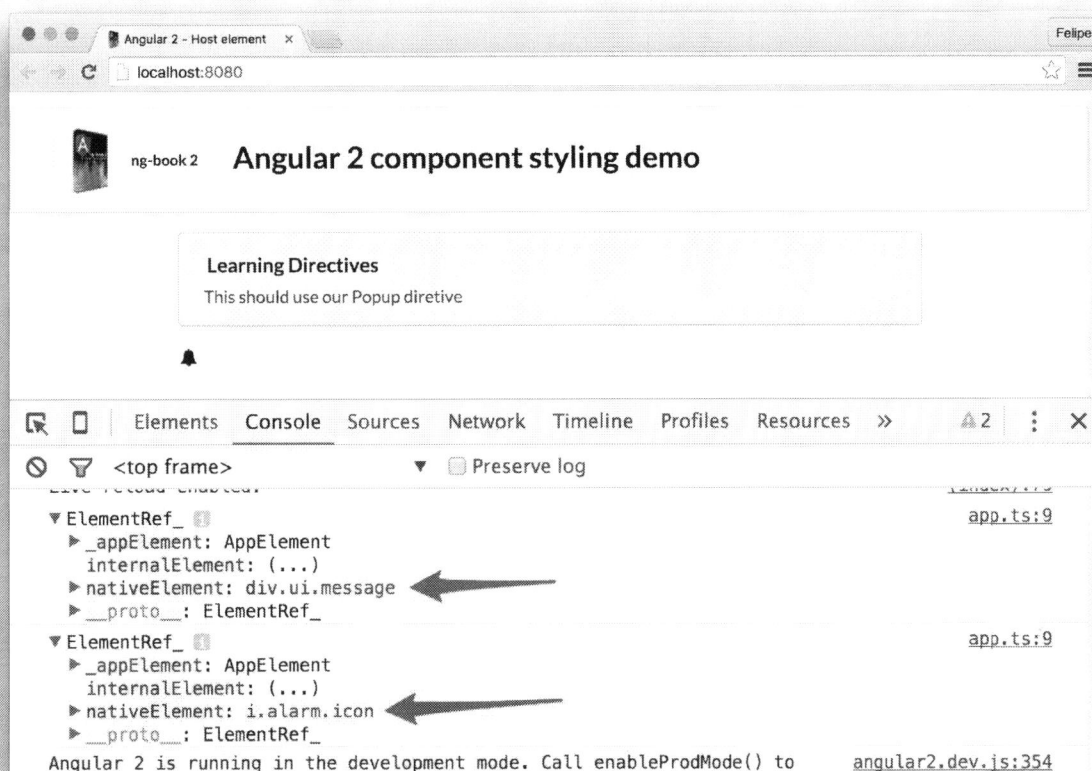

ElementRefs

Binding to the host

Moving on, our next goal is to do something when the host element is clicked.

We learned before that the way we bind events in elements in Angular is using the (event) syntax.

In order to bind events of the host element, we'll do something very similar, but the syntax is different. In order to bind the directive to a host's click event, we're going to use the decorator HostListener.

The HostListener decorator allows a directive to listen to events on its host element.

We'll do this by decorating a function on the component with the @HostListener() decoration.

We also want the host element to define what message will pop up when the element is clicked, using the message attribute.

First, let's add an inputs attribute to the directive. We'll do this by importing Input and using the @Input decorator with the property we will use for this input:

```
1   import { Component, Input } from '@angular/core';
2   ...
3   class Popup {
4     @Input() message: String;
5     ...
6   }
```

We're saying that we're having a property with the name message and expect to receive an input with the same name.

Then, let's add the HostListener decoration. We'll do this by adding @HostLisener('click') on the function we want to call when the host is clicked:

code/advanced-components/src/app/host/popup-demo/steps/host-3.ts

```
14    HostListener
15  } from '@angular/core';
16
17  @Directive({
18    selector: '[popup]'
19  })
20  export class PopupDirective {
21    @Input() message: String;
22
23    constructor(_elementRef: ElementRef) {
24      console.log(_elementRef);
25    }
26
27    @HostListener('click') displayMessage(): void {
28      alert(this.message);
29    }
30  }
```

Then when the host element is clicked we'll call the directive's displayMessage method, which will display the message the host element defines.

And finally, we need to change our app template a bit to add the message we want displayed for each element:

code/advanced-components/src/app/host/popup-demo/steps/host-3.ts

```
32  @Component({
33    selector: 'app-popup-demo',
34    template: `
35    <div class="ui message" popup
36        message="Clicked the message">
37      <div class="header">
38        Learning Directives
39      </div>
40
41      <p>
42        This should use our Popup diretive
43      </p>
44    </div>
45
46    <i class="alarm icon" popup
47       message="Clicked the alarm icon"></i>
48    `
49  })
50  export class PopupDemoComponent3 {
51  }
```

Notice that we use the popup directive twice, and we pass a different message each time we use it. This means when we run the app, we're able to click either on the message or on the alarm icon, and we'll see different messages:

Popup 1

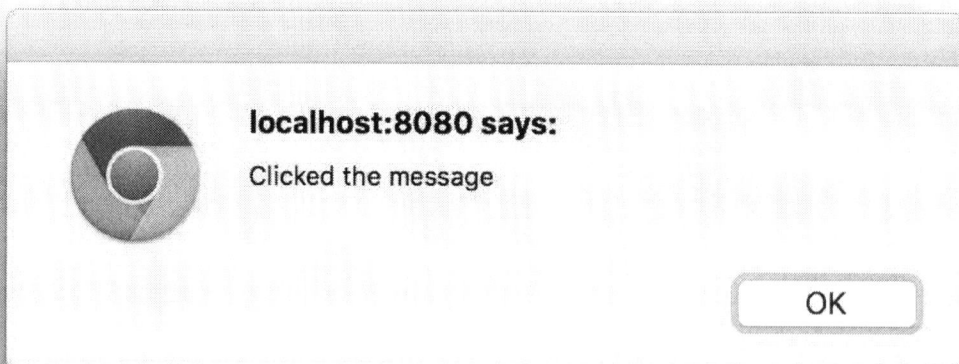

Popup 2

Adding a Button using exportAs

Now let's say we have a new requirement: we want to trigger the alert manually by clicking a button. How could we trigger the popup message from **outside** the host element?

In order to achieve this, we need to make the **directive available from elsewhere in the template**.

As we discussed in previous chapters, the way to reference a component is by using **template reference variable**. We can reference directives the same way.

In order to give the templates a reference to a directive we use the `exportAs` attribute. This will allow the host element (or a child of the host element) to define a template variable that references the directive using the `#var="exportName"` syntax.

Let's add the `exportAs` attribute to our directive:

code/advanced-components/src/app/host/popup-demo/steps/host-4.ts

```
17  @Directive({
18    selector: '[popup]',
19    exportAs: 'popup',
20  })
21  export class PopupDirective {
22    @Input() message: String;
23
24    constructor(_elementRef: ElementRef) {
25      console.log(_elementRef);
26    }
27
28    @HostListener('click') displayMessage(): void {
29      alert(this.message);
30    }
31  }
```

And now we need to change the two elements to export the template reference:

code/advanced-components/src/app/host/popup-demo/steps/host-4.ts

```
35    template: `
36    <div class="ui message" popup #popup1="popup"
37        message="Clicked the message">
38      <div class="header">
39        Learning Directives
40      </div>
41
42      <p>
43        This should use our Popup diretive
44      </p>
45    </div>
46
47    <i class="alarm icon" popup #popup2="popup"
48        message="Clicked the alarm icon"></i>
```

See that we used the template var #popup1 for the div.message and #popup2 for the icon.

Now let's add two buttons, one to trigger each popup:

code/advanced-components/src/app/host/popup-demo/steps/host-4.ts

```
49    <div style="margin-top: 20px;">
50      <button (click)="popup1.displayMessage()" class="ui button">
51        Display popup for message element
52      </button>
53
54      <button (click)="popup2.displayMessage()" class="ui button">
55        Display popup for alarm icon
56      </button>
57    </div>
```

Now reload the page and click each of the buttons and each message will appear as expected.

Creating a Message Pane with Content Projection

Sometimes when we are creating components we want to pass inner markup as an argument to the component. This technique is called *content projection*. The idea is that it lets us specify a bit of markup that will be expanded into a bigger template.

> **i** Angular 1 dug deep in the dictionary and called this *transclusion*.

Let's create a new directive that will render a nicely styled message like this:

> **Learning Directives**
> This should use our Popup diretive

Popup 1

Our goal is to write markup like this:

```
1  <div message header="My Message">
2    This is the content of the message
3  </div>
```

Which will render into the more complicated HTML like:

```
1  <div class="ui message">
2    <div class="header">
3      My Message
4    </div>
5
6    <p>
7      This is the content of the message
8    </p>
9  </div>
```

We have two challenges here: we need to change the host element <div> to add the ui and message CSS classes, and we need to add the div's contents to a specific place in our markup.

Changing the Host's CSS

To add attributes to the host element, we use a new decorator, similar to when we listened to events on the host: the HostBinding decorator. But now, instead of specifying the event name we want to listen for, we'll define the attribute name we want to 'bind' to. In this component, it looks like this:

```
1  @HostBinding('attr.class') cssClass = 'ui message';
```

This decoration tells angular that we want the value of cssClass to be kept in sync with the host's attribute class.

Using ng-content

Our next challenge is to include the original host element children in a specific part of a view. To do that, we use the ng-content directive.

Since this directive needs a template, let's use a component instead and write the following code:

code/advanced-components/src/app/content-projection/content-projection-demo/messageo.component.ts

```
1   /* tslint:disable:component-selector */
2   import {
3     Component,
4     OnInit,
5     Input,
6     HostBinding
7   } from '@angular/core';
8
9   @Component({
10    selector: '[app-message]',
11    template: `
12      <div class="header">
13        {{ header }}
14      </div>
15      <p>
16        <ng-content></ng-content>
17      </p>
18    `
19  })
20  export class MessageComponent implements OnInit {
21    @Input() header: string;
22    @HostBinding('attr.class') cssClass = 'ui message';
23
24    ngOnInit(): void {
25      console.log('header', this.header);
26    }
27  }
```

A few highlights:

- We use the @Input decorator to indicate we want to receive a header attribute, set on the host
  element
- We set the host element's class attribute to ui message using the host attribute of our
  component
- We use <ng-content></ng-content> to project the host element's children into a specific
  location of our template

When we open the app in the browser and inspect the message div, we see it worked exactly like we
planned:

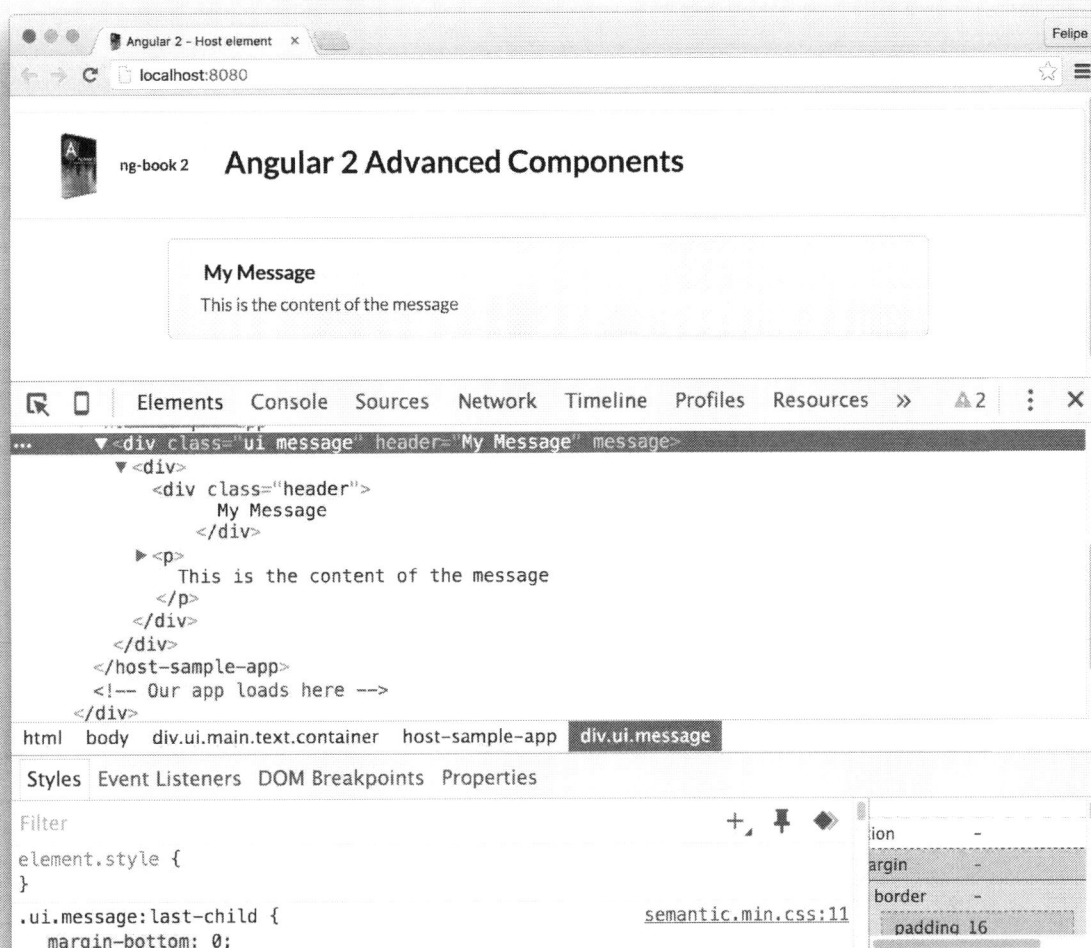

projected content

Querying Neighbor Directives - Writing Tabs

It's great when you can create a component that fully encapsulates its own behavior.

However, as a component grows in features, it might make sense to split it up into several smaller components that work together.

A great example of components that work together is a tab pane that has multiple tabs. The tab panel or *tabset*, as it's usually called, is composed of multiple *tabs*. In this scenario we have a parent component (the tabset) and multiple child components (the tabs). The tabset and the tabs don't make sense separately, but putting all of the logic in one component is cumbersome. So in this example, we're going to cover how to make separate components that work together.

Let's start writing those components in a way that we'll be able to use the following markup:

```
1  <tabset>
2    <tab title="Tab 1">Tab 1</tab>
3    <tab title="Tab 2">Tab 2</tab>
4    ...
5  </tabset>
```

We're going to use Semantic UI Tab styles[123] to render the tabs.

ContentTabComponent

Let's start by writing the ContentTabComponent

code/advanced-components/src/app/tabs/content-tabs-demo/content-tab.component.ts

```
1  import {
2    Component,
3    OnInit,
4    Input
5  } from '@angular/core';
6
7  @Component({
8    selector: 'tab',
9    templateUrl: './content-tab.component.html'
10  })
11  export class ContentTabComponent implements OnInit {
12    @Input() title: string;
13    active = false;
14    name: string;
15
16    constructor() { }
17
18    ngOnInit() { }
19  }
```

and the template:

code/advanced-components/src/app/tabs/content-tabs-demo/content-tab.component.html

```
1  <div class="ui bottom attached tab segment"
2    [class.active]="active">
3
4    <ng-content></ng-content>
5
6  </div>
```

There are not many new concepts here. We're declaring a component that will use the ContentTab-Component selector, and it will allow a title input to be set.

Then we're rendering a <div> and using the content projection concept we learned in the previous section to inline the contents of the <tab> directive inside the div.

Next we declare 3 properties on our components: *title*, *active* and *name*. One thing to notice is the @Input('title') decorator we added to the title property. This decorator is a way to ask Angular to automatically bind the value of the *input* title into the *property* title.

ContentTabsetComponent **Component**

Now let's move on to the ContentTabsetComponent component that will be used to wrap the tabs:

code/advanced-components/src/app/tabs/content-tabs-demo/content-tabset.component.ts

```
1  import {
2    Component,
3    AfterContentInit,
4    QueryList,
5    ContentChildren
6  } from '@angular/core';
7
8  import { ContentTabComponent } from './content-tab.component';
9
10 @Component({
11   selector: 'tabset',
12   templateUrl: './content-tabset.component.html'
13 })
14 export class ContentTabsetComponent implements AfterContentInit {
15   @ContentChildren(ContentTabComponent) tabs: QueryList<ContentTabComponent>;
16
17   ngAfterContentInit(): void {
18     this.tabs.toArray()[0].active = true;
19   }
```

```
20
21    setActive(tab: ContentTabComponent): void {
22      this.tabs.toArray().forEach((t) => t.active = false);
23      tab.active = true;
24    }
25
26    constructor() { }
27  }
```

and the template:

code/advanced-components/src/app/tabs/content-tabs-demo/content-tabset.component.html

```
1   <div class="ui top attached tabular menu">
2     <a *ngFor="let tab of tabs"
3       class="item"
4       [class.active]="tab.active"
5       (click)="setActive(tab)">
6
7       {{ tab.title }}
8
9     </a>
10  </div>
11  <ng-content></ng-content>
```

Let's break down the implementation so we can learn about the new concepts it introduces.

ContentTabsetComponent @Component **Decorator**

The @Component section doesn't have many new ideas. We're using the <tabset> tab as our selector.

The template itself uses ngFor to iterate through the tabs and if the tab has the *active* flag set to true, it will add the *active* CSS class to the <a> element that renders the tab.

We also specify that we are rendering the tabs themselves after the initial *div*, right where ng-content is.

ContentTabsetComponent **class**

Now let's turn our attention to the ContentTabsetComponent class. The first new idea we see here is that the ContentTabsetComponent class is implementing AfterContentInit. This *lifecycle hook* will tell Angular to call a method of our class (ngAfterContentInit) once the contents of the child directives have been initialized.

`ContentTabsetComponent` `ContentChildren` **and** `QueryList`

Next thing we do is declare the `tabs` property that will hold every `ContentTabComponent` component we declare inside the `ContentTabsetComponent`. Notice that instead of declaring this list as an array of `ContentTabComponents`, we use the class `QueryList`, passing a generic of `ContentTabComponent`. Why is this?

`QueryList` is a class provided by Angular and when we use `QueryList` with a `ContentChildren` Angular populates this with the **components that match the query** and then **keeps the items up to date** if the state of the application changes.

However, `QueryList` requires a `ContentChildren` to populate it, so let's take a look at that now.

On the `tabs` instance variable, we add the `@ContentChildren(Tab)` decorator. This decorator will tell Angular to inject all the direct child directives (of the `ContentTabComponent` type) into the `tabs` parameter. We then assign it to the `tabs` property of our component. With this **we now have access to all the child `ContentTabComponent` components**.

Initializing the `ContentTabsetComponent`

When this component is initialized, we want to make the first tab active. To do this we use the `ngAfterContentInit` function (that is described by the `AfterContentInit` hook). Notice that we use `this.tabs.toArray()` to cast Angular's `QueryList` into a native TypeScript array.

`ContentTabsetComponent` `setActive`

Finally we define a `setActive` method. This method is used when we click a tab on our template e.g. using `(click)="setActive(tab)"`. This function will iterate through all the tabs, setting their `active` properties to false. Then we set the tab we clicked to active.

Using the `ContentTabsetComponent`

Now the next step is to code the application component that makes use of both of the components we created. Here's how we write the component:

code/advanced-components/src/app/tabs/content-tabs-demo/content-tabs-demo.component.ts

```
1  import { Component, OnInit } from '@angular/core';
2
3  @Component({
4    selector: 'app-content-tabs-demo',
5    templateUrl: './content-tabs-demo.component.html'
6  })
7  export class ContentTabsDemoComponent implements OnInit {
8    tabs: any;
```

```
 9
10    constructor() { }
11
12    ngOnInit() {
13      this.tabs = [
14        { title: 'About', content: 'This is the About tab' },
15        { title: 'Blog', content: 'This is our blog' },
16        { title: 'Contact us', content: 'Contact us here' },
17      ];
18    }
19
20  }
```

and template:

code/advanced-components/src/app/tabs/content-tabs-demo/content-tabs-demo.component.html

```
 1  <tabset>
 2    <tab title="First tab">
 3      Lorem ipsum dolor sit amet, consectetur adipisicing elit.
 4      Quibusdam magni quia ut harum facilis, ullam deleniti porro
 5      dignissimos quasi at molestiae sapiente natus, neque voluptatum
 6      ad consequuntur cupiditate nemo sunt.
 7    </tab>
 8
 9    <tab
10      *ngFor="let tab of tabs"
11      [title]="tab.title">
12      {{ tab.content }}
13    </tab>
14  </tabset>
```

We're declaring that we're using tabs-sample-app as our component's selector and using the ContentTabsetComponent and ContentTabComponent components.

On the template we then create a ContentTabsetComponent and we add first a static tab (First tab) and we add a few more tabs from the tabs property of the component controller class, to illustrate how we can render tabs dynamically.

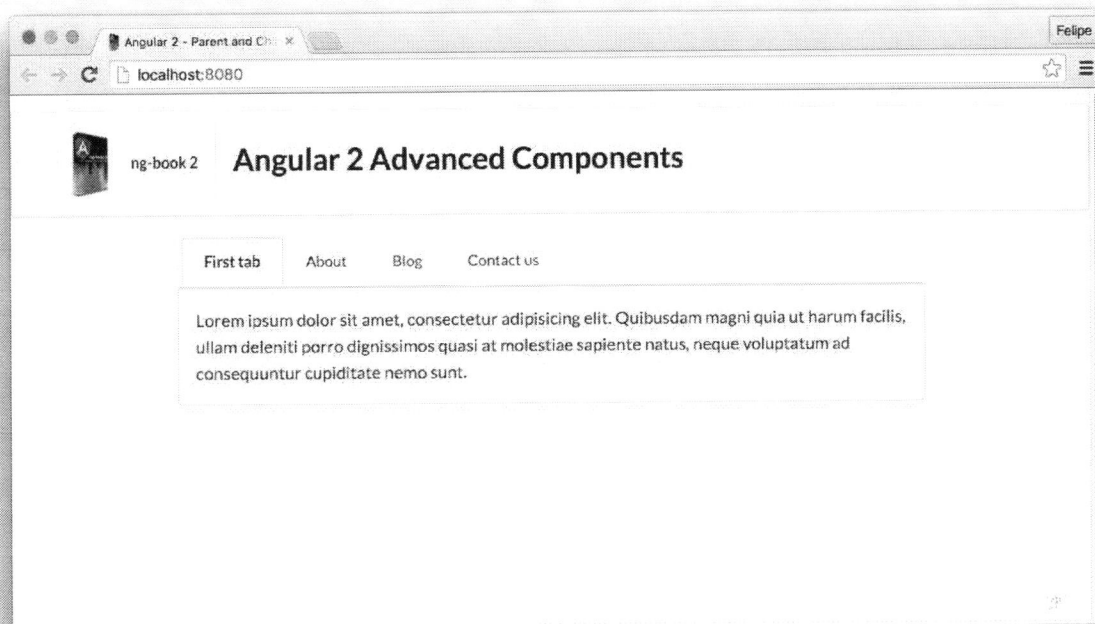

Tabset application

Lifecycle Hooks

Lifecycle hooks are the way Angular allows you to add code that runs before or after each step of the directive or component lifecycle.

The list of hooks Angular offers are:

- `OnInit`
- `OnDestroy`
- `DoCheck`
- `OnChanges`
- `AfterContentInit`
- `AfterContentChecked`
- `AfterViewInit`
- `AfterViewChecked`

Using these hooks each follow a similar pattern:

In order to be notified about those events you

1. declare that your directive or component class implements the interface and then
2. declare the ng method of the hook (e.g. ngOnInit)

Every method name is ng plus the name of the hook. For example, for OnInit we declare the method ngOnInit, for AfterContentInit we declare ngAfterContentInit and so on.

When Angular knows that a component implements these functions, it will invoke them at the appropriate time.

Let's take a look at each hook individually and when we would use each of them.

> It is actually not mandatory for the class to implement the interface, one could just create the method of the hook. But it is considered good practice[124] and has benefits from strong typing and editor tooling.

OnInit **and** OnDestroy

The OnInit hook is called when your directive properties have been initialized, and before any of the child directive properties are initialized.

Similarly, the OnDestroy hook is called when the directive instance is destroyed. This is typically used if we need to do some cleanup every time our directive is destroyed.

In order to illustrate let's write a component that implements both OnInit and OnDestroy:

code/advanced-components/src/app/lifecycle/on-init/on-init.component.ts

```
 1  import {
 2    Component,
 3    OnInit,
 4    OnDestroy
 5  } from '@angular/core';
 6
 7  @Component({
 8    selector: 'app-on-init',
 9    template: `
10    <div class="ui label">
11      <i class="cubes icon"></i> Init/Destroy
12    </div>
13    `
14  })
15  export class OnInitComponent implements OnInit, OnDestroy {
```

---

[124]https://angular.io/docs/ts/latest/guide/lifecycle-hooks.html

```
16    constructor() { }
17
18    ngOnInit(): void {
19      console.log('On init');
20    }
21
22    ngOnDestroy(): void {
23      console.log('On destroy');
24    }
25  }
```

For this component, we're just logging *On init* and *On destroy* to the console when the hooks are called.

Now in order to test those hooks let's use our component in our app component using ngFor to conditionally display it based on a boolean property. Let's also add a button that allows us to toggle that flag. This way, when the flag is false, our component will be *removed* from the page, causing the OnDestroy hook to be called. Similarly when the flag is toggled to true, the OnInit hook will be called.

Here's how our app component will look:

code/advanced-components/src/app/lifecycle/on-init/on-init-demo.component.ts

```
1  import { Component } from '@angular/core';
2
3  @Component({
4    selector: 'app-on-init-demo',
5    templateUrl: './on-init-demo.component.html'
6  })
7  export class OnInitDemoComponent {
8    display: boolean;
9
10   constructor() {
11     this.display = true;
12   }
13
14   toggle(): void {
15     this.display = !this.display;
16   }
17 }
```

and the template:

code/advanced-components/src/app/lifecycle/on-init/on-init-demo.component.html

```
1  <h4 class="ui horizontal divider header">
2    OnInit and OnDestroy
3  </h4>
4
5  <button class="ui primary button" (click)="toggle()">
6    Toggle
7  </button>
8  <app-on-init *ngIf="display"></app-on-init>
```

When we first run the application, we can see that the OnInit hook was called when the component was first instantiated:

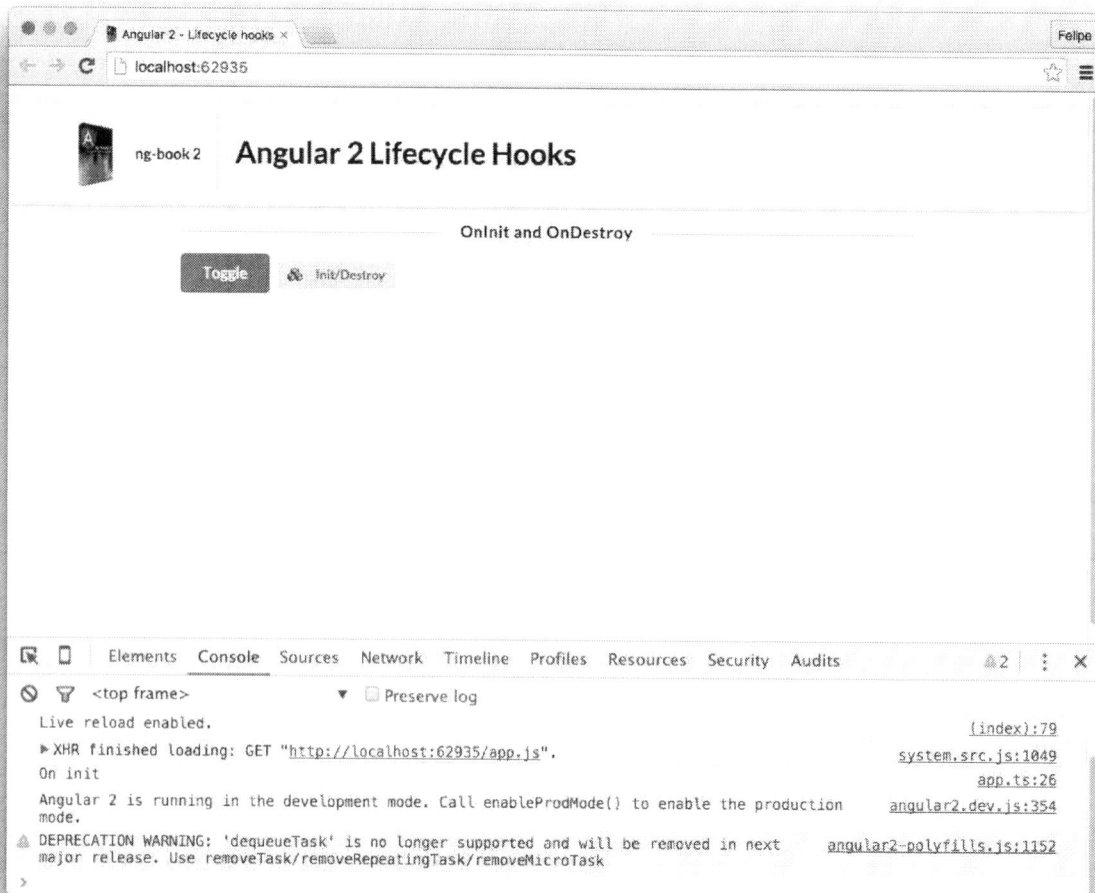

Initial state of our component

When I click the `Toggle` button for the first time, the component is destroyed and the hook is called as expected:

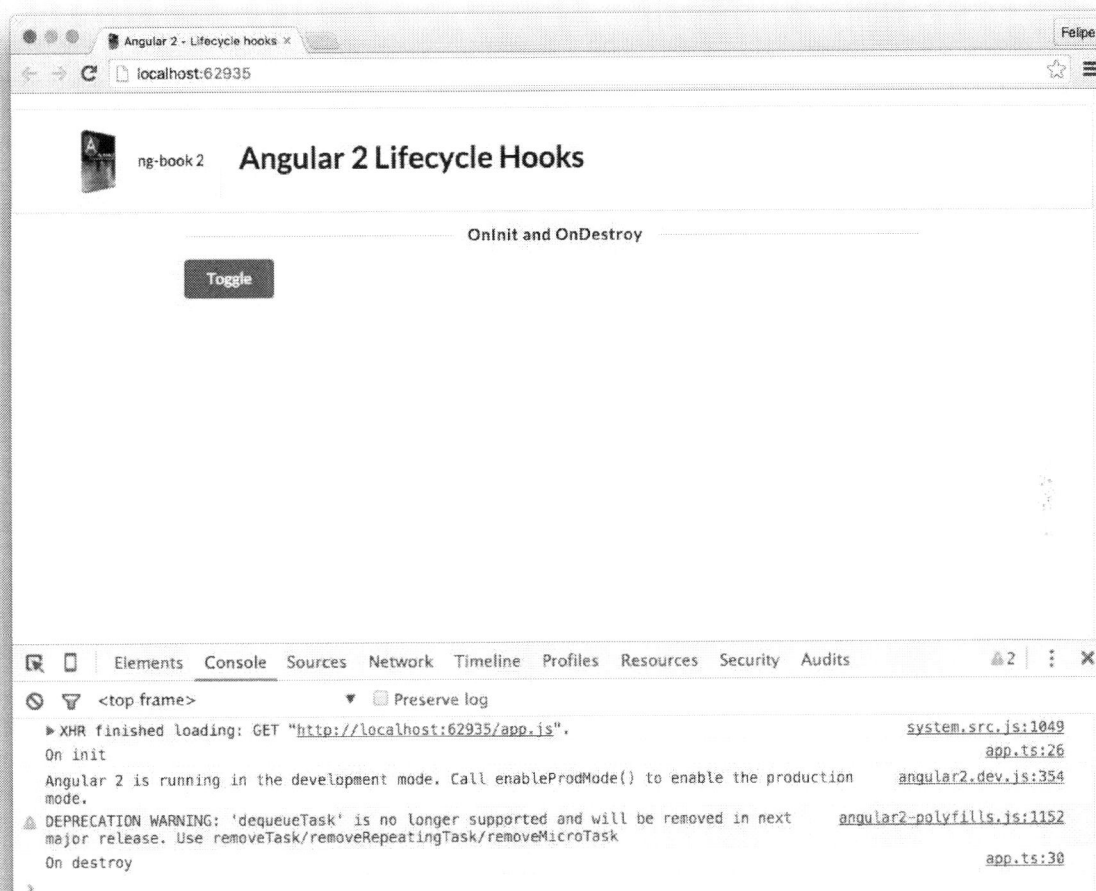

OnDestroy hook

And if we click it another time:

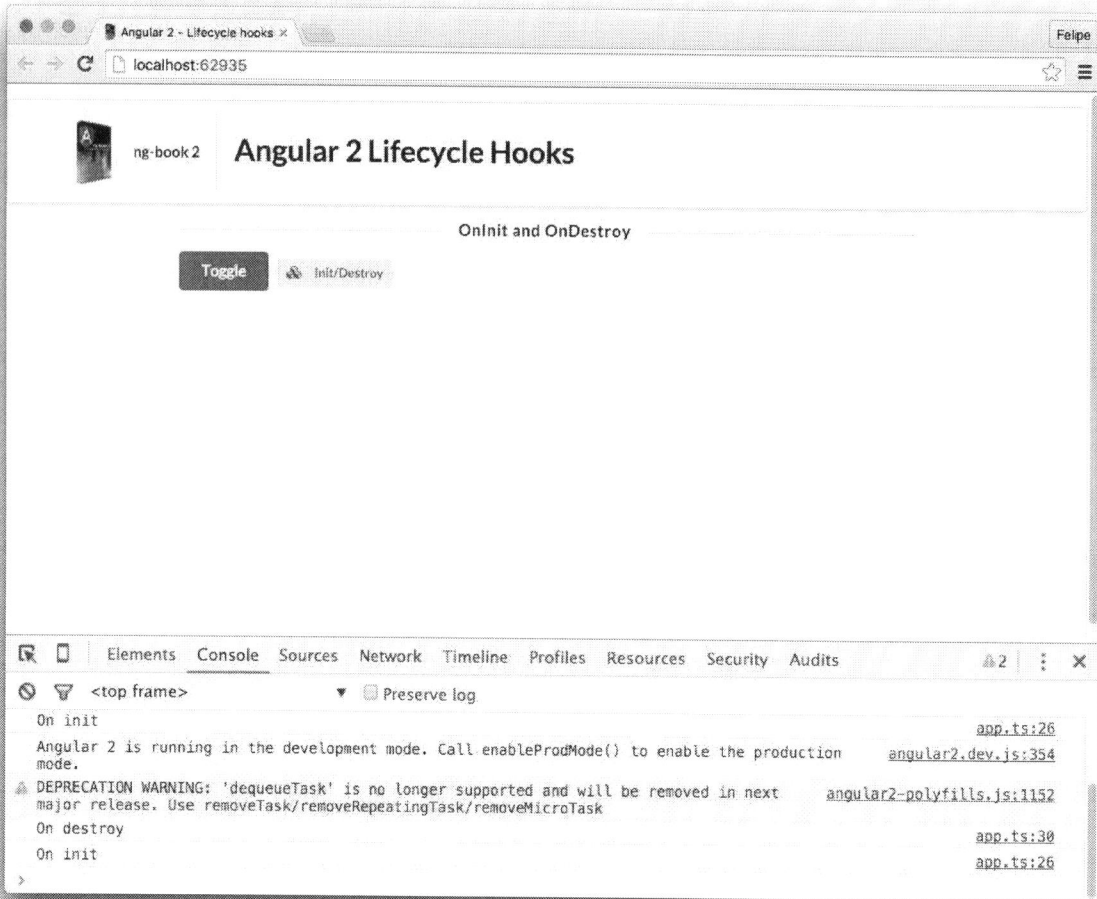

OnDestroy hook

OnChanges

The OnChanges hook is called after one or more of our component properties have been changed. The ngOnChanges method receives a parameter which tells which properties have changed.

To understand this better, let's write a comment block component that has two inputs: *name* and *comment*:

code/advanced-components/src/app/lifecycle/on-changes/on-changes.component.ts

```
1  import {
2    Component,
3    OnInit,
4    OnChanges,
5    Input,
6    SimpleChange
7  } from '@angular/core';
8
9  @Component({
10   selector: 'app-on-changes',
11   templateUrl: './on-changes.component.html'
12 })
13 export class OnChangesComponent implements OnChanges {
14   @Input('name') name: string;
15   @Input('comment') comment: string;
16
17   ngOnChanges(changes: {[propName: string]: SimpleChange}): void {
18     console.log('Changes', changes);
19   }
20 }
```

and template:

code/advanced-components/src/app/lifecycle/on-changes/on-changes.component.html

```
1  <div class="ui comments">
2    <div class="comment">
3      <a class="avatar">
4        <img src="assets/images/avatars/matt.jpg">
5      </a>
6      <div class="content">
7        <a class="author">{{name}}</a>
8        <div class="text">
9          {{comment}}
10       </div>
11     </div>
12   </div>
13 </div>
```

The important thing about this component is that it implements the OnChanges interface, and it declares the ngOnChanges method with this signature:

code/advanced-components/src/app/lifecycle/on-changes/on-changes.component.ts

```
17    ngOnChanges(changes: {[propName: string]: SimpleChange}): void {
18      console.log('Changes', changes);
19    }
```

This method will be triggered whenever the values of either the *name* or *comment* properties change. When that happens, we receive an object that maps changed fields to SimpleChange objects.

Each SimpleChange instance has two fields: currentValue and previousValue. If both name and comment properties change for our component, we expect the value of changes in our method to be something like:

```
1   {
2     name: {
3       currentValue: 'new name value',
4       previousValue: 'old name value'
5     },
6     comment: {
7       currentValue: 'new comment value',
8       previousValue: 'old comment value'
9     }
10  }
```

Now, let's change the app component to use our component and also add a little form where we can play with the name and comment properties of our component:

code/advanced-components/src/app/lifecycle/on-changes/on-changes-demo.component.ts

```
1   import { Component, OnInit } from '@angular/core';
2
3   @Component({
4     selector: 'app-on-changes-demo',
5     templateUrl: './on-changes-demo.component.html',
6     styles: []
7   })
8   export class OnChangesDemoComponent implements OnInit {
9     display: boolean;
10    name: string;
11    comment: string;
12
13    constructor() { }
14
```

```
15    ngOnInit() {
16      this.display = true;
17      this.name = 'Felipe Coury';
18      this.comment = 'I am learning so much!';
19    }
20
21    setValues(namefld, commentfld): void {
22      this.name = namefld.value;
23      this.comment = commentfld.value;
24    }
25
26    toggle(): void {
27      this.display = !this.display;
28    }
29
30    }
```

and template:

code/advanced-components/src/app/lifecycle/on-changes/on-changes-demo.component.html

```
1   <h4 class="ui horizontal divider header">
2     OnChanges
3   </h4>
4
5   <div class="ui form">
6     <div class="field">
7       <label>Name</label>
8       <input
9         type="text"
10        #namefld
11        value="{{name}}"
12       (keyup)="setValues(namefld, commentfld)">
13    </div>
14
15    <div class="field">
16      <label>Comment</label>
17      <textarea
18        #commentfld
19        (keyup)="setValues(namefld, commentfld)"
20        rows="2">{{comment}}</textarea>
21    </div>
22  </div>
```

```
23
24    <app-on-changes
25      [name]="name"
26      [comment]="comment"
27      ></app-on-changes>
```

Note the important pieces we added to the template. We declare a new form with name and comment fields.

When the keyup event is fired for either the name or comment fields, we are calling setValues with the template references namefld and commentfld that represent the input and textarea.

This method just takes the value from those fields and updates the name and comment properties accordingly:

code/advanced-components/src/app/lifecycle/on-changes/on-changes-demo.component.ts

```
21    setValues(namefld, commentfld): void {
22      this.name = namefld.value;
23      this.comment = commentfld.value;
24    }
```

So now, the first time we open the app, we can see that our OnChanges hook is called:

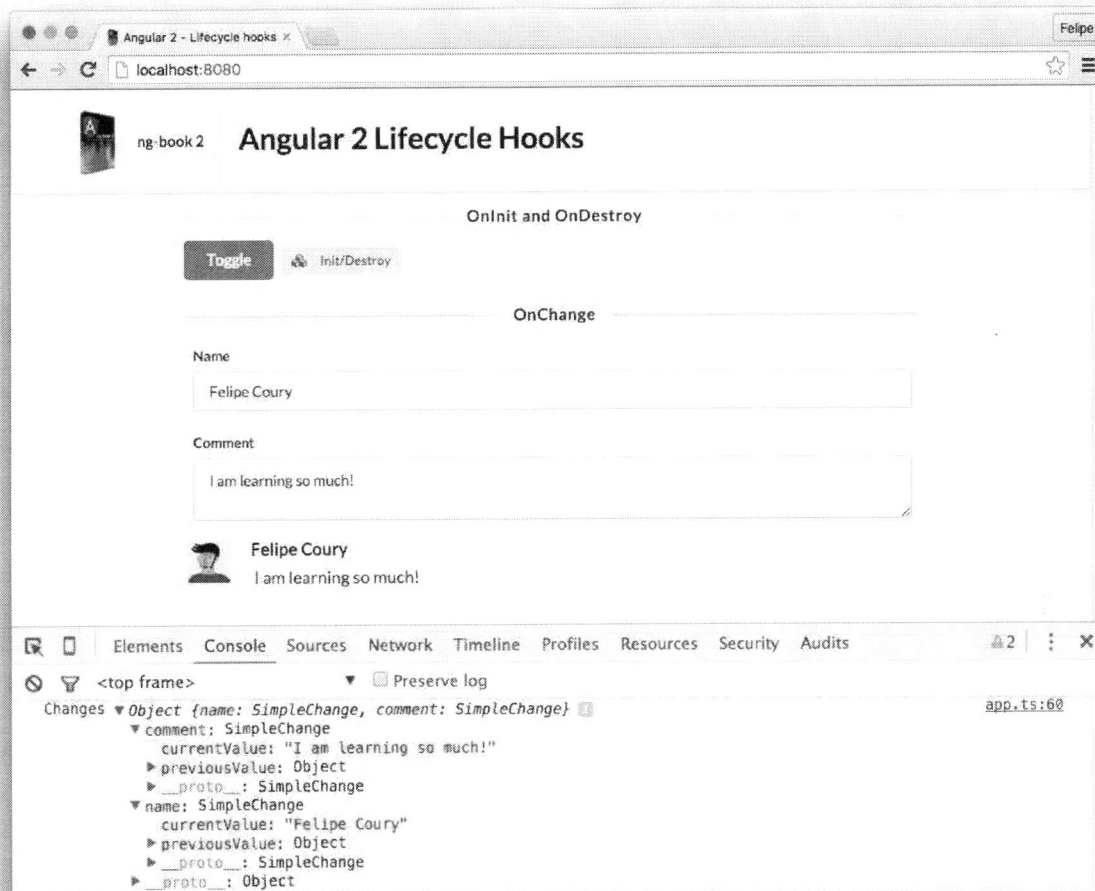

OnChanges

This happens when the initial values are set, on the constructor of the `LifecycleSampleApp` component.

Now if we play with the name, we can see that the hook is called repeatedly. In the case below, we pasted the name *Nate Murray* on top of the previous name, and the values for the changes are displayed as expected:

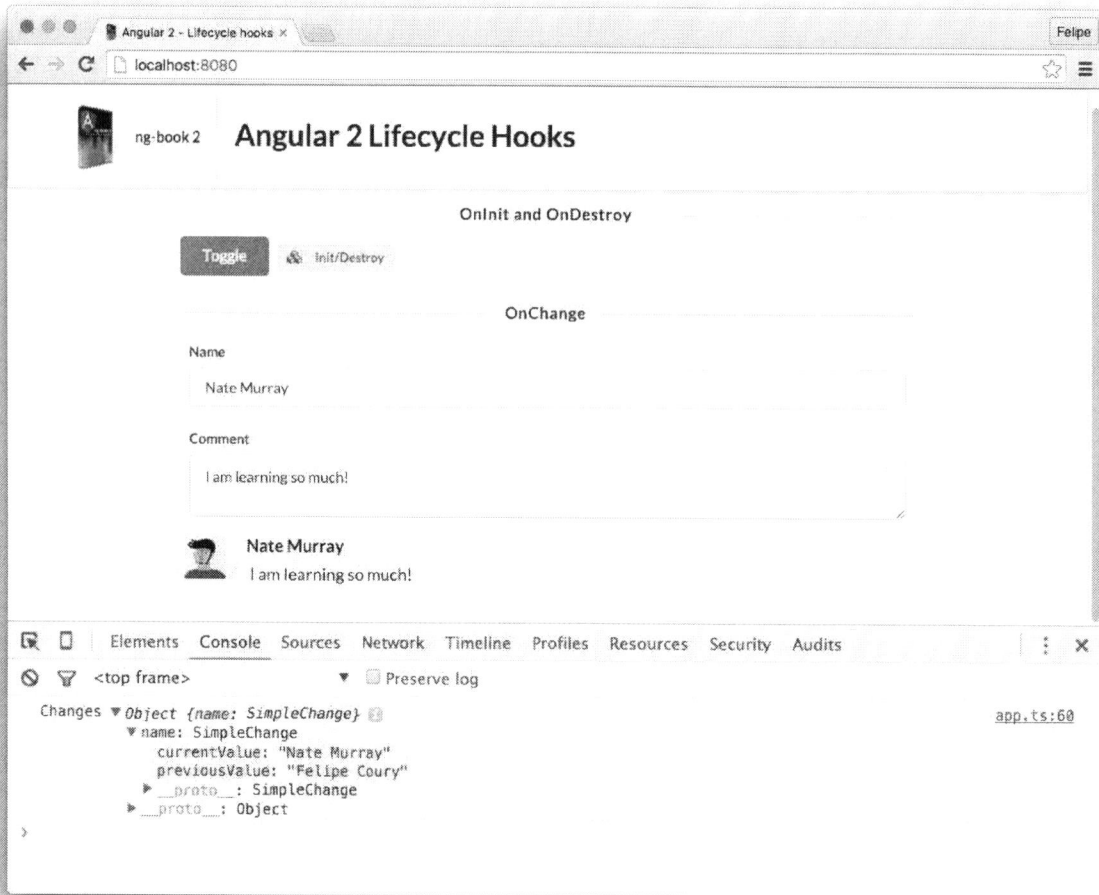

OnChanges

DoCheck

The default notification system implemented by OnChanges is triggered every time the Angular change detection mechanism notices there was a change on any of the directive properties.

However, there may be times when the overhead added by this change notification may be too much, especially if performance is a concern.

There may be times when we just want to do something in case an item was removed or added, or if only a particular property changed, for instance.

If we run into one of these scenarios, we can use the DoCheck hook.

> ⚠ It's important to note that the OnChanges hook gets overridden by DoCheck so if we implement both, OnChanges will be ignored.

Checking for changes

In order to evaluate what changed, Angular provides *differs*. **Differs will evaluate a given property of your directive to determine *what* changed.**

There are two types of built-in differs: *iterable differs* and *key-value differs.*

Iterable differs

Iterable differs should be used when we have a list-like structure and we're only interested in knowing things that were added or removed from that list.

Key-value differs

Key-value differs should be used for dictionary-like structures, and work at the key level. This differ will identify changes when a new key is added, when a key removed and when the value of a key changed.

Rendering a comment with DoCheck

To illustrate these concepts, let's build a component that renders a stream of comments, like below:

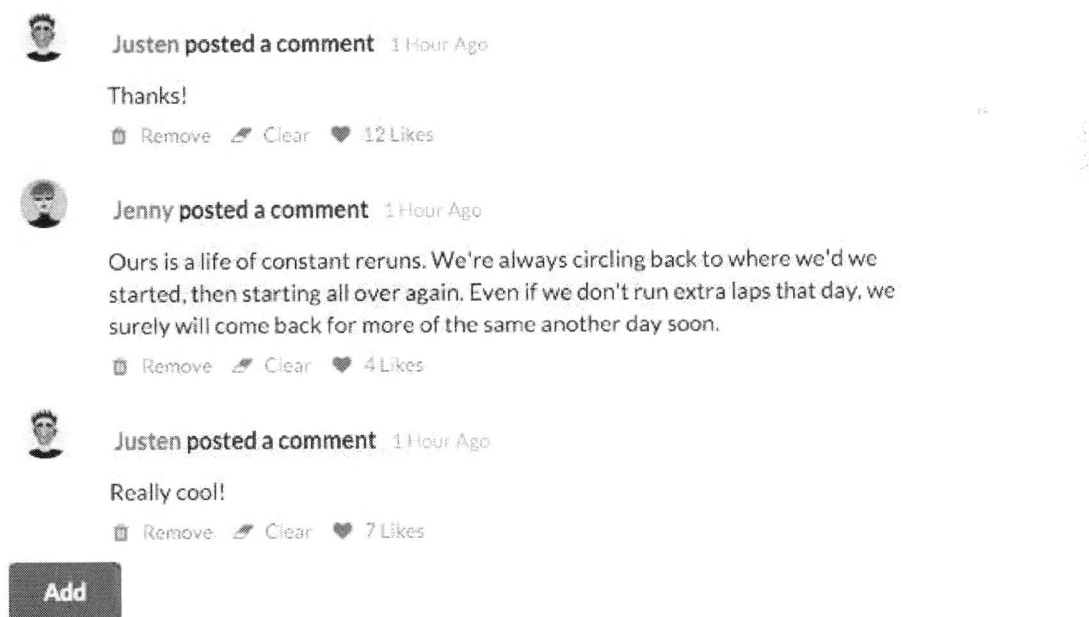

Justen posted a comment 1 Hour Ago

Thanks!

🗑 Remove ✏ Clear ♥ 12 Likes

Jenny posted a comment 1 Hour Ago

Ours is a life of constant reruns. We're always circling back to where we'd we started, then starting all over again. Even if we don't run extra laps that day, we surely will come back for more of the same another day soon.

🗑 Remove ✏ Clear ♥ 4 Likes

Justen posted a comment 1 Hour Ago

Really cool!

🗑 Remove ✏ Clear ♥ 7 Likes

Add

DoCheck example

Let's write a component that will render one individual comment. First, the template:

code/advanced-components/src/app/lifecycle/differs/comment.component.html

```
1   <div class="ui feed">
2     <div class="event">
3       <div class="label" *ngIf="comment.author">
4         <img src="assets/images/avatars/{{comment.author.toLowerCase()}}.jpg">
5       </div>
6       <div class="content">
7         <div class="summary">
8           <a class="user">
9             {{comment.author}}
10          </a> posted a comment
11          <div class="date">
12            1 Hour Ago
13          </div>
14        </div>
15        <div class="extra text">
16          {{comment.comment}}
17        </div>
18        <div class="meta">
19          <a class="trash" (click)="remove()">
20            <i class="trash icon"></i> Remove
21          </a>
22          <a class="trash" (click)="clear()">
23            <i class="eraser icon"></i> Clear
24          </a>
25          <a class="like" (click)="like()">
26            <i class="like icon"></i> {{comment.likes}} Likes
27          </a>
28        </div>
29      </div>
30    </div>
31  </div>
```

and in the component:

code/advanced-components/src/app/lifecycle/differs/comment.component.ts

```
 1  import {
 2    Component,
 3    Input,
 4    Output,
 5    EventEmitter,
 6    KeyValueDiffers,
 7    DoCheck
 8  } from '@angular/core';
 9
10  @Component({
11    selector: 'app-comment',
12    templateUrl: './comment.component.html'
13  })
14  export class CommentComponent implements DoCheck {
15    @Input() comment: any;
16    @Output() onRemove: EventEmitter<any>;
17    differ: any;
```

Here we are declaring the component metadata. Our component will receive the comment that should be rendered and it will emit an event with the remove button icon clicked.

On the class declaration we indicate we're implementing the DoCheck interface. We then declare the input property comment, and the output event onRemove. We also declare a differ property.

code/advanced-components/src/app/lifecycle/differs/comment.component.ts

```
19    constructor(differs: KeyValueDiffers) {
20      this.differ = differs.find([]).create();
21      this.onRemove = new EventEmitter();
22    }
```

On the constructor we're receiving a KeyValueDiffers instance on the differs variable. We then use this variable to create an instance of the key value differ using this syntax differs.find([]).create(null). We're also initializing our event emitter onRemove.

Next, let's implement the ngDoCheck method, required by the interface:

code/advanced-components/src/app/lifecycle/differs/comment.component.ts

```
24    ngDoCheck(): void {
25      const changes = this.differ.diff(this.comment);
26
27      if (changes) {
28        changes.forEachAddedItem(r =>
29          this.logChange('added', r)
30        );
31        changes.forEachRemovedItem(r =>
32          this.logChange('removed', r)
33        );
34        changes.forEachChangedItem(r =>
35          this.logChange('changed', r)
36        );
37      }
38    }
```

This is how you check for changes, if you're using a key-value differ. You call the `diff` method, providing the property you want to check. In our case, we want to know if there were changes to the `comment` property.

When no changes are detected, the returned value will be `null`. Now, if there are changes, we can call three different iterable methods on the differ:

- `forEachAddedItem`, for *keys* that were added
- `forEachRemovedItem`, for *keys* that were removed
- `forEachChangedItem`, for *keys* that were changed

Each method will call the provided callback with a *record*. For the key-value differ, this record will be an instance of the `KVChangeRecord` class.

```
▼ KVChangeRecord {key: "likes", previousValue: null, currentValue: 10, _nextPrevious: null, _next: null…}
    _next: null
    _nextAdded: null
    _nextChanged: null
    _nextPrevious: null
    _nextRemoved: null
    _prevRemoved: null
    currentValue: 10
    key: "likes"
    previousValue: 10
```

Example of a KVChangeRecord instance

The important fields for understanding what changed are *key*, *previousValue* and *currentValue*.

Next, let's write a method that will log to the console a nice sentence about what changed:

code/advanced-components/src/app/lifecycle/differs/comment.component.ts

```
40    logChange(action, r) {
41      if (action === 'changed') {
42        console.log(
43          r.key,
44          action,
45          'from',
46          r.previousValue,
47          'to',
48          r.currentValue
49        );
50      }
51      if (action === 'added') {
52        console.log(action, r.key, 'with', r.currentValue);
53      }
54      if (action === 'removed') {
55        console.log(
56          action,
57          r.key,
58          '(was ' + r.previousValue + ')'
59        );
60      }
61    }
```

Finally, let's write the methods that will help us change things on our component, to trigger our DoCheck hook:

code/advanced-components/src/app/lifecycle/differs/comment.component.ts

```
63    remove(): void {
64      this.onRemove.emit(this.comment);
65    }
66
67    clear(): void {
68      delete this.comment.comment;
69    }
70
71    like(): void {
72      this.comment.likes += 1;
73    }
```

The remove() method will emit the event indicating that the user asked for this comment to be removed, the clear() method will remove the comment text from the comment object, and the like() method will increase the like counter for the comment.

Rendering a list of comments with CommentsListComponent

Now that we have written a component for one individual comment, let's write a second component that will be responsible for rendering the list of comments. First the template:

code/advanced-components/src/app/lifecycle/differs/comments-list.component.html

```
 1   <app-comment
 2     *ngFor="let comment of comments"
 3     [comment]="comment"
 4     (onRemove)="removeComment($event)">
 5   </app-comment>
 6
 7   <button
 8     class="ui primary button"
 9     (click)="addComment()">
10     Add
11   </button>
```

The component template is straightforward: we're using the component we created above, and then using ngFor to iterate through a list of comments, rendering them. We also have a button that will allow the user to add more comments to the list.

Now let's implement our comment list class CommentsListComponent:

code/advanced-components/src/app/lifecycle/differs/comments-list.component.ts

```
 1   /* tslint:disable:max-line-length,quotemark */
 2   import {
 3     Component,
 4     IterableDiffers,
 5     DoCheck
 6   } from '@angular/core';
 7
 8   @Component({
 9     selector: 'app-comments-list',
10     templateUrl: './comments-list.component.html'
11   })
12   export class CommentsListComponent implements DoCheck {
13     comments: any[];
```

```
14    iterable: boolean;
15    authors: string[];
16    texts: string[];
17    differ: any;
```

Here we declare the variables we'll use: comments, iterable, authors, and texts.

code/advanced-components/src/app/lifecycle/differs/comments-list.component.ts

```
19    constructor(differs: IterableDiffers) {
20      this.differ = differs.find([]).create(null);
21      this.comments = [];
22
23      this.authors = ['Elliot', 'Helen', 'Jenny', 'Joe', 'Justen', 'Matt'];
24      this.texts = [
25        "Ours is a life of constant reruns. We're always circling back to where we\
26    'd we started, then starting all over again. Even if we don't run extra laps tha\
27    t day, we surely will come back for more of the same another day soon.",
28        'Really cool!',
29        'Thanks!'
30      ];
31
32      this.addComment();
33    }
```

For this component, we'll be using an iterable differ. We can see that the class we're using to create the differ is now IterableDiffers. However, the way we create a differ remains the same.

On the constructor we also initialize a list of authors and a list of comment texts to be used when adding new comments.

Finally, we call the addComment() method so we don't initialize the app with an empty list of comments.

The next three methods are used to add a new comment:

code/advanced-components/src/app/lifecycle/differs/comments-list.component.ts

```
33    getRandomInt(max: number): number {
34      return Math.floor(Math.random() * (max + 1));
35    }
36
37    getRandomItem(array: string[]): string {
38      const pos: number = this.getRandomInt(array.length - 1);
39      return array[pos];
40    }
41
42    addComment(): void {
43      this.comments.push({
44        author: this.getRandomItem(this.authors),
45        comment: this.getRandomItem(this.texts),
46        likes: this.getRandomInt(20)
47      });
48    }
49
50    removeComment(comment) {
51      const pos = this.comments.indexOf(comment);
52      this.comments.splice(pos, 1);
53    }
```

We are declaring two methods that will return a random integer and a random item from an array, respectively.

Finally, the addComment() method will push a new comment to the list, with a random author, random text and a random number of likes.

Next, we have the removeComment() method, that will be used to remove one comment from the list:

code/advanced-components/src/app/lifecycle/differs/comments-list.component.ts

```
50    removeComment(comment) {
51      const pos = this.comments.indexOf(comment);
52      this.comments.splice(pos, 1);
53    }
```

And finally we declare our change detection method ngDoCheck():

code/advanced-components/src/app/lifecycle/differs/comments-list.component.ts

```
55    ngDoCheck(): void {
56      const changes = this.differ.diff(this.comments);
57
58      if (changes) {
59        changes.forEachAddedItem(r => console.log('Added', r.item));
60        changes.forEachRemovedItem(r => console.log('Removed', r.item));
61      }
62    }
```

The iterable differ behaves the same way as the key-value differ but it only provides methods for items that were added or removed.

When we run the app now, we get the list of comments with one comment:

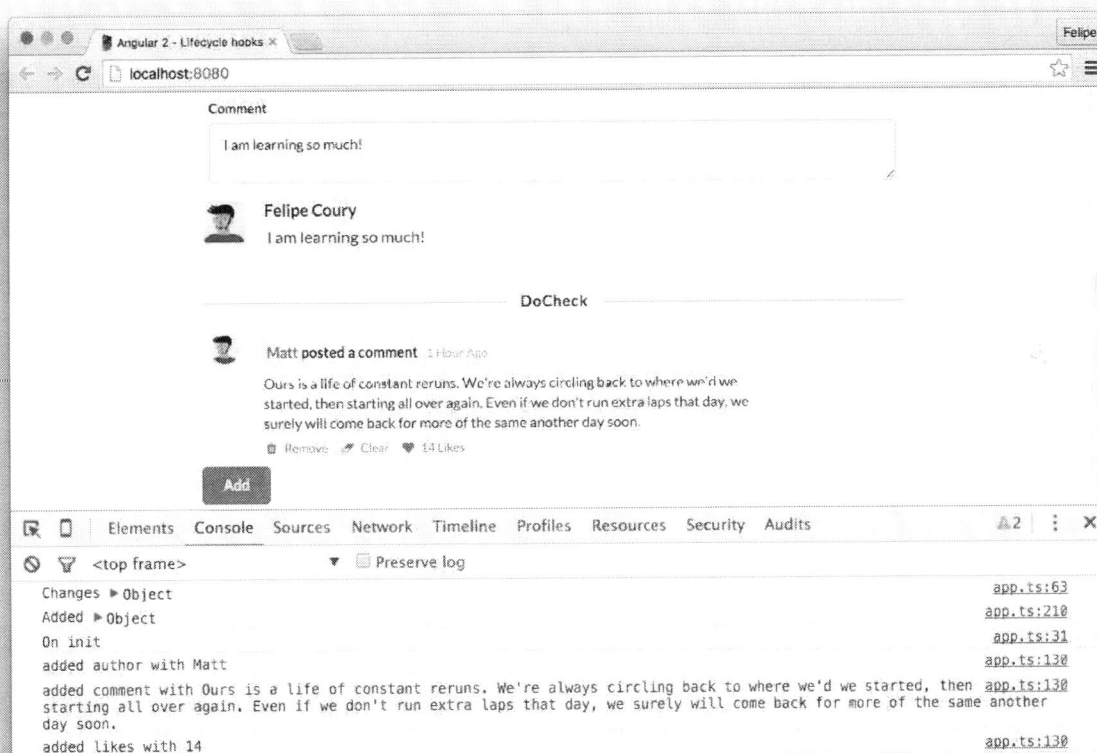

Initial state

We can also see that a few things were logged to the console, like:

```
1  added author with Matt
2  ...
3  added likes with 14
```

Let's see what happens when we add a new comment to the list by clicking the Add button:

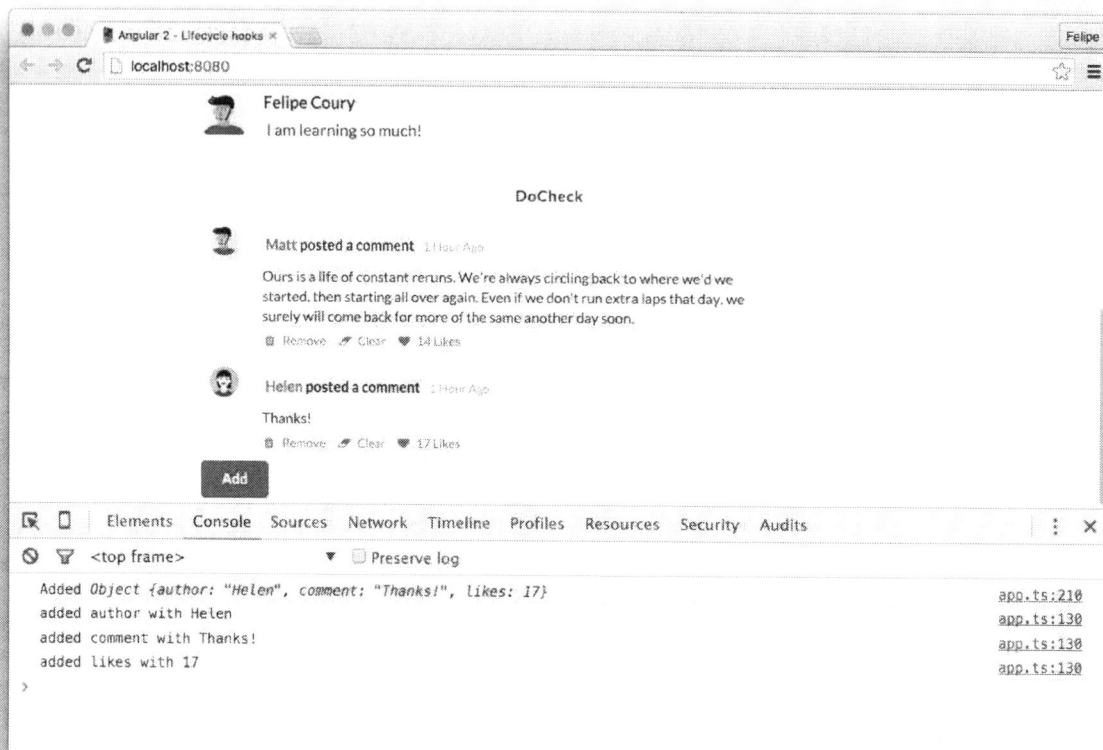

Comment added

We can see that the iterable differs identified that we added a new object to the list {author: "Hellen", comment: "Thanks!", likes: 17}.

We also got individual changes to the comment object logged, as detected by the key-value differ:

```
1  added author with Helen
2  added comment with Thanks!
3  added likes with 17
```

Now we can click the like button for this new comment:

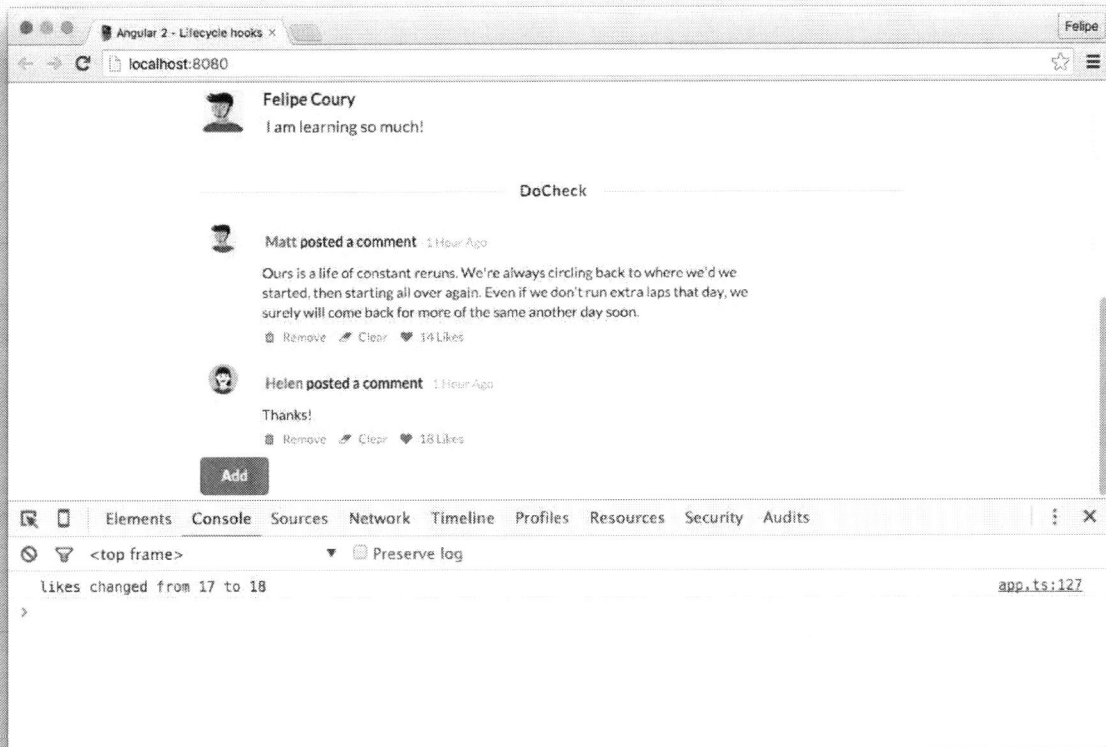

Number of likes changed

And now only the like change was detected.

If we click the *Clear* icon, it will remove the `comment` key from the comment object:

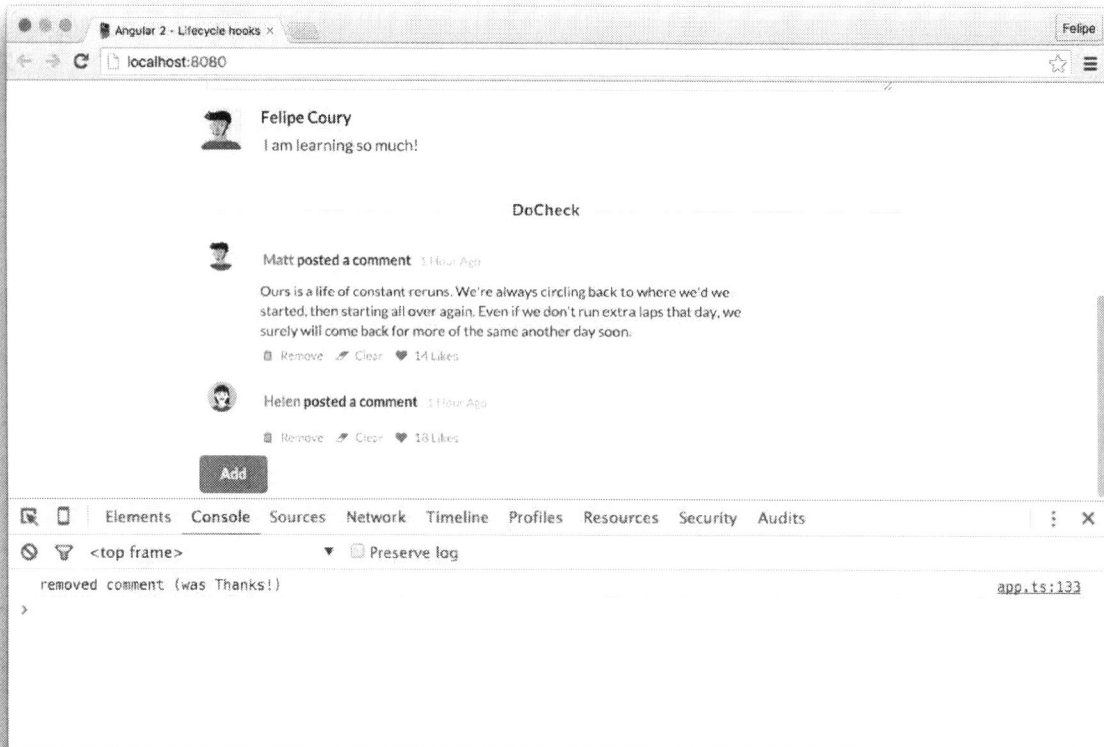

Comment text cleared

And the log confirms that we removed that key.

Finally, let's remove the last comment, by clicking the *Remove* icon:

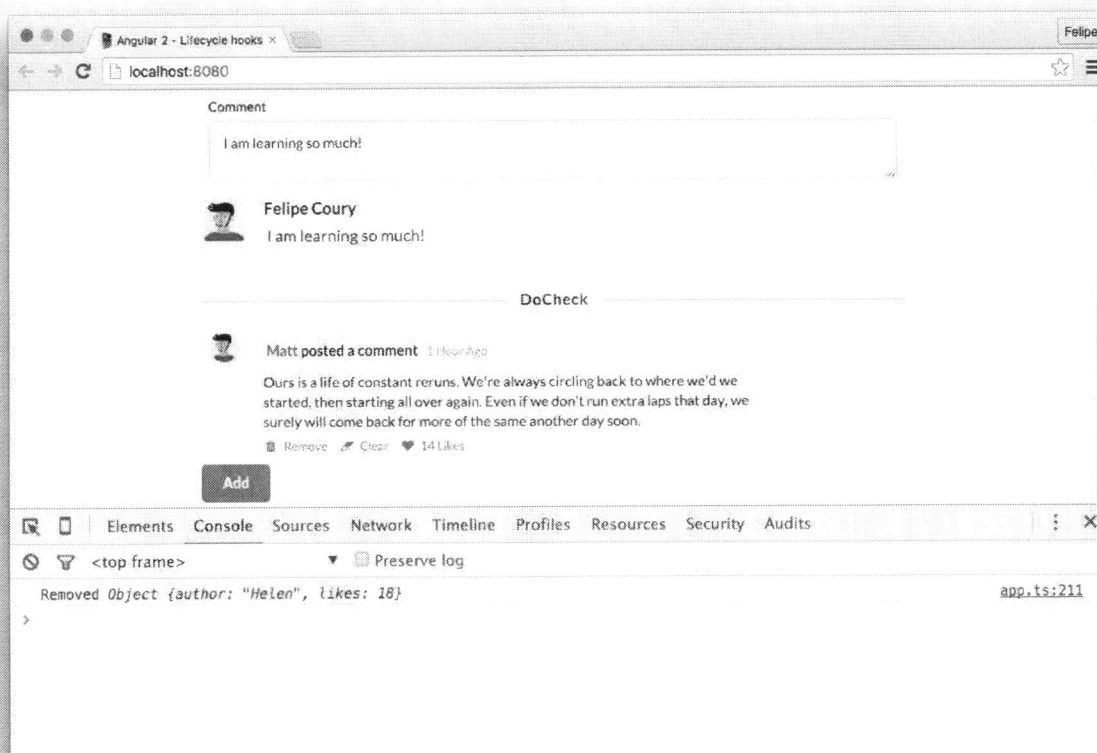

Comment removed

And as expected, we get a removed object log.

AfterContentInit, AfterViewInit, AfterContentChecked and AfterViewChecked

The AfterContentInit hook is called after OnInit, right after the initialization of the content of the component or directive has finished.

The AfterContentChecked works similarly, but it's called after the directive check has finished. The check, in this context, is the change detection system check.

The other two hooks: AfterViewInit and AfterViewChecked are triggered right after the content ones above, right after the view has been fully initialized. Those two hooks are only applicable to components, and not to directives.

Also, the AfterXXXInit hooks are only called once during the directive lifecycle, while the AfterXXXChecked hooks are called after every change detection cycle.

To better understand this, let's write another component that logs to the console during each lifecycle hook. It will also have a counter that we can increment by clicking a button:

code/advanced-components/src/app/lifecycle/all-hooks/all-hooks.component.ts

```
 1  import {
 2    Component,
 3    OnInit,
 4    OnDestroy,
 5    DoCheck,
 6    OnChanges,
 7    AfterContentInit,
 8    AfterContentChecked,
 9    AfterViewInit,
10    AfterViewChecked
11  } from '@angular/core';
12
13  @Component({
14    selector: 'app-all-hooks',
15    templateUrl: './all-hooks.component.html'
16  })
17  export class AllHooksComponent implements OnInit,
18    OnDestroy, DoCheck,
19    OnChanges, AfterContentInit,
20    AfterContentChecked, AfterViewInit,
21    AfterViewChecked {
22    counter: number;
23
24    constructor() {
25      console.log('AllHooksComponent --------- [constructor]');
26      this.counter = 1;
27    }
28    inc() {
29      console.log('AllHooksComponent --------- [counter]');
30      this.counter += 1;
31    }
32    ngOnInit() {
33      console.log('AllHooksComponent - OnInit');
34    }
35    ngOnDestroy() {
36      console.log('AllHooksComponent - OnDestroy');
37    }
38    ngDoCheck() {
39      console.log('AllHooksComponent - DoCheck');
40    }
41    ngOnChanges() {
```

```
42      console.log('AllHooksComponent - OnChanges');
43    }
44    ngAfterContentInit() {
45      console.log('AllHooksComponent - AfterContentInit');
46    }
47    ngAfterContentChecked() {
48      console.log('AllHooksComponent - AfterContentChecked');
49    }
50    ngAfterViewInit() {
51      console.log('AllHooksComponent - AfterViewInit');
52    }
53    ngAfterViewChecked() {
54      console.log('AllHooksComponent - AfterViewChecked');
55    }
56
57  }
```

Now let's add it to the app component, along with a `Toggle` button, like the one we used for the `OnDestroy` hook:

code/advanced-components/src/app/lifecycle/all-hooks/all-hooks-demo.component.html

```
1   <h4 class="ui horizontal divider header">
2     AfterContentInit, AfterViewInit, AfterContentChecked and AfterViewChecked
3   </h4>
4
5   <app-all-hooks
6     *ngIf="displayAfters"
7     ></app-all-hooks>
8
9   <button class="ui primary button" (click)="toggleAfters()">
10    Toggle
11  </button>
```

The final implementation for the app demo component now will look like this:

code/advanced-components/src/app/lifecycle/all-hooks/all-hooks-demo.component.ts

```
 1  import { Component, OnInit } from '@angular/core';
 2
 3  @Component({
 4    selector: 'app-all-hooks-demo',
 5    templateUrl: './all-hooks-demo.component.html',
 6    styles: []
 7  })
 8  export class AllHooksDemoComponent implements OnInit {
 9    displayAfters = true;
10
11    constructor() { }
12
13    ngOnInit() { }
14
15    toggleAfters(): void {
16      this.displayAfters = !this.displayAfters;
17    }
18  }
```

When the application starts, we can see each hook is logged:

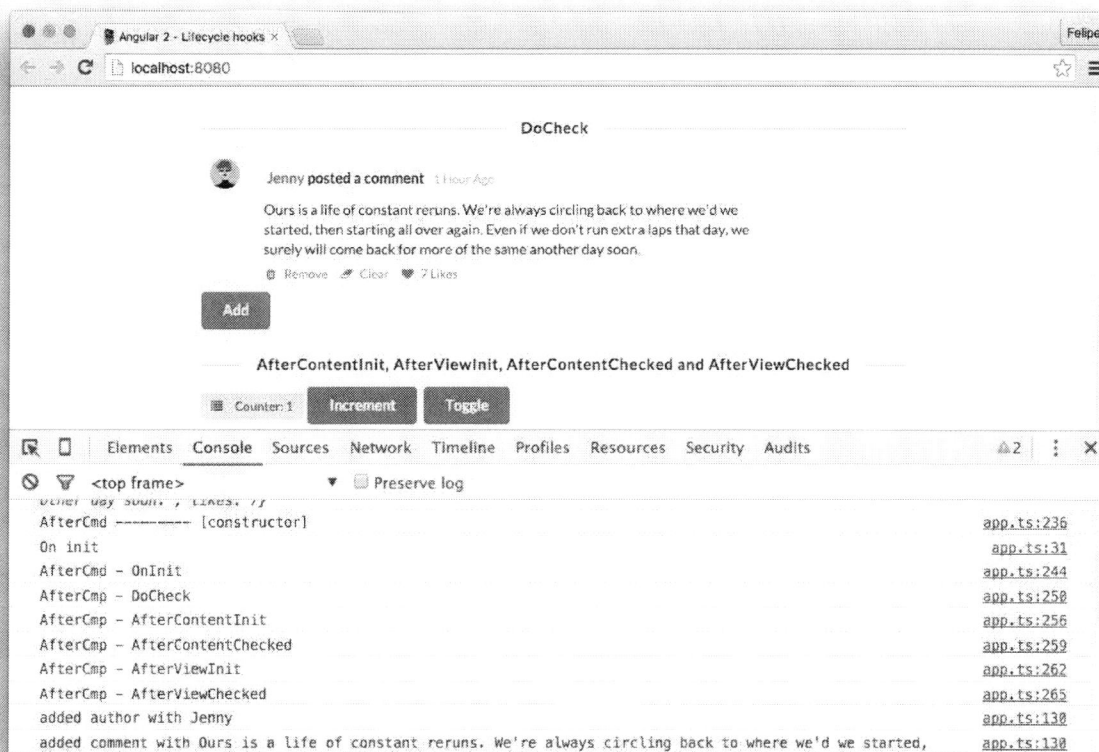

App started

Now let's clear the console and click the Increment button:

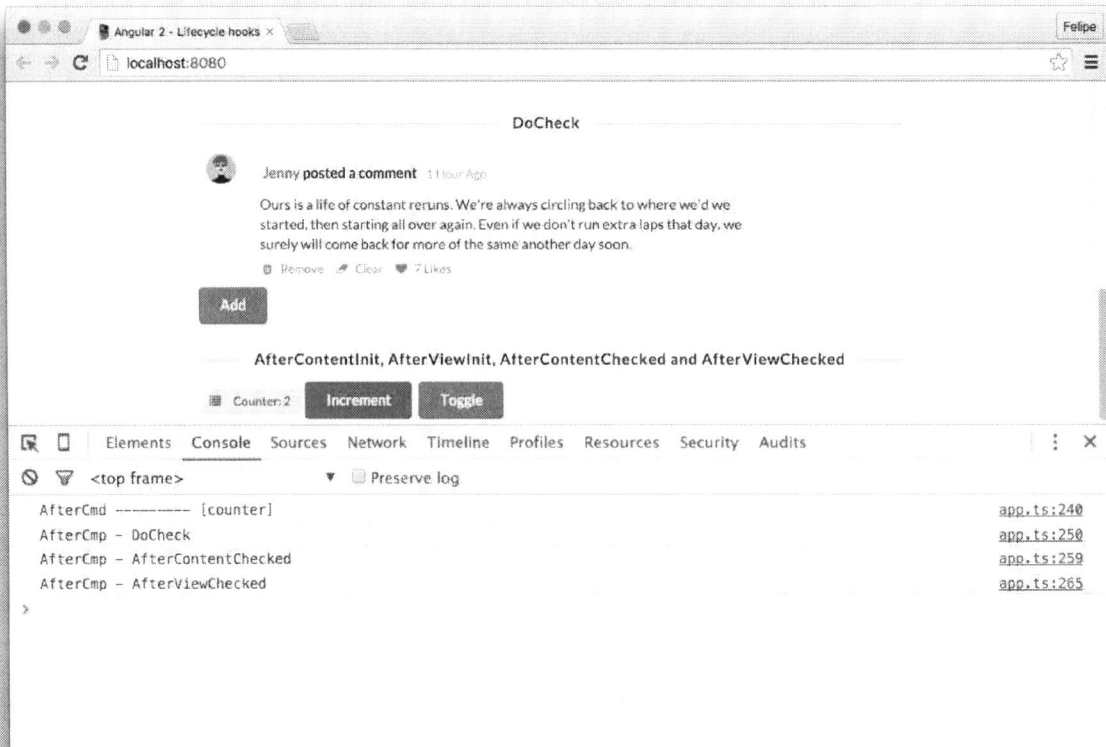

After counter increment

You can see that now only the `DoCheck`, `AfterContentCheck` and `AfterViewCheck` hooks were triggered.

Sure enough, if we click the `Toggle` button:

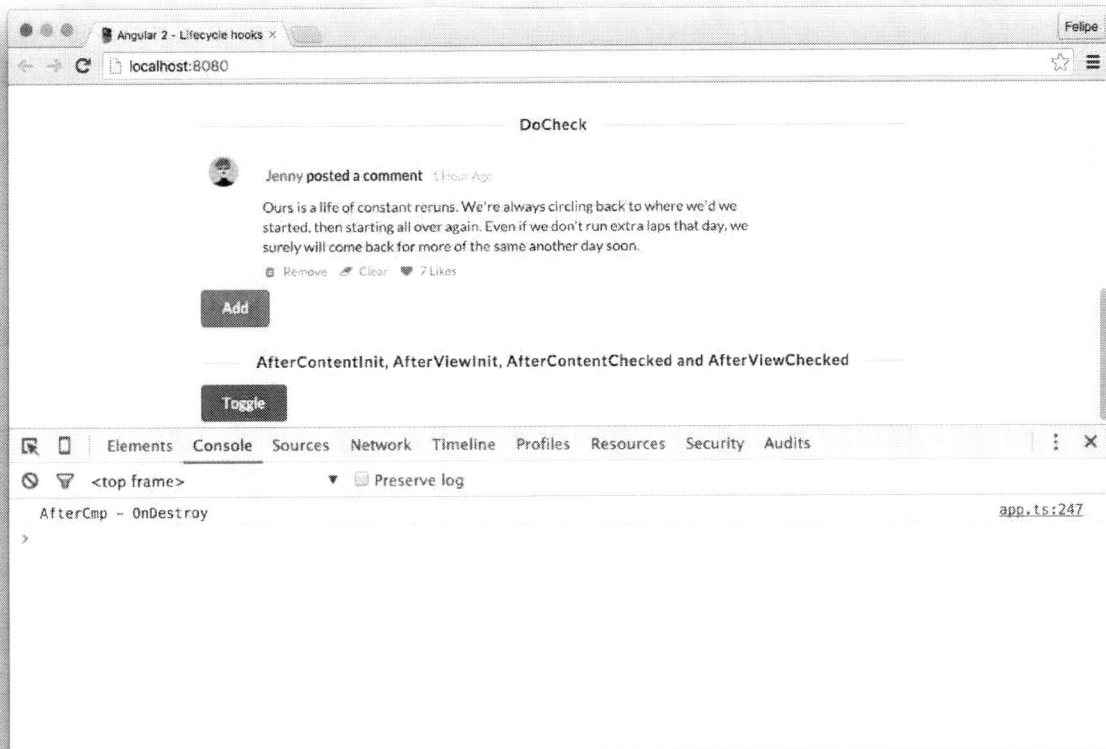

App started

And click it again:

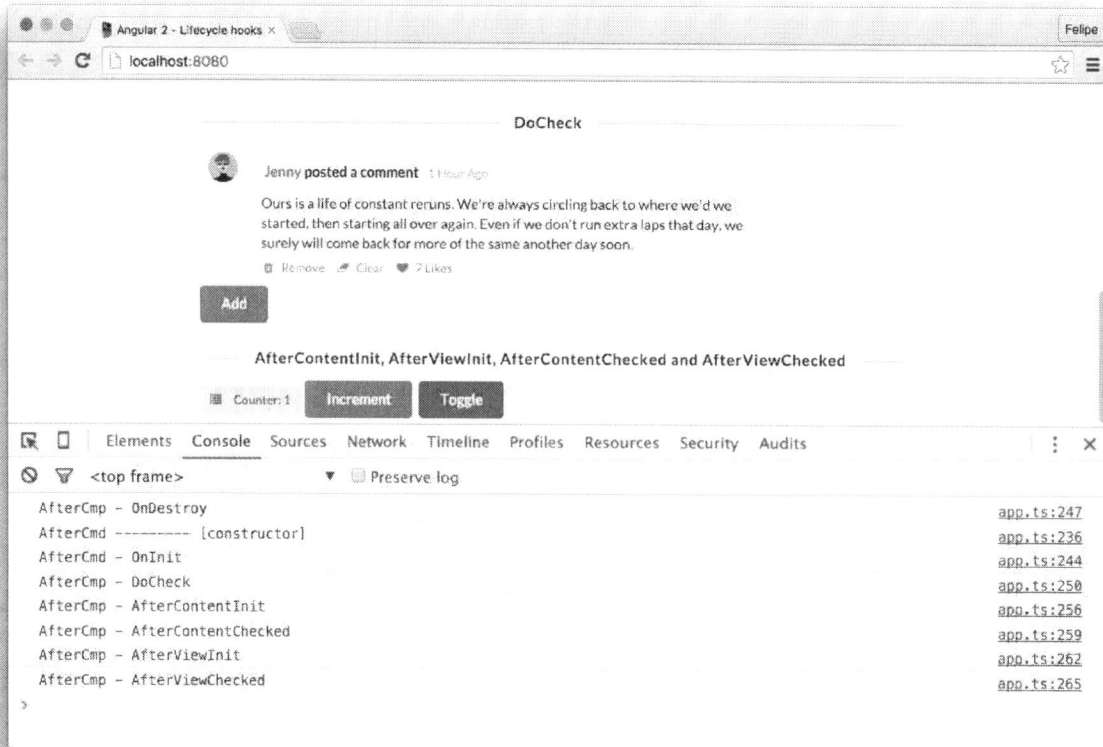

App started

All the hooks are triggered.

Advanced Templates

Template elements are special elements used to create views that can be dynamically manipulated.

In order to make working with templates simpler, Angular provides some syntactic sugar to create templates, so we often don't create them by hand.

For instance, when we write:

```
1  <app-comment
2    *ngFor="let comment of comments"
3    [comment]="comment"
4    (onRemove)="removeComment($event)">
5  </app-comment>
```

This gets converted into:

```
1  <app-comment
2    template="ngFor let comment of comments; #i=index"
3    [comment]="comment"
4    (onRemove)="removeComment($event)">
5  </app-comment>
```

Which then gets converted into:

```
1  <template
2    ngFor
3    [ngForOf]="comments"
4    let-comment="$implicit"
5    let-index="i">
6    <app-comment
7      [comment]="comment"
8      (onRemove)="removeComment($event)">
9    </app-comment>
10 </template>
```

It's important that we understand this underlying concept so we can build our own directives.

Rewriting ngIf - ngBookIf

Let's create a directive that does exactly what ngIf does. Let's call it ngBookIf.

ngBookIf @Directive

We start by declaring the @Directive decorator for our class:

```
1  @Directive({
2    selector: '[ngBookIf]'
3  })
```

We're using [ngBookIf] as the selector because, as we learned above, when we use *ngBookIf="condition", it will be converted to:

```
1  <template ngBookIf [ngBookIf]="condition">
```

Since ngBookIf is also an attribute we need to indicate that we're expecting to receive it as an input.

The job of this directive should be to add the directive template contents when the condition is true and remove it when it's false.

So when the condition is true, we will use a *view container*. The view container is used to attach one or more views to the directive.

We will use the view container to either:

- create a new view with our directive template embedded or
- clear the view container contents.

Before we do that, we need to inject the ViewContainerRef and the TemplateRef. They will be injected with the directive's view container and template.

Here's the code we'll need:

code/advanced-components/src/app/templates/ng-book-if/ng-book-if.directive.ts

```
11  export class NgBookIfDirective {
12    constructor(private viewContainer: ViewContainerRef,
13                private template: TemplateRef<any>) {}
```

Now that we have references to both the view container and the template, we will use a TypeScript property setter construct and also specify that this is an input using the Input() decorator:

code/advanced-components/src/app/templates/ng-book-if/ng-book-if.directive.ts

```
15    @Input() set ngBookIf(condition) {
16      if (condition) {
17        this.viewContainer.createEmbeddedView(this.template);
18      } else {
19        this.viewContainer.clear();
20      }
21    }
22  }
```

This method will be called every time we set a value on the ngBookIf property of our class. That is, this method will be called anytime the condition in ngBookIf="condition" changes.

Now we use the view container's createEmbeddedView method to attach the directive's template if the condition is true, or the clear method to remove everything from the view container.

Using ngBookIf

In order to use our directive, we can write the following demo component:

code/advanced-components/src/app/templates/ng-book-if/ng-book-if-demo.component.ts

```
1   import { Component } from '@angular/core';
2
3   @Component({
4     selector: 'app-ng-book-if',
5     templateUrl: './ng-book-if-demo.component.html',
6   })
7   export class NgBookIfDemoComponent {
8     display: boolean;
9
10    constructor() {
11      this.display = true;
12    }
13
14    toggle() {
15      this.display = !this.display;
16    }
17  }
```

and template:

code/advanced-components/src/app/templates/ng-book-if/ng-book-if-demo.component.html

```
1   <button class="ui primary button" (click)="toggle()">
2     Toggle
3   </button>
4
5   <div *ngBookIf="display">
6     The message is displayed
7   </div>
```

When we run the application, we can see that the directive works as expected: when we click the
Toggle button the message *This message is displayed* is toggled on and off the page.

Rewriting ngFor - NgBookFor

Now let's write a simplified version of the ngFor directive that Angular provides to handle repetition
of templates for a given collection.

`NgBookFor` **template deconstruction**

This directive will be used with the *`NgBookFor`*`="let var of collection"` notation.

Like we did for the previous directive, we need to declare the selector as being `[NgBookFor]`. However the input parameter, in this case, won't be `NgBookFor` only.

If we look back at how Angular converts the `*something="let var in collection"` notation, we can see that the final form of the element is the equivalent of:

```
1  <template something [somethingOf]="collection" let-var="$implicit">
2    <!-- ... -->
3  </template>
```

As we can see, the attribute that's being passed isn't `something` but `somethingOf` instead. That's where our directive receives the collection we're iterating on.

In the template that is generated, we're going to have a local view variable `#var`, that will receive the value from the `$implicit` local variable. That's the name of the local variable that Angular uses when "de-sugaring" the syntax into a `template`.

`NgBookFor` `@Directive`

Time to write the directive.

code/advanced-components/src/app/templates/ng-book-for/ng-book-for.directive.ts

```
1  import {
2    Directive,
3    IterableDiffer,
4    IterableDiffers,
5    ViewRef,
6    ViewContainerRef,
7    TemplateRef,
8    ChangeDetectorRef,
9    DoCheck,
10   Input
11 } from '@angular/core';
12
13 @Directive({
14   selector: '[ngBookFor]'
15 })
16 export class NgBookForDirective implements DoCheck {
17   private items: any;
18   private differ: IterableDiffer<any>;
```

```
19    private views: Map<any, ViewRef> = new Map<
20      any,
21      ViewRef
22    >();
23
24    constructor(
25      private viewContainer: ViewContainerRef,
26      private template: TemplateRef<any>,
27      private differs: IterableDiffers
28    ) {}
```

We are declaring some properties for our class:

- `items` holds the collection we're iterating on
- `differ` is an `IterableDiffer` (which we learned about in the Lifecycle Hooks section above) that will be used for change detection purposes
- `views` is a `Map` that will link a given item on the collection with the view that contains it

The constructor will receive the `viewContainer`, the template and an `IterableDiffers` instance (we discussed each of these things earlier in this chapter above).

Now, the next thing that's being injected is a change detector. We will have a deep dive in change detection in the next section. For now, let's say that this is the class that Angular creates to trigger the detection when properties of our directive change.

The next step is to write code that will trigger when we set the `ngBookForOf` input:

code/advanced-components/src/app/templates/ng-book-for/ng-book-for.directive.ts

```
31    set ngBookForOf(items) {
32      this.items = items;
33      if (this.items && !this.differ) {
34        this.differ = this.differs.find(items).create();
35      }
36    }
```

When we set this attribute, we're keeping the collection on the directive's `items` property and if the collection is valid and we don't have a differ yet, we create one.

To do that, we're creating an instance of `IterableDiffer` that reuses the directive's change detector (the one we injected in the constructor).

Now it's time to write the code that will react to a change on the collection. For this, we're going to use the **DoCheck** lifecycle hook by implementing the `ngDoCheck` method as follows:

code/advanced-components/src/app/templates/ng-book-for/ng-book-for.directive.ts

```
38    ngDoCheck(): void {
39      if (this.differ) {
40        const changes = this.differ.diff(this.items);
41        if (changes) {
42          changes.forEachAddedItem(change => {
43            const view = this.viewContainer.createEmbeddedView(
44              this.template,
45              { $implicit: change.item }
46            );
47            this.views.set(change.item, view);
48          });
49          changes.forEachRemovedItem(change => {
50            const view = this.views.get(change.item);
51            const idx = this.viewContainer.indexOf(view);
52            this.viewContainer.remove(idx);
53            this.views.delete(change.item);
54          });
55        }
56      }
57    }
```

Let's break this down a bit. First thing we do in this method is make sure we already instantiated the differ. If not, we do nothing.

Next, we ask the differ what changed. If there are changes, we first iterate through the items that were added using changes.forEachAddedItem. This method will receive a CollectionChangeRecord object for every element that was added.

Then for each element, we create a new embedded view using the view container's createEmbeddedView method.

```
1  let view = this.viewContainer.createEmbeddedView(this.template, {'$implicit': ch\
2  ange.item});
```

The second argument to createEmbeddedView is the *view context*. In this case, we're setting the $implicit local variable to change.item. This will allow us to reference the variable we declared back on the *NgBookFor="let var of collection" as var on that view. That is, the var in let var is the $implicit variable. We use $implicit because we don't know what name the user will assign to it when we're writing this component.

The final thing we need to do is to connect the item with the collection to its view. The reason behind this is that, if an item gets removed from the collection, we need to get rid of the correct view, as we do next.

Now for each item that was removed from the collection, we use the item-to-view map we keep to find the view. Then we ask the view container for the index of that view. We need that because the view container's `remove` method needs an index. Finally, we also remove the view from the item-to-view map.

Trying out our directive

To test our new directive, let's write the following component:

code/advanced-components/src/app/templates/ng-book-for/ng-book-for-demo.component.ts

```
1  import { Component, OnInit } from '@angular/core';
2
3  @Component({
4    selector: 'app-ng-book-for-demo',
5    templateUrl: './ng-book-for-demo.component.html'
6  })
7  export class NgBookForDemoComponent implements OnInit {
8    people: any[];
9
10   constructor() { }
11
12   ngOnInit() {
13     this.people = [
14       {name: 'Joe', age: 10},
15       {name: 'Patrick', age: 21},
16       {name: 'Melissa', age: 12},
17       {name: 'Kate', age: 19}
18     ];
19   }
20
21   remove(p) {
22     const idx: number = this.people.indexOf(p);
23     this.people.splice(idx, 1);
24     return false;
25   }
26
27   add(name, age) {
28     this.people.push({name: name.value, age: age.value});
29     name.value = '';
30     age.value = '';
31   }
32 }
```

and template:

code/advanced-components/src/app/templates/ng-book-for/ng-book-for-demo.component.html

```
1  <ul>
2    <li *ngBookFor="let p of people">
3      {{ p.name }} is {{ p.age }}
4      <a href (click)="remove(p)">Remove</a>
5    </li>
6  </ul>
7
8  <div class="ui form">
9    <div class="fields">
10     <div class="field">
11       <label>Name</label>
12       <input type="text" #name placeholder="Name">
13     </div>
14     <div class="field">
15       <label>Age</label>
16       <input type="text" #age placeholder="Age">
17     </div>
18   </div>
19 </div>
20 <div class="ui submit button"
21      (click)="add(name, age)">
22   Add
23 </div>
```

We're using our directive to iterate through a list of people:

code/advanced-components/src/app/templates/ng-book-for/ng-book-for-demo.component.html

```
1  <ul>
2    <li *ngBookFor="let p of people">
3      {{ p.name }} is {{ p.age }}
4      <a href (click)="remove(p)">Remove</a>
5    </li>
6  </ul>
```

When we click **Remove** we remove the item from the collection, triggering the change detection.

We also provide a form that allows adding items to the collection:

```
 8  <div class="ui form">
 9    <div class="fields">
10      <div class="field">
11        <label>Name</label>
12        <input type="text" #name placeholder="Name">
13      </div>
14      <div class="field">
15        <label>Age</label>
16        <input type="text" #age placeholder="Age">
17      </div>
18    </div>
19  </div>
20  <div class="ui submit button"
21       (click)="add(name, age)">
22    Add
23  </div>
```

Change Detection

As a user interacts with our app, data (state) changes and our app needs to respond accordingly.

One of the big problems any modern JavaScript framework needs to solve is how to figure out when changes have happened and re-render components accordingly.

In order to make the view react to changes to components state, Angular uses *change detection*.

What are the things that can trigger changes in a component's state? The most obvious thing is user interaction. For instance, if we have a component:

```
 1  @Component({
 2    selector: 'my-component',
 3    template: `
 4    Name: {{name}}
 5    <button (click)="changeName()">Change!</button>
 6    `
 7  })
 8  class MyComponent {
 9    name: string;
10    constructor() {
11      this.name = 'Felipe';
12    }
```

```
13
14    changeName() {
15      this.name = 'Nate';
16    }
17  }
```

We can see that when the user *clicks* on the **Change!** button, the component's *name* property will change.

Another source of change could be, for instance, a HTTP request:

```
1  @Component({
2    selector: 'my-component',
3    template: `
4    Name: {{name}}
5    `
6  })
7  class MyComponent {
8    name: string;
9    constructor(private http: Http) {
10     this.http.get('/names/1')
11       .map(res => res.json())
12       .subscribe(data => this.name = data.name);
13   }
14 }
```

And finally, we could have a timer that would trigger the change:

```
1  @Component({
2    selector: 'my-component',
3    template: `
4    Name: {{name}}
5    `
6  })
7  class MyComponent {
8    name: string;
9    constructor() {
10     setTimeout(() => this.name = 'Felipe', 2000);
11   }
12 }
```

But how does Angular become aware of these changes?

The first thing to know is that each component gets a change detector.

Like we've seen before, a typical application will have a number of components that will interact with each other, creating a dependency tree like below:

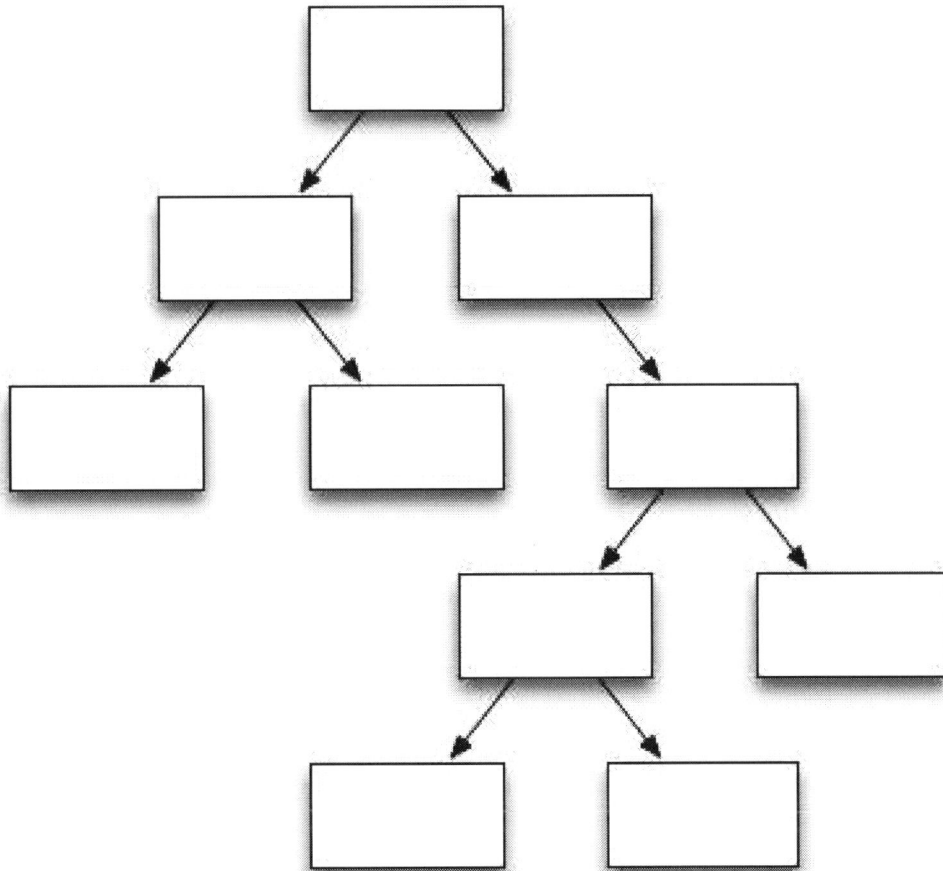

Component tree

For each component on our tree, a change detector is created and so we end up with a tree of change detectors:

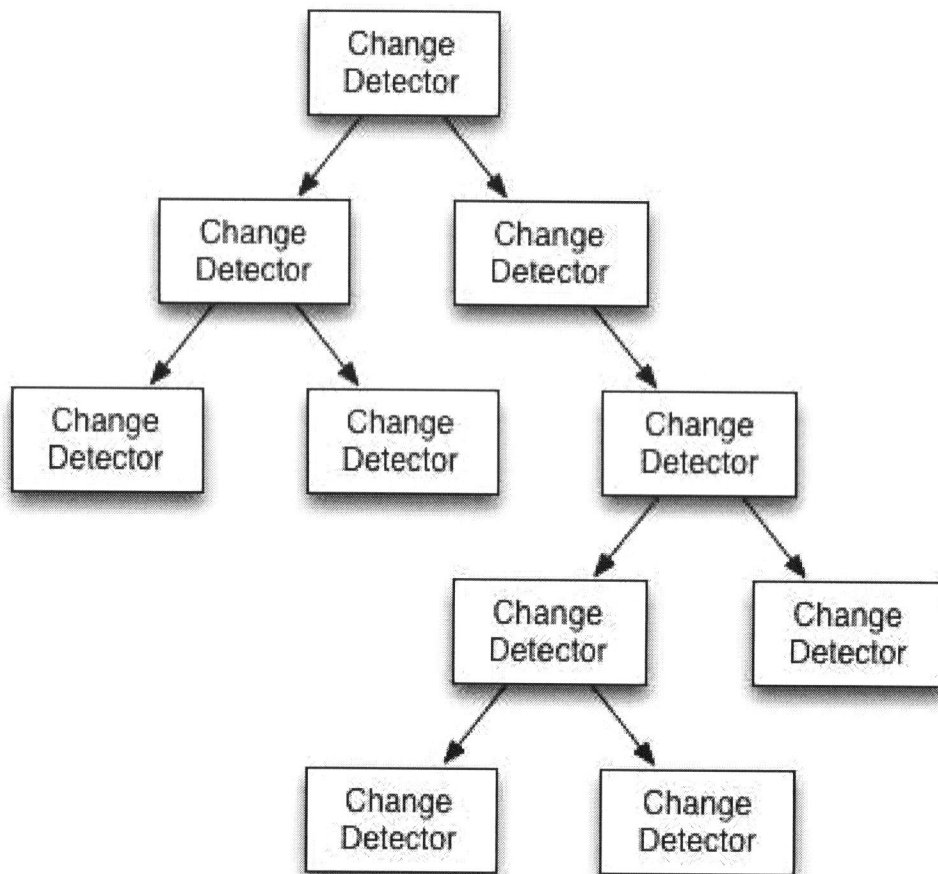

Change detector tree

When one of the components change, no matter where it is in the tree, a change detection pass is triggered for the whole tree. This happens because Angular scans for changes from the top component node, all the way to the bottom leaves of the tree.

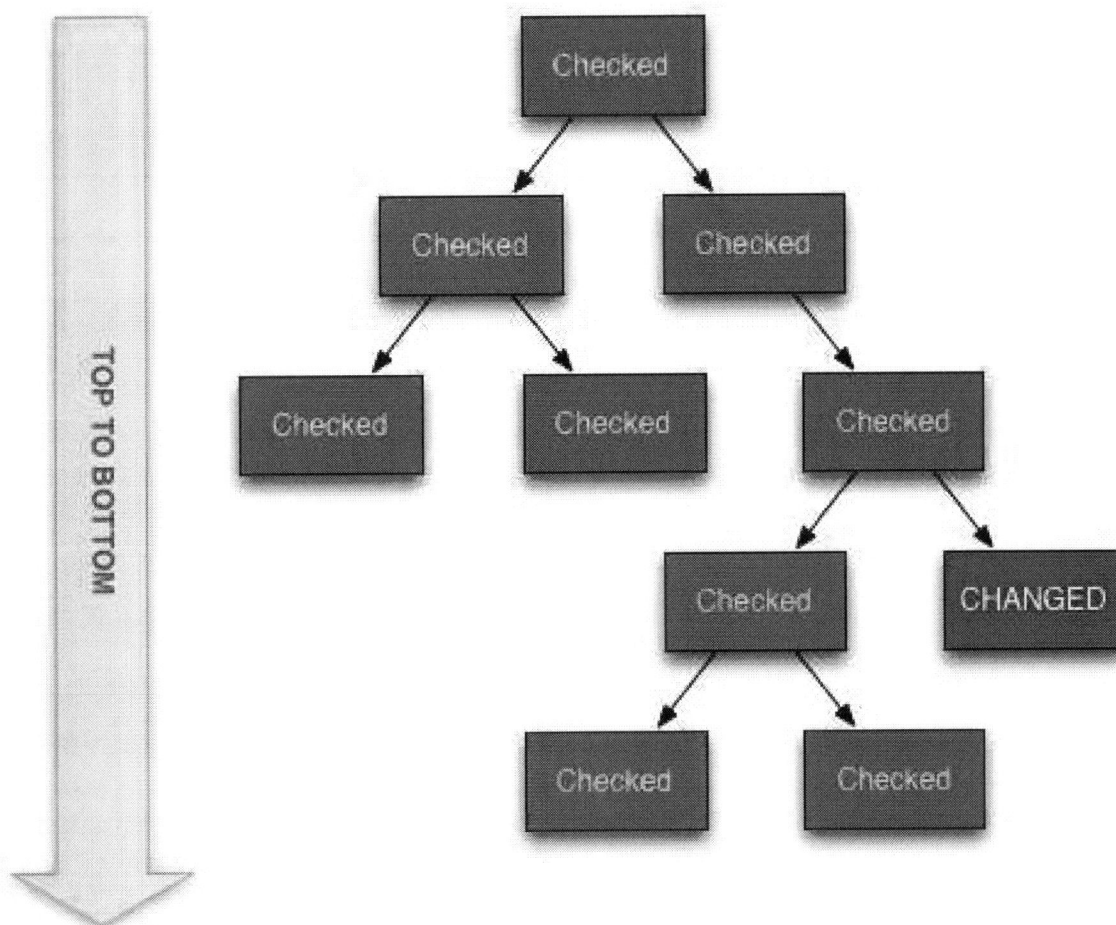

Default change detection

In our diagram above, the component in blue changed, but as we can see, it triggered checks for the whole component tree. Objects that were checked are indicated in red (note that the component itself was also checked).

It is natural to think that this check may be a very expensive operation. However, due to a number of optimizations (that make Angular code eligible for further optimization by the JavaScript engine), it's actually surprisingly fast.

Customizing Change Detection

There are times that the built-in or default change detection mechanism may be overkill. One example is if you're using immutable objects or if your application architecture relies on observables. In these cases, Angular provides mechanisms for configuring the change detection system so that you get very fast performance.

The first way to change the change detector behavior is by telling a component that it should only be checked if one of its *input values* change.

To recap, an input value is an attribute your component receives from the outside world. For instance, in this code:

```
1  class Person {
2    constructor(public name: string, public age: string) {}
3  }
4
5  @Component({
6    selector: 'mycomp',
7    template: `
8      <div>
9        <span class="name">{{ person.name }}</span>
10       is {{ person.age }} years old.
11     </div>
12     `
13  })
14  class MyComp {
15    @Input() person: Person;
16  }
```

We have person as an input attribute. Now, if we want to make this component change only when its input attribute changes, we just need to change the change detection strategy, by setting its changeDetection attribute to ChangeDetectionStrategy.OnPush.

> By the way, if you're curious, the default value for changeDetection is ChangeDetectionStrategy.Default.

Let's write a small experiment with two components. The first one will use the default change detection behavior and the other will use the OnPush strategy:

code/advanced-components/src/app/change-detection/on-push-demo/profile.model.ts

```
1  /**
2   * User Profile object, stores the first and
3   * last name as well as a function that gives the time
4   **/
5  export class Profile {
6    constructor(public first: string, public last: string) {}
7
8    lastChanged() {
```

```
 9      return new Date();
10    }
11  }
```

So we start with some imports and we declare a `Profile` class that will be used as the input in both of our components. Notice that we also created a method called `lastChange()` on the `Profile` class. It will help us determine when the change detection is triggered. When a given component is marked as needing to be checked, this method will be called, since it's present on the template. So this method will reliably indicate the last time the component was checked for changes.

Next, we declare the `DefaultChangeDetectionComponent` that will use the default change detection strategy:

code/advanced-components/src/app/change-detection/on-push-demo/default-change-detection.component.ts

```
 1  import {
 2    Component,
 3    Input
 4  } from '@angular/core';
 5  import { Profile } from './profile.model';
 6
 7  @Component({
 8    selector: 'app-default-change-detection',
 9    templateUrl: './default-change-detection.component.html'
10  })
11  export class DefaultChangeDetectionComponent {
12    @Input() profile: Profile;
13  }
```

and template:

code/advanced-components/src/app/change-detection/on-push-demo/default-change-detection.component.html

```
 1  <h4 class="ui horizontal divider header">
 2    Default Strategy
 3  </h4>
 4
 5  <form class="ui form">
 6    <div class="field">
 7      <label>First Name</label>
 8      <input
 9      type="text"
10      [(ngModel)]="profile.first"
```

```
11        name="first"
12        placeholder="First Name">
13     </div>
14     <div class="field">
15       <label>Last Name</label>
16       <input
17       type="text"
18       [(ngModel)]="profile.last"
19       name="last"
20       placeholder="Last Name">
21     </div>
22   </form>
23
24   <h5><em>Updates if either changes (e.g. more often)</em></h5>
25   <div>
26     {{profile.lastChanged() | date:'medium'}}
27   </div>
```

And a second component using OnPush strategy:

code/advanced-components/src/app/change-detection/on-push-demo/on-push-change-detection.component.ts

```
1  import {
2    Component,
3    Input,
4    ChangeDetectionStrategy
5  } from '@angular/core';
6  import { Profile } from './profile.model';
7
8  @Component({
9    selector: 'app-on-push-change-detection',
10   changeDetection: ChangeDetectionStrategy.OnPush,
11   templateUrl: './on-push-change-detection.component.html'
12 })
13 export class OnPushChangeDetectionComponent {
14   @Input() profile: Profile;
15 }
```

As we can see, both components use the same template. The only thing that is different is the header.

Finally, let's add the component that will render both components side by side:

code/advanced-components/src/app/change-detection/on-push-demo/on-push-demo.component.ts

```
1   import { Component } from '@angular/core';
2   import { Profile } from './profile.model';
3
4   @Component({
5     selector: 'app-on-push-demo',
6     template: `
7     <div class="ui page grid">
8       <div class="two column row">
9         <div class="column area">
10          <app-default-change-detection
11            [profile]="profile1">
12          </app-default-change-detection>
13        </div>
14        <div class="column area">
15          <app-on-push-change-detection
16            [profile]="profile2">
17          </app-on-push-change-detection>
18        </div>
19      </div>
20    </div>
21    `
22  })
23  export class OnPushDemoComponent {
24    profile1: Profile = new Profile('Felipe', 'Coury');
25    profile2: Profile = new Profile('Nate', 'Murray');
26  }
```

When we run this application, we should see both components rendered like below:

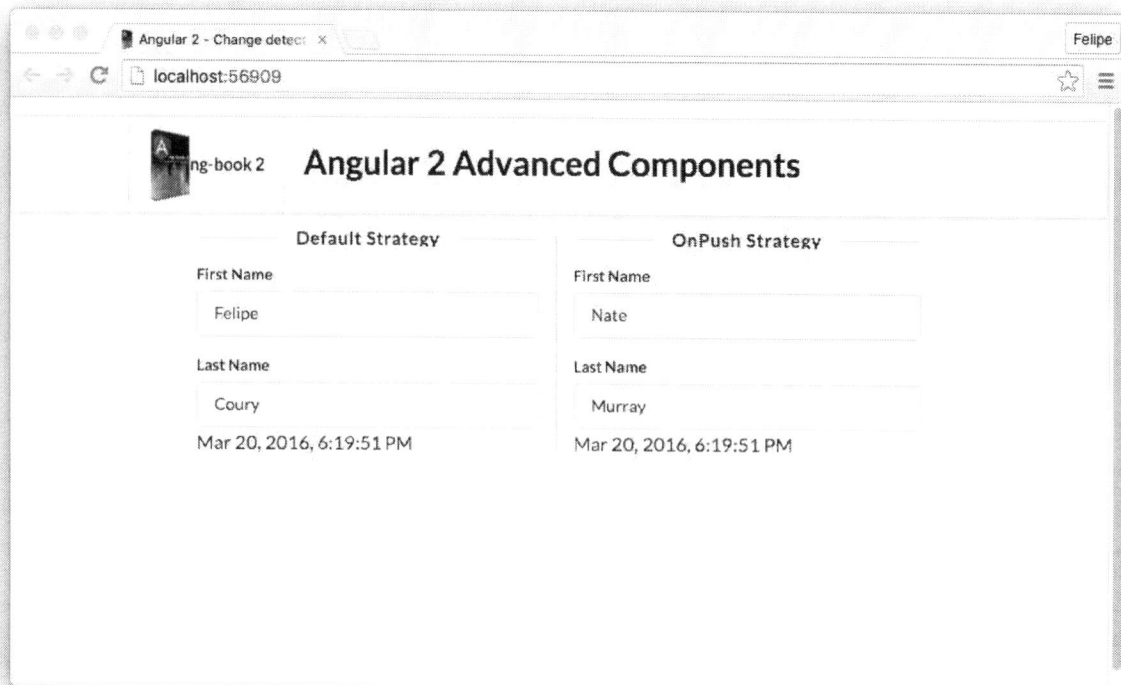

Default vs. OnPush strategies

When we change something on the component on the left, with the default strategy, we notice that the timestamp for the component on the right doesn't change:

OnPush changed, default got checked

To understand why this happened, let's check this new tree of components:

Tree of components

Angular checks for changes from the top to the bottom, so it queried first `OnPushDemoComponent`, then `DefaultChangeDetectionComponent` and finally `OnPushChangeDetectionComponent`. When it inferred that OnPushChangeDetectionComponent changed, it updates all the components of the tree, from top to bottom, making the DefaultChangeDetectionComponent to be rendered again.

Now when we change the value of the component on the right:

Default changed, OnPush didn't get checked

So now the change detection engine kicked in, the DefaultChangeDetectionComponent component was checked but OnPushChangeDetectionComponent wasn't. This happened because when we set the OnPush strategy for this component, it made the change detection kick in for this component *only* when one of its input attributes change. Changing other components of the tree doesn't trigger this component's change detector.

Zones

Under the hood, Angular uses a library called Zones to automatically detect changes and trigger the change detection mechanism. Zones will automatically tell Angular that something changed under the most common scenarios:

- when a DOM Event occurs (like *click, change,* etc.)
- when an HTTP request is resolved
- when a Timer is triggered (*setTimeout* or *setInterval*)

However, there are scenarios where Zones won't be able to automatically identify that something changed. That's another scenario where the **OnPush** strategy can be very useful.

A few examples of things that are out of the Zones control, would be:

- using a third party library that runs asynchronously
- immutable data
- Observables

these are perfect candidates for using **OnPush** along with a technique to manually hint Angular that something changed.

Observables and OnPush

Let's write a component that receives an **Observable** as a parameter. Every time we receive a value from this observable, we will increment a counter that is a property of the component.

If we were using the regular change detection strategy, any time we incremented the counter, we would get change detection triggered by Angular. However, we will have this component use the **OnPush** strategy and, instead of letting the change detector kick in for each increment, we'll only kick it when the number is a multiple of 5 or when the observable completes.

In order to do that, let's write our component:

code/advanced-components/src/app/change-detection/observables-demo/observable-change-detection.component.ts

```
1   import {
2     Component,
3     OnInit,
4     Input,
5     ChangeDetectionStrategy,
6     ChangeDetectorRef
7   } from '@angular/core';
8   import { Observable } from 'rxjs/Rx';
9
10  @Component({
11    selector: 'app-observable-change-detection',
12    changeDetection: ChangeDetectionStrategy.OnPush,
13    template: `
14    <div>
15      <div>Total items: {{counter}}</div>
16    </div>
17    `
```

```
18  })
19  export class ObservableChangeDetectionComponent implements OnInit {
20    @Input() items: Observable<number>;
21    counter = 0;
22
23    constructor(private changeDetector: ChangeDetectorRef) {
24    }
25
26    ngOnInit() {
27      this.items.subscribe((v) => {
28        console.log('got value', v);
29        this.counter++;
30        if (this.counter % 5 === 0) {
31          this.changeDetector.markForCheck();
32        }
33      },
34      null,
35      () => {
36        this.changeDetector.markForCheck();
37      });
38    }
39  }
```

Let's break down the code a bit so we can make sure we understand. First, we're declaring the component to take items as the input attribute and to use the OnPush detection strategy:

code/advanced-components/src/app/change-detection/observables-demo/observable-change-detection.component.ts

```
10  @Component({
11    selector: 'app-observable-change-detection',
12    changeDetection: ChangeDetectionStrategy.OnPush,
13    template: `
14    <div>
15      <div>Total items: {{counter}}</div>
16    </div>
17    `
18  })
```

Next, we're storing our input attribute on the items property of the component class, and setting another property, called counter, to 0.

code/advanced-components/src/app/change-detection/observables-demo/observable-change-detection.component.ts

```
19  export class ObservableChangeDetectionComponent implements OnInit {
20    @Input() items: Observable<number>;
21    counter = 0;
```

Then we use the constructor to get hold of the component's change detector:

code/advanced-components/src/app/change-detection/observables-demo/observable-change-detection.component.ts

```
23    constructor(private changeDetector: ChangeDetectorRef) {
24    }
```

Then, during the component initialization, on the ngOnInit hook:

code/advanced-components/src/app/change-detection/observables-demo/observable-change-detection.component.ts

```
26    ngOnInit() {
27      this.items.subscribe((v) => {
28        console.log('got value', v);
29        this.counter++;
30        if (this.counter % 5 === 0) {
31          this.changeDetector.markForCheck();
32        }
33      },
34      null,
35      () => {
36        this.changeDetector.markForCheck();
37      });
38    }
```

We're subscribing to the Observable. The subscribe method takes three callbacks as arguments: onNext, onError and onCompleted.

Our onNext callback will print out the value we got, then increment the counter. Finally, if the current counter value is a multiple of 5, we call the change detector's markForCheck method. That's the method we use whenever we want to tell Angular that a change has been made, so the change detector should kick in.

Then for the onError callback, we're using null, indicating we don't want to handle this scenario.

Finally, for the onComplete callback, we're also triggering the change detector, so the final counter can be displayed.

Now, on to the application component code, that will create the subscriber:

code/advanced-components/src/app/change-detection/observables-demo/observables-demo.component.ts

```
1   import { Component, OnInit } from '@angular/core';
2   import { Observable } from 'rxjs/Rx';
3
4   @Component({
5     selector: 'app-observables-demo',
6     template: `
7     <app-observable-change-detection
8       [items]="itemObservable">
9       </app-observable-change-detection>
10    `
11  })
12  export class ObservablesDemoComponent implements OnInit {
13    itemObservable: Observable<number>;
14
15    constructor() { }
16
17    ngOnInit() {
18      this.itemObservable = Observable.timer(100, 100).take(101);
19    }
20
21  }
```

The important line here is the following:

```
1   this.itemObservable = Observable.timer(100, 100).take(101);
```

This line creates the Observable we're passing to the component on the items input attribute. We're passing two parameters to the timer method: the first is the number of milliseconds to wait before producing the first value and the second is the milliseconds to wait between values. So this observable will generate sequential values every 100 values forever.

Since we don't want the observable to run forever, we use the take method, to take only the first 101 values.

When we run this code, we'll see that the counter will only be updated for each 5 values obtained from the observer and also when the observable completes, generating a final value of 101:

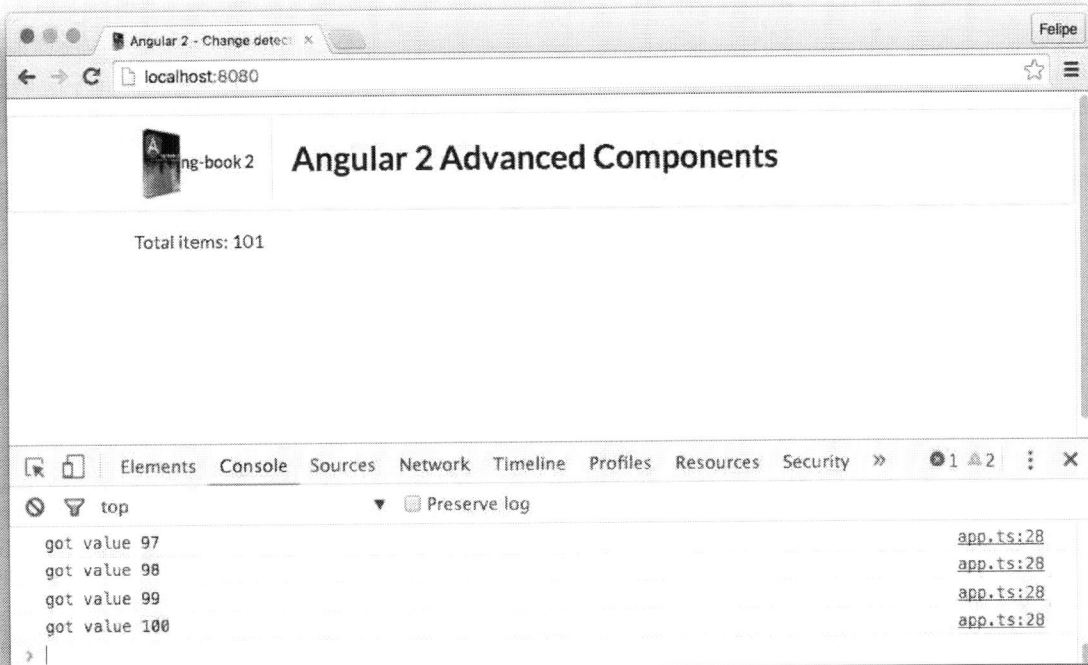

Manually triggering change detection

Summary

Angular provides us with many tools we can use for writing advanced components. Using the techniques in this chapter you will be able to write nearly any component functionality you wish.

Testing

After spending hours, days, months on a web app you're finally ready to release it to the world. Plenty of hard work and time has been poured into it and now it's time for it to pay off... and then boom: a blocking bug shows up that prevents anyone from signing up.

Test driven?

Testing can help reveal bugs before they appear, instill confidence in your web application, and makes it easy to onboard new developers into the application. There is little doubt about the power of testing amongst the world of software development. However, there is debate about how to go about it.

Is it better to write the tests first and then write the implementation to make those tests pass or would it be better to validate that code that we've already written is correct? It's pretty odd to think that this is a source of contention across the development community, but there is a debate that can get pretty heated as to which is the *right* way to handle testing.

In our experience, particularly when coming from a prototype-heavy background, we focus on building test-able code. Although your experience may differ, we have found that while we are prototyping applications, testing individual pieces of code that are likely to change can double or triple the amount of work it takes to keep them up. In contrast, we focus on building our applications in small components, keeping large amounts of functionality broken into several methods which allows us to test the functionality of a part of the larger picture. This is what we mean when we say *testable* code.

> An alternative methodology to prototyping (and then testing after) is called "Red-Green-Refactor". The idea is that you **write your tests first** and they fail (red) because you haven't written any code yet. Only after you have failing tests do you go on to write your implementation code until it all passes (green).

Of course, the decision of *what* to test is up to you and your team, however we'll focus on *how* to test your applications in this chapter.

End-to-end vs. Unit Testing

There are two major ways to test your applications: *end-to-end testing* or *unit testing*.

If you take a top-down approach on testing you write tests that see the application as a "black box" and you interact with the application like a user would and evaluate if the app seems to work from the "outside". This top-down technique of testing is called *End to End testing*.

> In the Angular world, the tool that is mostly used is called Protractor[125]. Protractor is a tool that opens a browser and interacts with the application, collecting results, to check whether the testing expectations were met.

The second testing approach commonly used is to isolate each part of the application and test it in isolation. This form of testing is called *Unit Testing*.

In Unit Testing we write tests that provide a given input to a given aspect of that unit and evaluate the output to make sure it matches our expectations.

In this chapter we're going to be covering how to **unit test** your Angular apps.

Testing Tools

In order to test our apps, we'll use two tools: Jasmine and Karma.

Jasmine

Jasmine[126] is a behavior-driven development framework for testing JavaScript code.

Using Jasmine, you can set expectations about what your code should do when invoked.

For instance, let's assume we have a sum function on a Calculator object. We want to make sure that adding 1 and 1 results in 2. We could express that test (also called a _spec), by writing the following code:

```
1  describe('Calculator', () => {
2    it('sums 1 and 1 to 2', () => {
3      var calc = new Calculator();
4      expect(calc.sum(1, 1)).toEqual(2);
5    });
6  });
```

One of the nice things about Jasmine is how readable the tests are. You can see here that we expect the calc.sub operation to equal 2.

We organize our tests with describe blocks and it blocks.

---

[125] https://angular.github.io/protractor/#/
[126] http://jasmine.github.io/2.4/introduction.html

Normally we use describe for each logical unit we're testing and inside that we use one it for each expectation you want to assert. However, this isn't a hard and fast rule. You'll often see an it block contain several expectations.

On the Calculator example above we have a very simple object. For that reason, we used one describe block for the whole class and one it block for each method.

This is not the case most of the times. For example, methods that produce different outcomes depending on the input will probably have more than one it block associated. On those cases, it's perfectly fine to have nested describes: one for the object and one for each method, and then different assertions inside individual it blocks.

We'll be looking at a lot of describe and it blocks throughout this chapter, so don't worry if it isn't clear when to use one vs. the other. We'll be showing lots of examples.

For more information about Jasmine and all its syntax, check out the Jasmine documentation page[127].

Karma

With Jasmine we can describe our tests and their expectations. Now, in order to actually run the tests we need to have a browser environment.

That's where Karma comes in. Karma allows us to run JavaScript code within a browser like Chrome or Firefox, or on a **headless** browser (or a browser that doesn't expose a user interface) like PhantomJS.

Writing Unit Tests

Our main focus on this section will be to understand how we write unit tests against different parts of our Angular apps.

We're going to learn to test **Services**, **Components**, **HTTP requests** and more. Along the way we're also going to see a couple of different techniques to make our code more testable.

Angular Unit testing framework

Angular provides its own set of classes that build upon the Jasmine framework to help writing unit testing for the framework.

The main testing framework can be found on the @angular/core/testing package. (Although, for testing components we'll use the @angular/compiler/testing package and @angular/platform-browser/testing for some other helpers. But more on that later.)

---

[127]http://jasmine.github.io/2.4/introduction.html

⚠ If this is your first time testing Angular I want to prepare you for something: When you write tests for Angular, there is a bit of setup.

For instance, when we have dependencies to inject, we often manually configure them. When we want to test a component, we have to use testing-helpers to initialize them. And when we want to test routing, there are quite a few dependencies we need to structure.

If it feels like there is a lot of setup, don't worry: you'll get the hang of it and find that the setup doesn't change that much from project to project. Besides, we'll walk you through each step in this chapter.

As always, you can find all of the sample code for this chapter in the code download. Looking over the code directly in your favorite editor can provide a good overview of the details we cover in this chapter. We'd encourage you to keep the code open as you go through this chapter.

Setting Up Testing

Earlier in the Routing Chapter we created an application for searching for music. In this chapter, let's write tests for that application.

Karma requires a configuration in order to run. So the first thing we need to do to setup Karma is to create a `karma.conf.js` file.

Let's `karma.conf.js` file on the root path of our project, like so:

🔑 Since we're using Angular CLI, this `karma.conf.js` file is already created for us! However, if your project does not use Angular CLI, you may need to setup Karma on your own.

code/routes/music/karma.conf.js

```
1   // Karma configuration file, see link for more information
2   // https://karma-runner.github.io/1.0/config/configuration-file.html
3
4   module.exports = function(config) {
5     let configuration = {
6       basePath: '',
7       frameworks: ['jasmine', '@angular-devkit/build-angular'],
8       plugins: [
9         require('karma-jasmine'),
10        require('karma-chrome-launcher'),
11        require('karma-jasmine-html-reporter'),
12        require('karma-coverage-istanbul-reporter'),
13        require('@angular-devkit/build-angular/plugins/karma')
```

```
14      ],
15      client: {
16        clearContext: false // leave Jasmine Spec Runner output visible in browser
17      },
18      coverageIstanbulReporter: {
19        dir: require('path').join(__dirname, '../coverage'),
20        reports: ['html', 'lcovonly'],
21        fixWebpackSourcePaths: true
22      },
23      reporters: ['progress', 'kjhtml'],
24      port: 9876,
25      colors: true,
26      logLevel: config.LOG_INFO,
27      autoWatch: true,
28      browsers: ['Chrome'],
29      singleRun: false
30    };
31
32    if (process.env.TRAVIS) {
33      configuration.customLaunchers = {
34        Chrome_travis_ci: {
35          base: 'Chrome',
36          flags: ['--no-sandbox']
37        }
38      };
39      configuration.browsers = ['Chrome_travis_ci'];
40    }
41
42    config.set(configuration);
43  };
```

Don't worry too much about this file's contents right now, just keep in mind a few things about it:

- sets PhantomJS as the target testing browser;
- uses Jasmine karma framework for testing;
- uses a WebPack bundle called `test.bundle.js` that basically wraps all our testing and app code;

The next step is to create a new `test` folder to hold our test files.

```
1    mkdir test
```

Testing Services and HTTP

Services in Angular start out their life as plain classes. In one sense, this makes our services easy to test because we can sometimes test them directly without using Angular.

With Karma configuration done, let's start testing the SpotifyService class. If we remember, this service works by interacting with the Spotify API to retrieve album, track and artist information.

Inside the test folder, let's create a service subfolder where all our service tests will go. Finally, let's create our first test file inside it, called spotify.service.spec.ts.

Now we can start putting this test file together. The first thing we need to do is import the test helpers from the @angular/core/testing package:

code/routes/music/src/app/spotify.service.spec.ts

```
1    import {
2      inject,
3      fakeAsync,
4      tick,
5      TestBed
6    } from '@angular/core/testing';
```

Next, we'll import a couple more classes:

code/routes/music/src/app/spotify.service.spec.ts

```
7    import {MockBackend} from '@angular/http/testing';
8    import {
9      Http,
10     ConnectionBackend,
11     BaseRequestOptions,
12     Response,
13     ResponseOptions
14   } from '@angular/http';
```

Since our service uses HTTP requests, we'll import the MockBackend class from @angular/http/testing package. This class will help us set expectations and verify HTTP requests.

The last thing we need to import is the class we're testing:

code/routes/music/src/app/spotify.service.spec.ts

```
16   import { SpotifyService } from './spotify.service';
```

HTTP Considerations

We could start writing our tests right now, but during each test execution we would be calling out and hitting the Spotify server. This is far from ideal for two reasons:

1. HTTP requests are relatively slow and as our test suite grows, we'd notice it takes longer and longer to run all of the tests.
2. Spotify's API has a quota, and if our whole team is running the tests, we might use up our API call resources needlessly
3. If we are offline or if Spotify is down or inaccessible our tests would start breaking, even though our code might technically be correct

This is a good hint when writing unit tests: isolate everything that you don't control before testing.

In our case, this piece is the Spotify service. The solution is that we will replace the HTTP request with something that would behave like it, but will **not hit the real Spotify server**.

Doing this in the testing world is called *mocking* a dependency. They are sometimes also called *stubbing* a dependency.

> You can read more about the difference between Mocks and Stubs in this article Mocks are not Stubs[128]

Let's pretend we're writing code that depends on a given Car class.

This class has a bunch of methods: you can start a car instance, stop it, park it and getSpeed of that car.

Let's see how we could use stubs and mocks to write tests that depend on this class.

Stubs

Stubs are objects we create on the fly, with a subset of the behaviors our dependency has.

Let's write a test that just interacts with the start method of the class.

You could create a *stub* of that Car class on-the-fly and inject that into the class you're testing:

---

[128] http://martinfowler.com/articles/mocksArentStubs.html

```
1  describe('Speedtrap', function() {
2    it('tickets a car at more than 60mph', function() {
3      var stubCar = { getSpeed: function() { return 61; } };
4      var speedTrap = new SpeedTrap(stubCar);
5      speedTrap.ticketCount = 0;
6      speedTrap.checkSpeed();
7      expect(speedTrap.ticketCount).toEqual(1);
8    });
9  });
```

This would be a typical case for using a stub and we'd probably only use it locally to that test.

Mocks

Mocks in our case will be a more complete representation of objects, that overrides parts or all of the behavior of the dependency. Mocks can, and most of the time will be reused by more than one test across our suite.

They will also be used sometimes to assert that given methods were called the way they were supposed to be called.

One example of a mock version of our Car class would be:

```
1  class MockCar {
2    startCallCount: number = 0;
3
4    start() {
5      this.startCallCount++;
6    }
7  }
```

And it would be used to write another test like this:

```
1  describe('CarRemote', function() {
2    it('starts the car when the start key is held', function() {
3      var car = new MockCar();
4      var remote = new CarRemote();
5      remote.holdButton('start');
6      expect(car.startCallCount).toEqual(1);
7    });
8  });
```

The biggest difference between a mock and a stub is that:

- a stub provides a subset of functionality with "manual" behavior overrides whereas
- a mock generally sets expectations and verifies that certain methods were called

Http MockBackend

Now that we have this background in mind, let's go back to writing our service test code.

Interacting with the live Spotify service every time we run our tests is a poor idea but thankfully Angular provides us with a way to create fake HTTP calls with MockBackend.

This class can be injected into a Http instance and gives us control of how we want the HTTP interaction to act. We can interfere and assert in a variety of different ways: we can manually set a response, simulate an HTTP error, and add expectations, like asserting the URL being requested matches what we want, if the provided request parameters are correct and a lot more.

So the idea here is that we're going to provide our code with a "fake" Http library. This "fake" library will appear to our code to be the real Http library: all of the methods will match, it will return responses and so on. However, we're not *actually* going to make the requests.

In fact, beyond not making the requests, our MockBackend will actually allow us to setup *expectations* and watch for behaviors we expect.

TestBed.configureTestingModule **and Providers**

When we test our Angular apps we need to make sure we configure the top-level NgModule that we will use for this test. When we do this, we can configure providers, declare components, and import other modules: just like you would when using NgModules generally.

Sometimes when testing Angular code, we *manually setup injections*. This is good because it gives us more control over what we're actually testing.

So in the case of testing Http requests, we don't want to inject the "real" Http class, but instead we want to inject something that looks like Http, but really intercepts the requests and returns the responses we configure.

To do that, we create a version of the Http class that uses MockBackend internally.

To do this, we use the TestBed.configureTestingModule in the beforeEach hook. This hook takes a callback function that will be called before each test is run, giving us a great opportunity to configure alternative class implementations.

code/routes/music/src/app/spotify.service.spec.ts

```
18  describe('SpotifyService', () => {
19    beforeEach(() => {
20      TestBed.configureTestingModule({
21        providers: [
22          BaseRequestOptions,
23          MockBackend,
24          SpotifyService,
25          { provide: Http,
```

```
26          useFactory: (backend: ConnectionBackend,
27                       defaultOptions: BaseRequestOptions) => {
28                         return new Http(backend, defaultOptions);
29                       }, deps: [MockBackend, BaseRequestOptions] },
30       ]
31    });
32  });
```

Notice that `TestBed.configureTestingModule` accepts an **array of providers** in the `providers` key to be used by the test injector.

`BaseRequestOptions` and `SpotifyService` are just the default implementation of those classes. But the last provider is a little more complicated :

code/routes/music/src/app/spotify.service.spec.ts
```
25          { provide: Http,
26            useFactory: (backend: ConnectionBackend,
27                         defaultOptions: BaseRequestOptions) => {
28                           return new Http(backend, defaultOptions);
29                         }, deps: [MockBackend, BaseRequestOptions] },
30       ]
```

This code uses `provide` with `useFactory` to create a version of the `Http` class, using a factory (that's what `useFactory` does).

That factory has a signature that expects `ConnectionBackend` and a `BaseRequestOption` instances. The second key on that object is `deps: [MockBackend, BaseRequestOptions]`. That indicates that we'll be using `MockBackend` as the first parameter of the factory and `BaseRequestOptions` (the default implementation) as the second.

Finally, we return our customized `Http` class with the `MockBackend` as a result of that function.

What benefit do we get from this? Well now every time (in our test) that our code requests `Http` as an injection, it will instead receive our customized `Http` instance.

This is a powerful idea that we'll use a lot in testing: use dependency injection to customize dependencies and isolate the functionality you're trying to test.

Testing getTrack

Now, when writing tests for the service, we want to verify that we're calling the correct URL.

> If you haven't looked at the Routing chapter music example in a while, you can find the code for this example here

Let's write a test for the `getTrack` method:

code/routes/music/src/app/spotify.service.ts

```
54    getTrack(id: string): Observable<any[]> {
55      return this.query(`/tracks/${id}`);
56    }
```

If you remember how that method works, it uses the `query` method, that builds the URL based on the parameters it receives:

code/routes/music/src/app/spotify.service.ts

```
22    query(
23      URL: string,
24      params?: Array<string>
25    ): Observable<any[]> {
26      let queryURL = `${SpotifyService.BASE_URL}${URL}`;
27      if (params) {
28        queryURL = `${queryURL}?${params.join('&')}`;
29      }
30      const apiKey = environment.spotifyApiKey;
31      const headers = new Headers({
32        Authorization: `Bearer ${apiKey}`
33      });
34      const options = new RequestOptions({
35        headers: headers
36      });
37
38      return this.http
39        .request(queryURL, options)
40        .map((res: any) => res.json());
41    }
```

Since we're passing /tracks/${id} we assume that when calling getTrack('TRACK_ID') the expected URL will be https://api.spotify.com/v1/tracks/TRACK_ID.

Here is how we write the test for this:

```
1   describe('getTrack', () => {
2     it('retrieves using the track ID',
3       inject([SpotifyService, MockBackend], fakeAsync((spotifyService, mockBackend\
4   ) => {
5         var res;
6         mockBackend.connections.subscribe(c => {
7           expect(c.request.url).toBe('https://api.spotify.com/v1/tracks/TRACK_ID');
8           let response = new ResponseOptions({body: '{"name": "felipe"}'});
9           c.mockRespond(new Response(response));
10        });
11        spotifyService.getTrack('TRACK_ID').subscribe((_res) => {
12          res = _res;
13        });
14        tick();
15        expect(res.name).toBe('felipe');
16      }))
17    );
18  });
```

This seems like a lot to grasp at first, so let's break it down a bit:

Every time we write tests with dependencies, we need to ask Angular injector to provide us with the instances of those classes. To do that we use:

```
1   inject([Class1,    /* ..., */ ClassN],
2          (instance1, /* ..., */ instanceN) => {
3   // ... testing code ...
4   })
```

When you are testing code that returns either a Promise or an RxJS Observable, you can use fakeAsync helper to test that code as if it were synchronous. This way Promises are fulfilled and Observables are notified immediately after you call tick().

So in this code:

```
1   inject([SpotifyService, MockBackend],
2          fakeAsync((spotifyService, mockBackend) => {
3   // ... testing code ...
4   }));
```

We're getting two variables: spotifyService and mockBackend. The first one has a concrete instance of the SpotifyService and the second is an instance MockBackend class. Notice that the arguments to the inner function (`spotifyService`, `mockBackend`) are injections of the classes specified in the first argument array of the `inject` function (`SpotifyService` and `MockBackend`).

We're also running inside `fakeAsync` which means that async code will be run synchronously when `tick()` is called.

Now that we've setup the injections and context for our test, we can start writing our "actual" test. We start by declaring a `res` variable that will eventually get the HTTP call response. Next we subscribe to `mockBackend.connections`:

```
1  var res;
2  mockBackend.connections.subscribe(c => { ... });
```

Here we're saying that whenever a new connection comes in to `mockBackend` we want to be notified (e.g. call this function).

We want to verify that the `SpotifyService` is calling out to the correct URL given the track id `TRACK_ID`. So what we do is specify an *expectation* that the URL is as we would expect. We can get the URL from the connection `c` via `c.request.url`. So we setup an expectation that `c.request.url` should be the string `'https://api.spotify.com/v1/tracks/TRACK_ID'`:

```
1  expect(c.request.url).toBe('https://api.spotify.com/v1/tracks/TRACK_ID');
```

When our test is run, if the request URL doesn't match, then the test will fail.

Now that we've received our request and verified that it is correct, we need to craft a response. We do this by creating a new `ResponseOptions` instance. Here we specify that it will return the JSON string: `{"name": "felipe"}` as the body of the response.

```
1  let response = new ResponseOptions({body: '{"name": "felipe"}'});
```

Finally, we tell the connection to replace the response with a `Response` object that wraps the `ResponseOptions` instance we created:

```
1  c.mockRespond(new Response(response));
```

> An interesting thing to note here is that your callback function in `subscribe` can be as sophisticated as you wish it to be. You could have conditional logic based on the URL, query parameters, or anything you can read from the request object etc.
>
> This allows us to write tests for nearly every possible scenario our code might encounter.

We have now everything setup to call the `getTrack` method with `TRACK_ID` as a parameter and tracking the response in our `res` variable:

```
1  spotifyService.getTrack('TRACK_ID').subscribe((_res) => {
2    res = _res;
3  });
```

If we ended our test here, we would be waiting for the HTTP call to be made and the response to be fulfilled before the callback function would be triggered. It would also happen on a different execution path and we'd have to orchestrate our code to sync things up. Thankfully using fakeAsync takes that problem away. All we need to do is call tick() and, like magic, our async code will be executed:

```
1  tick();
```

We now perform one final check just to make sure our response we setup is the one we received:

```
1  expect(res.name).toBe('felipe');
```

If you think about it, the code for all the methods of this service are *very* similar. So let's extract the snippet we use to setup the URL expectation into a function called expectURL:

code/routes/music/src/app/spotify.service.spec.ts

```
35    function expectURL(backend: MockBackend, url: string) {
36      backend.connections.subscribe(c => {
37        expect(c.request.url).toBe(url);
38        const response = new ResponseOptions({body: '{"name": "felipe"}'});
39        c.mockRespond(new Response(response));
40      });
41    }
```

Following the same lines, it should be very simple to create similar tests for getArtist and getAlbum methods:

code/routes/music/src/app/spotify.service.spec.ts

```
57    describe('getArtist', () => {
58      it('retrieves using the artist ID',
59        inject([SpotifyService, MockBackend], fakeAsync((svc, backend) => {
60          let res;
61          expectURL(backend, 'https://api.spotify.com/v1/artists/ARTIST_ID');
62          svc.getArtist('ARTIST_ID').subscribe((_res) => {
63            res = _res;
64          });
```

```
65          tick();
66          expect(res.name).toBe('felipe');
67       }))
68     );
69   });
70
71   describe('getAlbum', () => {
72     it('retrieves using the album ID',
73       inject([SpotifyService, MockBackend], fakeAsync((svc, backend) => {
74         let res;
75         expectURL(backend, 'https://api.spotify.com/v1/albums/ALBUM_ID');
76         svc.getAlbum('ALBUM_ID').subscribe((_res) => {
77           res = _res;
78         });
79         tick();
80         expect(res.name).toBe('felipe');
81       }))
82     );
83   });
```

Now `searchTrack` is slightly different: instead of calling `query`, this method uses the `search` method:

code/routes/music/src/app/spotify.service.ts

```
50   searchTrack(query: string): Observable<any[]> {
51     return this.search(query, 'track');
52   }
```

And then `search` calls `query` with `/search` as the first argument and an Array containing `q=<query>` and `type=track` as the second argument:

code/routes/music/src/app/spotify.service.ts

```
43   search(query: string, type: string): Observable<any[]> {
44     return this.query(`/search`, [
45       `q=${query}`,
46       `type=${type}`
47     ]);
48   }
```

Finally, `query` will transform the parameters into a URL `path` with a `QueryString`. So now, the URL we expect to call ends with `/search?q=<query>&type=track`.

Let's now write the test for `searchTrack` that takes into consideration what we learned above:

code/routes/music/src/app/spotify.service.spec.ts

```
85   describe('searchTrack', () => {
86     it('searches type and term',
87       inject([SpotifyService, MockBackend], fakeAsync((svc, backend) => {
88         let res;
89         expectURL(backend, 'https://api.spotify.com/v1/search?q=TERM&type=track'\
90   );
91         svc.searchTrack('TERM').subscribe((_res) => {
92           res = _res;
93         });
94         tick();
95         expect(res.name).toBe('felipe');
96       }))
97     );
98   });
```

The test ended up also being very similar to the ones we wrote so far. Let's review what this test does:

- it hooks into the HTTP lifecycle, by adding a callback when a new HTTP connection is initiated
- it sets an expectation for the URL we expect the connection to use including the query type and the search term
- it calls the method we're testing, searchTrack
- it then tells Angular to complete all the pending async calls
- it finally asserts that we have the expected response

In essence, when testing services our goals should be:

1. Isolate all the dependencies by using stubs or mocks
2. In case of async calls, use fakeAsync and tick to make sure they are fulfilled
3. Call the service method you're testing
4. Assert that the returning value from the method matches what we expect

Now let's move on to the classes that usually consume the services: components.

Testing Routing to Components

When testing components, we can either:

1. write tests that will interact with the component from the outside, passing attributes in and checking how the markup is affected or
2. test individual component methods and their output.

Those test strategies are known as **black box** and **white box** testing, respectively. During this section, we'll see a mix of both.

We'll begin by writing tests for the ArtistComponent class, which is one of the simpler components we have. This initial set of tests will test the component's internals, so it falls into the **white box** category of testing.

Before we jump into it, let's remember what ArtistComponent does:

The first thing we do on the class constructor is retrieve the **id** from the routeParams collection:

code/routes/music/src/app/artist/artist.component.ts

```
22    constructor(private route: ActivatedRoute, private spotify: SpotifyService,
23                private location: Location) {
24      route.params.subscribe(params => { this.id = params['id']; });
25    }
```

And with that we have our first obstacle. How can we retrieve the ID of a route without an available running router?

Creating a Router for Testing

Remember that when we write tests in Angular we manually configure many of the classes that are injected. Routing (and testing components) has a daunting number of dependencies that we need to inject. That said, once it's configured, it isn't something we change very much and it's very easy to use.

When we write tests it's often convenient to use beforeEach with TestBed.configureTestingModule to set the dependencies that can be injected. In the case of testing our ArtistComponent we're going to create a custom function that will create and configure our router for testing:

code/routes/music/src/app/artist/artist.component.spec.ts

```
21  describe('ArtistComponent', () => {
22    beforeEach(async(() => {
23      configureMusicTests();
24    }));
```

We define `configureMusicTests` in the helper file `MusicTestHelpers.ts`. Let's look at that now.

Here's the implementation of `configureMusicTests`. Don't worry, we'll explain each part:

code/routes/music/src/app/test/test.module.ts

```
68  export function configureMusicTests() {
69    const mockSpotifyService: MockSpotifyService = new MockSpotifyService();
70
71    TestBed.configureTestingModule({
72      imports: [
73        { // TODO RouterTestingModule.withRoutes coming soon
74          ngModule: RouterTestingModule,
75          providers: [provideRoutes(routerConfig)]
76        },
77        TestModule
78      ],
79      providers: [
80        mockSpotifyService.getProviders(),
81        {
82          provide: ActivatedRoute,
83          useFactory: (r: Router) => r.routerState.root, deps: [ Router ]
84        }
85      ]
86    });
87  }
```

We start by creating an instance of `MockSpotifyService` that we will use to mock the real implementation of `SpotifyService`.

Next we use a class called `TestBed` and call `configureTestingModule`. `TestBed` is a helper library that ships with Angular to help make testing easier.

In this case, `TestBed.configureTestingModule` is used to configure the `NgModule` used for testing. You can see that we provide an `NgModule` configuration as the argument which has:

- imports and

- providers

In our `imports` we're importing

- The `RouterTestingModule` and configuring it with our `routerConfig` - this configures the routes for testing
- The `TestModule` - which is the `NgModule` which declares all of the components we will test (see `MusicTestHelpers.ts` for the full details)

In `providers`

- We provide the `MockSpotifyService` (via `mockSpotifyService.getProviders()`)
- and the `ActivatedRoute`

Let's take a closer look at these starting with the `Router`.

Router

One thing we haven't talked about yet is what routes we want to use when testing. There are many different ways of doing this. First we'll look at what we're doing here:

code/routes/music/src/app/test/test.module.ts

```
32  @Component({
33    selector: 'blank-cmp',
34    template: ``
35  })
36  export class BlankCmp {
37  }
38
39  @Component({
40    selector: 'root-cmp',
41    template: `<router-outlet></router-outlet>`
42  })
43  export class RootCmp {
44  }
45
46  export const routerConfig: Routes = [
47    { path: '', component: BlankCmp },
48    { path: 'search', component: SearchComponent },
49    { path: 'artists/:id', component: ArtistComponent },
50    { path: 'tracks/:id', component: TrackComponent },
51    { path: 'albums/:id', component: AlbumComponent }
52  ];
```

Here instead of redirecting (like we do in the real router config) for the empty URL, we're just using `BlankCmp`.

Of course, if you want to use the same `RouterConfig` as in your top-level app then all you need to do is `export` it somewhere and `import` it here.

If you have a more complex scenario where you need to test lots of different route configurations, you could even accept a parameter to the `musicTestProviders` function where you use a new router configuration each time.

There are many possibilities here and you'll need to pick whichever fits best for your team. This configuration works for cases where your routes are relatively static and one configuration works for all of the tests.

Now that we have all of the dependencies, we create the `new Router` and call `r.initialNavigation()` on it.

ActivatedRoute

The `ActivatedRoute` service keeps track of the "current route". It requires the `Router` itself as a dependency so we put it in `deps` and inject it.

MockSpotifyService

Earlier we tested our `SpotifyService` by mocking out the HTTP library that backed it. Instead here, we're going to **mock out the whole service itself**. Let's look at how we can mock this out, or any, service.

Mocking dependencies

If you look inside `music/test` you'll find a `mocks/spotify.ts` file. Let's take a look:

code/routes/music/src/app/test/spotify.service.mock.ts

```
1  import {SpyObject} from './test.helpers';
2  import {SpotifyService} from '../spotify.service';
3
4  export class MockSpotifyService extends SpyObject {
5    getAlbumSpy;
6    getArtistSpy;
7    getTrackSpy;
8    searchTrackSpy;
9    mockObservable;
10   fakeResponse;
```

Here we're declaring the `MockSpotifyService` class, which will be a mocked version of the real `SpotifyService`. These instance variables will act as *spies*.

Spies

A *spy* is a specific type of mock object that gives us two benefits:

1. we can simulate return values and
2. count how many times the method was called and with which parameters.

In order to use spies with Angular, we're using the internal SpyObject class (it's used by Angular to test itself).

You can either declare a class by creating a new SpyObject on the fly or you can make your mock class inherit from SpyObject, like we're doing in our code.

The great thing inheriting or using this class gives us is the spy method. The spy method lets us override a method and force a return value (as well as watch and ensure the method was called). We use spy on our class constructor:

code/routes/music/src/app/test/spotify.service.mock.ts

```
12    constructor() {
13      super(SpotifyService);
14
15      this.fakeResponse = null;
16      this.getAlbumSpy = this.spy('getAlbum').and.returnValue(this);
17      this.getArtistSpy = this.spy('getArtist').and.returnValue(this);
18      this.getTrackSpy = this.spy('getTrack').and.returnValue(this);
19      this.searchTrackSpy = this.spy('searchTrack').and.returnValue(this);
20    }
```

The first line of the constructor call's the SpyObject constructor, passing the concrete class we're mocking. Calling super(...) is optional, but when you do the mock class it will inherit all the concrete class methods, so you can override just the pieces you're testing.

> If you're curious about how SpyObject is implemented you can check it on the angular/angular repository, on the file /modules/angular2/src/testing/testing_-internal.ts[129]

After calling super, we're initializing the fakeResponse field, that we'll use later to null.

Next we declare spies that will replace the concrete class methods. Having a reference to them will be helpful to set expectations and simulate responses while writing our tests.

When we use the SpotifyService within the ArtistComponent, the real getArtist method returns an Observable and the method we're calling from our components is the subscribe method:

---

[129]https://github.com/angular/angular/blob/b0cebdba6b65c1e9e7eb5bf801ea42dc7c4a7f25/modules/angular2/src/testing/testing_internal.ts#L205

code/routes/music/src/app/artist/artist.component.ts

```
27    ngOnInit(): void {
28      this.spotify
29        .getArtist(this.id)
30        .subscribe((res: any) => this.renderArtist(res));
31    }
```

However, in our mock service, we're going to do something tricky: instead of returning an observable from getArtist, we're returning this, the MockSpotifyService itself. That means the return value of this.spotify.getArtist(this.id) above will be the MockSpotifyService.

There's one problem with doing this though: our ArtistComponent was expecting to call subscribe on an Observable. To account for this, we're going to define subscribe on our MockSpotifyService:

code/routes/music/src/app/test/spotify.service.mock.ts

```
22    subscribe(callback) {
23      callback(this.fakeResponse);
24    }
```

Now when subscribe is called on our mock, we're immediately calling the callback, making the async call happen synchronously.

The other thing you'll notice is that we're calling the callback function with this.fakeResponse. This leads us to the next method:

code/routes/music/src/app/test/spotify.service.mock.ts

```
26    setResponse(json: any): void {
27      this.fakeResponse = json;
28    }
```

This method doesn't replace anything on the concrete service, but is instead a helper method to allow the test code to set a given response (that would come from the service on the concrete class) and with that simulate different responses.

code/routes/music/src/app/test/spotify.service.mock.ts

```
30    getProviders(): Array<any> {
31      return [{ provide: SpotifyService, useValue: this }];
32    }
```

This last method is a helper method to be used in TestBed.configureTestingModule providers like we'll see later when we get back to writing component tests.

Here's what our MockSpotifyService looks like altogether:

code/routes/music/src/app/test/spotify.service.mock.ts

```
1   import {SpyObject} from './test.helpers';
2   import {SpotifyService} from '../spotify.service';
3
4   export class MockSpotifyService extends SpyObject {
5     getAlbumSpy;
6     getArtistSpy;
7     getTrackSpy;
8     searchTrackSpy;
9     mockObservable;
10    fakeResponse;
11
12    constructor() {
13      super(SpotifyService);
14
15      this.fakeResponse = null;
16      this.getAlbumSpy = this.spy('getAlbum').and.returnValue(this);
17      this.getArtistSpy = this.spy('getArtist').and.returnValue(this);
18      this.getTrackSpy = this.spy('getTrack').and.returnValue(this);
19      this.searchTrackSpy = this.spy('searchTrack').and.returnValue(this);
20    }
21
22    subscribe(callback) {
23      callback(this.fakeResponse);
24    }
25
26    setResponse(json: any): void {
27      this.fakeResponse = json;
28    }
29
30    getProviders(): Array<any> {
31      return [{ provide: SpotifyService, useValue: this }];
32    }
33  }
```

Back to Testing Code

Now that we have all our dependencies under control, it is easier to write our tests. Let's write our test for our `ArtistComponent`.

As usual, we start with imports:

code/routes/music/src/app/artist/artist.component.spec.ts

```
1   import {
2     async,
3     ComponentFixture,
4     TestBed,
5     inject,
6     fakeAsync,
7   } from '@angular/core/testing';
8   import { Router } from '@angular/router';
9   import { Location } from '@angular/common';
10  import {
11    advance,
12    createRoot,
13    RootCmp,
14    configureMusicTests
15  } from '../test/test.module';
16
17  import { MockSpotifyService } from '../test/spotify.service.mock';
18  import { SpotifyService } from '../spotify.service';
19  import { ArtistComponent } from './artist.component';
```

Next, before we can start to describe our tests configureMusicTests to ensure we can access our musicTestProviders in each test:

code/routes/music/src/app/artist/artist.component.spec.ts

```
21  describe('ArtistComponent', () => {
22    beforeEach(async(() => {
23      configureMusicTests();
24    }));
```

Next, we'll write a test for everything that happens during the initialization of the component. First, let's take a refresh look at what happens on initialization of our ArtistComponent:

code/routes/music/src/app/artist/artist.component.ts

```
18  export class ArtistComponent implements OnInit {
19    id: string;
20    artist: Object;
21
22    constructor(private route: ActivatedRoute, private spotify: SpotifyService,
23                private location: Location) {
24      route.params.subscribe(params => { this.id = params['id']; });
25    }
26
27    ngOnInit(): void {
28      this.spotify
29        .getArtist(this.id)
30        .subscribe((res: any) => this.renderArtist(res));
31    }
```

Remember that during the creation of the component, we use route.params to retrieve the current route id param and store it on the id attribute of the class.

When the component is initialized ngOnInit is triggered by Angular (because we declared that this component implements OnInit. We then use the SpotifyService to retrieve the artist for the received id, and we subscribe to the returned observable. When the artist is finally retrieved, we call renderArtist, passing the artist data.

An important idea here is that we used dependency injection to get the SpotifyService, but remember, **we created a MockSpotifyService**!

So in order to test this behavior, let's:

1. Use our router to navigate to the ArtistComponent, which will initialize the component
2. Check our MockSpotifyService and ensure that the ArtistComponent did, indeed, try to get the artist with the appropriate id.

Here's the code for our test:

code/routes/music/src/app/artist/artist.component.spec.ts

```
26    describe('initialization', () => {
27      it('retrieves the artist', fakeAsync(
28        inject([Router, SpotifyService],
29              (router: Router,
30                mockSpotifyService: MockSpotifyService) => {
31          const fixture = createRoot(router, RootCmp);
32
33          router.navigateByUrl('/artists/2');
34          advance(fixture);
35
36          expect(mockSpotifyService.getArtistSpy).toHaveBeenCalledWith('2');
37        })));
38    });
```

Let's take it step by step.

fakeAsync **and** advance

We start by wrapping the test in `fakeAsync`. Without getting too bogged down in the details, by using `fakeAsync` we're able to have more control over when change detection and asynchronous operations occur. A consequence of this is that we need to explicitly tell our components that they need to detect changes after we make changes in our tests.

Normally you don't need to worry about this when writing your apps, as zones tend to do the right thing, but during tests we manipulate the change detection process more carefully.

If you skip a few lines down you'll notice that we're using a function called `advance` that comes from our `MusicTestHelpers`. Let's take a look at that function:

code/routes/music/src/app/test/test.module.ts

```
54    export function advance(fixture: ComponentFixture<any>): void {
55      tick();
56      fixture.detectChanges();
57    }
```

So we see here that `advance` does two things:

1. It tells the component to detect changes and
2. Calls `tick()`

When we use `fakeAsync`, timers are actually synchronous and we use `tick()` to simulate the asynchronous passage of time.

Practically speaking, in our tests we'll call `advance` whenever we want Angular to "work it's magic". So for instance, whenever we navigate to a new route, update a form element, make an HTTP request etc. we'll call `advance` to give Angular a chance to do it's thing.

inject

In our test we need some dependencies. We use `inject` to get them. The `inject` function takes two arguments:

1. An array of *tokens* to inject
2. A function into which to provide the injections

And what classes will `inject` use? The providers we defined in `TestBed.configureTestingModule` `providers`.

Notice that we're injecting:

1. `Router`
2. `SpotifyService`

The `Router` that will be injected is the `Router` we configured in `musicTestProviders` above.

For `SpotifyService`, notice that we're requesting injection of the *token* `SpotifyService`, but we're receiving a `MockSpotifyService`. A little tricky, but hopefully it makes sense given what we've talked about so far.

Testing `ArtistComponent`'s Initialization

Let's review the contents of our actual test:

code/routes/music/src/app/artist/artist.component.spec.ts

```
31      const fixture = createRoot(router, RootCmp);
32
33      router.navigateByUrl('/artists/2');
34      advance(fixture);
35
36      expect(mockSpotifyService.getArtistSpy).toHaveBeenCalledWith('2');
```

We start by creating an instance of our `RootCmp` by using `createRoot`. Let's look at the `createRoot` helper function:

code/routes/music/src/app/test/test.module.ts

```
59  export function createRoot(router: Router,
60                               componentType: any): ComponentFixture<any> {
61    const f = TestBed.createComponent(componentType);
62    advance(f);
63    (<any>router).initialNavigation();
64    advance(f);
65    return f;
66  }
```

Notice here that when we call `createRoot` we

1. Create an instance of the root component
2. advance it
3. Tell the router to setup it's `initialNavigation`
4. advance again
5. return the new root component.

This is something we'll do a lot when we want to test a component that depends on routing, so it's handy to have this helper function around.

Notice that we're using the `TestBed` library again to call `TestBed.createComponent`. This function creates a component of the appropriate type.

> `RootCmp` is an empty component that we created in `MusicTestHelpers`. You definitely don't need to create an empty component for your root component, but I like to do it this way because it lets us test our child component (`ArtistComponent`) more-or-less in isolation. That is, we don't have to worry about the effects of the parent app component.
>
> That said, maybe you *want* to make sure that the child component operates correctly in context. In that case instead of using `RootCmp` you'd probably want to use your app's normal parent component.

Next we use `router` to navigate to the url `/artists/2` and `advance`. When we navigate to that URL, `ArtistComponent` should be initialized, so we assert that the `getArtist` method of the `SpotifyService` was called with the proper value.

Testing `ArtistComponent` **Methods**

Recall that the `ArtistComponent` has an `href` which calls the `back()` function.

code/routes/music/src/app/artist/artist.component.ts

```
33    back(): void {
34      this.location.back();
35    }
```

Let's test that when the `back` method is called, the router will redirect the user back to the previous location.

The current location state is controlled by the `Location` service. When we need to send the user back to the previous location, we use the `Location`'s `back` method.

Here is how we test the `back` method:

code/routes/music/src/app/artist/artist.component.spec.ts

```
40    describe('back', () => {
41      it('returns to the previous location', fakeAsync(
42        inject([Router, Location],
43              (router: Router, location: Location) => {
44          const fixture = createRoot(router, RootCmp);
45          expect(location.path()).toEqual('/');
46
47          router.navigateByUrl('/artists/2');
48          advance(fixture);
49          expect(location.path()).toEqual('/artists/2');
50
51          const artist = fixture.debugElement.children[1].componentInstance;
52          artist.back();
53          advance(fixture);
54
55          expect(location.path()).toEqual('/');
56        })));
57    });
```

The initial structure is similar: we inject our dependencies and create a new component.

We have a new expectation - we assert that the `location.path()` is equal to what we expect it to be.

We also have another new idea: we're accessing the methods on the `ArtistComponent` itself. We get a reference to our `ArtistComponent` instance through the line

`fixture.debugElement.children[1].componentInstance`.

Now that we have the instance of the component, we're able to call methods on it directly, like
back().

After we call back() we advance and then verify that the location.path() is what we expected it
to be.

Testing ArtistComponent **DOM Template Values**

The last thing we need to test on ArtistComponent is the template that renders the artist.

code/routes/music/src/app/artist/artist.component.html

```
1  <div *ngIf="artist">
2    <h1>{{ artist.name }}</h1>
3
4    <p>
5      <img src="{{ artist.images[0].url }}">
6    </p>
7
8    <p><a href (click)="back()">Back</a></p>
9  </div>
```

Remember that the instance variable artist is set by the result of the SpotifyService getArtist
call. Since we're mocking the SpotifyService with MockSpotifyService, the data we should have
in our template should be whatever the mockSpotifyService returns. Let's look at how we do this:

code/routes/music/src/app/artist/artist.component.spec.ts

```
59  describe('renderArtist', () => {
60    it('renders album info', fakeAsync(
61      inject([Router, SpotifyService],
62            (router: Router,
63              mockSpotifyService: MockSpotifyService) => {
64      const fixture = createRoot(router, RootCmp);
65
66      const artist = {name: 'ARTIST NAME', images: [{url: 'IMAGE_1'}]};
67      mockSpotifyService.setResponse(artist);
68
69      router.navigateByUrl('/artists/2');
70      advance(fixture);
71
72      const compiled = fixture.debugElement.nativeElement;
73
74      expect(compiled.querySelector('h1').innerHTML).toContain('ARTIST NAME');
```

```
75      expect(compiled.querySelector('img').src).toContain('IMAGE_1');
76    })));
77  });
```

The first thing that's new here is that we're *manually setting the response* of the mockSpotifyService with setResponse.

The artist variable is a *fixture* that represents what we get from the Spotify API when we call the artists endpoint at GET https://api.spotify.com/v1/artists/{id}.

Here's what the real JSON looks like:

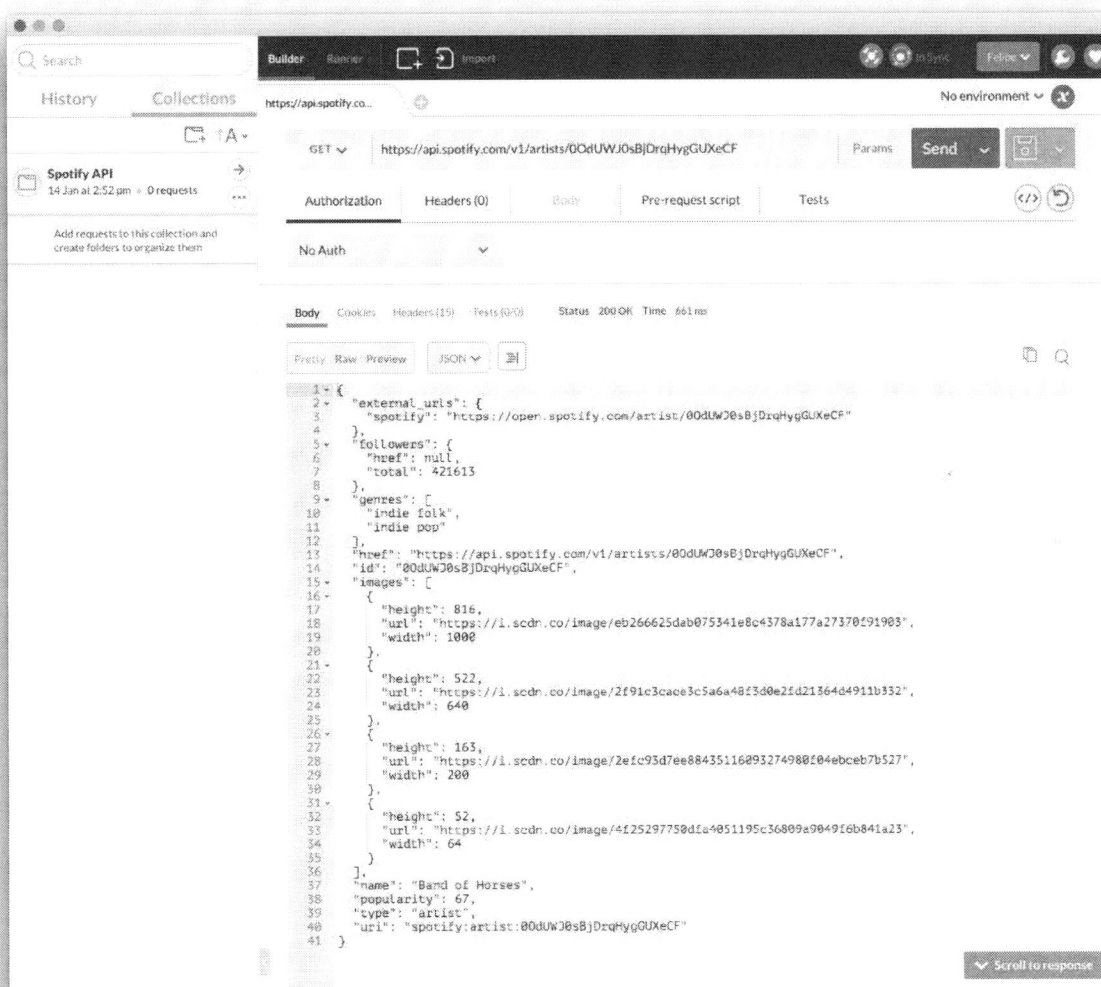

Postman - Spotify Get Artist Endpoint

However, for this test we need only the name and images properties.

When we call the `setResponse` method, that response will be used for the next call we make to any of the service methods. In this case, we want the method `getArtist` to return this response.

Next we navigate with the router and `advance`. Now that the view is rendered, we can use the DOM representation of the component's view to check if the artist was properly rendered.

We do that by getting the `nativeElement` property of the `DebugElement` with the line `fixture.debugElement.nativeElement`.

In our assertions, we expect to see H1 tag containing the artist's name, in our case the string `ARTIST NAME` (because of our `artist` fixture above).

To check those conditions, we use the `NativeElement`'s `querySelector` method. This method will return the first element that matches the provided CSS selector.

For the H1 we check that the text is indeed `ARTIST NAME` and for the image, we check its `src` property is `IMAGE 1`.

With this, we are done testing the `ArtistComponent` class.

Testing Forms

To write form tests, let's use the `DemoFormWithEventsComponent` component we created back in the `Forms` chapter. This example is a good candidate because it uses a few features of Angular's forms:

- it uses a `FormBuilder`
- has validations
- handles events

As a reminder, here's the full code for that class:

code/forms/src/app/demo-form-with-events/demo-form-with-events.component.ts

```
1  import { Component, OnInit } from '@angular/core';
2  import {
3    FormBuilder,
4    FormGroup,
5    Validators,
6    AbstractControl
7  } from '@angular/forms';
8
9  @Component({
10   selector: 'app-demo-form-with-events',
11   templateUrl: './demo-form-with-events.component.html',
12   styles: []
```

```
13  })
14  export class DemoFormWithEventsComponent implements OnInit {
15    myForm: FormGroup;
16    sku: AbstractControl;
17
18    ngOnInit() {
19    }
20
21    constructor(fb: FormBuilder) {
22      this.myForm = fb.group({
23        'sku':  ['', Validators.required]
24      });
25
26      this.sku = this.myForm.controls['sku'];
27
28      this.sku.valueChanges.subscribe(
29        (value: string) => {
30          console.log('sku changed to:', value);
31        }
32      );
33
34      this.myForm.valueChanges.subscribe(
35        (form: any) => {
36          console.log('form changed to:', form);
37        }
38      );
39
40    }
41
42    onSubmit(form: any): void {
43      console.log('you submitted value:', form.sku);
44    }
45
46  }
```

And the template:

code/forms/src/app/demo-form-with-events/demo-form-with-events.component.html

```
1   <div class="ui raised segment">
2     <h2 class="ui header">Demo Form: with events</h2>
3     <form [formGroup]="myForm"
4           (ngSubmit)="onSubmit(myForm.value)"
5           class="ui form">
6
7       <div class="field"
8            [class.error]="!sku.valid && sku.touched">
9         <label for="skuInput">SKU</label>
10        <input type="text"
11               class="form-control"
12               id="skuInput"
13               placeholder="SKU"
14               [formControl]="sku">
15          <div *ngIf="!sku.valid"
16            class="ui error message">SKU is invalid</div>
17          <div *ngIf="sku.hasError('required')"
18            class="ui error message">SKU is required</div>
19      </div>
20
21      <div *ngIf="!myForm.valid"
22        class="ui error message">Form is invalid</div>
23
24      <button type="submit" class="ui button">Submit</button>
25    </form>
26  </div>
```

Just to recap, this code will have the following behavior:

- when no value is present for the SKU field, two validation error will be displayed: *SKU is invalid* and *SKU is required*
- when the value of the SKU field changes, we are logging a message to the console
- when the form changes, we are also logging to the console
- when the form is submitted, we log yet another final message to the console

It seems that one obvious external dependency we have is the console. As we learned before, we need to somehow mock all external dependencies.

Creating a `ConsoleSpy`

This time, instead of using a `SpyObject` to create a mock, let's do something simpler, since all we're using from the `console` is the `log` method.

We will replace the original `console` instance, that is held on the `window.console` object and replace by an object we control: a `ConsoleSpy`.

code/forms/src/app/utils.ts

```
14  export class ConsoleSpy {
15    public logs: string[] = [];
16    log(...args) {
17      this.logs.push(args.join(' '));
18    }
19    warn(...args) {
20      this.log(...args);
21    }
22  }
```

The `ConsoleSpy` is an object that will take whatever is `logged`, naively convert it to a string, and store it in an internal list of things that were logged.

> To accept a variable number of arguments on our version of the `console.log` method, we are using ES6 and TypeScript's *Rest parameters*[130].
>
> This operator, represented by an ellipsis, like `...theArgs` as our function argument. In a nutshell using it indicates that we're going to capture all the remaining arguments from that point on. If we had something like `(a, b, ...theArgs)` and called `func(1, 2, 3, 4, 5)`, a would be 1, b would be 2 and `theArgs` would have `[3, 4, 5]`.
>
> You can play with it yourself if you have a recent version of Node.js[131] installed:
>
> ```
> 1  $ node --harmony
> 2  > var test = (a, b, ...theArgs) => console.log('a=',a,'b=',b,'theArgs=',theArgs);
> 3  undefined
> 4  > test(1,2,3,4,5);
> 5  a= 1 b= 2 theArgs= [ 3, 4, 5 ]
> ```

So instead of writing it to the console itself, we'll be storing them on an array. If the code under test calls `console.log` three times:

---

[130] https://developer.mozilla.org/en/docs/Web/JavaScript/Reference/Functions/rest_parameters

[131] https://nodejs.org/en/

```
1  console.log('First message', 'is', 123);
2  console.log('Second message');
3  console.log('Third message');
```

We expect the _logs field to have an array of ['First message is 123', 'Second message', 'Third message'].

Installing the ConsoleSpy

To use our spy in our test we start by declaring two variables: originalConsole will keep a reference to the original console instance, and fakeConsole that will hold the *mocked* version of the console. We also declare a few variables that will be helpful in testing our input and form elements.

code/forms/src/app/demo-form-with-events/demo-form-with-events.component.spec.ts

```
20  describe('DemoFormWithEventsComponent', () => {
21    let component: DemoFormWithEventsComponent;
22    let fixture: ComponentFixture<DemoFormWithEventsComponent>;
23
24    let originalConsole, fakeConsole;
25    let el, input, form;
```

And then we can install the fake console and specify our providers:

code/forms/src/app/demo-form-with-events/demo-form-with-events.component.spec.ts

```
27    beforeEach(async(() => {
28      // replace the real window.console with our spy
29      fakeConsole = new ConsoleSpy();
30      originalConsole = window.console;
31      (<any>window).console = fakeConsole;
32
33      TestBed.configureTestingModule({
34        imports: [ FormsModule, ReactiveFormsModule ],
35        declarations: [ DemoFormWithEventsComponent ]
36      })
37      .compileComponents();
38    }));
```

Back to the testing code, the next thing we need to do is replace the real console instance with ours, saving the original instance.

Finally, on the afterAll method, we restore the original console instance to make sure it doesn't *leak* into other tests.

code/forms/src/app/demo-form-with-events/demo-form-with-events.component.spec.ts

```
49    // restores the real console
50    afterAll(() => (<any>window).console = originalConsole);
```

Configuring the Testing Module

Notice that in the `beforeEach` we call `TestBed.configureTestingModule` - remember that `configureTestingModule` sets up the root `NgModule` for our tests.

In this case we're importing the two forms modules and declaring the `DemoFormWithEvents` component.

Now that we have control of the console, let's begin testing our form.

Testing The Form

Now we need to test the validation errors and the events of the form.

The first thing we need to do is to get the references to the SKU input field and to the form elements:

code/forms/src/app/demo-form-with-events/demo-form-with-events.component.1.spec.ts

```
43    it('validates and triggers events', fakeAsync( () => {
44      fixture = TestBed.createComponent(DemoFormWithEventsComponent);
45      component = fixture.componentInstance;
46      el = fixture.debugElement.nativeElement;
47      input = fixture.debugElement.query(By.css('input')).nativeElement;
48      form = fixture.debugElement.query(By.css('form')).nativeElement;
49      fixture.detectChanges();
```

The last line tells Angular to commit all the pending changes, similar to what we did in the routing section above. Next, we will set the SKU input value to the empty string:

code/forms/src/app/demo-form-with-events/demo-form-with-events.component.1.spec.ts

```
51      input.value = '';
52      dispatchEvent(input, 'input');
53      fixture.detectChanges();
54      tick();
```

Here we use `dispatchEvent` to notify Angular that the input element changed, and then we trigger the change detection a second time. Finally we use `tick()` to make sure all asynchronous code triggered up to this point gets executed.

The reason we are using `fakeAsync` and `tick` on this test, is to assure the form events are triggered. If we used `async` and `inject` instead, we would finish the code before the events were triggered.

Now that we have changed the input value, let's make sure the validation is working. We ask the component element (using the `el` variable) for all child elements that are error messages and then making sure we have both error messages displayed:

code/forms/src/app/demo-form-with-events/demo-form-with-events.component.1.spec.ts

```
57    let msgs = el.querySelectorAll('.ui.error.message');
58    expect(msgs[0].innerHTML).toContain('SKU is invalid');
59    expect(msgs[1].innerHTML).toContain('SKU is required');
```

Next, we will do something similar, but this time we set a value to the SKU field:

code/forms/src/app/demo-form-with-events/demo-form-with-events.component.1.spec.ts

```
62    input.value = 'XYZ';
63    dispatchEvent(input, 'input');
64    fixture.detectChanges();
65    tick();
```

And make sure all the error messages are gone:

code/forms/src/app/demo-form-with-events/demo-form-with-events.component.1.spec.ts

```
67    msgs = el.querySelectorAll('.ui.error.message');
68    expect(msgs.length).toEqual(0);
```

Finally, we will trigger the submit event of the form:

code/forms/src/app/demo-form-with-events/demo-form-with-events.component.1.spec.ts

```
70    fixture.detectChanges();
71    dispatchEvent(form, 'submit');
72    tick();
```

And finally we make sure the event was kicked by checking that the message we log to the console when the form is submitted is there:

```
74    // checks for the form submitted message
75    expect(fakeConsole.logs).toContain('you submitted value: XYZ');
```

We could continue and add new verifications for the other two events our form triggers: the SKU change and the form change events. However, our test is growing quite long.

When we run our tests, we see it passes:

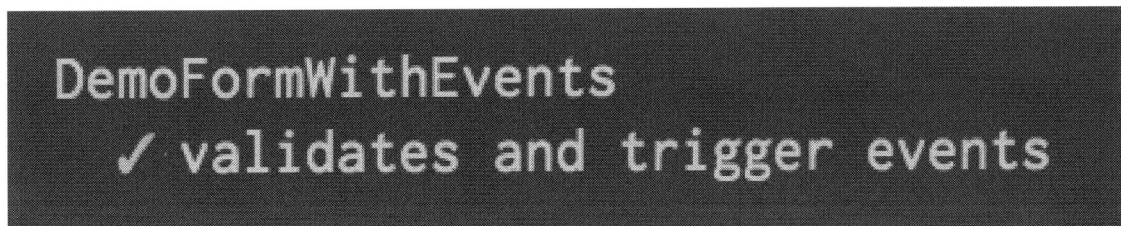

DemoFormWithEvents test output

This test works, but stylistically we have some code smells:

- a really long `it` condition (more than 5-10 lines)
- more than one or two `expects` per `it` condition
- the word **and** on the test description

Refactoring Our Form Test

Let's fix that by first extracting the code that creates the component and gets the component element and also the elements for the input and for the form:

code/forms/src/app/demo-form-with-events/demo-form-with-events.component.spec.ts

```
41    fixture = TestBed.createComponent(DemoFormWithEventsComponent);
```

The `createComponent` code is pretty straightforward: Creates the component with

`TestBed.createComponent`, retrieves all the elements we need and calls `detectChanges`.

Now the first thing we want to test is that given an empty SKU field, we should see two error messages:

code/forms/src/app/demo-form-with-events/demo-form-with-events.component.spec.ts

```
52    it('displays errors with no sku', fakeAsync( () => {
53      input.value = '';
54      dispatchEvent(input, 'input');
55      fixture.detectChanges();
56
57      // no value on sku field, all error messages are displayed
58      const msgs = el.querySelectorAll('.ui.error.message');
59      expect(msgs[0].innerHTML).toContain('SKU is invalid');
60      expect(msgs[1].innerHTML).toContain('SKU is required');
61    }));
```

See how much cleaner this is? Our test is focused and tests only one thing. Great job!

This new structure makes adding the second test easy. This time we want to test that, once we add a value to the SKU field, the error messages are gone:

code/forms/src/app/demo-form-with-events/demo-form-with-events.component.spec.ts

```
63    it('displays no errors when sku has a value', fakeAsync( () => {
64      input.value = 'XYZ';
65      dispatchEvent(input, 'input');
66      fixture.detectChanges();
67
68      const msgs = el.querySelectorAll('.ui.error.message');
69      expect(msgs.length).toEqual(0);
70    }));
```

One thing you may have noticed is that so far, our tests are not using `fakeAsync`, but `async` plus `inject` instead.

That's another bonus of this refactoring: we will only use `fakeAsync` and `tick()` when we want to check if something was added to the console, because that's all our form's event handlers do.

The next test will do exactly that - when the SKU value changes, we should have a message logged to the console:

code/forms/src/app/demo-form-with-events/demo-form-with-events.component.spec.ts

```
72    it('handles sku value changes', fakeAsync( () => {
73      input.value = 'XYZ';
74      dispatchEvent(input, 'input');
75      tick();
76
77      expect(fakeConsole.logs).toContain('sku changed to: XYZ');
78    }));
```

We can write similar code for both the form change...

code/forms/src/app/demo-form-with-events/demo-form-with-events.component.spec.ts

```
80    it('handles form changes', fakeAsync(() => {
81      input.value = 'XYZ';
82      dispatchEvent(input, 'input');
83      tick();
84
85      expect(fakeConsole.logs).toContain('form changed to: [object Object]');
86    }));
```

... and the form submission events:

code/forms/src/app/demo-form-with-events/demo-form-with-events.component.spec.ts

```
88    it('handles form submission', fakeAsync((tcb) => {
89      input.value = 'ABC';
90      dispatchEvent(input, 'input');
91      tick();
92
93      fixture.detectChanges();
94      dispatchEvent(form, 'submit');
95      tick();
96
97      expect(fakeConsole.logs).toContain('you submitted value: ABC');
98    }));
```

When we run the tests now, we get a much nicer output:

```
DemoFormWithEvents
  ✓ displays errors with no sku
  ✓ displays no errors when sku has a value
  ✓ handles sku value changes
  ✓ handles form changes
  ✓ handles form submission
```

DemoFormWithEvents test output after refactoring

Another great benefit from this refactor can be seen when something goes wrong. Let's go back to the component code and change the message when the form gets submitted, in order to force one of our tests to fail:

```
1  onSubmit(form: any): void {
2    console.log('you have submitted the value:', form.sku);
3  }
```

If we ran the previous version of the test, here's what would happen:

```
DemoFormWithEvents
  ✗ validates and trigger events
      Expected [ 'sku changed to: ', 'form changed to: [object Object]', 'sku changed to: XYZ', 'form cha
nged to: [object Object]', 'you have submitted the value: XYZ' ] to contain 'you submitted value: XYZ'.
          at /Users/fcoury/code/ng-book2/manuscript/code/forms/test.bundle.js:41894
          at run (/Users/fcoury/code/ng-book2/manuscript/code/forms/test.bundle.js:5942)
          at zoneBoundFn (/Users/fcoury/code/ng-book2/manuscript/code/forms/test.bundle.js:5915)
          at lib$es6$promise$$internal$$tryCatch (/Users/fcoury/code/ng-book2/manuscript/code/forms/test.
```

DemoFormWithEvents error output before refactoring

It's not immediately obvious what failed. We have to read the error code to realize it was the submission message that failed. We also can't be sure if that was the only thing that broke on the component code, since we may have other test conditions after the one that failed that never had a chance to be executed.

Now, compare that to the error we get from our refactored code:

```
DemoFormWithEvents
    ✓ displays errors with no sku
    ✓ displays no errors when sku has a value
    ✓ handles sku value changes
    ✓ handles form changes
    ✗ handles form submission
        Expected [ 'sku changed to: ABC', 'form changed to: [object Object]', 'you have submitted the
value: ABC' ] to contain 'you submitted value: ABC'.
            at /Users/fcoury/code/ng-book2/manuscript/code/forms/test.bundle.js:41673
            at run (/Users/fcoury/code/ng-book2/manuscript/code/forms/test.bundle.js:5942)
            at zoneBoundFn (/Users/fcoury/code/ng-book2/manuscript/code/forms/test.bundle.js:5915)
            at lib$es6$promise$$internal$$tryCatch (/Users/fcoury/code/ng-book2/manuscript/code/forms/
```

DemoFormWithEvents error output after refactoring

This version makes it pretty obvious that the only thing that failed was the form submission event.

Testing HTTP requests

We could test the HTTP interaction in our apps using the same strategy as we used so far: write a mock version of the `Http` or `HttpClient` class, since it is an external dependency.

But since the vast majority of single page apps written using frameworks like Angular use HTTP interaction to talk to APIs, the Angular testing library already provides a built in alternative: `HttpTestingController`.

Let's dive a little deeper now and see some more testing scenarios and also some good practices. In order to do this, let's write tests for the examples from the *HTTP chapter*.

First, let's see how we test different HTTP methods, like POST or DELETE and how to test the correct HTTP headers are being sent.

Back on the HTTP chapter, we created this example that covered how to do those things using `HttpClient`.

Testing a POST

The first test we'll write is to make sure we're doing a proper POST request on the `makePost` method:

code/http/src/app/more-http-requests/more-http-requests.component.ts

```
20    makePost(): void {
21      this.loading = true;
22      this.http
23        .post(
24          'https://jsonplaceholder.typicode.com/posts',
25          JSON.stringify({
26            body: 'bar',
27            title: 'foo',
28            userId: 1
29          })
30        )
31        .subscribe(data => {
32          this.data = data;
33          this.loading = false;
34        });
35    }
```

When writing our test for this method, our goal is to test two things:

1. the request method (POST) is correct and that
2. the URL we're hitting is also correct.

Here's how we turn that into a test:

First, we'll need to setup our tests to use the HttpClientTestingModule and HttpTestingController:

code/src/app/more-http-requests/more-http-requests.component.spec.ts

```
1   import {
2     async,
3     inject,
4     ComponentFixture,
5     TestBed
6   } from '@angular/core/testing';
7
8   import { HttpClient, HttpRequest, HttpHeaders } from '@angular/common/http';
9   import {
10    HttpTestingController,
11    HttpClientTestingModule
12  } from '@angular/common/http/testing';
```

```
13
14  import { MoreHttpRequestsComponent } from './more-http-requests.component';
15
16  describe('MoreHttpRequestsComponent', () => {
17    let component: MoreHttpRequestsComponent;
18    let fixture: ComponentFixture<MoreHttpRequestsComponent>;
19    let httpMock: HttpTestingController;
20
21    beforeEach(
22      async(() => {
23        TestBed.configureTestingModule({
24          declarations: [MoreHttpRequestsComponent],
25          imports: [HttpClientTestingModule]
26        });
27      })
28    );
29
30    beforeEach(
31      async(
32        inject([HttpTestingController], _httpMock => {
33          fixture = TestBed.createComponent(MoreHttpRequestsComponent);
34          component = fixture.componentInstance;
35          fixture.detectChanges();
36          httpMock = _httpMock;
37        })
38      )
39    );
40
41    afterEach(
42      inject([HttpTestingController], (httpMock: HttpTestingController) => {
43        httpMock.verify();
44      })
45    );
```

Above, we configure our testing module to import the `HttpClientTestingModule`. Then we inject `HttpTestingController` and store it as a variable in `httpMock`.

Now we're ready to write our test:

code/src/app/more-http-requests/more-http-requests.component.spec.ts

```
47   it(
48     'performs a POST',
49     async(() => {
50       component.makePost();
51
52       const req = httpMock.expectOne(
53         'https://jsonplaceholder.typicode.com/posts'
54       );
55       expect(req.request.method).toEqual('POST');
56       req.flush({ response: 'OK' });
57       expect(component.data).toEqual({ response: 'OK' });
58
59       httpMock.verify();
60     })
61   );
```

We start by call the `makePost()` function directly on the component. This might look odd because we don't typically call functions directly on our components. But what we're trying to do here is cause the HTTP request to be made, that way we can test expectations on it.

Next we use the instance variable `httpMock` and expect that one request was made to `jsonplaceholder` by using the `expectOne` function.

The line `req.flush` will send a "mock" response to that HTTP request, and then we `expect` that the `component.data` matches that response.

Lastly, we call `httpMock.verify()` to finalize any remaining expectations.

Now that we understand how this works, adding a second test for DELETE method is straightforward.

Testing DELETE

Here's how the `makeDelete` method is implemented:

code/http/src/app/more-http-requests/more-http-requests.component.ts

```
37    makeDelete(): void {
38      this.loading = true;
39      this.http
40        .delete('https://jsonplaceholder.typicode.com/posts/1')
41        .subscribe(data => {
42          this.data = data;
43          this.loading = false;
44        });
45    }
```

And this is the code we use to test it:

src/app/more-http-requests/more-http-requests.component.spec.ts

```
63    it(
64      'performs a DELETE',
65      async(() => {
66        component.makeDelete();
67
68        const req = httpMock.expectOne(
69          'https://jsonplaceholder.typicode.com/posts/1'
70        );
71
72        expect(req.request.method).toEqual('DELETE');
73        req.flush({ response: 'OK' });
74        expect(component.data).toEqual({ response: 'OK' });
75
76        httpMock.verify();
77      })
78    );
```

Everything here is the same, except for the URL that changes a bit and the HTTP method, which is now RequestMethod.Delete.

Testing HTTP Headers

The last method we have to test on this class is makeHeaders:

code/http/src/app/more-http-requests/more-http-requests.component.ts

```
47    makeHeaders(): void {
48      const headers: HttpHeaders = new HttpHeaders({
49        'X-API-TOKEN': 'ng-book'
50      });
51
52      const req = new HttpRequest(
53        'GET',
54        'https://jsonplaceholder.typicode.com/posts/1',
55        {
56          headers: headers
57        }
58      );
59
60      this.http.request(req).subscribe(data => {
61        this.data = data['body'];
62      });
63    }
```

In this case, what our test should focus on is making sure the header X-API-TOKEN is being properly set to ng-book:

src/app/more-http-requests/more-http-requests.component.spec.ts

```
80    it(
81      'sends correct headers',
82      async(() => {
83        component.makeHeaders();
84
85        const req = httpMock.expectOne(
86          req =>
87            req.headers.has('X-API-TOKEN') &&
88            req.headers.get('X-API-TOKEN') == 'ng-book'
89        );
90
91        req.flush({ response: 'OK' });
92        expect(component.data).toEqual({ response: 'OK' });
93
94        httpMock.verify();
95      })
96    );
```

The req.headers attribute returns the headers and we're using two methods to perform two different assertions:

- the has method to check whether a given header was set, ignoring it's value
- the get method, that returns the value that was set

If having the header set is sufficient, use has. Otherwise, if you need to inspect the set value, use get.

Now let's move to a more complex example.

Testing YouTubeSearchService

Back in the HTTP chapter we also built a YouTube video search. The HTTP interaction for that example takes place on a service called YouTubeSearchService:

code/http/src/app/you-tube-search/you-tube-search.service.ts

```
26  /**
27   * YouTubeService connects to the YouTube API
28   * See: * https://developers.google.com/youtube/v3/docs/search/list
29   */
30  @Injectable()
31  export class YouTubeSearchService {
32    constructor(
33      private http: HttpClient,
34      @Inject(YOUTUBE_API_KEY) private apiKey: string,
35      @Inject(YOUTUBE_API_URL) private apiUrl: string
36    ) {}
37
38    search(query: string): Observable<SearchResult[]> {
39      const params: string = [
40        `q=${query}`,
41        `key=${this.apiKey}`,
42        `part=snippet`,
43        `type=video`,
44        `maxResults=10`
45      ].join('&');
46      const queryUrl = `${this.apiUrl}?${params}`;
47      return this.http.get(queryUrl).map(response => {
48        return <any>response['items'].map(item => {
49          // console.log("raw item", item); // uncomment if you want to debug
50          return new SearchResult({
```

```
51              id: item.id.videoId,
52              title: item.snippet.title,
53              description: item.snippet.description,
54              thumbnailUrl: item.snippet.thumbnails.high.url
55          });
56        });
57      });
58    }
59 }
```

It uses the YouTube API to search for videos and parse the results into a SearchResult instance:

code/http/src/app/you-tube-search/search-result.model.ts

```
5  export class SearchResult {
6    id: string;
7    title: string;
8    description: string;
9    thumbnailUrl: string;
10   videoUrl: string;
11
12   constructor(obj?: any) {
13     this.id            = obj && obj.id            || null;
14     this.title         = obj && obj.title         || null;
15     this.description   = obj && obj.description    || null;
16     this.thumbnailUrl  = obj && obj.thumbnailUrl   || null;
17     this.videoUrl      = obj && obj.videoUrl       ||
18                          `https://www.youtube.com/watch?v=${this.id}`;
19   }
20 }
```

The important aspects of this service we need to test are that:

- given a JSON response, the service is able to parse the video id, title, description and thumbnail
- the URL we are requesting uses the provided search term
- the URL starts with what is set on the YOUTUBE_API_URL constant
- the API key used matches the YOUTUBE_API_KEY constant

With that in mind, let's start writing our test:

code/http/src/app/you-tube-search/you-tube-search.component.before.spec.ts

```
25  describe('YouTubeSearchComponent (before)', () => {
26    let component: YouTubeSearchComponent;
27    let fixture: ComponentFixture<YouTubeSearchComponent>;
28
29    beforeEach(
30      async(() => {
31        TestBed.configureTestingModule({
32          declarations: [
33            YouTubeSearchComponent,
34            SearchResultComponent,
35            SearchBoxComponent
36          ],
37          imports: [HttpClientTestingModule],
38          providers: [
39            YouTubeSearchService,
40            { provide: YOUTUBE_API_KEY, useValue: 'YOUTUBE_API_KEY' },
41            { provide: YOUTUBE_API_URL, useValue: 'YOUTUBE_API_URL' }
42          ]
43        });
44      })
45    );
```

As we did for every test we wrote on this chapter, we start by declaring how we want to setup our dependencies: we're using the real YouTubeSearchService instance, but setting fake values for YOUTUBE_API_KEY and YOUTUBE_API_URL constants. We're also importing the HttpClientTesting-Module.

Now, let's begin to write our first test case:

code/http/src/app/you-tube-search/you-tube-search.component.before.spec.ts

```
53    describe('search', () => {
54      it(
55        'parses YouTube response',
56        inject(
57          [YouTubeSearchService, HttpTestingController],
58          fakeAsync((service, httpMock) => {
59            let res;
60
61            service.search('hey').subscribe(_res => {
62              res = _res;
```

```
63              });
64
65              const req = httpMock.expectOne({ method: 'GET' });
66              req.flush({
67                items: [
68                  {
69                    id: { videoId: 'VIDEO_ID' },
70                    snippet: {
71                      title: 'TITLE',
72                      description: 'DESCRIPTION',
73                      thumbnails: {
74                        high: { url: 'THUMBNAIL_URL' }
75                      }
76                    }
77                  }
78                ]
79              });
80
81              tick();
82
83              const video = res[0];
84              expect(video.id).toEqual('VIDEO_ID');
85              expect(video.title).toEqual('TITLE');
86              expect(video.description).toEqual('DESCRIPTION');
87              expect(video.thumbnailUrl).toEqual('THUMBNAIL_URL');
88
89              httpMock.verify();
90            })
91          )
92        );
93      });
```

Here we're calling the method we're testing: search. We're calling it with the term *hey* and capturing the response on the res variable.

Here we are telling HttpClient to return a fake response that will match the relevant fields what we expect the YouTube API to respond when we call the real URL. We do that by using the req.flush method of the connection.

code/http/src/app/you-tube-search/you-tube-search.component.before.spec.ts

```
66        req.flush({
67          items: [
68            {
69              id: { videoId: 'VIDEO_ID' },
70              snippet: {
71                title: 'TITLE',
72                description: 'DESCRIPTION',
73                thumbnails: {
74                  high: { url: 'THUMBNAIL_URL' }
75                }
76              }
77            }
78          ]
79        });
```

If you noticed before, we're using fakeAsync that requires us to manually sync asynchronous code by calling tick(). When we do that here, we expect that the search finished executing and our res variable to have a value.

Now is the time to evaluate that value:

code/http/src/app/you-tube-search/you-tube-search.component.before.spec.ts

```
83        const video = res[0];
84        expect(video.id).toEqual('VIDEO_ID');
85        expect(video.title).toEqual('TITLE');
86        expect(video.description).toEqual('DESCRIPTION');
87        expect(video.thumbnailUrl).toEqual('THUMBNAIL_URL');
```

We are getting the first element from the list of responses. We know it's a SearchResult, so we're now checking that each attribute was set correctly, based on our provided response: the id, title, description and thumbnail URL should all match.

With this, we completed our first goal when writing this test. However, didn't we just say that having a huge it method and having too many expects are testing code smells?

We did, so before we continue let's refactor this code to make isolated assertions easier.

Add the following helper function inside our describe('search', ...):

code/http/src/app/you-tube-search/you-tube-search.component.spec.ts

```
81    function search(term: string, response: any, callback) {
82      return inject(
83        [YouTubeSearchService, HttpTestingController],
84        fakeAsync((service, httpMock) => {
85          let res;
86
87          // search
88          service.search(term).subscribe(_res => {
89            res = _res;
90          });
91
92          const req = httpMock.expectOne({ method: 'GET' });
93          req.flush(response);
94          tick();
95
96          callback(req.request, res);
97        })
98      );
99    }
```

Let's see what this function does: it uses inject and fakeAsync to perform the same thing we were doing before, but in a configurable way. We take a *search term*, a *response* and a *callback function*. We use those parameters to call the search method with the search term, set the fake response and call the callback function after the request is finished, providing the request and the response objects.

This way, all our test need to do is call the function and check one of the objects.

Let's break the test we had before into four tests, each testing one specific aspect of the response:

code/http/src/app/you-tube-search/you-tube-search.component.spec.ts

```
101    it(
102      'parses YouTube video id',
103      search('hey', defaultResponse, (req, res) => {
104        const video = res[0];
105        expect(video.id).toEqual('VIDEO_ID');
106      })
107    );
108
109    it(
110      'parses YouTube video title',
111      search('hey', defaultResponse, (req, res) => {
```

```
112          const video = res[0];
113          expect(video.title).toEqual('TITLE');
114        })
115      );
116
117      it(
118        'parses YouTube video description',
119        search('hey', defaultResponse, (req, res) => {
120          const video = res[0];
121          expect(video.description).toEqual('DESCRIPTION');
122        })
123      );
124
125      it(
126        'parses YouTube video thumbnail',
127        search('hey', defaultResponse, (req, res) => {
128          const video = res[0];
129          expect(video.description).toEqual('DESCRIPTION');
130        })
131      );
```

Doesn't it look good? Small, focused tests that test only one thing. Great!

Now it should be really easy to add tests for the remaining goals we had:

code/http/src/app/you-tube-search/you-tube-search.component.spec.ts

```
133      it(
134        'sends the query',
135        search('term', defaultResponse, (req, res) => {
136          expect(req.url).toContain('q=term');
137        })
138      );
139
140      it(
141        'sends the API key',
142        search('term', defaultResponse, (req, res) => {
143          expect(req.url).toContain('key=YOUTUBE_API_KEY');
144        })
145      );
146
147      it(
148        'uses the provided YouTube URL',
```

```
149        search('term', defaultResponse, (req, res) => {
150          expect(req.url).toMatch(/^YOUTUBE_API_URL\?/);
151        })
152      );
```

Feel free to add more tests as you see fit. For example, you could add a test for when you have more than one item on the response, with different attributes. See if you can find other aspects of the code you'd like to test.

Conclusion

The Angular team has done a great job building testing right into Angular. It's easy to test all of the aspects of our application: from controllers, to services, forms and HTTP. Even testing asynchronous code that was a difficult to test is now a breeze.

Converting an AngularJS 1.x App to Angular

If you've been using Angular for a while, then you probably already have production AngularJS 1 apps. Angular is great, but there's no way we can drop everything and rewrite our entire production apps in Angular. What we need is a way to *incrementally* upgrade our AngularJS 1 app. Thankfully, Angular has a fantastic way to do that.

The interoperability of AngularJS 1 (ng1) and Angular (ng2) works really well. In this chapter, we're going to talk about how to upgrade your ng1 app to ng2 by writing a *hybrid* app. A hybrid app is running ng1 and ng2 simultaneously (and we can exchange data between them).

Peripheral Concepts

When we talk about interoperability between AngularJS 1 and Angular, there's a lot of peripheral concepts. For instance:

Mapping AngularJS 1 Concepts to Angular: At a high level, ng2 Components are ng1 directives. We also use Services in both. However, this chapter is about using both ng1 and ng2, so we're going to assume you have basic knowledge of both. If you haven't used ng2 much, checkout the chapter on How Angular Works before reading this chapter.

Preparing ng1 apps for ng2: AngularJS 1.5 provides a new .component method to make "component-directives". .component is a great way to start preparing your ng1 app for ng2. Furthermore, creating thin controllers (or banning them altogether[132]) is a great way to refactor your ng1 app such that it's easier to integrate with ng2.

Another way to prepare your ng1 app is to reduce or eliminate your use of two-way data-binding in favor of a one-way data flow. In-part, you'd do this by reducing $scope changes that pass data between directives and instead use services to pass your data around.

These ideas are important and warrant further exploration. However, we're not going to extensively cover best-practices for pre-upgrade refactoring in this chapter.

Instead, here's what we **are** going to talk about:

Writing hybrid ng1/ng2 apps: ng2 provides a way to bootstrap your ng1 app and then write ng2 components and services. You can write ng2 components that will mix with ng1 components and it "just works". Furthermore, the dependency injection system supports passing between ng1 and ng2 (both directions), so you can write services which will run in either ng1 or ng2.

---

[132]http://teropa.info/blog/2014/10/24/how-ive-improved-my-angular-apps-by-banning-ng-controller.html

The best part? Change detection runs within Zones, so you don't need to call `$scope.apply` or worry much about change-detection at all.

What We're Building

In this chapter, we're going to be converting an app called "Interest" - it's a Pinterest-like clone. The idea is that you can save a "Pin" which is a link with an image. The Pins will be shown in a list and you can "fav" (or unfav) a pin.

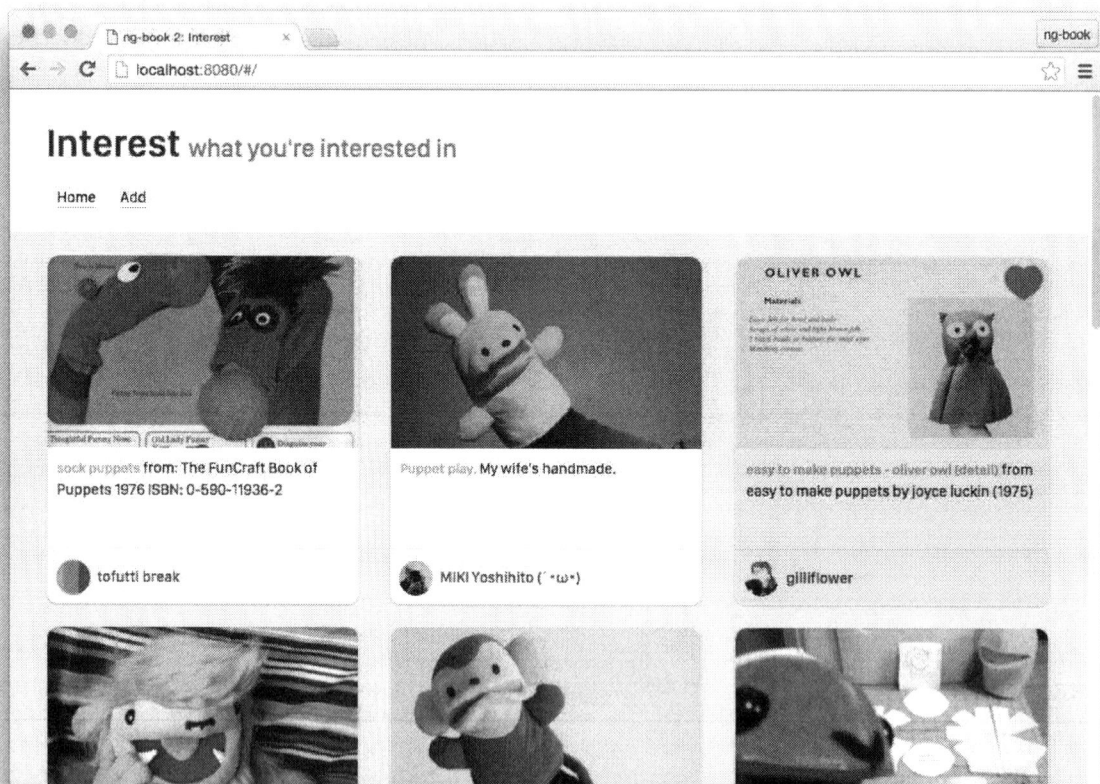

Our completed Pinterest-like app

You can find the completed code for both the ng1 version and the completed hybrid version in the sample code download under `code/upgrade/ng1` and `code/conversion/hybrid`

The hybrid app is written using Angular CLI. In order to run it, change into the directory and type:

```
1  npm install
2  npm start
```

Before we dive in, let's set the stage for interoperability between ng1 and ng2

Mapping AngularJS 1 to Angular

From a high level, the five main parts of AngularJS 1 are:

- Directives
- Controllers
- Scopes
- Services
- Dependency Injection

Angular changes this list significantly. You might have heard that at ngEurope 2014 Igor and Tobias from the Angular core team announced that they were killing off several "core" ideas in AngularJS 1 (video here[133]). Specifically, they announced that Angular was killing off:

- $scope (& two-way binding by default)
- Directive Definition Objects
- Controllers
- `angular.module`

---

[133] https://www.youtube.com/watch?v=gNmWybAyBHI

Igor and Tobias killing off many APIs from 1.x. at ngEurope 2014. Photo Credit: Michael Bromley (used with permission)

As someone who's built AngularJS 1 apps and is used to thinking in ng1, we might ask: if we take those things away, what is left? How can you build Angular apps without Controllers and $scope?

Well, as much as people like to dramatize how **different** Angular is, it turns out, a lot of the same ideas are still with us and, in fact, Angular provides just as much functionality but with **a much simpler model**.

At a high-level Angular core is made up of:

- Components (think "directives") and
- Services

Of course there's tons of infrastructure required to make those things work. For instance, you need Dependency Injection to manage your Services. And you need a strong change detection library to efficiently propagate data changes to your app. And you need an efficient rendering layer to handle rendering the DOM at the right time.

Requirements for Interoperability

So given these two different systems, what features do we need for easy interoperability?

- **Use Angular Components in AngularJS 1**: The first thing that comes to mind is that we need to be able to write new ng2 components, but use them within our ng1 app.
- **Use AngularJS 1 Components in Angular**: It's likely that we won't replace a whole branch of our component-tree with all ng2 components. We want to be able to re-use any ng1 components we have *within* a ng2 component.
- **Service Sharing**: If we have, say, a `UserService` we want to share that service between both ng1 and ng2. Services are normally plain JavaScript objects so, more generally, what we need is an interoperable **dependency injection** system.
- **Change Detection**: If we make changes in one side, we want those changes to propagate to the other.

Angular provides solutions for all of these situations and we'll cover them in this chapter.

In this chapter we're going to do the following:

- Describe the ng1 app we'll be converting
- Explain how to setup your hybrid app by using ng2's `UpgradeAdapter`
- Explain step-by-step how to share components (directives) and services between ng1 and ng2 by converting the ng1 app to a hybrid app

The AngularJS 1 App

To set the stage, let's go over the AngularJS 1 version of our app.

> This chapter assumes some knowledge of AngularJS 1 and ui-router[134]. If you're not comfortable with AngularJS 1 yet, check out ng-book 1[135].
>
> We won't be diving too deeply into explaining each AngularJS 1 concept. Instead, we're going to review the structure of the app to prepare for our upgrade to a ng2/hybrid app.

To run the ng1 app, `cd` into `conversion/ng1` in the code samples, install the dependencies, and run the app.

---

[134]https://github.com/angular-ui/ui-router
[135]http://ng-book.com

```
1  cd code/upgrade/ng1   # change directories
2  npm install           # install dependencies
3  npm run go            # run the app
```

If your browser doesn't open automatically, open the url: http://localhost:8080[136].

> Note that the AngularJS 1 app in ng1 will run on port 8080 whereas the hybrid app (discussed below) will run on port 4200.

In this app, you can see that our user is collecting puppets. We can hover over an item and click the heart to "fav" a pin.

Red heart indicates a faved pin

We can also go to the /add page and add a new pin. Try submitting the default form.

> Handling image uploads is more complex than we want to handle in this demo. For now, just paste the full URL to an image if you want to try a different image.

---

[136]http://localhost:8080

The ng1-app HTML

The `index.html` in our ng1 app uses a common structure:

code/upgrade/ng1/index.html

```
1   <!DOCTYPE html>
2   <html ng-app='interestApp'>
3   <head>
4     <meta charset="utf-8">
5     <title>Interest</title>
6     <link rel="stylesheet" href="css/bootstrap.min.css">
7     <link rel="stylesheet" href="css/sf.css">
8     <link rel="stylesheet" href="css/interest.css">
9   </head>
10  <body class="container-fullwidth">
11
12    <div class="page-header">
13      <div class="container">
14        <h1>Interest <small>what you're interested in</small></h1>
15
16        <div class="navLinks">
17          <a ui-sref='home' id="navLinkHome">Home</a>
18          <a ui-sref='add' id="navLinkAdd">Add</a>
19        </div>
20      </div>
21    </div>
22
23    <div id="content">
24      <div ui-view=''></div>
25    </div>
26
27    <script src="js/vendor/lodash.js"></script>
28    <script src="js/vendor/angular.js"></script>
29    <script src="js/vendor/angular-ui-router.js"></script>
30    <script src="js/app.js"></script>
31  </body>
32  </html>
```

- Notice that we're using `ng-app` in the `html` tag to specify that this app uses the module `interestApp`.
- We load our javascript with `script` tags at the bottom of the body.
- The template contains a `page-header` which stores our navigation

- We're using ui-router which means we:
    - Use ui-sref for our links (Home and Add) and
    - We use ui-view where we want the router to populate our content.

Code Overview

We'll look at each section in code, but first, let's briefly describe the moving parts.

In our app, we have two routes:

- / uses the HomeController
- /add uses the AddController

We use a PinsService to hold an array of all of the current pins. HomeController renders the list of pins and AddController adds a new element to that list.

Our root-level route uses our HomeController to render pins. We have a pin directive that renders each pin.

The PinsService stores the data in our app, so let's look at the PinsService first.

ng1: PinsService

code/upgrade/ng1/js/app.js

```
1  angular.module('interestApp', ['ui.router'])
2  .service('PinsService', function($http, $q) {
3    this._pins = null;
4
5    this.pins = function() {
6      var self = this;
7      if(self._pins == null) {
8        // initialize with sample data
9        return $http.get("/js/data/sample-data.json").then(
10         function(response) {
11           self._pins = response.data;
12           return self._pins;
13         })
14     } else {
15       return $q.when(self._pins);
16     }
17   }
18
```

```
19    this.addPin = function(newPin) {
20      // adding would normally be an API request so lets mock async
21      return $q.when(
22        this._pins.unshift(newPin)
23      );
24    }
25  })
```

The `PinsService` is a `.service` that stores an array of pins in the property `_.pins`.

The method `.pins` returns a promise that resolves to the list of pins. If `_.pins` is `null` (i.e. the first time), then we will load sample data from `/js/data/sample-data.json`.

code/upgrade/ng1/js/data/sample-data.json

```
1   [
2     {
3       "title": "sock puppets",
4       "description": "from:\nThe FunCraft Book of Puppets\n1976\nISBN: 0-590-11936\
5   -2",
6       "user_name": "tofutti break",
7       "avatar_src": "images/avatars/42826303@N00.jpg",
8       "src": "images/pins/106033588_167d811702_o.jpg",
9       "url": "https://www.flickr.com/photos/tofuttibreak/106033588/",
10      "faved": false,
11      "id": "106033588"
12    },
13    {
14      "title": "Puppet play.",
15      "description": "My wife's handmade.",
16      "user_name": "MIKI Yoshihito (´ロwロ)",
17      "avatar_src": "images/avatars/7940758@N07.jpg",
18      "src": "images/pins/4422575066_7d5c4c41e7_o.jpg",
19      "url": "https://www.flickr.com/photos/mujitra/4422575066/",
20      "faved": false,
21      "id": "4422575066"
22    },
23    {
24      "title": "easy to make puppets - oliver owl (detail)",
25      "description": "from easy to make puppets by joyce luckin (1975)",
26      "user_name": "gilliflower",
27      "avatar_src": "images/avatars/26265986@N00.jpg",
28      "src": "images/pins/6819859061_25d05ef2e1_o.jpg",
```

```
29      "url": "https://www.flickr.com/photos/gilliflower/6819859061/",
30      "faved": false,
31      "id": "6819859061"
32    },
```

Snippet from Sample Data

The method .addPin simply adds the new pin to the array of pins. We use $q.when here to return a promise, which is likely what would happen if we were doing a real async call to a server.

ng1: Configuring Routes

We're going to configure our routes with ui-router.

If you're unfamiliar with ui-router you can read the docs here[137].

As we mentioned, we're going to have two routes:

code/upgrade/ng1/js/app.js

```
26  .config(function($stateProvider, $urlRouterProvider) {
27    $stateProvider
28      .state('home', {
29        templateUrl: '/templates/home.html',
30        controller: 'HomeController as ctrl',
31        url: '/',
32        resolve: {
33          'pins': function(PinsService) {
34            return PinsService.pins();
35          }
36        }
37      })
38      .state('add', {
39        templateUrl: '/templates/add.html',
40        controller: 'AddController as ctrl',
41        url: '/add',
42        resolve: {
43          'pins': function(PinsService) {
44            return PinsService.pins();
```

---

[137]https://github.com/angular-ui/ui-router/wiki

```
45          }
46        }
47      })
48
49      $urlRouterProvider.when('', '/') ;
50  })
```

The first route / maps to the `HomeController`. It has a template, which we'll look at in a minute. Notice that we also are using the `resolve` functionality of `ui-router`. This says that before we load this route for the user, we want to call `PinsService.pins()` and inject the result (the list of pins) into the controller (`HomeController`).

The `/add` route as similarly, except that it has a different template and a different controller.

Let's first look at our `HomeController`.

ng1: `HomeController`

Our `HomeController` is straightforward. We save `pins`, which is injected because of our `resolve`, to `$scope.pins`.

code/upgrade/ng1/js/app.js

```
60  .controller('HomeController', function(pins) {
61    this.pins = pins;
62  })
```

ng1: / `HomeController` template

Our home template is small: we use an `ng-repeat` to repeat over the pins in `$scope.pins`. Then we render each pin with the `pin` directive.

code/upgrade/ng1/templates/home.html

```
1  <div class="container">
2    <div class="row">
3      <pin item="pin" ng-repeat="pin in ctrl.pins">
4      </pin>
5    </div>
6  </div>
```

Let's dive deeper and look at this `pin` directive.

ng1: `pin` Directive

The `pin` directive is restricted to matching an element (E) and has a `template`.

We can input our `pin` via the `item` attribute, as we did in the `home.html` template.

Our `link` function, defines a function on the scope called `toggleFav` which toggles the pin's `faved` property.

code/upgrade/ng1/js/app.js

```
92  })
93  .directive('pin', function() {
94    return {
95      restrict: 'E',
96      templateUrl: '/templates/pin.html',
97      scope: {
98        'pin': "=item"
99      },
100     link: function(scope, elem, attrs) {
101       scope.toggleFav = function() {
102         scope.pin.faved = !scope.pin.faved;
103       }
104     }
105   }
106 })
```

> This directive shouldn't be taken as an example of directive using the current best-practices. For instance, if I was writing this component anew (in ng1) I would probably use the new `.component` directive available in AngularJS 1.5+. At the very least, I'd probably use `controllerAs` instead of `link` here.
>
> But this section is less about how to write ng1 code, as much as **how to work with the ng1 code you already have.**

ng1: `pin` Directive template

The template `templates/pin.html` renders an individual pin on our page.

code/upgrade/ng1/templates/pin.html

```
1   <div class="col-sm-6 col-md-4">
2     <div class="thumbnail">
3       <div class="content">
4         <img ng-src="{{pin.src}}" class="img-responsive">
5         <div class="caption">
6           <h3>{{pin.title}}</h3>
7           <p>{{pin.description | truncate:100}}</p>
8         </div>
9         <div class="attribution">
10          <img ng-src="{{pin.avatar_src}}" class="img-circle">
11          <h4>{{pin.user_name}}</h4>
12        </div>
13      </div>
14      <div class="overlay">
15        <div class="controls">
16          <div class="heart">
17            <a ng-click="toggleFav()">
18              <img src="/images/icons/Heart-Empty.png" ng-if="!pin.faved"></img>
19              <img src="/images/icons/Heart-Red.png"   ng-if="pin.faved"></img>
20            </a>
21          </div>
22        </div>
23      </div>
24    </div>
25  </div>
```

The directives we use here are ng1 built-ins:

- We use `ng-src` to render the `img`.
- Next we show the `pin.title` and `pin.description`.
- We use `ng-if` to show either the red or empty heart

The most interesting thing here is the `ng-click` that will call `toggleFav`. `toggleFav` changes the `pin.faved` property and thus the red or empty heart will be shown accordingly.

Red vs. Black Heart

Now let's turn our attention to the `AddController`.

ng1: `AddController`

Our `AddController` has a bit more code than the `HomeController`. We open by defining the controller and specifying the services it will inject:

code/upgrade/ng1/js/app.js

```
63  .controller('AddController', function($state, PinsService, $timeout) {
64    var ctrl = this;
65    ctrl.saving = false;
```

We're using `controllerAs` syntax in our router and template, which means we set properties on `this` instead of on $scope. Scoping `this` in ES5 JavaScript can be tricky, so we assign `var ctrl = this;` which helps disambiguate when we're referencing the controller in nested functions.

code/upgrade/ng1/js/app.js

```
67    var makeNewPin = function() {
68      return {
69        "title": "Steampunk Cat",
70        "description": "A cat wearing goggles",
71        "user_name": "me",
72        "avatar_src": "images/avatars/me.jpg",
73        "src": "/images/pins/cat.jpg",
74        "url": "http://cats.com",
75        "faved": false,
76        "id": Math.floor(Math.random() * 10000).toString()
77      }
78    }
79
80    ctrl.newPin = makeNewPin();
```

We create a function `makeNewPin` that contains the default structure and data for a pin.

We also initialize this controller by setting `ctrl.newPin` to the value of calling this function.

The last thing we need to do is define the function to submit a new pin:

code/upgrade/ng1/js/app.js

```
82   ctrl.submitPin = function() {
83     ctrl.saving = true;
84     $timeout(function() {
85       PinsService.addPin(ctrl.newPin).then(function() {
86         ctrl.newPin = makeNewPin();
87         ctrl.saving = false;
88         $state.go('home');
89       });
90     }, 2000);
91   }
92 })
```

Essentially, this article is calling out to `PinService.addPin` and creating a new pin. But there's a few other things going on here.

In a real application, this would almost certainly call back to a server. We're mimicking that effect by using `$timeout`. (That is, you could remove the `$timeout` function and this would still work. It's just here to deliberately slow down the app to give us a chance to see the "Saving" indicator.)

We want to give some indication to the user that their pin is saving, so we set the `ctrl.saving = true`.

We call `PinsService.addPin` giving it our `ctrl.newPin`. `addPin` returns a promise, so in our promise function we

1. revert `ctrl.newPin` to the original value
2. we set `ctrl.saving` to `false`, because we're done saving the pin
3. we use the `$state` service to redirect the user to the homepage where we can see our new pin

Here's the whole code of the `AddController`:

code/upgrade/ng1/js/app.js

```
63 .controller('AddController', function($state, PinsService, $timeout) {
64   var ctrl = this;
65   ctrl.saving = false;
66
67   var makeNewPin = function() {
68     return {
69       "title": "Steampunk Cat",
70       "description": "A cat wearing goggles",
71       "user_name": "me",
```

```
72        "avatar_src": "images/avatars/me.jpg",
73        "src": "/images/pins/cat.jpg",
74        "url": "http://cats.com",
75        "faved": false,
76        "id": Math.floor(Math.random() * 10000).toString()
77      }
78    }
79
80    ctrl.newPin = makeNewPin();
81
82    ctrl.submitPin = function() {
83      ctrl.saving = true;
84      $timeout(function() {
85        PinsService.addPin(ctrl.newPin).then(function() {
86          ctrl.newPin = makeNewPin();
87          ctrl.saving = false;
88          $state.go('home');
89        });
90      }, 2000);
91    }
92  })
```

ng1: AddController template

Our /add route renders the add.html template.

Adding a New Pin Form

The template uses ng-model to bind the input tags to the properties of the newPin on the controller. The interesting things here are that:

- We use ng-click on the submit button to call ctrl.submitPin and
- We show a "Saving..." message if ctrl.saving is truthy

code/upgrade/ng1/templates/add.html

```
1  <div class="container">
2    <div class="row">
3
4      <form class="form-horizontal">
5
6        <div class="form-group">
7          <label for="title"
8                 class="col-sm-2 control-label">Title</label>
```

```
 9              <div class="col-sm-10">
10                <input type="text"
11                       class="form-control"
12                       id="title"
13                       placeholder="Title"
14                       ng-model="ctrl.newPin.title">
15              </div>
16            </div>
17
18            <div class="form-group">
19              <label for="description"
20                     class="col-sm-2 control-label">Description</label>
21              <div class="col-sm-10">
22                <input type="text"
23                       class="form-control"
24                       id="description"
25                       placeholder="Description"
26                       ng-model="ctrl.newPin.description">
27              </div>
28            </div>
29
30            <div class="form-group">
31              <label for="url"
32                     class="col-sm-2 control-label">Link URL</label>
33              <div class="col-sm-10">
34                <input type="text"
35                       class="form-control"
36                       id="url"
37                       placeholder="Link URL"
38                       ng-model="ctrl.newPin.url">
39              </div>
40            </div>
41
42            <div class="form-group">
43              <label for="url"
44                     class="col-sm-2 control-label">Image URL</label>
45              <div class="col-sm-10">
46                <input type="text"
47                       class="form-control"
48                       id="url"
49                       placeholder="Image URL"
50                       ng-model="ctrl.newPin.src">
```

```
51              </div>
52            </div>
53
54            <div class="form-group">
55              <div class="col-sm-offset-2 col-sm-10">
56                <button type="submit"
57                        class="btn btn-default"
58                        ng-click="ctrl.submitPin()">Submit</button>
59              </div>
60            </div>
61            <div ng-if="ctrl.saving">
62              Saving...
63            </div>
64          </form>
65
66        </div>
67      </div>
```

ng1: Summary

There we have it. This app has just the right amount of complexity that we can start porting it to Angular.

Building A Hybrid

Now we're ready to start putting some Angular in our AngularJS 1 app.

Before we start using Angular in our browser, we're going to need to make some modifications to our project structure.

> You can find the code for this example in code/conversion/hybrid.
>
> To run it, run:
>
> 1 npm install
> 2 npm start
>
> Then open your browser to http://localhost:4200 – note that this is a **different URL** than the pure-AngularJS 1 app above.

Hybrid Project Structure

The first step to creating a hybrid app is to make sure you have both ng1 and ng2 loaded as dependencies. Everyone's situation is going to be slightly different.

In this example we've **vendored** the AngularJS 1 libraries (in js/vendor) and we're loading the Angular libraries from npm.

In your project, you might want to vendor them both, use bower[138], etc. However, using npm is very convenient for Angular, and so we suggest using npm to install Angular.

One of the first challenges we face when making a hybrid app is ensuring our build-process can support both JavaScript and TypeScript files, as well as resolving our assets, type-definitions, and so on.

Here we're using Angular CLI (which is based on Webpack) in order to build this app. We'll describe the specific steps necessary to get our app running within Angular CLI, but if you have an existing build process, it might take some additional work to get it in order.

Dependencies with package.json

You install dependencies with npm using the package.json file. Here's our package.json for the hybrid example:

code/upgrade/hybrid/package.json

```
 1  {
 2    "name": "hybrid",
 3    "version": "0.0.0",
 4    "license": "MIT",
 5    "scripts": {
 6      "ng": "ng",
 7      "start": "ng serve",
 8      "build": "ng build",
 9      "test": "ng test",
10      "lint": "ng lint",
11      "e2e": "ng e2e"
12    },
13    "private": true,
14    "dependencies": {
15      "@angular/common": "6.0.0",
16      "@angular/compiler": "6.0.0",
17      "@angular/core": "6.0.0",
18      "@angular/forms": "6.0.0",
```

---

[138]http://bower.io/

```
19      "@angular/http": "6.0.0",
20      "@angular/platform-browser": "6.0.0",
21      "@angular/platform-browser-dynamic": "6.0.0",
22      "@angular/router": "6.0.0",
23      "@angular/upgrade": "6.0.0",
24      "@types/jasmine": "2.5.53",
25      "@types/jasminewd2": "2.0.2",
26      "core-js": "2.4.1",
27      "reflect-metadata": "0.1.3",
28      "rxjs": "6.0.0",
29      "ts-node": "3.2.0",
30      "zone.js": "0.8.26"
31    },
32    "devDependencies": {
33      "@angular-devkit/build-angular": "~0.5.0",
34      "@angular-devkit/build-optimizer": "0.5.7",
35      "@angular/cli": "6.0.0",
36      "@angular/compiler-cli": "6.0.0",
37      "@types/angular-ui-router": "^1.1.40",
38      "@types/jasmine": "2.5.38",
39      "@types/node": "~6.0.60",
40      "codelyzer": "~2.0.0",
41      "jasmine-core": "~2.5.2",
42      "jasmine-spec-reporter": "~3.2.0",
43      "karma": "~1.4.1",
44      "karma-chrome-launcher": "~2.0.0",
45      "karma-cli": "~1.0.1",
46      "karma-coverage-istanbul-reporter": "0.2.0",
47      "karma-jasmine": "~1.1.0",
48      "karma-jasmine-html-reporter": "0.2.2",
49      "protractor": "~5.1.0",
50      "ts-node": "~2.0.0",
51      "tslint": "~4.4.2",
52      "typescript": "2.7.x"
53    }
54  }
```

> If you're unfamiliar with what one of these packages does, it's a good idea to find out. `rxjs`, for example, is the library that provides our observables.

Notice that we've included the `@angular/upgrade` package. This module contains the tools necessary for booting a hybrid app.

Compiling our code

We're going to be using TypeScript in this example alongside our JavaScript AngularJS 1 code. To do this, we're going to put all of our "old" JavaScript code in the folder `js/`.

We also want to load AngularJS, as well as `angular-ui-router` and our AngularJS 1 app. Here, to do this we're going to include them in the `scripts` tag of our `.angular-cli.json`

```
 1  {
 2    "apps": [
 3      {
 4        // ...
 5        "scripts": [
 6          "js/vendor/angular.js",
 7          "js/vendor/angular-ui-router.js",
 8          "js/app.js"
 9        ],
10      }
11    ]
12  }
```

> This step may vary depending on your build process. For instance, if you have an existing AngularJS app you may have an existing build process that builds that app into one or a few files (e.g. using Gulp or another build system). In that case, if you want to bring that build into your Angular CLI project, you could have a separate step that would build those files and import them into "scripts" here.
>
> In the case that you want a more unified workflow, you'll need to run `ng eject` and modify the generated Webpack file from there.
>
> That said, building custom Webpack configurations is beyond the scope of this book.

When we write hybrid ng2 apps **the Angular code becomes the entry point**. This makes sense because **it's Angular that's providing the backwards compatibility with AngularJS 1**. Let's take a closer look at the bootstrapping process.

Bootstrapping our Hybrid App

Now that we have our project structure in place, let's bootstrap the app.

If you recall, with AngularJS 1 you can bootstrap the app in 1 of two ways:

1. You can use the `ng-app` directive, such as `ng-app='interestApp'`, in your HTML or

2. You can use `angular.bootstrap` in JavaScript

In hybrid apps we use a **new bootstrap** method that comes from an `UpgradeAdapter`.

Since we'll be bootstrapping the app in code, **make sure you remove the `ng-app` from your `index.html`.**

Here's what a minimal bootstrapping of our code would look like:

```
1   // code/upgrade/hybrid/src/app/app.module.ts
2   import {
3     NgModule,
4     forwardRef
5   } from '@angular/core';
6   import { CommonModule } from '@angular/common';
7   import { BrowserModule } from '@angular/platform-browser';
8
9   import { UpgradeAdapter } from '@angular/upgrade';
10  declare var angular: any;
11
12  /*
13   * Create our upgradeAdapter
14   */
15  const upgradeAdapter: UpgradeAdapter = new UpgradeAdapter(
16    forwardRef(() => MyAppModule)); // <-- notice forward reference
17
18  // ...
19  // upgrade and downgrade components in here
20  // ...
21
22  /*
23   * Create our app's entry NgModule
24   */
25  @NgModule({
26    declarations: [ MyNg2Component, ... ],
27    imports: [
28      CommonModule,
29      BrowserModule
30    ],
31    providers: [ MyNg2Services, ... ]
32  })
33  class MyAppModule { }
34
```

```
35  /*
36   * Bootstrap the App
37   */
38  upgradeAdapter.bootstrap(document.body, ['interestApp']);
```

We start by importing the `UpgradeAdapter` and then we create an instance of it: `upgradeAdapter`.

However, the constructor of `UpgradeAdapter` requires an `NgModule` that we'll be using for our Angular up - but we haven't defined it yet! To get around this we use the `forwardRef` function which allows us to take a 'forward reference' to our `NgModule` which we declare below.

When we define our `NgModule` `MyAppModule` (or specifically in this app it will be `InterestAppModule`), we define it like we would any other Angular `NgModule`: we put in our declarations, imports, providers, etc.

Lastly, we tell the `upgradeAdapter` to `bootstrap` our app on the element `document.body` and we specify the module name of our **AngularJS 1 app**.

This will bootstrap our AngularJS 1 app within our Angular app! Now we can start replacing pieces with Angular.

What We'll Upgrade

Let's discuss what we're going to port to ng2 in this example and what will stay in ng1.

The Homepage

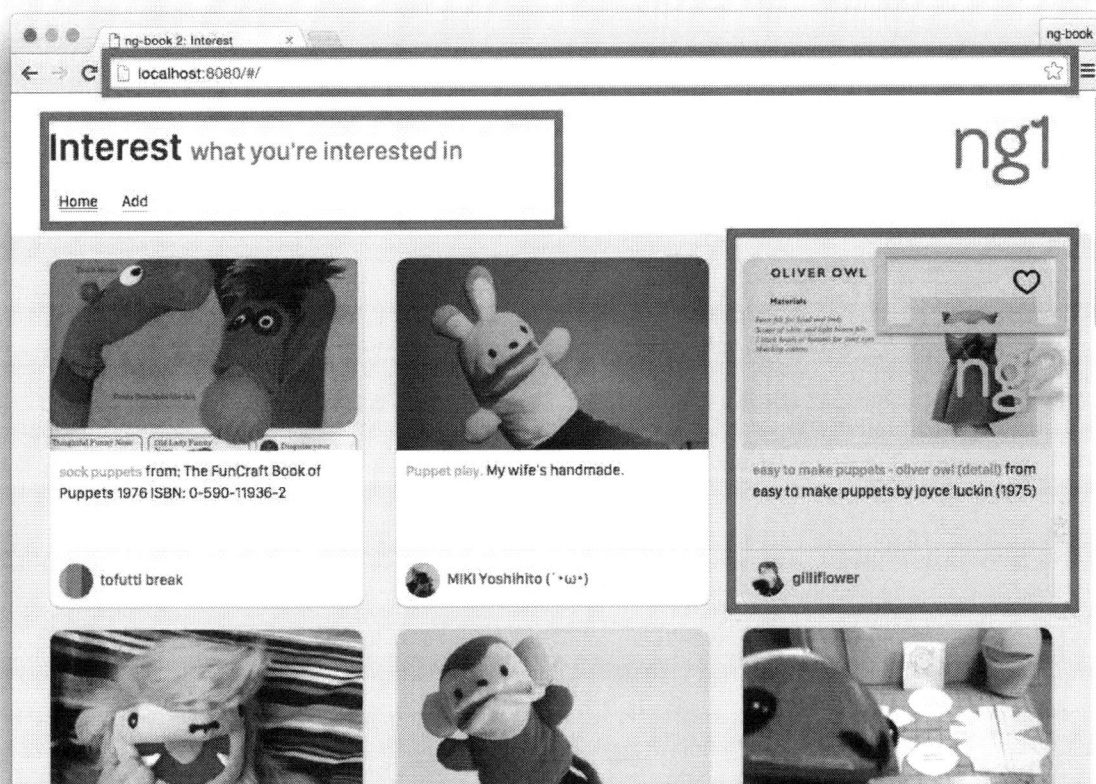

Homepage ng1 and ng2 Components

The first thing to notice is that we're going to continue to manage routing with ng1. Of course, Angular has its own routing, which you can read about in our routing chapter. But if you're building a hybrid app, you probably have lots of routes configured with AngularJS 1 and so in this example we'll continue to use `ui-router` for the routing.

On the homepage, we're going to nest a ng2 component within an ng1 directive. In this case, we're going to convert the "pin controls" to a ng2 component. That is, our ng1 `pin` directive, will call out to the ng2 `pin-controls` component and `pin-controls` will render the fav heart.

It's a small example that shows a powerful idea: how to seamlessly exchange data between ng versions.

The About Page

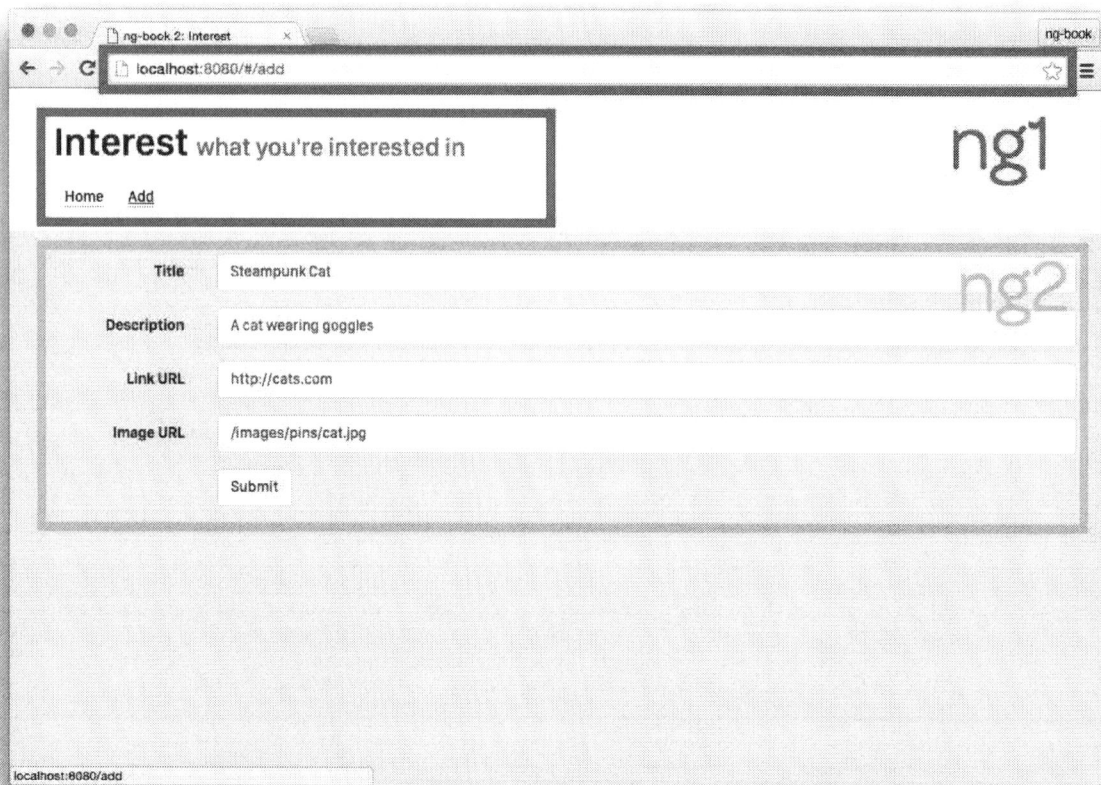

About Page ng1 and ng2 Components

We're going to use ng1 for the router and header on the about page as well. However on the about page, we're going to replace the whole form with a ng2 component: AddPinComponent.

If you recall, the form will add a new pin to the PinsService, and so in this example we're going to need to somehow make the (ng1) PinsService accessible to the (ng2) AddPinComponent.

Also, remember that when a new pin is added, the app should be redirected to the homepage. However, to change routes we need to use the ui-router $state service (ng1) in the AddPinComponent (ng2). So we also need to make sure the $state service can be used in AddPinComponent as well.

Services

So far we've talked about two ng1 services that will be *upgraded* to ng2:

- PinsService and
- $state

We also want to explore "downgrading" a ng2 service to be used by ng1. For this, later on in the chapter, we'll create an `AnalyticsService` in TypeScript/ng2 that we share with ng1.

Taking Inventory

So to recap we're going to "cross-expose" the following:

- Downgrade the ng2 `PinControlsComponent` to ng1 (for the fav buttons)
- Downgrade the ng2 `AddPinComponent` to ng1 (for the add pin page)
- Downgrade the ng2 `AnalyticsService` to ng1 (for recording events)
- Upgrade the ng1 `PinsService` to ng2 (for adding new pins)
- Upgrade the ng1 `$state` service to ng2 (for controlling routes)

A Minor Detour: Typing Files

One of the great things about TypeScript is the compile-time typing. However, if you're building a hybrid app, I suspect that you've got a lot of untyped JavaScript code that you're going to be integrating into this project.

When you try to use your JavaScript code from TypeScript you may get compiler errors because the compiler doesn't know the structure of your JavaScript objects. You could try casting everything to `<any>` but that is ugly and error prone.

The better solution is to, instead, provide your TypeScript compiler with custom *type decorators*. Then the compiler will be able to enforce the types of your JavaScript code.

For instance, remember how in our ng1 app we created a pin object in `makeNewPin`?

code/upgrade/ng1/js/app.js

```
67   var makeNewPin = function() {
68     return {
69       "title": "Steampunk Cat",
70       "description": "A cat wearing goggles",
71       "user_name": "me",
72       "avatar_src": "images/avatars/me.jpg",
73       "src": "/images/pins/cat.jpg",
74       "url": "http://cats.com",
75       "faved": false,
76       "id": Math.floor(Math.random() * 10000).toString()
77     }
78   }
79
80   ctrl.newPin = makeNewPin();
```

It would be nice if we could tell the compiler about the structure of these objects and not resort to using any everywhere.

Furthermore, we're going to be using the ui-router $state service in Angular / TypeScript, and we need to tell the compiler what functions are available there, too.

So while providing TypeScript custom type definitions is a TypeScript (and not an Angular-specific) chore, it's a chore we need to do nonetheless. And it's something that many people haven't done yet because TypeScript is, at time of publishing, relatively new.

So in this section I want to walk through how you deal with custom typings in TypeScript.

If you're already familiar with how to create and use TypeScript type definition files, you can safely skim this section.

Typing Files

In TypeScript we can describe the structure of our code by writing *typing definition files*. Typing definition files generally end in the extension .d.ts.

Generally, when you write TypeScript code, you don't need to write a .d.ts because your TypeScript code itself contains types. We write .d.ts files when we have some external JavaScript code that we want to add typing to after the fact.

For instance, in describing our pin object, we could write an interface for it like so:

code/upgrade/hybrid/src/js/app.d.ts

```
1  interface Pin {
2    title: string;
3    description: string;
4    user_name: string;
5    avatar_src: string;
6    src: string;
7    url: string;
8    faved: boolean;
9    id: string;
10 }
```

Notice that we're not declaring a class, and we're not creating an instance. Instead, we're defining the shape (types) of an interface.

In order to use .d.ts files, you need to tell the TypeScript compiler where they are. The easiest way to do this is by adding a reference to typings.d.ts. For instance in typings.d.ts we'll add this:

```
1   /// <reference path="./js/app.d.ts"/>
```

We'll write `app.d.ts` in a little bit. First, let's explore a tool that exists to help us with third-party TypeScript definition files: `typings`.

Third-party libraries with `@types`

Typescript allows for loading third-party types via NPM.

We're going to use `angular-ui-router` with our app, so let's install the typings for `angular-ui-router`. To get this setup, all we have to do is install the `@types/angular-ui-router` package.

```
1   npm install @types/angular-ui-router --save
```

Now, by default, TypeScript will read types from the `node_modules/@types/` directory. We'll look at how we uses these types in our code in a moment.

Custom Typing Files

Being able to use third-party typing files is great, but there are going to be situations where typing files don't already exist: especially in the case of our own code.

Generally, when we write custom typing files we co-locate the file alongside its respective JavaScript code. So let's create the file `js/app.d.ts`:

code/upgrade/hybrid/src/js/app.d.ts

```
1   interface Pin {
2     title: string;
3     description: string;
4     user_name: string;
5     avatar_src: string;
6     src: string;
7     url: string;
8     faved: boolean;
9     id: string;
10  }
11
12  interface PinsService {
13    pins(): Promise<Pin[]>;
14    addPin(pin: Pin): Promise<any>;
15  }
```

Here we're making an "ambient declaration" and the idea is that we're defining a variable that didn't originate from a TypeScript file. In this case, we're defining two interfaces:

1. `Pin`
2. `PinsService`

The `Pin` interface describes the keys and value-types of a pin object.

The `PinsService` interface describes the types of our two methods on our `PinsService`.

- `pins()` returns a `Promise` of an array of `Pins`
- `addPin()` takes a `Pin` as an argument and returns a `Promise`

Learn More about Writing Type Definition Files

If you'd like to learn more about writing `.d.ts` files, checkout these helpful links:

- TypeScript Handbook: Working with other JavaScript Libraries[139]
- TypeScript Handbook: Writing definition files[140]
- Quick tip: Typescript declare keyword[141]

Now that we have this file setup, TypeScript will know about the `Pin` and `PinsService` types in our code.

Writing ng2 `PinControlsComponent`

Now that we have the typings figured out, let's turn our attention back to the hybrid app.

The first thing we're going to do is write the ng2 `PinControlsComponent`. This will be an ng2 component nested within an ng1 directive. The `PinControlsComponent` displays the fav hearts and toggles fav'ing a pin.

Next, let's write our component:

---

[139] http://www.typescriptlang.org/Handbook#modules-working-with-other-javascript-libraries

[140] https://github.com/Microsoft/TypeScript-Handbook/blob/master/pages/Writing%20Definition%20Files.md

[141] http://blogs.microsoft.co.il/gilf/2013/07/22/quick-tip-typescript-declare-keyword/

code/upgrade/hybrid/src/app/pin-controls/pin-controls.component.ts

```
1  import {
2    Component,
3    Input,
4    Output,
5    EventEmitter
6  } from '@angular/core';
7
8  @Component({
9    selector: 'pin-controls',
10   templateUrl: './pin-controls.component.html',
11   styleUrls: ['./pin-controls.component.css']
12 })
13 export class PinControlsComponent {
14   @Input() pin: Pin;
15   @Output() faved: EventEmitter<Pin> = new EventEmitter<Pin>();
16
17   toggleFav(): void {
18     this.faved.emit(this.pin);
19   }
20 }
```

Notice here that we'll match the element pin-controls.

Our template looks very similar to the ng1 version except we're using the ng2 template syntax for (click) and *ngIf.

Now the component definition class:

code/upgrade/hybrid/src/app/pin-controls/pin-controls.component.html

```
1  <div class="controls">
2    <div class="heart">
3      <a (click)="toggleFav()">
4        <img src="/assets/images/icons/Heart-Empty.png" *ngIf="!pin.faved" />
5        <img src="/assets/images/icons/Heart-Red.png"   *ngIf="pin.faved" />
6      </a>
7    </div>
8  </div>
```

Notice that instead of specifying inputs and outputs in the @Component decorator, in this case we're annotating the properties on the class directly with the @Input and @Output decorators. This is a convenient way to us to provide typings to these properties.

This component will take an input of `pin`, which is the `Pin` object we're controlling.

This component specifies an output of `faved`. This is a little bit different than how we did it in the ng1 app. If you look at `toggleFav` all we're doing is emitting (on the `EventEmitter`) the current pin.

The idea here is that we've already implemented how to change the `faved` state in ng1 and we may not want to re-implement that functionality ng2 (you may want to, it just depends on your team conventions).

Using ng2 `PinControlsComponent`

Now that we have an ng2 `pin-controls` component, we can now use it in a **AngularJS 1** template. Here's what our `pin.html` template looks like now:

code/upgrade/hybrid/src/assets/templates/pin.html

```
1  <div class="col-sm-6 col-md-4">
2    <div class="thumbnail">
3      <div class="content">
4        <img ng-src="{{pin.src}}" class="img-responsive">
5        <div class="caption">
6          <h3>{{pin.title}}</h3>
7          <p>{{pin.description | truncate:100}}</p>
8        </div>
9        <div class="attribution">
10          <img ng-src="{{pin.avatar_src}}" class="img-circle">
11          <h4>{{pin.user_name}}</h4>
12        </div>
13      </div>
14      <div class="overlay">
15        <pin-controls [pin]="pin"
16                      (faved)="toggleFav($event)"></pin-controls>
17      </div>
18    </div>
19  </div>
```

This template is for an ng1 directive, and we can use ng1 directives such as `ng-src`. However, notice the line where we use our ng2 `pin-controls` component:

```
1  <pin-controls [pin]="pin"
2                (faved)="toggleFav($event)"></pin-controls>
```

What's interesting here is that we're using the ng2 input bracket syntax [pin] and the ng2 output parentheses syntax (faved).

In a hybrid app **when you use ng2 directives in ng1, you still use the ng2 syntax.**

With our input [pin] we're passing the pin which comes from the scope of the ng1 directive.

With our output (faved) we're calling the toggleFav function on the scope of the ng1 directive. Notice what we did here: we didn't modify the pin.faved state within the ng2 directive (although, we could have). Instead, we asked the ng2 PinControlsComponent to simply emit the pin when toggleFav is called there. (If this is confusing, take a second look at toggleFav of PinControlsComponent.)

Again, the reason we do this is because we're showing how you can keep your existing functionality (scope.toggleFav) in ng1, but start porting over components to ng2. In this case, the ng1 pin directive listens for the faved event on the ng2 PinControlsComponent.

If you refresh your page now, you'll notice that it doesn't work. That's because there's one more thing we need to do: downgrade PinControlsComponent to ng1.

Downgrading ng2 PinControlsComponent to ng1

The final step to using our components across ng2/ng1 borders is to use our UpgradeAdapter to downgrade our components (or upgrade, as we'll see in a bit).

We perform this downgrade in our app.module.ts file

First we need to import the necessary libraries and declare the angular variable:

code/upgrade/hybrid/src/app/app.module.ts

```
1  import {
2    NgModule,
3    forwardRef
4  } from '@angular/core';
5  import { UpgradeAdapter } from '@angular/upgrade';
6  import { BrowserModule } from '@angular/platform-browser';
7
8  import { FormsModule } from '@angular/forms';
9  import { HttpModule } from '@angular/http';
10
11 import { AppComponent } from './app.component';
12 import { AddPinComponent } from './add-pin/add-pin.component';
13 import { PinControlsComponent } from './pin-controls/pin-controls.component';
14 import { AnalyticsService } from './analytics.service';
15
16 declare var angular: any;
```

Then we create a `.directive` in (almost) the normal ng1 way:

code/upgrade/hybrid/src/app/app.module.ts

```
16   declare var angular: any;
17
18   /*
19    * Create our upgradeAdapter
20    */
21   export const upgradeAdapter: UpgradeAdapter = new UpgradeAdapter(
22     forwardRef(() => AppModule));
23
24     /*
25    * Expose our ng2 content to ng1
26    */
27   angular.module('interestApp')
28     .directive('pinControls',
29                 upgradeAdapter.downgradeNg2Component(PinControlsComponent))
```

Remember that our ng1 app calls `angular.module('interestApp', [])`. That is, our ng1 app has already registered the `interestApp` module with `angular`.

Now we want to look up that module by calling `angular.module('interestApp')` and then add directives to it, just like we do in ng1 normally.

> **angular.module getter and setter syntax**
>
> If you recall, when we pass an array as the second argument to `angular.module`, we are *creating* a module. That is, `angular.module('foo', [])` will *create* the module `foo`. Informally, we call this the "setter" syntax.
>
> Similarly, if we omit the array we are *getting* a module (that is assumed to already exist). That is, `angular.module('foo')` will *get* the module `foo`. We call this the "getter" syntax.

> In this example, if you forget this distinction and call `angular.module('interestApp', [])` in `app.ts` (ng2) then you will accidentally overwrite your existing `interestApp` module and your app won't work. Careful!

We're calling `.directive` and creating a directive called `'pinControls'`. This is standard ng1 practice. For the second argument, the directive definition object (DDO), we don't create the DDO manually. Instead, we call `upgradeAdapter.downgradeNg2Component`.

`downgradeNg2Component` will convert our `PinControlsComponent` into an ng1-compatible directive. Pretty neat.

1. Present a form to the user for describing the pin
2. Use the `PinsService` to add the new pin to the list of pins
3. Redirect the user to the homepage

Let's think through how we're going to do these things from ng2.

Angular provides a robust forms library. So there's no complication here. We're going to write a straight ng2 form.

However the `PinsService` comes from ng1. Often we have many existing services in ng1 and we don't have time to upgrade them all. So for this example, we're going to keep `PinsService` as an ng1 object, and *inject it into ng2*.

Similarly, we're using `ui-router` in ng1 for our routing. To change pages in `ui-router` we have to use the $state service, which is an ng1 service.

So what we're going to do is **upgrade** the `PinsService` and the $state service from ng1 to ng2. And this couldn't be any easier.

Upgrading ng1 `PinsService` and $state to ng2

To upgrade ng1 services we call `upgradeAdapter.upgradeNg1Provider`:

code/upgrade/hybrid/src/app/app.module.ts

```
37  /*
38   * Expose our ng1 content to ng2
39   */
40  upgradeAdapter.upgradeNg1Provider('PinsService');
41  upgradeAdapter.upgradeNg1Provider('$state');
```

And that's it. Now we can `@Inject` our ng1 services into ng2 components like so:

```
1   // angular.ui.IStateService is available because we've
2   // installed @types/angular-ui-router in our package.json
3   type IStateService = angular.ui.IStateService;
4
5   class AddPinComponent {
6     constructor(@Inject('PinsService') public pinsService: PinsService,
7                 @Inject('$state') public uiState: IStateService) {
8     }
9     // ...
10    // now you can use this.pinsService
11    // or this.uiState
12    // ...
13  }
```

In this constructor, there's a few things to look at:

The `@Inject` decorator, says that we want the next variable to be assigned the value of what the injection will resolve to. In the first case, that would be our ng1 `PinsService`.

In TypeScript, in a `constructor` when you use the `public` keyword, it is a shorthand for assigning that variable to `this`. That is, here when we say `public pinsService` what we're saying is, 1. declare a property `pinsService` on instances of this class and 2. assign the constructor argument `pinsService` to `this.pinsService`.

The result is that we can access `this.pinsService` throughout our class.

Lastly we define the type of both services we're injecting: `PinsService` and `IStateService`.

`PinsService` comes from the `app.d.ts` we defined previously:

code/upgrade/hybrid/src/js/app.d.ts

```
12   interface PinsService {
13     pins(): Promise<Pin[]>;
14     addPin(pin: Pin): Promise<any>;
15   }
```

And `IStateService` comes from the typings for `ui-router`, which we installed with `typings`.

By telling TypeScript the types of these services we can enjoy type-checking as we write our code.

Let's write the rest of our `AddPinComponent`.

Writing ng2 `AddPinComponent`

We start by importing the types we need:

code/upgrade/hybrid/src/app/add-pin/add-pin.component.ts

```
1   declare var angular: any;
2   import {
3     Component,
4     Inject
5   } from '@angular/core';
6   // angular.ui.IStateService is available because we've
7   // installed @types/angular-ui-router in our package.json
8   type IStateService = angular.ui.IStateService;
```

Again, notice that we're importing our custom types `Pin` and `PinsService`. And we're also importing `IStateService` from `angular-ui-router`.

AddPinComponent `@Component`

Our `@Component` is straightforward:

code/upgrade/hybrid/src/app/add-pin/add-pin.component.ts

```
10   @Component({
11     selector: 'add-pin',
12     templateUrl: './add-pin.component.html',
13     styleUrls: ['./add-pin.component.css']
14   })
```

AddPinComponent **template**

We're loading our template using a `templateUrl`. In that template, we setup our form much like the ng1 form, only we're using ng2 form directives.

> We're not going to describe `ngModel` / `ngSubmit` deeply here. If you'd like to know more about how Angular forms work, checkout the forms chapter, where we describe forms in depth.

code/upgrade/hybrid/src/app/add-pin/add-pin.component.html

```
1    <div class="container">
2      <div class="row">
3
4        <form (ngSubmit)="onSubmit()"
5              class="form-horizontal">
6
7          <div class="form-group">
8            <label for="title"
9                   class="col-sm-2 control-label">Title</label>
10           <div class="col-sm-10">
11             <input type="text"
12                    class="form-control"
13                    id="title"
14                    name="title"
15                    placeholder="Title"
16                    [(ngModel)]="newPin.title">
17           </div>
```

We're using two directives here: `ngSubmit` and `ngModel`.

We use `(ngSubmit)` on the form to call the `onSubmit` function when the form is submitted. (We'll define `onSubmit` on the `AddPinComponent` controller below.)

We use `[(ngModel)]` to bind the value of the `title` input tag to the value of `newPin.title` on the controller.

Here's the full listing of the template:

code/upgrade/hybrid/src/app/add-pin/add-pin.component.html

```
1   <div class="container">
2     <div class="row">
3
4       <form (ngSubmit)="onSubmit()"
5             class="form-horizontal">
6
7         <div class="form-group">
8           <label for="title"
9                 class="col-sm-2 control-label">Title</label>
10          <div class="col-sm-10">
11            <input type="text"
12                  class="form-control"
13                  id="title"
14                  name="title"
15                  placeholder="Title"
16                  [(ngModel)]="newPin.title">
17          </div>
18        </div>
19
20        <div class="form-group">
21          <label for="description"
22                class="col-sm-2 control-label">Description</label>
23          <div class="col-sm-10">
24            <input type="text"
25                  class="form-control"
26                  id="description"
27                  name="description"
28                  placeholder="Description"
29                  [(ngModel)]="newPin.description">
30          </div>
31        </div>
32
33        <div class="form-group">
34          <label for="url"
35                class="col-sm-2 control-label">Link URL</label>
36          <div class="col-sm-10">
37            <input type="text"
38                  class="form-control"
39                  id="url"
40                  name="url"
41                  placeholder="Link URL"
```

```
42                          [(ngModel)]="newPin.url">
43                </div>
44            </div>
45
46            <div class="form-group">
47              <label for="url"
48                     class="col-sm-2 control-label">Image URL</label>
49              <div class="col-sm-10">
50                <input type="text"
51                       class="form-control"
52                       id="url"
53                       name="url"
54                       placeholder="Image URL"
55                       [(ngModel)]="newPin.src">
56              </div>
57            </div>
58
59            <div class="form-group">
60              <div class="col-sm-offset-2 col-sm-10">
61                <button type="submit"
62                        class="btn btn-default"
63                        >Submit</button>
64              </div>
65            </div>
66            <div *ngIf="saving">
67              Saving...
68            </div>
69          </form>
```

`AddPinComponent` **Controller**

Now we can define `AddPinComponent`. We start by setting up two instance variables:

code/upgrade/hybrid/src/app/add-pin/add-pin.component.ts

```
15  export class AddPinComponent {
16    saving = false;
17    newPin: Pin;
```

We use `saving` to indicate to the user that the save is in progress and we use `newPin` to store the `Pin` we're working with.

code/upgrade/hybrid/src/app/add-pin/add-pin.component.ts

```
19    constructor(@Inject('PinsService') private pinsService: PinsService,
20                @Inject('$state') private uiState: IStateService) {
21      this.newPin = this.makeNewPin();
22    }
```

In our `constructor` we `Inject` the services, as we discussed above. We also set `this.newPin` to the value of `makeNewPin`, which we'll define now:

code/upgrade/hybrid/src/app/add-pin/add-pin.component.ts

```
24    makeNewPin(): Pin {
25      return {
26        title: 'Steampunk Cat',
27        description: 'A cat wearing goggles',
28        user_name: 'me',
29        avatar_src: '/assets/images/avatars/me.jpg',
30        src: '/assets/images/pins/cat.jpg',
31        url: 'http://cats.com',
32        faved: false,
33        id: Math.floor(Math.random() * 10000).toString()
34      };
35    }
```

This looks a lot like how we defined it in ng1, only now we have the benefit of it being typed.

When the form is submitted, we call `onSubmit`. Let's define that:

code/upgrade/hybrid/src/app/add-pin/add-pin.component.ts

```
37    onSubmit(): void {
38      this.saving = true;
39      console.log('submitted', this.newPin);
40      setTimeout(() => {
41        this.pinsService.addPin(this.newPin).then(() => {
42          this.newPin = this.makeNewPin();
43          this.saving = false;
44          this.uiState.go('home');
45        });
46      }, 2000);
47    }
```

Again, we're using a timeout to *simulate* the effect of what would happen if we had to call out to a server to save this pin. Here, we're using `setTimeout`. Compare that to how we defined this function in ng1:

code/upgrade/ng1/js/app.js

```
82    ctrl.submitPin = function() {
83      ctrl.saving = true;
84      $timeout(function() {
85        PinsService.addPin(ctrl.newPin).then(function() {
86          ctrl.newPin = makeNewPin();
87          ctrl.saving = false;
88          $state.go('home');
89        });
90      }, 2000);
91    }
```

Notice that in ng1 we had to use the $timeout service. Why is that? Because ng1 is based around the digest loop. If you use setTimeout in ng1, then when the callback function is called, it's "outside" of angular and so your changes aren't propagated unless something kicks off a digest loop (e.g. using $scope.apply).

However in ng2, we can use setTimeout directly because change detection in ng2 uses Zones and is therefore, more or less automatic. We don't need to worry about the digest loop in the same way, which is really nice.

In onSubmit we're calling out to the PinsService by:

```
1  this.pinsService.addPin(this.newPin).then(() => {
2    // ...
3  });
```

Again, the PinsService is accessible via this.pinsService because of how we defined the constructor. The compiler doesn't complain because we said that addPin takes a Pin as the first argument in our app.d.ts:

code/upgrade/hybrid/src/js/app.d.ts

```
13    pins(): Promise<Pin[]>;
14    addPin(pin: Pin): Promise<any>;
15  }
```

And we defined this.newPin to be a Pin.

After addPin resolves, we reset the pin using makeNewPin and set this.saving = false.

To go back to the homepage, we use the ui-router $state service, which we stored as this.uiState. So we can change states by calling this.uiState.go('home').

Using AddPinComponent

Now let's use the AddPinComponent.

Downgrade ng2 AddPinComponent

To use AddPinComponent we need to downgrade it:

code/upgrade/hybrid/src/app/app.module.ts

```
27  angular.module('interestApp')
28    .directive('pinControls',
29            upgradeAdapter.downgradeNg2Component(PinControlsComponent))
30    .directive('addPin',
31            upgradeAdapter.downgradeNg2Component(AddPinComponent));
```

This will create the addPin directive in ng1, which will match the tag <add-pin>.

Routing to add-pin

In order to use our new AddPinComponent page, we need to place it somewhere within our ng1 app. What we're going to do is take the add state in our router and just set the <add-pin> directive to be the template:

code/upgrade/hybrid/src/js/app.js

```
39      .state('add', {
40        template: "<add-pin></add-pin>",
41        url: '/add',
42        resolve: {
43          'pins': function(PinsService) {
44            return PinsService.pins();
45          }
46        }
47      })
```

Exposing an ng2 service to ng1

So far we've downgraded ng2 components to be used in ng2, and upgraded ng1 services to be used in ng2. But as our application start converting over to ng2, we'll probably start writing services in Typescript/ng2 that we'll want to expose to our ng1 code.

Let's create a simple service in ng2: an "analytics" service that will record events.

The idea is that we have an AnalyticsService in our app that we use to recordEvents. In reality, we're just going to console.log the event and store it in an array. But it gives us a chance to focus on what's important: describing how we share a ng2 service with ng1.

Writing the AnalyticsService

Let's take a look at the AnalyticsService implementation:

code/upgrade/hybrid/src/app/analytics.service.ts

```
 1   import { Injectable } from '@angular/core';
 2
 3   /**
 4    * Analytics Service records metrics about what the user is doing
 5    */
 6   @Injectable()
 7   export class AnalyticsService {
 8     events: string[] = [];
 9
10     public recordEvent(event: string): void {
11       console.log(`Event: ${event}`);
12       this.events.push(event);
13     }
14   }
```

There are two things to note here: 1. recordEvent and 2. being Injectable

recordEvent is straightforward: we take an event: string, log it, and store it in events. In your application you would probably send the event to an external service like Google Analytics or Mixpanel.

To make this service injectable, we do two things: 1. Annotate the class with @Injectable and 2. bind the token AnalyticsService to this class.

> ℹ️ The @Injectable decorator really means that other dependencies can be injected into this service, but it's recommended to add it to all services, even those that don't have dependencies. Read more about @Injectable in the chapter on dependency injection

Now Angular will manage a singleton of this service and we will be able to inject it where we need it.

Downgrade ng2 AnalyticsService to ng1

Before we can use the AnalyticsService in ng1, we need to downgrade it.

The process of downgrading an ng2 service to ng1 is similar to the process of downgrading a directive, but there is one extra step: we need to make sure AnayticsService is in the list of providers for our NgModule:

code/upgrade/hybrid/src/app/app.module.ts

```
43  @NgModule({
44    declarations: [
45      AppComponent,
46      AddPinComponent,
47      PinControlsComponent
48    ],
49    imports: [
50      BrowserModule,
51      FormsModule,
52      HttpModule
53    ],
54    providers: [
55      AnalyticsService
56    ]
57  })
58  export class AppModule { }
```

Then we can use downgradeNg2Provider:

code/upgrade/hybrid/src/app/app.module.ts

```
33  angular.module('interestApp')
34    .factory('AnalyticsService',
35            upgradeAdapter.downgradeNg2Provider(AnalyticsService));
```

We call angular.module('interestApp') to get our ng1 module and then call .factory like we would in ng1. To downgrade the service, we call

upgradeAdapter.downgradeNg2Provider(AnalyticsService), which wraps our AnalyticsService in a function that adapts it to an ng1 factory.

Using AnalyticsService in ng1

Now we can inject our ng2 AnalyticsService into ng1. Let's say we want to record whenever the HomeController is visited. We could record this event like so:

code/upgrade/hybrid/src/js/app.js

```
60  .controller('HomeController', function(pins, AnalyticsService) {
61    AnalyticsService.recordEvent('HomeControllerVisited');
62    this.pins = pins;
63  })
```

Here we inject `AnalyticsService` as if it was a normal ng1 service we call `recordEvent`. Fantastic!

We can use this service anywhere we would use injection in ng1. For instance, we can also inject the `AnalyticsService` into our ng1 `pin` directive:

code/upgrade/hybrid/src/js/app.js

```
64  .directive('pin', function(AnalyticsService) {
65    return {
66      restrict: 'E',
67      templateUrl: '/assets/templates/pin.html',
68      scope: {
69        'pin': "=item"
70      },
71      link: function(scope, elem, attrs) {
72        scope.toggleFav = function() {
73          AnalyticsService.recordEvent('PinFaved');
74          scope.pin.faved = !scope.pin.faved;
75        }
76      }
77    }
78  })
```

Summary

Now you have all the tools you need to start upgrading your ng1 app to a hybrid ng1/ng2 app. The interoperability between ng1 and ng2 works very well and we owe a lot to the Angular team for making this so easy.

Being able to exchange directives and services between ng1 and ng2 make it super easy to start upgrading your apps. We can't always upgrade our apps to ng2 overnight, but the `UpgradeAdapter` lets us start using ng2 - without having to throw our old code away.

References

If you're looking to learn more about hybrid Angular apps, here are a few resources:

- The Official Angular Upgrade Guide[142]
- The Angular2 Upgrade Spec Test[143]
- The Angular2 Source for `DowngradeNg2ComponentAdapter`[144]

---

[142] https://angular.io/docs/ts/latest/guide/upgrade.html

[143] https://github.com/angular/angular/blob/master/modules/angular2/test/upgrade/upgrade_spec.ts

[144] https://github.com/angular/angular/blob/master/modules/angular2/src/upgrade/downgrade_ng2_adapter.ts

Printed in Great Britain
by Amazon